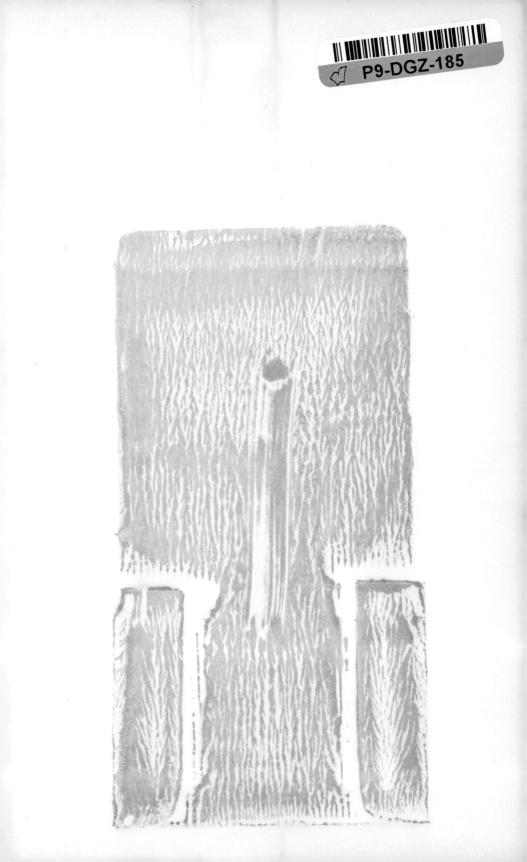

Theories of Counseling

GUIDANCE, COUNSELING
AND STUDENT PERSONNEL
IN EDUCATION

WALTER F. JOHNSON, *Consulting Editor*

Arbuckle, *Counseling and Psychotherapy: An Overview*
Bennett, *Guidance and Counseling in Groups*
Bernhardt, *Discipline and Child Guidance*
Detjen and Detjen, *Elementary School Guidance*
Dinkmeyer and Caldwell, *Developmental Counseling and Guidance in the Elementary School*
Downing, *Guidance and Counseling Services: An Introduction*
Hoppock, *Occupational Information*
Johnson, Stefflre, and Edelfelt, *Pupil Personnel and Guidance Services*
Jones, Stefflre, and Stewart, *Principles of Guidance*
Kemp, *Foundations of Group Counseling*
Stefflre and Grant, *Theories of Counseling*
Tolbert, *Introduction to Counseling*
Warters, *Techniques of Counseling*
Williamson, *Vocational Counseling*

McGRAW-HILL SERIES IN EDUCATION

Arno A. Bellack   *Teachers College, Columbia University*
Consulting Editor, Supervisor, Curriculum, and Methods in Education

Walter F. Johnson   *Michigan State University*
Consulting Editor, Guidance, Counseling,
and Student Personnel in Education

The late Harold A. Benjamin was Consulting Editor
of the Foundation of Education Series from
its inception in 1935 until January 1969.

Theories of Counseling

Second Edition

Buford Stefflre
Michigan State University

W. Harold Grant
Auburn University

McGraw-Hill Book Company
New York   St. Louis   San Francisco   Düsseldorf   Johannesburg   Kuala Lumpur
London   Mexico   Montreal   New Delhi   Panama   Rio de Janeiro   Singapore
Sydney   Toronto

Theories of Counseling

Library of Congress Catalog Card Number 70-172668

07-060971-3

1 2 3 4 5 6 7 8 9 0   DODO   7 9 8 7 6 5 4 3 2

This book was set in Times Roman by Rocappi, Inc.,
and printed and bound by R. R. Donnelley, & Sons Company.
The designer was Merrill Haber. The editors were Robert C. Morgan
and David Dunham. Matt Martino supervised production.

Contents

Foreword

There have been a great many developments in the field of counseling since the first edition of this book was published. The field has changed its dimensions in both breadth and depth as a result of such factors as more careful delineation of philosophies about counseling processes and human behavior; vastly expanded research efforts; the empirical evidence that comes from widespread practice; and a shift in counseling practices.

Just as new developments have occurred, time-worn methods are being questioned. The result has been a demand for counselors with a greater diversity of backgrounds and of professional preparation to respond to the needs of people in a much greater variety of sociocultural settings. It has been a period of growth and professional maturation for counselors, as well as a time to challenge and reexamine the theories upon which counseling practices rest.

The contributors' revisions reflect the changes which have occurred since their first writing. Their contributions bespeak the thorough knowledge that comes from intimate involvement in their particular theory or specialty. Comments on the first edition have usually included the readability and mature writing style of the respective authors. Readers will find this edition has not lost these qualities.

With the untimely death of Buford Stefflre, the profession lost one of its most competent critics and spokesmen. He was troubled by the inconsistencies and incongruities which were all too prevalent in what practitioners chose to call "counseling." He was convinced that a better understanding of the theoretical underpinnings by the practitioner would make his conduct more consistent at the very least. At the same time, he was deeply sensitive to the social ills of our time and sought constantly to relate the significance of what counselors do as one means of correcting some of society's inequities. A brilliant and articulate scholar, with a keen wit, he was also a sharp critic— always a delightful adversary and a lovable colleague. We miss him immensely.

Dr. Harold Grant has accepted the responsibility for editing this edition. He and "Steff" had worked together on numerous occasions and were in close agreement on most professional concerns, as well as being good personal friends. This personal mutual regard and Hal Grant's demonstrated competency as a scholar and editor made this choice a very fortuitous one.

We are pleased to be able to present this new edition for counselors— those in training as well as those already in practice.

WALTER F. JOHNSON

Introduction

I am a counselor, and my relationship with students is called counseling. The goal of our relationship is the same as the goal of education and of life itself—the development of self-direction. Because self-direction is the primary characteristic we ascribe to the being called God, we view it as the ultimate good; thus, each human being seeks that ultimate good in himself, and each spends a lifetime trying to realize his potential. While we share a common goal, we also are involved with each other in attaining it. The relationships we create with others can deter or facilitate our development. What kind of relationship contributes most to the attainment of this goal? Jesus called it love and defined it as an act of the spirit, an act of the mind, and an act of the heart.

The act of the spirit we call faith. A relationship that facilitates self-directedness includes a belief or an assumption that each person has the potential to be self-directed. If I doubt a person's potential to become self-directed, this doubt severely limits a relationship's power to help him develop self-direction. Since I cannot rely on science to prove that someone has the potential to be self-directed, I must assume that he does—I must have faith. There is no substitute for this faith; it is an essential ingredient in the relationship called love.

The act of the mind we call understanding. While I may believe a man has potential to be self-directed, I must understand his present status of development or have information about him individually. If I lack this understanding, I tend to act toward him as a member of a species rather than as an individual person. Fortunately, man's nature and experiences give him countless ways to understanding others and thus help them to achieve self-direction.

The act of the heart we call acceptance. Acceptance is acting congruently with the faith and understanding one has of another. It is not limited to affective behavior. Acceptance is also logical, assertive, practical, and abstract. In other words, acceptance includes any and all behavior through which a person demonstrates his faith and understanding to help another become more self-directed. If I refuse to behave as another needs me, I am not accepting him, and I am impeding his potential for self-direction.

A person will seek a relationship with me—or counseling—when he perceives that he is not the kind of person he wants to be. This feeling usually is accompanied by his lack of love for himself. In the sense described above, it becomes my role to love him with unqualified faith and with as much understanding as my skills permit; and I must show acceptance by behaving in ways that facilitate his development. This will enable him to increase his love for himself and to begin to become the kind of person he wants to be. He can begin to be self-directed.

This book is about a particular kind of relationship called counseling. Through personal experience and professional practice, the four theorists represented here evolved approaches and formulated theories about the relationship of counseling.

Each of the theories described in this book is a blueprint of the counseling relationship, and each describes a kind of faith or assumption about man's nature and provides a framework for understanding. Techniques for accepting or applying the assumptions and understanding of a counseling relationship are included in each theory. The client-centered approach places more emphasis on faith than the others. The trait-factor and psychoanalytic approaches involve more ways to understand. The behavioral approach places more emphasis on acceptance or doing something to modify the counselee's behavior.

You already relate to people. You already have a theory. Perhaps it's more personal at this point, as mine is. The principal difference between ours and the four outlined in this book is the level of development. A good way to develop your personal theory is to become more aware of it. Carefully examining the more highly developed theories of others will help you to do this. You are also likely to find that aspects of these theories are actually extensions of your own. Thus you can develop your theory more quickly than if you depended totally on your own experiences.

The four theories described here are the ones most counselors find particularly meaningful to their professional practice. Each is described by an outstanding practitioner who has found this particular theory meaningful. He is sharing himself with you as I have in a less scholarly way in this preface. This makes the theories much more alive than they would be if they were impersonally analyzed in an impartial academic fashion.

While the theories are useful to you regardless of the context in which you plan to use them, they are presented here with the expectation that most students using this book plan to use them in an educational context. This makes the application of the theories for the prospective school counselor easier to make.

Perhaps your choice of counseling as a career is a continuation of your search for self-direction and identity. If so, you'll find this book a rich resource. Knowing yourself more accurately and completely, you'll be better prepared to collaborate with others in their quest.

W. HAROLD GRANT

About the Authors

Kent F. Bennington is a clinical instructor of psychology in the Department of Psychiatry and the Department of Physical Medicine and Rehabilitation at the University of California's Davis Medical School. His bachelor's degree is from Ohio State University, his master's from the University of New Mexico, and his doctorate from the University of Missouri. Dr. Bennington previously served as psychological consultant for Headstart and Day Care Center programs in the eleven-state North Central Region of the United States and also was an instructor in the College of Education at the University of Missouri.

Leonard D. Goodstein is a professor of psychology and director of professional training in psychology at the University of Cincinnati. He was formerly director of the University Counseling Service and professor of psychology at the University of Iowa, Iowa City. During the summer of 1960 he was research consultant to the Counseling Center at the University of California, Berkeley. Dr. Goodstein received his bachelor's degree cum laude and with honors in psychology from the City University of New York. His graduate degrees are from Columbia University, and he is a diplomate in clinical psychology of the American Board of Professional Psychology. He is the author of many articles in the professional literature on counseling and clinical psychology and serves as a consulting editor of the *Journal of Consulting and Clinical Psychology, Psychological Reports,* and the *Journal of Experimental Research in Personality.* Dr. Goodstein has served as a consultant to the Peace Corps, the Veterans Administration, the Teacher Corps, and a number of other educational and industrial organizations. He is a fellow of the American Psychological Association and a life member of the American Personnel and Guidance Association.

W. Harold Grant is director of Student Development Services and professor of counselor education at Auburn University. He was formerly assistant dean of students at Auburn and Cornell Universities and professor of education at Michigan State University. He received his bachelor's degree with honor in psychology from Auburn and his doctorate in guidance and student personnel from Columbia Teachers College. A doctor of humanities (*honoris causa*) degree was conferred on Dr. Grant by Mt. Angel College.

Donald L. Grummon is professor of psychology and is a counseling psychologist with the Counseling Center at Michigan State University. He previously served as director of the Counseling Center. His bachelor's degree is from dePauw University, his master's from Ohio State University, and his doctorate from the University of Chicago. He served for two years as a psychologist at the Cheltenham School for Boys (a training school for court-committed delinquents) and then was at the University of Chicago where he was an assistant professor of psychology, a counselor, and administrative and research coordinator in the counseling center. He has written in the fields of both counseling and clinical psychology. While at Ohio State University and at the University of Chicago, Dr. Grummon worked closely with Carl Rogers.

Paul T. King is director of the Counseling Center and a counseling psychologist at the University of Missouri. His bachelor's degree is in journalism from the University of Kentucky where he also received his master's degree. His doctorate is from Pennsylvania State University. Dr. King is a diplomate in counseling psychology of the American Board of Examiners in Professional Psychology. He has served as a psychologist in child guidance clinics, speech pathology clinics, and psychological clinics. For the last sixteen years he worked as a counseling psychologist in the Counseling Center at Michigan State University and at the University of Missouri.

William Ratigan is guidance director at Charlevoix, Michigan, and senior extension lecturer for Michigan State University where he studied for his doctorate in the Department of Counseling, Personnel Services, and Educational Psychology. His bachelor's degree is in the humanities from the University of Tennessee at Chattanooga. Former chief of NBC's Far Eastern Listening Post, he supervised war correspondents and commentators in the PTO, then served as editor and scriptwriter for the network at the first UN Conference. Designated one of the most significant authors in his native state, his manuscripts and private papers are now a part of the University of Michigan Historical Collections. He is also a co-author of ASCA's first yearbook. Recent counselor-educator assignments include visiting lecturer at Florida State University, the University of Wisconsin—Milwaukee, and the University of Miami (Coral Gables). Previously, in connection with his NBC duties, he lectured on broadcasting at the University of Denver and acted as an instructor in journalism for UCLA.

Buford Stefflre was a professor in the College of Education at Michigan State University until his death. His bachelor's degree was in English from the University of California and his graduate degrees in guidance are from the University of Southern California. He worked for fifteen years with the Los Angeles City Schools as a teacher, counselor, and supervisor of counseling. He had been at Michigan State University since 1955 in the Department of Guidance and Pupil Personnel Services. He served as editor of the *Personnel and Guidance Journal* and was issue chairman of the "Guidance and Pupil Personnel" issue of the *Review of Educational Research* which was published in April, 1963. He was the author of numerous articles in professional psychological and educational journals and two school guidance texts.

Edmund G. Williamson is professor emeritus of psychology and dean emeritus of students at the University of Minnesota. His bachelor's degree is from the University of Illinois and his doctorate from the University of Minnesota. Dean Williamson was the recipient of the research award in 1953 and the Nancy C. Wimmer award in 1962 from the American Personnel and Guidance Association. He was a Fulbright visiting lecturer at Tokyo University in 1955. From 1950 to 1970 he was chairman of the Veterans Administration Advisory Committee on Counseling Services for Vocational Rehabilitation and Education. Dean Williamson is the author of numerous books and articles in the field of psychology and education and has been active in a number of organizations in these fields.

1

Function of Theory in Counseling

BUFORD STEFFLRE

As counseling becomes a more recognized service of educational institutions, it is necessary to make an effort to conceptualize this process so that its purposes and methods are more amenable to study and understanding. The experienced counselor may need to make a more systematic effort to look at what happens in the counseling interview so that he may understand it within a framework which makes sense in the light of his knowledge about human behavior. The inexperienced counselor, or the counselor in training, may need to develop some guidelines regarding what he should do during the counseling interview—guidelines which logically evolve from overarching theories. This chapter will attempt to define theory and show its values and limitations. It will also attempt to define counseling and distinguish it both from psychotherapy on the one hand and instruction on the other. Subsequent chapters will show the place of counseling theory in school settings and will delineate four of the most important theories currently in use.

What Is a Theory?

Scientists and philosophers have given us many definitions of theory. One has called it a human convention for keeping data in order. This philosopher points out that if human memories were better than they are, we should have no need for theory since we could simply refer to raw data whenever we wanted to consider a problem. Because our memories are fallible, theories are not only convenient but necessary since they enable us to reduce complexities to manageable proportions so that we can deal with an otherwise overwhelming amount of information. To perform this function, a theory must consist of data plus an interrelating structure which tell us how one piece of information has relevance for another (Pepper, 1961, p. 72). Another definition says that a theory is a provisional systemization of events. Again, we are being told that a theory is a device which enables us to see relationships between one event or fact and another (McCabe, 1958, p. 49). Currently it seems fashionable to think of theories as models. A theory, then, may be called a conceptual model—for example, the id— which is postulated to explain a process inferred from observed behavior. This definition says that we see certain happenings and that we strive to have them make sense. They make sense only if we are able to postulate some process which if it operated, would result in the behavior (McCabe, 1958, p. 49). In a widely used discussion of theory in the field of psychology, the definition evolved indicates that theory is a cluster of relevant assumptions systematically related to each other and a set of empirical definitions (Hall & Lindzey, 1957, p. 10). Here again are the elements of data—empirical definitions, postulates or conventions, and relevant assumptions—which have appeared in previous definitions. Finally, we come to a most usable and memorable definition which states merely that a theory is a possible world which can be checked against the real world (Pepinsky & Pepinsky, 1954, p. 18).

What these definitions have in common are the elements of reality and belief. Reality is the data or behavior which we see and strive to explain. Belief is the way that we try to make sense out of the data by relating what we see to conceivable explanations of it. Theory building, then, grows out of our need to make sense of life. A theory is a map on which a few points are known, and the road between them is inferred. Good maps can be filled in as we learn more about the world, and, poor ones will need to be thrown away when we find that they are leading us astray.

Do We Need Theory?

Often the experienced counselor, and even the trainee, is scornful of theory and questions its value to him. Students frequently say that they want more practical courses and "not all this theory." A dichotomy between theory and practicality is often assumed. In reality, however, nothing is as practical as a good theory. [Like a good map, it tells us what to look for, what to expect, and where to go.] The use of theory can be analogous to the learning about life that helps the neonate make sense out of the booming, buzzing confusion which is his world. The phenomena of nature are not in themselves necessarily ordered. But to operate, we must impose order on them, and this ordering is a function of theory.

Those who feel that they can operate entirely without theory and even assume an antitheoretical position are usually basing their behavior on vaguely defined but implicit theory. There is no other way that they can decide what to do. Intuition, often advanced as a substitute for theory, is itself but a crude type of hypothesizing (McDanfel, Lallas, Saum, & Gilmore, 1959, p. 148). "The views of the 'practical men' are usually derived from assumptions and arguments no less complex than those on which theory is based; they are more and not less liable to error because they are less openly expressed" (Campbell, 1953, p. 289). The real question then is not whether we shall operate from theory since we have no choice in this matter, but rather what theories shall we use and how shall we use theories. Specifically, in a counseling situation when a client says "I hate my mother," the counselor's reactions are limited only by his biological status. He can slap the client, he can run out of the room, he can jump up on his chair, he can reply "It makes you bitter just thinking about her," or he can do any of a number of things. When he makes a choice among the responses open to him, he must act from theory. That is, he must act from some notion as to what the client means by his statement, what his statement means in the life of the client, what the proper goals of counseling are, what the function of the counselor is, what techniques are successful in moving toward the determined goals, and the other elements which taken together constitute for him a theory of counseling.

What Underlying Bases Do Theories Have?

Just as phenomena which we observe can be seen in many ways, so countless theories can possibly be constructed. To explain why we have the theories which we do, we must look at the bases of theory.

Personal Basis

One of the underlying sources of theory is the personal need structure of the theory builder or user. This dimension of theory has been pointed up by Shoben (1962, p. 619), who says that since there is little in the way of research evidence that points to one theory as being superior to another in the field of counseling, we must look within the counselor who uses a given theory to determine why he is attracted to that particular one. Certainly this same personal element would seem to be present in theory building. The character, the genius, the personality of the theory constructor is expressed in the theory which ne develops.

Historical Basis

A good example of the influence of history on the possibility of theory building is given by Theobald:

> The stated aims of the physical and social sciences are indeed very similar. Their object is to reduce the overwhelming diversity and complexity of reality to simple theoretical regularities so that events can be understood, and, if possible, the future predicted on the basis of the laws discovered. Two steps are generally considered necessary in the evolution of a theory. First, observations of the facts of phenomena to be described, and, second, the formulation of a theory that will cover all the observed facts. It can then be tested by using it for the purposes of prediction: as long as it gives valid results, it remains useful. However, if exceptions are found, it should be modified so that it will cover all the observed facts (1961, p. 40).

Theobald goes on to point out that up to about five hundred years ago theory building in the physical sciences was bound by emotional attachment and belief. The examples of the difficulties of Copernicus are known to us. People could not build and believe in a theory which did not put the earth at the center of the universe.

The social sciences are today, and perhaps forever, in the position of the physical sciences of five hundred years ago in the limits placed upon them. It is impossible to be completely free of emotional and value elements as theory builders in the social science. The social sciences are such that we must always consider "ends," and at least at this time in history desirable ends, or goals, are apt to be "given" and so not subject to investigation. We cannot escape ethical theory which points toward what should be, even though it may limit the acceptance of psychological theories regarding what is or what can be. Psychological theory may tell us the relative distance and the type of surface of several roads, but only ethical theory can tell us which one is worth taking. For example, we cannot meaningfully and freely construct theories to answer the question "Which is more efficient, communism or free enterprise?" because we must first ask a prior ethical question "Which is right?"

Still another limitation on theory building in social science is the fact that research itself, at least with our present techniques, may alter objective reality. In the physical science this influence of the researcher on his data is called "the principle of indeterminancy." In social science it is quite clear that in many contexts as soon as we begin to do research, the situation we wanted to understand vanishes. A good example of this principle is shown by the placebo effect in counseling. When a client changes his behavior after counseling, it is difficult to determine whether the change is associated with the personality of the counselor, the technique of counseling, or the attention given him. This last factor—sympathetic attention—has been likened to the physician's placebo. An extension to another area is illustrated by some research on causes of leaving school which was done in a large school system. A group of potential dropouts was identified and randomized into two groups. One group—the experimental—got all kinds of special treatment and attention and the other—the control group—did not. True, the experimental group began to behave in a more desirable fashion, but unfortunately for science, the control group began to respond in much the same way. In other words, as soon as research was done in the school, it altered the reality of the situation. The classrooms were different, the halls were different, and objective reality was not what it was when the research began. We must conclude then that theories in the social sciences are bound by space and bound by time. The theories that explain behavior in 1850 may not explain it in the year 2000. The theory that seems reasonable in America may not be useful in Vietnam.

Sociological Basis

Theories are influenced not only by the personal context but by the cultural context in which the theory builder and user lives. Americans are said to live in a world which is orderly, and so we are attracted to theory in general and particularly to theories which attempt to make sense of natural phenomena. We believe that it is a man's job to discover the order in the universe and build models (theories) which reflect it (Hall, 1961, p. 133). In such an orderly universe we are apt to look for causality and assume that it is present. The usual arguments against complete causality (determinism) include the belief that the individual is unique and complex, that causality may imply teleology, and finally that if behavior is caused, we are left without the concept of guilt. On the other hand, those arguing for the acceptance of causality would reply first than uniqueness is relative in psychology if not in etymology and that in the history of science many previously complex problems now seem understandable. With regard to teleology the espousers of a position assuming causality would say that perhaps it is the present expectation and not the future goal which motivates. Finally, they would say that we may still punish antisocial behavior, but our motives would be to affect the future and not to correct the past. Regardless of the logic of the position, most counselors behave "as if" behavior is both caused and to some extent free. Logical contradictions notwithstanding, we believe that there is sufficient order in the psychological universe so that we can to some extent understand and predict behavior, but sufficient freedom in an individual that he has some choices which are relatively free of genetics and of history. We ask not "Is man free?" but "How free is man?" The sociological base of theory in America, then, is an orderly one. We look for order in the world, and we find it.

Americans are also concerned with recent times rather than with remote history, and therefore our theories are apt to explain behavior in terms of relatively recent events. Because of this point of view, we may sometimes slip into the error of thinking that since *A* happened after *B, B* must have caused *A*. Instruction in formal logic will not always free us of this fallacy because the culture within which we operate tends to value such explanations. A good example of the American concern with the present as opposed to the concern of some other peoples with the past was given recently by an American researcher working in Florence, Italy. The researcher was trying to discover the effects of university services on community life in small villages. His research designs always called for counting and analyzing the relationships among events that were happening or had just happened. His Italian colleagues, however, who were also interested in the problem were more apt to approach the hypotheses through a discussion of what the Etruscans did and how this influenced the Romans, what the Romans did and how this influenced the Goths, and so on to the present. The theories built and held by Americans are apt to be time-bound in the sense that they look not very far in the past and not very far in the future, for Americans are most comfortable in "possible worlds" of this kind.

Still another sociological influence in American theory building and theory holding is the English language itself.

> The categories and types that we isolate from the world of phenomena we do not find there because they stare every observer in the face: on the contrary, the world is presented in a kaleidoscopic flux of impressions which has to be organized by our minds. We cut nature up, organize it into concepts, and ascribe significance as we do, largely because we are parties to an agreement organized in this way—an agreement that holds throughout our speech community and is codified in the patterns of our language ... no individual is free to describe nature with absolute impartiality ... (From *The Silent Language* by Edward T. Hall. Copyright ⊙ 1959 by Edward T. Hall. Reprinted by permission of Doubleday & Company, Inc.)

Perhaps the best known example of the influence of language on perception is that some Eskimo dialects have as many as twenty different words for snow in its various forms and stages. A language like English with its relative lack of concern for snow would not lend itself to the same kinds of theory about snow as an Eskimo theorist might build. It has been further suggested that even such a seemingly objective phenomenon as the color spectrum itself is sliced up arbitrarily and differently by different languages. Therefore, there would be people who would be incapable of developing a theory involving, for example, "purple," for purple is not *seen* by the speakers of the language. Purple would not be seen because it could not be isolated and labeled. Our language, too, by arbitrary designations forbids us to see what others may see or to think thoughts that others might think

Philosophical Basis

[Although there would seem to be a logical connection between philosophy and practice, it does not yet seem clear whether a given philosophical position will necessarily lead to a specific counseling theory.] Perhaps Wrenn (1959) in the *NSSE Yearbook* has made the most ambitious attempt to relate philosophy to counseling. Essentially, however, Wrenn pointed to the several philosophical bases which could justify the various school personnel activities which have evolved rather than starting from philosophical positions and drawing conclusions about the type of services they would consistently suggest. Curriculum theorists have largely given up trying to show necessary bonds between philosophical positions and classroom experiences. Many of them rather postulate a series of principles between the philosophy and the practice. These principles might stem from a number of different philosophical positions, but they tend to narrow the field of practice if we assume them to be sound principles.

In the counseling field such guiding principles—halfway between philosophy and practice—might come from the area of mental health. In other words, regardless of the basic philosophy which we hold, perhaps we can agree that mental health is a desirable goal and come to some conclusion as to what constitutes desirable mental health and then construct a theory of counseling which we hope will lead toward desirable mental health. Unfortunately, however, there is not agreement on what constitutes mental health (Jahoda, 1958, p. 23). Jahoda summarizes current concepts of mental health and says that there are six criteria which seem most fruitful in considering this concept. The six criteria which she lists are (1) attitudes of an individual toward his own self; (2) growth, development, or self-actualization; (3) integration; (4) autonomy; (5) perception of reality; and (6) environmental mastery. One or more of these criteria would probably be accepted by most theorists in the counseling field as a legitimate goal of their activity. If we accept the first criterion as the best indicator of mental health, certain counseling theories might be suggested, while the last criterion might suggest quite different ones. Our theory building and use are guided, if not by our philosophy, at least by our acceptance of basic principles which are near philosophy in sweep and depth. It is only after such a goal has been clarified and accepted, however, that a reasonable theory can be built. If we operated from other principles or philosophical bases, we should have to construct other theories.

In summary, then, theories do not appear at random. [If we are to understand why certain theories are constructed and accepted, we need to know something about the philosophical assumptions that the theory builders and the theory holders operate from.] We need to know something about the historical context in which the theory appears. We need to understand the sociocultural milieu in which the theory developed. In this milieu we should want to pay particular attention to the language and to the life view which the inhabitant held. Finally, we can only understand the genesis of a theory by knowing something about the personality, needs, strengths, and genius of the theory builder.

What Do Theories Do?

Theories once constructed and accepted perform a variety of functions. A theory may lead us to observe relationships which we had previously overlooked. The germ theory pointed out relationships which had long been present in fact but made no sense until a theory was built which related one fact to another. The relationship between sleeping with the windows open in the malaria-ridden South and getting sick with malaria only became apparent after the theory regarding the disease was constructed.

Theories help us to incorporate our data because theories predict laws just as laws predict events (Campbell, 1953, p. 300). From theories we may define operational truths because theories involve assertions which lead to prediction which can be tested and verified (McCabe, 1958, p. 51). Theories focus our attention on relevant data by telling us what to look for and lead us to the use of consistent terminology. It was only after the construction and acceptance of self-theory that such matters as warmth and friendliness in the classroom received systematic attention from researchers. Theories may help us construct new methods of behaving in a counseling situation and point to ways of evaluating the old ones (Brammer & Shostrom, 1960, p. 6). A doctoral student indicated that he was interested in studying the problem of college students who did not have a declared academic major. When he asked what he should look for in doing research on these students, there was obviously no way to give him an answer until there was some clarification as to what theory he was holding about them. Without a theory he might have studied their intelligence, their blood types, the color of their hair, their height, or the names of their uncles. After the student had considered the problem, he decided that the most meaningful theory for his investigation was that developed by Super, who suggests that a selection of an occupation constitutes the implementation of a self-concept. It would seem to follow from this theory that a student who was unable to tentatively select an occupation would have a very unclear self-concept. Starting from this theoretical basis, the doctoral student was able to proceed with his research. The theory told him what to look for. At the end of his investigation it helped him incorporate his findings and make sense from them.

A special problem in the use of theory is its application to individual cases. Theories essentially lead to generalizations about averages, but for dealing with an individual, we often feel that we need principles which explain the unique personality. In dealing with an individual, we need to remember that laws are probability statements and that the more classes for which we have explanatory laws, the more effectively we can deal with an individual. It would seem that as we narrow the reference cases, we can become more explicit and helpful in explaining individual behavior (Phillips, 1956, p. 75; Pepinsky & Pepinsky, 1954, p. 20). The previously quoted article by Shoben (1962) refers to this problem and points out that the use of theory with an individual case both facilitates and inhibits our behavior. Theory facilitates by helping us see sense and meaning in the client's behavior, but it may inhibit us by blinding us to his uniqueness. We may force him to fit on the Procrustean bed of a theory applicable to the many.

We need, then, not only theory to help us see what is happening within an individual but skepticism stemming from the realization that present theories in social science will rarely, if ever, completely explain the behavior of a given individual.

How Do We Know a Good Theory?—Formal Attributes

There are pigs and pigs; there are theories and theories. A good theory may be said to have five formal attributes. *A good theory is clear* in that there is agreement among its general principles (philosophy), and agreement of its consequences with observation (science). It is clear in that it is communicable, and those who read it will understand what is meant. It is an easily read map.

A good theory is comprehensive in that it has scope and accounts for much behavior. It will explain what happens to many people in many situations. It approaches all-purpose utility.

A good theory is explicit, that is, it has precision. While it may make use of evocative statements such as "psychological warmth," and "fully functioning," these concepts will be translatable into denotative statements so that they can be checked against clear referents in the real world (Frank, 1949, p. 27). It is not the mystical or obscure talk of the theorist that spoils his theory, but it is his failure to translate his poetry into science.

A good theory is parsimonious and does not overexplain phenomena. A theory which explains a given event in five different ways is apt not to explain it at all.

Finally, *a good theory generates useful research.* Some theories may stand for decades untested because they lack this formal attribute. Other theories more heuristic may be excellent theories simply because they stimulate much research which itself proves them false.

In summary, then, a theory is always a map in the process of being filled in with greater detail. We do not so much ask is it true, but is it helpful.

How Do We Use Theory?

Among counselors we may find attitudes toward the value of various types of theory on a continuum from the dogmatically theoretical to the dogmatically antitheoretical. Six steps or gradations have been identified (Bone, 1959, p. 99). One person may see psychology as exactly the same as physical science in both goals and methods. He would search for the most rigorous behavioristic theories and attempt to find them apart from the influence of society, history, and personality. A second person may believe that the above position is true in principle but not completely so in fact, and he will temper his "rigor" with the realization that what is good for physical science may not be good for counseling. A third person would value the ideographic but press, to the extent that he could, toward the nomothetic. Such a person would attempt to wed the values of the physical science with the peculiarities of the social science. A fourth person might use both approaches but really feel that the ideographic is the best for his purposes. A fifth might make use of clinical insight in his work but try when possible to check it by an approximation of the scientific method. Such a person would have a basic commitment to the ideographic but some sense of responsibility for using the nomothetic. Finally, there are counselors who would use the completely clinical method and feel that attempts at theory building and rigorous research were inappropriate as well as impossible.

As we examine counseling theories, we may be appalled by the fact that they do not seem to be very soundly based on empirical data or always skillfully constructed to illuminate the relationships among the facts that we do have. Such a realization may tend to immobilize a new counselor. He may say, "How can I act when our theories are so poorly supported?" This dilemma seems best resolved by making a distinction between action and belief. We may have to act on less evidence than we can demand for belief since the basis of action is ethical and the basis of belief is cognitive. We cannot wait until theories are perfected but must operate on what evidence we have. As we choose among the approaches open to us, we may have to take the best of what appears to be a very poor lot. We may have to act "as if " we know, when, in fact, we know we do not know.

Conflicting theories also may be somewhat traumatizing to the student. Closer examination, however, may in some cases indicate that theories complement each other rather than contradict (McCabe, 1958, p. 50). The use of more than one theory may point to the same facts and give clarity where previously we had confusion. The analogy might be made of the use of a variety of stage lights in a theatrical production. Sometimes the overhead light will give us the view we want; sometimes the red spotlight or blue will illuminate what we are looking for.

A philosopher has suggested that we strive for rational clarity in theory and reasonable eclecticism in practice (Pepper, 1961, p. 330). This advice would permit us to be as rigorous as we should like in a cognitive area but as humane as we should be in action. "Rational clarity" demands that we hold our theory explicitly if we should make the best use of it because only then can we correct for our biases in theory selection and valuation. It is the theory we use without knowing we are using it that is dangerous to us and our clients. Just as personality defects and emotional problems in the counselor need not preclude the possibility of effective work if they are taken into account and corrected for, so theory may be better used in counseling if we are aware that the theory is held and acknowledge its limitations and some of the sources of its attraction to us.

Finally, it has been suggested that we make best use of theories in social science by remembering that they will not long remain useful. Since they are bound by space and time and the present level of our knowledge, the best of theories will not long serve. If we should accept this limitation, we should teach our students not only presently held theories but ways of building new ones (Theobald, 1961, p. 100). Theory building will need to be a constant process for those who remain in counseling. It is for this reason that there may be value in examining as we have the structure, function, and genesis of theory.

What Is Counseling?

Having considered the nature and function of theory, we must now discuss the activity to which it will be applied in this book—counseling. Defining counseling and distinguishing it from both psychotherapy and instruction is the next task which must be performed to enable us to consider various theories of counseling.

In defining counseling, we are again faced with the fact that various authorities have seen it in different lights. These differences are due not only to differences in point of view and philosophy among the specialists in this field but are due to historical changes in the perceptions which have been held of this art.

In 1945, the educational dictionary maker, Good, defined counseling as the "individualized and personalized assistance with personal, educational, vocational problems, in which all pertinent facts are studied and analyzed, and a solution is sought, often with the assistance of specialists, school and community resources, and personal interviews in which the counselee is taught to make his own decisions" (1945, p. 104). This older definition would now be seen as merely a statement supporting one point of view or theory of counseling. Its strong emphasis on cognitive material, immediate decision making, and use of external resources was characteristic of the views of counseling commonly held at that time and still held by certain proponents.

A more recent definition is that of English and English (1958, p. 127) in their dictionary in which they say that counseling is "a relationship in which one person endeavors to help another to understand and solve his adjustment problems. The area of adjustment is often indicated: educational counseling, vocational counseling, social counseling, et cetera." They go on to point out that "counseling is a two-way affair involving both counselor and counselee. Unfortunately, both noun and verb counsel retain an older meaning of advice giving, which is now conceived as only part of the counseling process."

Still another of the more modern and psychologically oriented definitions is the one by Pepinsky and Pepinsky in which they say that counseling is seen as "(a) diagnosis and treatment of minor (nonimbedded, nonincapacitating), functional (nonorganic) maladjustment and (b) as a relationship, primarily individual and face-to-face, between counselor and client" (1954). A middle-of-the road definition much valued and used is that given by Wrenn when he says that "counseling is a dynamic and purposeful relationship between two people in which procedures vary with the nature of the student's need, but in which there is always mutual participation by the counselor and the student with the focus upon self-clarification and self-determination by the student" (1951). It will be seen that Wrenn's definition is sufficiently broad to encompass both the activities of the earlier proponents of counseling and those of the more modern practitioners. Hahn (1953) points out that the reason for these different perceptions in the counseling process is that counseling itself seems to have three different bodies of supporters. He identifies the social welfare advocates who have primarily an ideographic interest. Typical of these would be Coombs and the others in the phenomenological school. A second group would be those who are more medically oriented and more nomothetic in their position. Foremost among these would be such men as Thorne. The final and third movement identified by Hahn would be those people who are primarily concerned with student personnel administration and who have great interest in measurement. Typical of this group would be Strong, Bingham, and probably Williamson (Hahn, 1953, p. 234). Because counseling practitioners approach the process from a variety of directions and backgrounds, it should not seem unusual that they view and define counseling in a variety of ways. Although they may be each patting the same elephant, they are getting quite different notions of what the beast is like.

A common element in many current definitions of counseling is the notion that counseling is aimed at helping people make choices and act on them—helping them answer the question, "What shall I do?" Perhaps the clearest advocate of this point of view is Tyler: "Counseling is one kind of psychological helping activity, the kind that concentrates on the growth of a clear sense of ego identity and the willingness to make choices and commitments in accordance with it" (1958, p. 8). Others have agreed that this element of choice is the key factor in counseling. Moore (1961, p. 63) in making the point that high school counselors should not do psychotherapy defines counseling in the high school setting as help with choice making. Traube says

> A counselor's task is helping the student to examine and analyze his own problem; to gather, evaluate, and organize pertinent data in regard to it; to think through the probable consequences of various possible solutions; to choose and try out the solution that seems to fit the known facts and needs most adequately; and to modify his plan of solution when it proves to be out of harmony with the facts and needs of the situation (1950, p. 932).

Shostrom and Brammer quote a definition which tells us that counseling is "a purposeful, reciprocal relationship between two people in which one, a trained person, helps the other to change himself or his environment" (1952, p. 1). And finally, Wolberg tells us that counseling is "a form of interviewing in which the client is helped to understand himself more completely in order to correct an environmental or adjustment difficulty" (1954, p. 12). An important element in any understanding of counseling is a recognition that many people see it as an aid in choice making prior to acting.

Learning is another element which is often used in defining counseling. Gustad says that

> counseling is a learning-oriented process, carried on in a simple, one-to-one social environment, in which a counselor, professionally competent in relevant psychological skills and knowledge, seeks to assist the client by methods appropriate to the latter's needs and within the context of the total personnel program, to learn more about himself, to learn how to put such understanding into effect in relation to more clearly perceived, realistically defined goals to the end that the client may become a happier and more productive member of his society (1953).

This concern with learning which we have seen was an element in earlier definitions of counseling has again come to the fore with research and study on the behavioral aspects of the counseling process. Indeed, most theorists in the field now would agree that counseling is a learning process, although they might have some sharp differences as to what facilitates learning and how learning occurs.

Still another element frequently found in definitions of counseling is that of personality development. Bordin says "The psychological counselor is a psychological practitioner who aids people with these problems of behavior in which the critical issues have to do with their emotions and motivations ... Counseling ... involves interactions . where the counselor ... has taken responsibility for making his role in the interaction process contribute positively to the other person's personality development" (1955, p. 3). Again, although almost all theorists might agree that counseling involves personality development, there might be relatively little agreement as to how personality development is best furthered.

One of the conceptions of counseling involves its effect on role clarification. Tyler (1961, p. 21) says that counseling is much concerned with role problems as opposed to psychotherapy with its emphasis on intrapersonal conflict. An authoritative report by the Division of Counseling Psychology of the American Psychological Association (1961) defines counseling as being involved primarily with role problems. This report points out that three trends merge in counseling psychology—vocational guidance, psychometrics, and personality development. The fact that these three streams have different sources may indicate some of the reasons for differences of opinion with regard to what counseling is or should be. The report goes on to say that the present emphasis in counseling embraces such goals for the client as clear self-perception and harmony with environment and such goals for society as the encouragement of society to recognize individual differences and encouragement of the full development of all people. This report would suggest that there will remain some differences in the specifics of what counseling should be but that there might be general agreement that one of the purposes of counseling is to help an individual understand one of his role commitments and carry it out more successfully.

The attempts at definitions that are quoted here have had in common the primarily instrumental character of counseling. Although some of them would suggest that counseling is basically concerned with dynamic problems, the bulk of counseling theorists seem to believe that counseling deals with such problems as choice, action, and role definition. It has been seen that many writers have attempted to define counseling without, on the one hand, succeeding to everyone's satisfaction, or, on the other hand, seriously damaging themselves or the profession. Thus encouraged, this author joins the line with his definition: "Counseling denotes a professional relationship between a trained counselor and a client. This relationship is usually person-to-person, although it may sometimes involve more than two people, and it is designed to help the client understand and clarify his view of his life space so that he may make meaningful and informed choices consonant with his essential nature in those areas where choices are available to him." This definition like many quoted above indicates that counseling is a process, that it is a relationship, that it is designed to help people make choices, that underlying better choice making are such matters as learning, personality development, and self-knowledge which can be translated into better role perception and more effective role behavior.

Distinctions between Counseling and Psychotherapy

Efforts to distinguish counseling from psychotherapy has not met with universal approval. Some people think that such a distinction should not be made and that the two terms should be used synonymously. Others, however, particularly those preparing secondary school counselors, are of the opinion that such a distinction *must* be made. If it is not present in nature, it must be invented. If no distinction is possible, then certainly all master's level counselor education programs should stop at once and twenty thousand secondary school counselors who are presently employed to do "counseling" should be dismissed, for few would hold that these people are properly trained psychotherapists. A distinction, then, must be found even though the edges of the distinction may blur and agreement on all particulars is unlikely. The problem is clearly posed by Hahn who writes,

> I know of few counselors or psychologists who are completely satisfied that clear distinctions (between counseling and psychotherapy) have been made. . . . Perhaps the most complete agreements are: 1- that counseling and psychotherapy cannot be distinguished clearly, 2- that counselors practice what psychotherapists consider psychotherapy, 3- that psychotherapists practice what counselors consider to be counseling, and 4- that despite the above they are different (1953, p. 232).

The difficulty of distinction was recognized by English and English in their previously quoted definition which goes on to say of counseling that "while usually applied to help the normal counselee it merges by imperceptible degrees into psychotherapy" (1958).

Before trying to make a distinction between counseling and psychotherapy, we might find it helpful to pause and define psychotherapy itself. Wolberg defines psychotherapy as "a form of treatment for problems of an emotional nature in which a trained person deliberately establishes a professional relationship with a patient with the object of removing, modifying or retarding existing symptoms, of mediating disturbed patterns of behavior, and of promoting positive personality growth and development" (1954, p. 1). Eysenck quotes an amusing definition which says that psychotherapy is "an unidentified technique applied to unspecified problems with unpredictable outcomes. For this technique we recommend rigorous training" (1961, p. 698). Eysenck then more seriously defines psychotherapy as containing such elements as (1) a prolonged interpersonal relationship, (2) the involvement of trained personnel, (3) a self-dissatisfaction with emotional and/or interpersonal adjustment on the part of the client, (4) the use of psychological methods, (5) an activity based on a theory of mental disorders, and (6) an aim through this relationship of ameliorating self-dissatisfaction.

To see some of the differences between counseling and psychotherapy, we shall look at their respective goals, clients, practitioners, settings, and methods. Although we shall examine these differences, no completely satisfactory, defensible, and clear distinctions are expected. It seems more likely that a continuum may exist from one activity to the other in regard to each of these elements. Just as first aid may shade into the practice of medicine so counseling may shade into psychotherapy, but no one thinks that it is impossible to distinguish the application of a band-aid from brain surgery. Or as Goldman (1964) writes, "True, there are times around dusk, when one is uncertain about turning on the lights. . . . Do these borderline decisions mean that there is no value in differentiating between day and night . . .?"

[This notion of a continuum of counseling to psychotherapy has been well expressed by Brammer and Shostrom who indicate that the two activities may overlap, but that in general counseling would be characterized by such terms as "educative, supportive, situational, problem solving, conscious awareness, and emphasis on normal," whereas therapy would be characterized by such terms as "reconstructive, depth emphasis, analytic, focus on unconscious and emphasis on neurotic or other emotional problems" (1960, p. 6). Patterson, in reviewing the literature on counseling, indicates that the counseling end of a counseling-psychotherapy continuum would be characterized by such elements as "normal, preventive, developmental, not severe, area versus total, reality oriented, positive, non-imbedded" (1959, p. 4). This emphasis on distinction by relative position on several continua provides a useful framework from which to attempt more specific differences with regard to goals, clients, practitioners, settings, and methods.

Goals

In looking at the goals of counseling as distinguished from the goals of psychotherapy, it would seem that frequently a goal of counseling is to help an individual deal with the developmental tasks which are appropriate to his age. The adolescent who is being helped with the problems of sexual definition, emotional independence from parents, preparation for an occupation, and the other tasks typical of his age and our culture would be receiving counseling. On the other hand, a middle-aged person who is grappling with these same problems might be closer to the appropriate concern of a psychotherapist.]

The previously cited report of Division 17 of the American Psychological Association says

When we consider these discussions and look at the contribution counseling psychologists are making and can make to society, we can summarize what is important about the specialty by saying that it focuses on *plans* individuals must make to play productive *roles* in their social environments. Whether the person being helped with such planning is sick or well, abnormal or normal, is really irrelevant. The focus is on assets, skills, strengths, possibilities for further development. Personality difficulties are dealt with only when they constitute obstacles to the individual's forward progress (1961, p. 6).

Another suggested distinction regarding goals has been made by Hahn and MacLean (1955), who indicate that the counselor would give heavy emphasis to prevention of disruptive deviations, whereas the psychotherapist might give primary emphasis to present deviations with secondary attention to prevention. They make another distinction with regard to reality testing and indicate that a goal of counseling is to permit reality testing in a somewhat sheltered situation, whereas in psychotherapy testing is permitted in an almost completely sheltered situation. Finally, they say that counseling has as a goal long-range educational and vocational planning. Their total emphasis seems to involve distinguishing counseling as being concerned with preventive mental health and psychotherapy with remediation.

Another distinction is sometimes made with regard to the goal of these two activities in that counseling is more concerned with narrowly situational matters, while psychotherapy is more concerned with changing the organisms so that the client can handle not only the present but future problems. In other words, counseling sometimes is defined as being more peripheral and psychotherapy more central.

Shaw (1957, p. 357) indicates that counseling should be more concerned with creative help, while psychotherapy is more concerned with mental illness. That is, counseling is not so much involved with curing or treating as with pointing out new vistas of opportunity. Mowrer (1953) has indicated the possibility of distinguishing the goals of counseling and psychotherapy on the basis of two kinds of anxiety. Normal anxiety is the proper business of counseling, whereas psychotherapy might more appropriately deal with neurotic anxiety.

Tyler (1961, p. 58) suggests that counseling is the process of helping the client to attain a clear sense of identity but that psychotherapy attempts to make changes in the basic developmental structure. Again Tyler (1961, p. 12) indicates that psychotherapy deals with personality change, while counseling deals with the utilization of resources; psychotherapy with intrapersonal conflict, counseling with role problems.

Vance and Volsky (1962, pp. 565-570) suggest that a common goal in much psychotherapy and counseling is the reduction of psychological discordance. When this discordance is accompanied by considerable psycho-pathology, it falls more appropriately into the domain of the psychothera-pist, but when it is reality-based as, for example, with a client whose goals call for abilities he lacks, it calls for counseling skills. However, these authors contend that the dimensions of discordance and psychopathology are correlated, and they therefore believe that all psychologists who offer person-alized treatment services will do both psychotherapy and psychological discordance reduction.

The most ambitious attempt to distinguish counseling from psychother-apy has been made by Wolberg (1954). Wolberg distinguishes three kinds of approaches to problems in this area: supportive, insight-reeducative, and insight-reconstructive. Supportive psychotherapy has as its object emotional equilibrium with a minimization of symptoms so that the individual can function near his norm. Examples of treatment in this area would be direc-tive guidance, environmental manipulation, externalization of interests, and persuasion. These and other supportive treatments might appropriately be given by a counselor. In passing, he suggests that indications for the ap-propriateness of this goal would include (1) a strong ego beset by temporary problems or (2) an ego so weak that even psychotherapy would not be useful. Contraindicators would include great authority problems and there-fore a tendency to resist persuasion or to succumb to it.

Insight psychotherapy with reeducated goals, according to Wolberg, attempts to modify attitudes of behavior to more adaptive life integration. The goal of such psychotherapy would be to further insight into conscious processes so that behavior might be changed or goals might be changed. Wolberg would include in this area counseling as well as social casework. By implication this treatment is indicated for those relatively slight prob-lems or problems in a circumscribed area.

Finally, Wolberg writes of insight psychotherapy with reconstructive goals. In this kind of psychotherapy the practitioner works toward an aware-ness of unconscious conflicts and hopes to make extensive alterations of the character structure of the client. He points out that although supportive therapy and reeducative psychotherapy may lead to reconstructive psycho-therapy, it is important to make distinctions among these three approaches in terms of their goals. Reconstructive therapy, particularly in the form of psychoanalysis, is indicated for those who have neuroses sufficiently severe to justify the considerable expenditure of time and money and who are, at the same time, bright and neither too young to be "reasonable" nor too old to be "flexible." Contraindicators include severe symptoms which demand rapid attention, psychosis, irremediable life situations provoking neurotic defenses, and great secondary gains which accrue to the neurosis. If we accept Wolberg's distinction, the psychotherapist would be concerned with reconstructive goals and the counselor with reeducative and supportive goals. Obviously, however, there might be occasions when a psychotherapist would properly work toward supportive or reeducative goals, and there also would be times when the counselor might find himself doing reconstructive psychotherapy.

In summary, the goals of psychotherapy usually involve quite a complete change of basic character structure. The goals of counseling are apt to be more limited, more concerned with aiding growth, more concerned with the immediate situation, more concerned with helping the individual function adequately in appropriate roles.

Clients

Some attempts have been made to distinguish counseling from psychotherapy on the basis of the clients they serve. Traditionally it has been said that the counselor deals with normal people, and the psychotherapist with the neurotic or psychotic. The most systematic delineation of this kind has been made by Hahn and MacLean (1955) who indicate that the normal is a major type of client for the counselor and a secondary type for the psychotherapist. The neurotic would be seen by the counselor only on an emergency basis or as a consultant to other specialists, whereas the neurotic would be the usual type of client for the psychotherapist. Finally, a psychotic would be seen by a counselor only in an emergency or on a consultative basis, whereas he might be treated by a psychotherapist working in collaboration with a medical doctor.

These distinctions while once widely accepted now seem to be under some attack. Tyler (1961, p. 13) specifically rejects a distinction between counseling and psychotherapy which is based on clients or settings. Others, too, have complained that while the distinction between normal and neurotic is easy to make clear, it may be difficult to make practical. Still many would say that one useful distinction between counseling and psychotherapy is that the counselor is primarily trained to deal with normal people and that the psychotherapist is primarily trained to deal with disturbed people.

Practitioners

Distinctions between counseling and psychotherapy necessarily involve some consideration of the practitioner himself. Black says "that a major share of therapy done today is performed by people who are not even called therapists" (1952, p. 302). The previously discussed report—Current Status of Counseling Psychology (1961)—points out that there is considerable overlap in membership in Division 17 (Counseling Psychology) and Division 12 (Clinical Psychology) in the American Psychological Association. In

1957 25 percent of the members of Division 17 also belonged to Division 12. There is indication, however, that this overlap is less among new members.

It should be remembered that although this report indicates that psychological therapists and counseling psychologists are very similar in their training and professional identification, we are speaking here only of the more highly trained counselors. It is estimated that there are about ten thousand full-time counselors operating in the American schools and perhaps another ten thousand part-time counselors. The average training for these people would probably be that represented by a master's degree in guidance in a college of education. Most counseling is done by people with considerably less training than that held by psychotherapists, even if we should agree that some psychotherapy is done by those with training at this level.

Perhaps it could be said that the better-trained counselors are scarcely distinguishable from the better-trained psychotherapist. Both will have basic training in personality theory, interviewing and research methods, considerable background in biological and physical sciences, in sociology, in mathematics, and in community organization. Both will have a formal internship of two or more years and will be apt to hold a doctor's degree. The relatively untrained psychotherapist, however, would be most apt to have either a master's degree in social work or in clinical psychology, whereas the relatively untrained counselor might have almost any kind of a background but generally a teaching credential plus a few guidance courses. Some will have a master's degree in counseling, but most will have not even this much preparation. The difference, then, in the practitioners may be great or minimal. It may be true on occasion, but certainly not always, that one can tell whether counseling or psychotherapy is going on by looking at who is doing it. Thompson and Super (1964) report the conclusions of a recent important conference on the training of counseling psychologists and point out that degrees may be granted by departments of either psychology or education.

Settings

Some attempt has been made to distinguish between counseling and psychotherapy in terms of where it is happening. It is observed that psychotherapists are more apt to work in hospital settings or in private practice; counselors are more apt to be working in educational settings. While this is true, to some extent, it is less a distinguishing feature than it once was. The Veterans Administration, for example, is hiring counselors to work in hospitals to do vocational counseling with disabled veterans. On the other hand, school systems and colleges are now hiring clinical psychologists and other therapeutically oriented practitioners. Still, as a generalization, it could be said that although counseling may more often occur in educational institutions and psychotherapy more in medical settings, we cannot always determine which activity is going on by noting where it is happening.

Methods

In distinguishing counseling from psychotherapy on the basis of difference of methods, we should run counter to the advice of Patterson (1959, p. 10), who sees no differences between them. This, of course, would be the general position of most client-centered counselors. Certainly commonality in method is great. Where universals or essentials of method have been listed for psychotherapy and for counseling, they have much overlap. Black (1952, p. 305) believes that all psychotherapists would have in common the building of rapport between patient and therapist, the acceptance and appreciation of the basic human worth of the individual (although not necessarily the complete negation of any possibility of evaluation as in the Rogerian theory), the supportive relationship of the psychotherapist to the patient, the status implicit or explicit of the psychotherapist, and the provision of controls and limits in the relationship. These universals of psychotherapy would be equally applicable to counseling. Counseling, too, involves rapport, acceptance, support, status, control, and limits.

Tyler lists what she feels are the essentials of any counseling relationship, and again they would seem to apply to psychotherapy (1961, p. 14): interest by the counselor in the client, confidence in the counselor by the client, limits on their relationship, the use of information as a resource when appropriate, and a relationship which has as a goal the facilitating of the development of the client. Black and Tyler seem to say that the methods of psychotherapy are varied and the methods of counseling are varied and that sometimes there would be more differences within the several approaches in therapy than between therapy and counseling and more differences within the several approaches in counseling than between counseling and psychotherapy.

Wolberg (1954) believes that concern with the conscious level is more characteristic of counselors and that concern with the unconscious level is more characteristic of therapists. Other distinctions between counseling (reeducative psychotherapy) and therapy (reconstructive psychotherapy) are these: (1) Counseling is usually of less duration than therapy; (2) the sessions are apt to occur less frequently; (3) less case history taking and more psychological examination is typical and characteristic of counseling; (4) more advice giving and less transference is characteristic of counseling. Whereas a therapist is more apt to make his individual assessment or diagnosis chiefly through a clinical interview, the counselor may frequently make use of psychometric tools.

Method has been discussed by Bordin who feels that the distinction should be primarily quantitative rather than qualitative. (He believes that both counseling and psychotherapy should be preceded by a medical examination.) Counseling would deal with less emotionally intense matters and be more generally positive than would therapy (1955, p. 160). Counseling more than therapy would deal with cognition and therapy more than counseling would deal with conative aspects. A major contribution of Bordin to the problem of definition is made when he deals with the concept of ambiguity (1955, p. 138). Statements can be ambiguous with regard to the topic to be discussed, the relationship between the counselor and the clients, or the goals of counseling. To the extent that the counselor moves toward a more ambiguous structure in his counseling, he is moving toward therapy. Ambiguity leads to anxiety, and the forcing of anxiety leads to a more therapeutic relationship. The method of counseling then would be to limit the ambiguity, and the method of therapy to maximize it.

To summarize some differences in method between counseling and psychotherapy, we can say that counseling is characterized by shorter duration of treatment, less frequent visits, more use of psychological examination, more concern with the client's present daily problems, more focus on his conscious activities, more advice giving, less concern with transference, more emphasis on the reality situation, more cognition and less emotional intensity, more clarity and less ambiguity.

Summary

The distinction between counseling and psychotherapy cannot be made with complete clarity and satisfaction. At the same time an attempt must be made to at least distinguish the master's level school counselor and the psychoanalyst as well as many intermediate positions. The total length of training for school counselors is presently averaging about one year of graduate work, and of that probably less than half is psychological in nature. Can we not make it clear to these counselors that they are not trained as therapists? The position of this chapter is that at least the extremes of differences between counseling and psychotherapy can be identified. While it is true that "tall" cannot be distinguished from "short" when men are roughly five-foot-nine, it is equally clear that five-foot-two is different from six-foot-five. An attempt to distinguish between these two activities—counseling and psychotherapy—is made particularly difficult by the prestige structure in American academic circles. In general, education is less valued than psychology as a discipline. Since education departments train most counselors, counseling does not have the prestige of psychotherapy. As a consequence master's level school counselors like to think of themselves as counseling psychologists, counseling psychologists sometimes like to think of themselves as clinical psychologists, and clinical psychologists like to muddy the distinction with psychiatry. Although snobbery and professional psychopathy makes these distinctions difficult, the distinctions themselves are not without value.

In attempting to point to some differences between counseling and psychotherapy, we can now look at the several elements we have considered and compare the two activities with regard to their position on various continua. (1) Counseling tends to be concerned with instrumental behavior, with role problems, with situations, with choices which must be made, and with actions which must be taken. Goals of counseling are more limited than those of psychotherapy, but this does not mean that these limited goals are unimportant or that changes in immediate behavior may not have lasting global effects. (2) Counselors deal primarily with normal individuals. (The distinction between "normal" and "neurotic" is as fraught with difficulties, of course, as the distinction between counseling and psychotherapy.) (3) The practitioner of counseling may be trained at the doctoral level with a two-year internship as would be his counterpart in clinical psychology. Many counselors, however, are trained at less than a doctoral level or at the doctoral level but with relatively little psychology and little or no formal supervised internship. These people because of the prestige rank of psychology and because of their own confused role concepts may quickly come to think of themselves as psychotherapists. Although they have difficulty making the distinction, there is no reason why more objective observers should. (4) The setting in which counseling takes place is most apt to be an educational setting or a community agency, although counselors may work in a medical setting or in private practice. (5) The methods used will indicate that counseling shows more concern than psychotherapy with present events than with those of the past, more concern with cognition than with affect, more concern with clarity than with ambiguity.

There seems to be no litmus paper which will distinguish counseling from psychotherapy as it changes from blue to red. Combinations of clues, however, may be helpful in distinguishing the two activities. If we see an interview relationship in which the professional person is trained at less than a doctoral level (or at the doctoral level without a formal two-year internship), if he is dealing with a normal client, if he is dealing with him in an educational setting, if he is primarily concerned with conscious processes, and if his goals are to help the client play one of his life roles more effectively by making better choices, we can say that counseling is going on. On the other hand, if the practitioner has been trained primarily in clinical psychology, if his client seems quite disturbed, if they are working in a medical setting, if the goals are to reconstruct the personality of the client, and if the methods are characterized by ambiguity, intense emotion, and concern for unconscious processes, we may more appropriately label the activity as psychotherapy.

Counseling Distinguished from Instruction

If to a counseling practitioner the thunder on the left is representative of psychotherapy, the thunder on the right is representative of instruction. There are educational theorists who see little distinction between counseling and teaching. Certainly in a broad sense their goals may be much the same since both are concerned with helping an individual develop to the point where he can assume responsibilities for himself and live a satisfying life. More narrowly, however, the goals of counseling are more determined by the needs of the individual as he sees them, whereas the goals of instruction are more apt to be societally determined. The most permissive and student-centered teacher of an algebra class has some views as to what should be covered in an instructional situation because society has, to some extent, defined those goals, but in the counseling situation the counselor has less preconception about what will be needed to help the individual.

With regard to the client (or student), instruction is thought to be for all. With regard to counseling, there are those who think counseling should be given to everyone, but frequently it happens that counseling is only given to those who voluntarily request it or perhaps to those seen as "needing" it.

The practitioner of teaching has been trained in specific instructional techniques and subject matter, while hopefully the counselor has had additional training in interviewing, psychometrics, occupational information, and other competencies required by his specialized role. It would seem to be true, however, that often teachers do counseling and sometimes counselors do teaching. The wisdom of having the same person play both roles can be questioned because the teacher is required to be judgmental and to operate as a representative of an educational institution with certain responsibilities determined by the function of that institution, whereas the counselor has primary responsibility to the individual and so can be less judgmental. Part of this confusion stems from the fact that educational institutions in America have two purposes—the developmental and the screening. They have the job of helping a student grow, but they also have the job of acting as gatekeeper to certain occupations and roles. This screening function, which is now being performed by the educational institution, would seem to inhibit the kind of relationship which is thought to be most helpful in counseling. The counseling, then, particularly if it concerns individual educational problems, may be difficult to distinguish from instruction.

The methods of teaching are more apt to be group methods, and the methods of counseling are more apt to be individual methods. However, teachers may teach one student at a time, and this tutoring function has long been recognized and valued, while more and more counselors are experimenting with group procedures.

If we see an individual in a group being dealt with by a teacher with some societally determined preconception as to the goals of the interaction, we are apt to call this activity instruction rather than counseling.

Substantive Elements in Theories of Counseling

Having considered the activity of counseling, let us now return to our discussion of theory.

We have previously considered the nature of theory and the formal attributes of a theory. Since we are concerned with a special kind of theory—one dealing with counseling—we need now to look at the substantive elements which would characterize such a theory. Substantive elements are determined by what the theory is about, what it deals with. Substantive elements in learning theory might involve such matters as environmentalism versus nativism and historical versus contemporary causation, while in administrative theory such matters as direction, staffing, and planning might be included. The substantive elements of a counseling theory would include (1) assumptions regarding the nature of man, (2) beliefs regarding learning theory and changes in behavior, (3) a commitment to certain goals of counseling, (4) a definition of the role of the counselor, and (5) research evidence supporting the theory.

While we have previously noted that counseling theory may not necessarily derive from a specific philosophy, some assumptions must be made about what kind of a creature man is in order to construct a theory about counseling him. As we examine specific theories, we shall note whether the theorist is assuming the innate goodness or evil of man, the problems attendant upon the human condition, and the pliability of man, that is, whether he is sufficiently plastic in nature that he can be shaped in one way or another by the interaction of genetic elements and environment.

Counseling theories also include beliefs about how people change or learn. There is some agreement that counseling constitutes a learning process, but theorists may disagree on how this learning takes place. Is it furthered by a general atmosphere or by specific stimulus-response situations? Change would seem to be a goal of counseling, but there may be great differences among theorists regarding how change comes about.

The goals of counseling will differ for different theories. We have indicated previously that even if we assume that mental health is the goal we are aiming at, there are various definitions as to what constitutes mental health. For example, the usual high school counseling seems to assume that mental health can be equated with a mastery of environment, particularly as exemplified by grades in school or the ability to get along in an educational institution and meet the expectations of the teachers. Glad (1959) at least by inference suggests that the goals of various therapeutic approaches are so different that one person could be considered to have been successfully treated by advocates of one theory and at the same time be seen as in need of therapy by advocates of another theory. A good counseling theory will be explicit and clear regarding its goals.

The role of the counselor will be different in different theories. This role will differ with regard to the place and importance of diagnosis, for example, and some may make much use of tests, case histories, and screening interviews, while others will not. Other elements on which there would be differences would be the extent to which interpretation, advice, and persuasion are thought to be proper behavior for the counselor. We may find differences in the extent to which theories permit and support the intrusion of counselor's values into the counseling situation. There may be differences with regard to what actually is done in the initial contact and to what attitude the therapist has toward group procedures. Above all, the basic counseling style and its clarification regarding such matters as acceptance as opposed to interpretation, advice as opposed to clarification, use of authority as opposed to denial of authority, and encouragement of transference versus denial of transference will typify a theory. Finally, there may be differences with regard to such special problems as dependency of the client, the communication problem, and other elements which may appear to help define the role of the counselor.

The different theories may lend themselves to illustrative case material which will tell us in more specific terms how the theory functions in a given case. It is only by examining such typescripts that we can see the relationship between logical constructs and the events of the counseling interview. Since a theory deals not only with logical structure but with specific data, we shall want to look for research evidence and support with regard to the theories which we are considering. A theory which is completely abstract is a poor theory not because it is wrong, but because it does not help us to understand the facts which are already available. In summary, a theory of counseling must meet not only certain formal criteria but must make explicit its position regarding certain substantive elements which have been isolated above and which are those that seem appropriate to the judgment of a theory in this field.

Bibliography

Black, J. D. Common factors in patient-therapist relationship in diverse psychotherapies. *J. clin. Psychol.,* 1952, **8**, 302-306.

Bone, H. Personality theory. In *American handbook of psychiatry.* New York: Basic Books, 1959. Pp. 88-113.

Bordin, E. S. *Psychological counseling.* New York: Appleton Century Crofts, 1955.

Brammer, L. M., & Shostrom, E. L. *Therapeutic psychology.* Englewood Cliffs, N.J.: Prentice-Hall, 1960.

Campbell, N. R. The structure of theories. In *Readings in the philosophy of science.* New York: Appleton Century Crofts, 1953. Pp. 288-308.

The current status of counseling psychology—A report of a special committee of the Division 17 of Counseling Psychology of the American Psychological Association, 1961.

English, H. B., & English, A. C. *A comprehensive dictionary of psychological and psychiatric terms.* New York: McKay, 1958.

Eysenck, H. J. The effects of psychotherapy. In *Handbook of abnormal psychology.* New York: Basic Books, 1961. Pp. 697-725.

Frank, P. *Modern science and its philosophy.* Cambridge, Mass.: Harvard, 1949.

Glad, D. D. *Operational values in psychotherapy.* Fair Lawn, N.J.: Oxford University Press, 1959.

Goldman, L. Another log. *Amer. Psychologist,* 1964, **19**, 418-419.

Good, C. V. (Ed.), *Dictionary of education.* New York: McGraw-Hill, 1945.

Gustad, J. W. In R. F. Berdie (Ed.), *Roles and relationships in counseling.* Minneapolis: University of Minnesota Press, 1953.

Hahn, M. E. Conceptual trends in counseling. *Personnel guid. J.,* 1953, **31**, 231-235.

Hahn, M. E., & MacLean, M. S. *Counseling psychology.* (2nd ed.) New York: McGraw-Hill, 1955.

Hall, C. S., & Lindzey, G. *Theories of personality.* New York: Wiley, 1957.

Hall, E. T. *The silent language.* Garden City, N. Y.: Doubleday; and Greenwich, Conn.: Fawcett, 1961.

Jahoda, M. *Current concepts of positive mental health.* New York: Basic Books, 1958.

McCabe, G. E. When is a good theory practical? *Personnel guid. J.,* 1958, **37**(1), 47-52.

McDaniel, H. B., Lallas, J. E., Saum, J. A., & Gilmore, J. L. *Readings in guidance.* New York: Holt, 1959.

Moore, G. D. A negative view toward therapeutic counseling in the public schools. *Counselor Educ. Suprv.,* 1961, **1**(2), 60-68.

Mowrer, O. H. *Psychotherapy—Theory and research.* New York: Ronald, 1953.

Patterson, C. H. *Counseling and psychotherapy: Theory and practice.* New York: Harper & Row, 1959.

Pepinsky, H. B., & Pepinsky, P. *Counseling—Theory and practice.* New York: Ronald, 1954.

Pepper, S. C. *World hypotheses.* Berkeley, Calif.: University of California Press, 1961.

Phillips, E. L. *Psychotherapy—A modern theory and practice.* Englewood Cliffs, N.J.: Prentice-Hall, 1956.

Shaw, F. J. Counseling. In *Annual review of psychology.* Palo Alto, Calif.: Annual Reviews, 1957.

Shoben, E. J., Jr. The counselor's theory as a personal trait. *Personnel guid. J.,* 1962, **40**, 617–621.

Shostrom, E. L., & Brammer, L. M. *The dynamics of the counseling process.* New York: McGraw-Hill, 1952.

Theobald, R. *The challenge of abundance.* New York: New American Library, 1961.

Thompson. A. S., & Super, D. E. *The professional preparation of counseling psychologists.* Report of the 1964 Greystone Conference, New York: Bureau of Publications, Teachers College, Columbia University, 1964.

Traube, M. R. Pupil personnel work. V. Counseling services. In *Encyclopedia of educational research.* New York: Macmillan, 1950. Pp. 930–938.

Tyler, L. E. Theoretical principles underlying the counseling process. *J. counsel. Psychol.,* 1958, 5(1), 3–8.

Tyler, L. E. *The work of the counselor.* New York: Appleton Century Crofts, 1961.

Vance, F. L., & Volsky, T. C., Jr. Counseling and psychotherapy: Split personalities or siamese twins. *Amer. Psychologist,* 1962, **17**, 565–570.

Wolberg, L. R. *The technique of psychotherapy.* New York: Grune & Stratton, 1954.

Wrenn, C. G. *Student personnel work in college.* New York: Ronald, 1951.

Wrenn, C. G. Philosophical and psychological bases of personnel services in education. *Personnel Services in Education.* 1958 Yearb. Nat. Soc. Stud. Educ., Part II. Chicago: The University of Chicago Press, 1959.

2

Counseling Theory and Practice in the School

WILLIAM RATIGAN

This chapter is concerned with the effect of the total environment on the theoretical approach of the counselor. The counselor's approach is shaped by environmental factors such as changes in society brought about by the cultural revolution; the developmental stage of both counselor and client, and the needs of each; the requirements and expectations of colleagues, superiors, and surrounding community; and the myriad environmental forces that determine roles.

The focus here will be on school counseling, with awareness that campus counseling, employment counseling, marriage counseling, rehabilitation counseling, pastoral counseling, and even draft counseling, among others, are alike shaped by setting and surroundings, and choices of where to work and what to do and whom to help. At each stage of life man needs counseling. The counselor who has chosen to be man's helper at any particular stage moves into a setting that will influence his theory of how to operate; i.e., a retirement counselor is not likely to be found in a child-guidance clinic, and there is little college counseling done in elementary schools.

Roeber (1965) studied the roles and functions of counselors in various settings, pointing out that "a counselor in the employment service is more concerned with the tangible or *product* aspects of counseling outcome than with reconstructing the emotive or *process* of a counselee's personality. His immediate task is helping a client become optimally employed as quickly as feasible, relying upon other agency or community resources when employment depends upon fundamental, long-term changes in attitudes, values, needs, and other personality dimensions."

Roeber saw a rehabilitation counselor as "constantly working within medical limits, those associated with his client's disabilities as well as those imposed by the nature of different work, and educational settings." He observed that an immediate role of the school counselor was to help pupils accept themselves and the world in which they live; and he concluded that the employment counselor's role was the only clear-cut role, in contrast to all other counseling groups examined.

Useful schematic models, pertaining to environmental forces affecting counselor role development and consequent theoretical position, are found in Getzels (1963) and Ivey and Robin (1966). Other useful schemata, clarifying social and organizational effect on role shaping, include those presented by Allport (1965) and Kahn et al. (1964).

The total setting for any counselor, of course, includes his inner world, his reactions to himself and to significant others within his orbit. Wrenn found a bookful of role definitions in four phrases by Bentley (1968), who examined role theory as developed in sociology: (1) role *expectation* (what others expect you to do); (2) role *concept* (what you conceive your role to be); (3) role *acceptance* (what you will accept of others' expectations of you within the framework of your own role perception); and (4) role *performance* (what you actually do on the job).

Counselors are found in business and industrial settings, in community agency settings, in churches, in private practice, in prisons, in the Peace Corps, in Veterans Administration installations, and in other locations. However, the settings that draw more counselors than all the other settings are the elementary and secondary schools. During the sixties about 50,000 counselors worked in educational environments, the majority in the traditional locus, the high school, but a significant and growing number at the elementary level. Government projections look ahead to a demand for at least 125,000 public school counselors by the mid-seventies, with a minimum of 54,000 counselors wanted to practice developmental counseling in the elementary grades. In other words, dramatizing the phenomenal public acceptance of these comparative newcomers to the scene, the demand for elementary school counselors alone outweighs the combined demand for college and university counselors, rehabilitation counselors, employment service counselors, and Office of Educational Opportunity counselors.

Numbers are significant in settings. For example, the ratio of the number of counselors in a school system to the number of pupils or students is a vital statistic operative in the development of counseling theory and practice.

In their perception of counselor ecology, Shertzer and Stone (1968) stated concisely that "Good counseling, like good teaching, is a highly complex activity which is situationally dependent upon the counselor, the counselee, the setting, the topic, and the conditions under which it is conducted."

Settings have as many individual differences as pupils. If "fingerprints" could be taken of schools, classrooms, or teacher lounges, no two would be found alike. Every setting is unique, just as each person within the setting defies duplication. The interaction may be subtle or otherwise, but behavior changes occur in the process.

Walz and Miller (1969) examined research dealing with the nature of educational climates and environments in schools and colleges, finding that there are definite differences which affect the behavior of students and staff. In a study of elementary schools, six types of climate were identified: open, autonomous, controlled, familiar, paternal, and closed. One implication revealed in this research review was the need for variety in counselor behavior—a need for school and college counselors to change their ways, to adjust to the climates of the different educational settings, and to serve as interpreters of the climatic mixes so that they might help both students and staff adjust to particular environmental factors.

A major difference between the ecologies of school and college counseling is that in the latter situation the clients no longer are captive and the campus climate is nowhere near as custodial. The public schools are like prisons and public mental hospitals in that they fall into the category of organizations where neither the client served by the organization nor the organization itself can reject participation (Willower, Hoy, and Eidell, 1967). This tends to put a premium on discipline and pressures the counselor to join teachers and administrators in enforcement roles. This occurs especially at the secondary level, as apart from the more humanistic setting of the elementary school where the counselor's whole-child-oriented approach is more familiar and congenial to instructional personnel. (More about discipline later.)

Perhaps the most saturating influence in the educational setting is that school personnel are overwhelmingly (the word is used advisedly) middle class. This means rejection of lower-class values and generally a sour-grapes or halo attitude toward upper-strata offspring. School personnel traditionally want to deal with conforming children, "nice clean-cut American kids from good homes." Deviations from the norm, such as creativity, are apt to be stifled by lack of understanding if nothing else.

In his comprehensive statement on the function of elementary school counseling, Costar (1966) directed attention to the fact that both the counselor's training and the nature of the work setting affect his duties. Since the counselor's clients at this level are young and relatively immature, he spends much time consulting with their parents and teachers. "The proportion of time spent in this capacity varies from school to school, depending upon the attitudes and wishes of the teachers and parents with whom he works. Second, since this is a relatively new position, the philosophy and objectives of training programs for elementary school counselors still vary considerably from university to university throughout the country. Thus not all people holding counseling positions at this level see their jobs in the same way."

That school counselors were extremely sensitive about their settings and job titles became evident in the late sixties. Arbuckle (1967) precipitated dialogue with school personnel when he examined the possibility of a closer relationship between the school counselor, the social worker, and the psychologist, going so far as to suggest that the new functional title for each of the three be *school counseling psychologist.*

In her public school "Riposte," personnel director Paulson (1967) wondered "if the school really exists for Arbuckle and where those are that he does know in which he cannot pick out any of the three workers on the basis of the differences of their functions," and concluded that it is doubtful "whether he needs to repeat his generous offer of the proud name, *school counseling psychologist.* School counselors and school social workers are justly proud of their own names."

Brammer (1968) touched another nerve involving counselor identity and setting when he wrote, "The Counselor is a Psychologist." He had quoted Brayfield as having said, "We counselors are always playing around in someone else's ball park," and wondered, "Where will school counselors, particularly, play ball?" Then he suggested "the counseling psychology ball park, not as an ideal solution but as the possibility most compatible with evolving school counseling functions."

From his school-oriented position, Felix (1968) made it another personnel and guidance journal dialogue by replying that "At best, the passage indicates considerable confusion about which is the home team. It puts one in mind of what happened last winter when some fellas from the West Coast went to Texas for a basketball game. Since the place where they were playing had been built with other sports in mind, they shipped a floor from Los Angeles. Even so, the Houston team came through with an important victory.

"Similarly, we have let some psychologists come into our park, even though the place is not really suited to the game at which they excel. They have put down the floor they brought with them. Now they want us to change the way we train and practice, and even change the name of our team. Next thing you know, they will want to rename the park."

Gammons (1969) spoke along the same line when he pointed out the danger in too much exposure to formal theories: "As counselors we should be well versed in current theory. It should serve as a useful reservoir of ideas for action. But we must interpret theory in the light of the practical limitations imposed by the realities of the average school. In short, we must make up our minds at the very outset whether we are going to be counselors or psychologists. We can't be both."

The theory-therapy issues continued to be a favorite bone of contention although a number of leading figures in the field regarded theory as either nonexistent or irrelevant. Cottingham (1969) noted that, except for position papers issued by Dinkmeyer (1965) and Krumboltz (1966) on developmental counseling and behavioral counseling, respectively, little had been written on counseling theories distinctly applicable to elementary school settings; and Krumboltz himself (1969) tended "not to talk about theory because our so-called theories don't provide a basis for practice in the schools—not useful."

Stiller (1969), city guidance director turned counselor-educator, saw little relation between formal theory and school counseling practice. He said the existing practices covered a wide range of activities, some of which are called counseling, some of which are not. Even the so-called counseling practices are implemented in a school setting whereas the theories are derived from observations in clinical or agency settings, and little attention is given to the influence of the setting upon the application of the theory.

"What is needed is an overall theory of the practice of school counseling into which the counseling function could fit and against which we can measure the adequacy of existing theories of counseling. Lacking that, we ask each counselor to develop his own 'style of life,' or working philosophy. The person who does so with understanding, at least has the advantage of consistency and knowledge of what he is doing. Unfortunately, students often attempt to develop their understandings in the vacuum created by the gaps between the theories and the requirements of the setting, and as a result, many of them don't really understand what they *say* they do, nor realize what they *actually* do."

Another guidance director (Aubrey, 1969) charged that two decades of counselor educators had borrowed heavily from psychotherapeutic theories in attempts to discover an adequate framework for counseling in a school context while, at the same time, the counselors departed significantly from this kind of approach in practice.

In pointing out the misapplication of therapy models to school settings, Aubrey cited the following as crucial factors in school counseling: training programs for counselors, the structure of the school, administrative attitude, the involuntary nature of much school counseling, the limitations of time, educational objectives, the transitoriness of school counseling, and the irregularity of counseling contacts:

"Researchers and theoreticians alike would be well advised to examine the sociological structure of the school before suggesting counseling frameworks directly antithetical to institutional norms and expectations. The school is simply not a guidance clinic or mental health center."

I interpreted the above exchanges between counselor-educators and counselors not as representing antagonistic fixed positions, but as give and take between professionals whose different vantages had given them different perspectives; both groups would gain mutual understanding and professional growth by sharing views, however conflicting they might seem.

Inherent in the situation was the fact that certain counselor-educators were dedicated to a "continuing education" strategy whereby they advanced controversial notions in hopes of stimulating involvement, discussions, and seminal ideas.

However, the exchange between educators and practitioners also signaled the strong sense of separate identity and awareness of dissimilar work settings developed by counselors interacting in their own ecology. School counseling "came of age" at the 1970 American School Counselor Association (ASCA) delegate assembly when it was moved "that the American School Counselor Association direct itself toward becoming an autonomous national organization which determines its own destiny and is responsible to the relevant needs of school counselors."

Although threatening to separate from the "parental establishment" and become their own men, the school counselors also voted to continue "the dialogue with co-professionals through establishing an appropriate liaison with APGA," thereby indicating that they would repudiate any such paraphrase of Kipling as, "Theorists are theorists and practitioners are practitioners, and never the twain shall meet."

In fact, when the issue was presented in the fall of 1970, a majority of school counselors voted to continue affiliation with American Personnel and Guidance Association (APGA) in a response (1,333 ballots from a membership of over 14,000) even lighter than ASCA President Don Peters (1970) had predicted to John Krumboltz:

"It's not that school counselors don't care about their profession, but they're busy being school counselors with kids in the front lines."

Ivory Tower Versus Firing Line

In school counseling, as in all education, there tends often to be a gap between theory and practice. The professing theorist, dedicated to the study of crucial issues, may be inclined to look down upon the school counselor as an assembly-line mechanic performing necessary tasks with appropriate tools but without insight regarding the real meaning of his job. In return the practicing counselor may stereotype the theorist as living in an ivory tower on a diet of dreams, with cobwebs his sole output.

The gap in understanding between the theory and the practice of counseling outwardly reflects an attitude of superiority that in certain cases might well be traced to compensatory reactions springing from suspicions of inferiority. Such suspicions are often rooted in reality. Many a professing theorist would find himself unable to meet the everyday problems of a school counselor. It is equally true that the mechanical-type school counselor, obsessed with time and tools and techniques, performs his stint on the assembly line of educational mass production with little awareness of what the total enterprise is all about.

As the school counselor becomes more oriented to the theory of counseling and the professor to its practice, the gap in understanding tends to be closed by mutual respect. Each begins to realize that practical success of any importance is based on sound theory and that any theory worth thinking about has to have eventually some capability for application or relevance for practice. In short, the most successful practitioners are theorists as well, and the most successful theorists are practical men (Benjamin, 1939, p. iii).

To paraphrase Keats: "Theory is practice and practice is theory; that's all you know and all you need to know." In other words, what a person does is really his translation of his theoretical position into behavior, whether or not he can verbalize or even understand his actions. Theory can be observed in practice. The roles a counselor plays and the functions he performs spell out his theory.

Since entering the profession, my main concern has been to explore the field of school counseling in an attempt to locate the influences that guide or pull or push counselors into the personal evolution of a theory befitting themselves, their counselees, and the environment in which they operate.

Pierson (1965) noted that the "adequately trained school counselor develops his own role, a role that tends to be unique with him and unique to the situation in which the role is developed."

Each newcomer counselor enters a unique situation, and he must find the answers that are most appropriate for him. Given a do-it-yourself kit, so to speak, he finds out that some of the parts are missing, nobody knows where. He is puzzled by various sets of directions that differ not only on the method of assembly and the time it takes to do the job but also on what is intended to be built. He begins to have the characteristics of the neurotic: He has conflicts, he is confused, he is concerned. But he clings to the basic faith of all counselors: "One person can help another, somehow."

Place of Personnel Services in Education

At least in many small conservative communities a still prevailing attitude toward personnel services in education is epitomized in the anecdote of the little old lady who stood on the bank of the Hudson River while attempts were made to get Fulton's steamboat under way. "They'll never start it," she predicted, shaking her head, "They'll never start it!" When the steamboat finally went into motion, the little old lady changed her words but not her basic doubts about the whole thing. "They'll never stop it," she cried forebodingly, "They'll never stop it!"

Despite the lingering doubts and a natural reaction against the proliferation of personnel services, other than classroom help is essential in education and always has been. Wherever the teaching-learning process takes place, there are attendant problems and needs. In the American secondary school such problems and needs, intensified by the excitements of adolescence, also have been multiplied by public commitment to the Jacksonian attitude of education rather than to the selective admission principle of Jefferson, which is often followed at the college and university level. "High School U.S.A." fulfills the Jacksonian doctrine as expressed by period historian Bancroft in phrases that carry a guidance personnel ring:

> Let the waters of intelligence, like the rains of heaven, descend upon the whole earth ... The prejudices of ignorance are more easily removed than the prejudices of interest; the first are blindly adopted; the second are wilfully preferred! Intelligence must be diffused among the whole people; truth must be scattered among those who have no interest to suppress its growth. ... It is alone by infusing such great principles into the common mind that revolutions in society are brought about. They never have been, they never can be, effected by superior intelligence (1954, pp. 271-272).

The modern "open-door" policy of the American secondary school, reflecting both national policy and the personnel viewpoint, has made other than classroom help increasingly necessary to more learners and nonlearners, all with their unique quotas of individual differences and inalienable rights, the heart of the matter to the personnel worker, whose professional goal and reason for being is to *personalize* education.

The Case for Personnel Services

Despite growth of acceptance of his program, the personnel worker learns by experience that, if not already equipped with the characteristic, he must develop a tolerance for ambiguity. He is neither here nor there in the world of education, not on the faculty, not in administration, but plying his trade in a never-never land somewhere in between, balancing himself on a high thin wire of uncertainty. He has at least four bosses: the faculty, the student body, the administration, the community. Which should he please to succeed? Lining up too closely with any one of these factions will result in the failure of his program, the loss of his job. He must keep the confidence of the student body and yet advise the faculty, report to the administration, and inform the community. He has to accept his marginal role, which is crucial in the educational process but always vulnerable.

Although now accepted by the majority of administrators and faculty members, highly trained personnel workers may be regarded by old-line administrators as necessary nuisances or potential rivals while veteran teachers may look upon them as free-wheelers with soft jobs and no pupil load, as nonessential, as cluttering up the place, and as people who only offer services to individuals who have no business to be in school anyway. Some teachers feel threatened by personnel workers, suspecting that they hear things from pupils about which teachers are sensitive, categorizing personnel workers as undercover agents spying out faculty weaknesses. These teachers resent the fact that personnel workers know things about pupils that they won't share, that they have to defend pupils against the faculty, and that they come into a school system announcing, in effect: "This guidance-personnel work is too complicated for the classroom teacher. To do a satisfactory job, a person must have specialized training and devote full time to the program with no divided allegiances to academic subject matter."

Recognizing the possibility of arousing negative attitudes, personnel workers are generally agreed that what happens between the classroom teacher and the learner is the most important thing that happens in any school, but they insist that their own program of welfare services is what puts democracy into education. In an era when individual values are being eroded away by tremendous forces, the personnel worker realizes that the budget of personal freedom is as rigidly fixed as any economic budget, that perhaps 90 percent must be allocated to society, leaving only 10 percent to manipulate, but he is convinced that the way the individual is allowed to manipulate his precious 10 percent of independence often decides between success and failure, between happiness and grief.

Place of Counseling in Personnel Services

There is a growing tendency at all school levels to classify guidance as one of the personnel services and to regard counseling as its basic function. Although there is no such general agreement as to what other specific services should be identified as guidance, a minimum program customarily includes individual inventory, occupational-educational and social-personal information, placement, and follow-up. After these services there is less agreement about what should be on the list. Are school activities such as orientation, career days, college nights, science fairs, or the hot lunch program a part of guidance? Agreed that counseling is the one basic service, does only the person who holds the title attempt the job? Observation replies that everyone in school, from classroom teacher to football coach to custodian, carries on some form of counseling.

In the field of personnel services the general guidance worker who had to stretch himself so thin across such a wide area that he lost identity and usefulness seems to be another vanishing American. The effective counselor is primarily a specialist, much as he may worry about Thorstein Veblen's definition, "trained incapacity," about the dangers of learning more and more about less and less, and about increasing his stock of tricks of the trade and losing his touch of empathy. Despite the preceding anxieties, most school counselors consider themselves specialists in such areas as test interpretation, occupational information, and human relations, the latter paramount along with knowledge of and ability to apply principles of learning.

The trend toward specialization involves the school counselor in one of the paradoxes that plague the profession. The guidance movement, intent on the consideration of individual differences and the unique personality, was conceived as a counteracting force to the assembly-line system of mass production in education that tended to produce specialists and render the entire process impersonal, with the individual learner reduced to a number or name in a roll book. But now the school counselor, as the leading expert in guidance, finds himself a specialist in combating the evils of specialization, a contradiction that bears watching and that points toward more training in the humanities rather than in the technologies because, essentially, guidance is the business of helping man reach full development as a human being.

Another Definition of Counseling

As treated on these pages counseling may be more fully defined as the profession of helping people make intelligent choices on their way to becoming self-respecting citizens in a culture that historically places maximum value on individual development. The school guidance program is a continuing and developmental attempt to provide a healthful climate for the ultimate mental, physical, and spiritual dignity of man with his conscience and free will in opposition to the other dominant social philosophy of the electronic age which requires the negation of the individual as a sacrifice to the growth of the state.

Every counselor faces another paradox of his own profession when he tries to follow the behavioral scientists in the belief that human behavior is caused and therefore can be predicted and controlled. If this is not so, then why is he wasting his time at impossible tasks? If this is so, then he is toiling hopelessly in a culture opposed to his efforts, a culture dedicated to the proposition that men are free and responsible for their actions rather than the captive victims of predestination.

The above paradox may be resolved by paraphrasing a message of Christ, Himself called Counselor: "Render unto Science the things that

relate to Science, but to Art the things that relate to Art." Although scientific behaviorism is useful as a guideline to school counselors, counseling
remains an art, with human values and intangible verities still the heart of
what takes place between the counselor and counselee.

Counseling Theory and the National Defense Education Act

School counselors may take pride in the knowledge that counseling is one of
the oldest and most honored of callings and yet so young a profession that
it may be dated from the first decade of this century. From the start the
"stripling" showed sturdy growth, rising and broadening from the vocational guidance-counseling movement, refusing to be swallowed up by progressive education, declining to join the mental hygienists because of reluc-
tance to believe that everyone who does wrong is an unresponsible victim of
disease (Pierson, 1961, p. 54). In 1958, on what might be called its fiftieth
birthday, guidance-counseling was ranked top priority in importance by the
federal government's passage of an education act "to insure trained manpower of sufficient quality and quantity to meet the national defense needs of
the United States."

Pleased by the opportunities that federal monies would provide their
profession, some counselors were nevertheless troubled by certain implications in the wording of the National Defense Education Act (NDEA). The
government's intentions were bluntly stated, and a definite policy stood out
in such passages as, "the security of the nation requires the fullest development of the mental resources and technical skills of its young men and
women. ... We must increase our efforts to identify and educate more of
the talent of our nation."

Title V, the section of the act specifically related to school counseling,
promised, in effect, to reward each state which planned "a program for
testing students in the public secondary schools to identify students with
outstanding aptitudes and ability ... and a program of guidance and counseling to advise students of courses of study best suited to their ability,
aptitudes, and skills, and to encourage students with outstanding aptitudes
and ability to complete their secondary school education, take the necessary
courses for admission in institutions of higher education, and enter such
institutions."

The provisions of the NDEA, logical enough on the surface to a nation
up in educational arms over Sputnik, failed to make any allowance for the
bright boy who might prefer becoming a truck driver rather than a space
pilot or for the gifted girl who might prefer to raise a family instead of
bacteria cultures. Young people were viewed as defense weapons rather
than as human beings. Ignored was the philosophy that courses in a curricu-

lum and the careers to which they lead are the means of education and not the ends. In this light the NDEA appeared as new pressure in an old American paradox: the individual impulse toward freedom and the social impulse to restrict that freedom in the name of national interests. Clearly, large numbers of people, including educators, were willing to accept ready-made values rather than search their souls for values appropriate to themselves.

The NDEA emphasis on testing programs also seemed to reflect a national mood naïve in its trust that the way to avert unprecedented disaster was to locate the talented through standardized tests and then process them for the public welfare. Pencil and paper performance does not necessarily predict behavior or discover much needed creativity.

School counselors, reacting with schoolmen in general against the flood of testing and the "quest of excellence," soon learned that professing theorists could indeed be practical men. NDEA Counseling and Guidance Institutes acted as checks and balances against the extreme implications in the National Defense Education Act itself by training counselors to deal more effectively with students representing the total range of academic talent, and at all school levels.

Counseling Goals in Schools

One definition of high scholarship equates it with skill in pleasing teachers, by practicing orderly conduct, and by memorizing trivia that can be easily test-measured. The worthy qualities of the creative and the nonacademic are not so glibly identifiable. Both as guidance experts and as schoolmen, counselors face the fact that broader goals of education have revolutionized the high school program. The many must be served, not the exclusive few, and the greatest good for the greatest number is no idle watchword. Responsible for the education of more than 90 percent of all American youth fourteen to seventeen years of age, the secondary schools cannot be operated as farm clubs for colleges and universities, as nothing more than training camps for talent earmarked for higher education (Testing, testing, testing, 1962, p. 25).

Although in the American culture a college education has become increasingly crucial in determining occupational and status levels, the college-bound remain a minority, and therefore much of the high school program must be for the benefit of the terminal pupils and must be maintained so against all pressures because this majority of school citizens has equal need for approval and of assurance that achievement in areas other than the traditionally academic is commendable.

Fortunately, the mushrooming of junior and community colleges across the nation opened doors to many classroom citizens who otherwise would have been barred from higher education early in school life. In addition to their regular academic programs, these new institutions, along with a number of vocationally oriented senior colleges, took over many functions formerly associated in the public mind with "trade schools" or technical institutes. Here, with school and college counselors cooperating on specialized programs for them, young people within a few months to two years may learn to become a salesman, a machinist, a forestry aide, an auto mechanic, a cook, etc. However, the scholarship and entrance examinations required for placement at many colleges continue to downgrade the general nonacademic programs in schools.

The merits of the Jeffersonian principle of selection at the college level need to be weighed against the merits of the Jacksonian principle of admission at the school level on a scale that can evaluate traits of originality, courage, and stability, essential qualities in any era but especially important today. Such traits, generally developed and fixed early in life, are by no means monopolized by those who excel academically, and the secondary school provides the last organized large-scale opportunity for adolescents to develop these qualities of originality, courage, and stability vital to continued national existence on a moonstruck world torn between its daydreams of reaching the stars and its nightmares of falling through space (Testing, testing, testing, 1962, pp. 11, 26, 27).

The educational, and therefore the counseling, goals of the public high school seem as clear and as inclusive as the welcome extended by the Statue of Liberty to all comers, but it is obvious that the counselor who leans toward the Jeffersonian principle of selection will choose a different theory of counseling than the one who favors the Jacksonian principle of "come one, come all." In fact, *whatever the counselor's personal bias toward theory, the choice may not be his at the secondary level but dictated by the educational philosophy of his particular school situation,* as has been implied from the start of this chapter.

Although reasonable compromises seem destined at the secondary level if the counselor and the counseling program are to have any chance for growth, the counselor must resist insofar as practical the pressures in high school, including the NDEA, pushing him toward goals that are not compatible with the purposes of counseling. It is not the purpose of counseling, for instance, to recruit pupils for occupations in which they are needed, nor is it the purpose of counseling to encourage bright pupils to go to college and dull pupils to go into the world of work. It is the purpose of counseling to help the pupil help himself toward goals that meet his own needs and satisfactions. If the individual is not permitted access to free choice, then he becomes a shadow of the school and of the larger society, a credit to neither of these because he has lost his own identity, the preservation and development of which is a primary goal of the democratic process. A literary reference appears in order here.

A Novelist Indicates His Counseling Theory

The following is a copy of a letter written by an American novelist to his father, a physician, who was furious at having counseled a young friend of the family only to find the counsel ignored:

> It's too bad that Edwin did not appreciate your efforts, but you must remember two things: First, West Point, though a good training physically, is none too wonderful intellectually ... Second, the boy had to decide for himself. He may not know what's best for him—but maybe you don't either. You answer, Well, then, he should have made up his mind before we took all that trouble. That's only partly true. Are there *any* of us who decide things right off, before partly going into arrangements? ... Stop sulking at Edwin, or you'll make him feel guilty and self-conscious, and you have no right to do that. If he's shiftless—ALL RIGHT ... Claude and you and even my perfect self are too confoundedly impatient with people who haven't our sort of ambitions. Why should they have? And we have no right to ... make them feel guilty—a frame of mind in which it's much harder to get on ... Huh? ... When you say "I am thru with him for he deceived us"—hang it, the best way to make the poor devil deceive all of you is to be impatient ... you give him another chance, if you have a chance to give him a chance! (Schorer, 1961, p. 379).

A definite stand on the purposes of counseling is indicated in the above letter by the novelist who scolded and satirized his fellow Americans for their tendency to relinquish individual freedom for group security, the first American writer to win the Nobel Prize for Literature, the creator of Babbitt and other forerunners of today's status seekers and organization men, Sinclair Lewis. Is there not room for reflection here by school counselors in general, and in particular by those who feel moved by personal compulsion or by external pressure to become recruiting officers or directive agents of another kind? Whatever the response, counseling theory is plainly a process of choice and evolution, here as elsewhere.

Role Expectation of the School Counselor (How is he seen?)

The saying, "We see ourselves as others see us," may be turned around: Others see us as we see ourselves, as we give the appearance of being. If the school counselor has a distinct impression of his own role, the faculty, the student body, the administration, and the community will tend to accept his self-image.

All too often the school counselor has no clear-cut definition of his role. There is the story of a counselor, now a university dean, who told of having been appointed guidance director of a school system so suddenly that he had not the vaguest idea of his duties. Finally he decided to hustle down the corridor several times a day with a batch of papers clutched in his hand, looking as if he were going somewhere on important business. This convinced school people that he knew what he was supposed to do, and it gave him a breathing spell to find out.

The school counselor who fails to brief the administration on what he should do and what he should not do soon finds his responsibilities defined for him, generally in an unhappy fashion for the success of the counseling program and for the counselor's autonomy. However, if he is competently trained and skillful in action, administrators will tend to give him a free hand, consult with him about school policy and public relations, and weigh his opinions heavily.

An indication of how administrators see the role of the school counselor is evident in the fact that he may be given such titles as Assistant Principal—Guidance and Counseling, and Assistant to the Superintendent for Personnel and Counseling. By these titles the counselor is viewed as a fellow administrator, although quite evidently under the paternal system of the public schools he is in danger of becoming less a counselor and more a "Daddy's helper."

Because school counseling is regarded as a step toward the administrative level, the counselor may be seen by some faculty members as a "mouse training to be a rat," but teachers who have received the services of an adequate counselor are prone to look on him as a welcome assistant in various areas of school work and a handy man to have around in an emergency.

School Counseling and Pragmatism

In analyzing his role, every experienced school counselor bears in mind that in many schools, and especially in the conservative school caricatured by the sabre-toothed curriculum, seniority and case load are what count. The teacher who, even under the ideal circumstances of facing only twenty-seven pupils in a classroom and an accredited limit of no more than one hundred and seventy during the school day, tends to be irritated by (or envious of) the apparently uncluttered life of someone who deals with perhaps three or five pupils during a clock hour and rarely more than twenty-five or thirty during a full-time counseling day. Case loads are not matters to be dismissed (or discussed) lightly. The school counselor's role here is the tactful one of showing respect for those carrying the quantitative burden, while at the same time gently emphasizing the essential importance of his own services to individuals.

Despite all efforts to the contrary, the school counselor may find it difficult to avoid being regarded as an authority figure by the student body. Even if he does not teach a single period, he belongs to the adult world and is therefore viewed as a potential antagonist. He may be seen as a tower of strength on which to lean or as a weakling who steers clear of discipline and looks the other way when misbehavior occurs. He may be labeled "an okay guy" or a "head-shrinker."

The student body of any school is made up of practical people. The school counselor stays aware that their philosophy is fundamental American pragmatism. Pupils care little about intentions; they are interested in results. If the counselor proves to be of some use, if he makes school more pleasant by rescheduling a slow learner, by helping a football player get back on the eligibility list, by steering an academic pupil into a college scholarship, then the student body will see the counselor as a worthwhile instrument and put him to use.

Half the girls who face the counselor will be married at the age of twenty, and it behooves him to be practical also or he will "lose" them. It is a challenge to orient girls, while they are daydreaming about kissing husbands home from work and pushing baby buggies, to the faraway fact that they will spend some twenty-five years of their adult lives at an occupation other than housewifery.

The school counselor faces many variations of the American youth. How he perceives them and how they in turn perceive him will serve to define and perhaps to change their respective roles. It is evident that *the very pupils the counselor interviews and that the teachers who work with him will bring persuasion and pressure to bear on his ultimate choice of counseling theory.*

Influence of Time on Counseling Theory

The counselor with a heavy case load, the rule rather than the exception at any school level, runs into his old dilemma, time. Although no rigid limit can be set to interviews insofar as satisfactory procedures and results are concerned, practical limits will be set by the counselor's schedule, and he must decide the limits applicable to his own situation. It is apparent that how he budgets his time will reflect a theory of counseling. For instance, he may feel that he is the expert who knows the answers, become didactic, and push toward the directive extreme; he may compromise (synthesize?) and become eclectic; he may borrow time from some counselees and lend it to others; he may consign time to perdition and attempt to remain client-centered with all. In any case *the pressure of the clock has influenced his choice of counseling theory.*

Depending on the philosophy of the community and the policy of the administration, the school counselor may find himself involved in functions that he does not consider part of his role. Although 98 percent of attendance problems are routine and only 2 percent of absenteeism and truancy are matters for counseling, he may be ordered to check attendance. As a result of false economy he may find his counseling time swamped by clerical chores. He may be expected to stand in for an absent principal, supervise study halls and other areas, police lunch lines, ride the spectator bus, chaperone dances, and, in short, share the myriad tasks that used to be assigned arbitrarily by an administrator to all faculty members. In the "early days" there were counselors who actually invited such assignments in hopes of being considered "one of the boys." That style and the arbitrary administrator went out of date in most schools when teachers, including counselors, started professional negotiations in the sixties, but no doubt there are still counselors in positions similar to the above outmoded model.

Since time is the counselor's dilemma at all school levels, he has a tendency to become an efficiency expert. As such, he runs the risk of changing his methods and his attitudes until, almost unconsciously, he may turn into a caricature whose business is compulsion rather than counseling.

As counselors acquire sophistication in theory and on the job, there tends to be closer agreement between their ideas on how they should spend their time and how they actually do spend it. During the sixties, secondary school counselors found in general that Darley's study (1943) of the problems of youth in the high schools of Minnesota still related to their own situation. About 95 percent of the problems presented to counselors at the secondary level remained vocational and educational, with vocational needs somewhat more frequent; the remaining 5 percent of the problems were in the personal-social-emotional category. However, at least rocking-chair research now indicates a more balanced situation. Perhaps this is due in part to the greater sophistication of both elementary and secondary school counselors who realize that counseling cannot be separated into neat compartments but is enveloped in psychological and sociological forces.

Problems of youth are becoming increasingly complex in a rapidly changing world. The exploding population, the changing pattern of American life, the generation gap with its alcohol versus drugs confrontation, the affluent society with its poverty pockets, the threat of nuclear accident, the shifting labor market, the disturbed ecology, the pollution time bombs—all these have focused attention on the special knowledge and training of school counselors at all levels.

Historically responsible for counseling their offspring, bewildered parents have shifted their responsibility to the schools, primarily insofar as vocational and educational matters are concerned. They look on the school counselor as a specialist in the foregoing areas, and they are beginning to picture him as playing an important role in helping with the personal-social-emotional problems that are interwoven with the others. However, the typical school counselor refers to the mental health clinic or to another appropriate source the 4 percent of the student body who indicate need of intensive therapy.

The above referrals may come as a shock to the type of school counselor who has fancied himself as dealing preeminently with personal-social-emotional problems and whose mirror reflects a practicing psychologist rather than the practical counselor. Obviously these two types of counselors, depending on how they distribute their time among the school population, act from different theories of counseling; the one sees himself as a clinical psychologist, the other as a developmental counselor with the conviction that the school is a place for normal learning, not a center for severely disturbed children.

Always the role of the counselor—"How is he seen?"—depends largely on how he sees himself and how successfully he projects his image. The effective school counselor realizes that professional behavior has been achieved only when the practitioner perceives that techniques and practices are means and not ends, when he knows not only how and what but *why.* He appreciates the fact that there are as many differences *within* people as between people. He strives toward the essence of counseling described in Kahlil Gibran's *The Prophet:*

> The teacher who walks in the shadow of the temple among his followers, gives not of his wisdom but rather of his faith and his lovingness. If he is indeed wise, he does not bid you enter the door of his wisdom, but rather leads you to the threshold of your own mind.

School counselors, doubtful of their wisdom, try to offer understanding, acceptance, and love above and beyond mere information. When they come face to face with hostile reactions, they examine themselves first on the possibility that they have projected feelings, perhaps frustrations, of their own onto others.

On the basic practical level every school counselor's best hope of being accepted in his role by his peers, the student body, the community (and not least of all by himself) is the recipe for success in any other walk of life: to fill needs and offer satisfactory services in spite of pressures from the clock and the calendar.

Role Enactment of the School Counselor (What does he actually do?)

The written job description, used with success in business and industry, may also be used effectively by the school counselor. A daily record should be kept, and he should take inventory each semester to determine the relation between role expectation and role enactment.

A counselor chosen to head a program in a school committed for the first time to a formal guidance program invariably meets the universal question: "Exactly what is this fellow supposed to do?" The sequential remark, not always complimentary, as events develop, becomes: "What doesn't this fellow do?"

The special services expected of a counselor may range from being able to teach at least one subject to handling every phase of the guidance program and coordinating the pupil personnel services by acting as contact man between such specialists as the school psychologist, school social worker, school health worker, and school attendance worker. The counselor's private office, if he is fortunate enough to have one, becomes a sounding board for personal problems, school gripes, occupational outlook information, career exploration, parental confessions, and probate reports. The counselor's files hold material relating to every pupil in school, with special data on disciplinary cases, dropouts, the retarded, the gifted, and the underprivileged. His research projects examine the changing characteristics of the school population, and he interprets this information to teachers and administrators for use in curriculum planning and in the development of administrative structure and regulations.

The counselor is expected to become a liaison officer between administration and faculty, a link between school and community resources. He is expected to establish better understanding between children and parents, student body and faculty, and among the pupils themselves. He is a go-between, a negotiator, a peacemaker, an expert in human relations and in interpersonal relations.

Even if he has a private office, the counselor tends to have encounters in halls, in doorways, or in a corner of the lunch room or library. He tends to favor the dynamic rather than the formal approach, willing to meet his counselees on the decisive spur of the moment, between classes, before or after school, in groups, or in the classic one-to-one situation. Despite all efforts, and perhaps because of them, the counselor is criticized for being too much of a specialist, too much of a generalist, too nondirective and wishy-washy, or too directive and bossy.

In brief, the school counselor wears many hats, and this tends to put him in the position outlined in the familiar cartoon strip where a gentleman in a derby is passing a public playground during a season when the snow is good packing. Personalities aside, the target is irresistible.

School Discipline and Counseling Theory

Because of his role as a defender and guardian of individualism, the school counselor faces innumerable problems in interpersonal relations. No matter how strongly he may feel about not becoming involved in punitive discipline, the pressures of faculty, administration, community, and even student body may be so strong as to force him to conform (at least with lip service) or resign. Not to engage in what others consider right and proper (and necessary) is a difficult task. It requires extreme tact and diplomacy to avoid the implication that disciplinarians are wrong or the suspicion on their part that the counselor is shirking responsibility to curry favor with pupils. An effective counselor must, in words and in actual practice, keep on redefining his role while simultaneously indicating acceptance of faculty roles: They are largely concerned with the group, he is largely concerned with the individual; they are largely concerned with control, he is largely concerned with self-expression; together as a team they carry on the educational program at the secondary level.

Professors of counseling generally recommend that even the sort of discipline implied in scheduling interviews with pupils should be eliminated where possible, claiming that counselors' contacts with adolescents should be voluntary on the part of the pupil, arguing that the slightest coercion may result in loss of support and confidence. Recommended are such mechanics as leaving a box supplied with slips and pencils outside the counselor's door, bearing the notice: "If you want to see me, sign the slip, and I'll get in touch with you." In the actual working situation, the assignment of pupils to counselors by sex, grade, program, random selection, or otherwise results in compulsory counseling sessions as a general practice. In smaller school systems the self-referral approach is more common, but even here counselors tend to use the interpretation of standardized tests as springboards for counseling.

Although there is much verbiage on such topics as "Do guidance and discipline mix?" the effective school counselor seems largely untroubled by the differing opinions, realizing what neophytes and certain of their educators may not—that discipline, if swiftly and justly administered, is a compliment seldom resented, a sign that the individual disciplined is worthy of attention. Such a counselor does *not* disassociate himself from discipline. In fact, he may even become punitive on occasion without losing the respect and trust of the student body. He recognizes, however, that his primary function is to prevent rather than to punish. He is concerned with cause rather than effect. His aim is to get at the roots of maladjustment rather than to deal with the obvious symptoms.

A step in counseling prior to punitive discipline is to explain alternatives to the student in much the same way that they are pointed out in occupational and educational matters. Just as the student must be told that unless he takes certain subjects and makes certain grades, he won't have much chance to get into certain jobs or schools of higher learning, so must he be told the consequences of disobeying rules. The school counselor must also be ready to accept the possibility that even when the consequences have been pointed out, the student may decide to disobey the rules any way. If disobedience results, the counselor becomes neither judge nor executioner.

Irrespective of innermost feelings, he adheres strictly to professional ethics and to school policy. When the rules are flouted, the general welfare of the student body must be safeguarded. Neither an informer (except in extreme situations involving great danger to self or others) nor an apprentice principal (except when he confuses his role), the school counselor recognizes that it is the administrator's duty to carry out punishment and enforce discipline.

The counselor's responsibility is to give the administrator all available (nonconfidential) information about the individual to provide the basis for making a fair judgment for a course of action. If the administrator refers a student for counseling, the counselor's appropriate role is to attempt to help the student achieve greater self-understanding, accept the consequences of his behavior, and profit from experience (Ratigan & Johnson, 1961, p. 49).

How the counselor sees his role in discipline and in a testing situation undeniably affects his choice of counseling theory. If he is inclined toward the client-centered position, tests may be regarded as clouding the issue. It is common experience, however, in the supervised practicum course conducted in university counseling laboratories, for the inexperienced or unsure counselor to hide his own inadequacies behind an immediate barrage of tests. Such counselors tend toward control of the individual through other forms of discipline as well as tests, and therefore they are inclined toward a directive counseling theory.

Modus Operandi: Implications for Counseling Theory

As the school counselor sits face-to-face with the pupil who has a problem, he reminds himself to look for the *single simple* cause first, then go on to the complex. He uses the law of probability instead of playing hunches. He asks himself: "Which is most likely? What's the best bet? *What's on his and my hidden agenda?*"

Counselors learn by experience that the original reason for seeking counsel often turns out not to be the real reason. They school themselves not to mistake symptoms for the cause, realizing that a headache is a symptom of something and that "I want to drop English Comp" is a symptom of something else. They learn to pay close attention to a typical counselee's theme song, asking themselves: "What's he harping about?

What tune does he always come back to?" On the other hand, counselors also "listen" for what the counselee *avoids* talking about.

In the course of his day, the school counselor encounters a variety of problems initiated by questions or statements similar to the following: "I want to be a doctor. How much do they make?" "What am I best suited for?" "I have this interest and ability. How can I turn it into money?" "I've got to drop out of school. What can I do in the way of work?" "I guess I'll join the Peace Corps. Tell me about it." "I want to be an engineer, but my parents want me to be a minister." "I'm graduating in Commercial. What kind of a job can I get in this community?" "I want to get married, but my folks think I'm too young." "I was kicked out of math and told not to come back, but if I don't get the credits, I can't graduate, and my Dad's got heart trouble." "I'm physically handicapped and I want some kind of suitable work." "I haven't got a single friend in the whole school." "My father would like to know my IQ so he can tell whether I should be a physicist or not." "Where's there a school that learns you how to operate Diesels"? "How can I get to be a butcher?" "Look at this mark on my report card, just because I wouldn't cheat on the test, and all the rest of them did." "I've decided on nursing. Where can I get a scholarship?"

During this counseling session the school counselor avoids "thinking ahead" because it prevents understanding of the counselee's immediate feelings. After the session he spends five minutes or so going over his notes and reviewing the interview. He examines himself, perhaps probing for the reason why his thoughts went wandering at a certain point, not necessarily a sign of boredom but of higher interest in other areas. He double-checks his observation of the slightest personality changes, realizing that these progress geometrically rather than arithmetically. For example, if a shy boy mentions that he asked a girl to dance during the noon hour, this may be a sign of what might become geometric progression, whereas it is no sign in an aggressive girl-happy boy.

The way in which he goes about his daily tasks, the degree of sensitivity he displays toward counselees, the methods he uses in problem-solving, the very schedule he sets himself, all these point the school counselor toward a theory of counseling. All counselors are more alike than they are different. They vary in depth and in degree. Their choice of counseling theory is based largely on emphasis in attitude rather than on any sharp dichotomy.

Relation of Goals to Counseling Theory

There are as many goals in counseling as there are problems, but in general the school counselor keeps to the three primary purposes of the interview: to get information, to give information, and to change behavior. He sees counseling as getting to learn about the personality of the individual and then attempting to remove the blocks preventing further personality development. His primary business is to lend his strength to support a person in undergoing behavior change.

In defining goals, school counselors are generally agreed that the pupil must make his own decisions, but they insist that the counselor may supply knowledge the pupil lacks. If youngsters have the right to fail, then the counselor has the responsibility to see that the failure amounts to a learning experience and not to a personal catastrophe.

There are implications for counseling theory in these beliefs. How much support does the counselor believe the counselee should get? How much attitude change is to be attempted? In answering these questions for himself, a counselor's theory of counseling may range anywhere from psychotherapy in depth to undiluted instruction.

The school counselor's broad goal may be summed up as a developmental process of helping the individual find himself in the present and, on the basis of apparent potential and desire, locate himself in the future. However, not to be lost sight of in the broad and lofty goals of counseling are such practical bits of business as hunting up and putting into the student's hand a scholarship blank or information about a job opportunity suited to his ability and needs. This simple and very obvious service may take only moments, but it might result in more geometric progression across a lifetime than the most brilliant applications of any counseling theory.

One vital goal of the school counselor is to identify and to encourage real nonconformists among the student body, not those who act differently for the sake of seeming different, but those who are truly divergent thinkers. For most of the school population they are uncomfortable people to have around but, far more than the academically talented whose very willingness to exhibit high performance is a pledge of allegiance to the status quo, these nonconformists are the potential bearers of new gifts to man's cultural heritage, and the counselor must bid them welcome, perhaps in spite of his own discomfort at their divergent ideas.

Relation of Theory to Behavior

What kind of personal philosophy does each school counselor build or borrow for himself? Is he fixated on middle-class values? Does he enjoy Buddha and Beethoven, or does he bowl every Wednesday and feel motivated by progressive jazz? Is he cosmopolitan or insular in outlook? Does he study the issues involved in his profession? Has he developed a style and a way of life that make him an individual, or is he trying to educate the young without having either an educational philosophy worth defining or a personal philosophy of life worth transmitting to others (Ratigan, 1964).

If each particular school counselor knows where he himself stands right now on such matters as are mentioned above, then he knows where he stands right now on counseling theory. His behavior, within the possibilities of the school situation, will tend to reflect a definite theory of counseling and to be consistent. The counselor who does not know where he stands *with himself* does not know where he stands on counseling. His behavior will tend to reflect his indecision and to be inconsistent. This means neither that the consistent counselor's stand on ways of life is an either-or manifesto nor that his stand is rigidly fixed. This does mean that a counselor's stand is a place from which to take new sightings and soundings before moving one way or another. In brief analysis the conflicts or issues in school counseling perhaps may be reduced to philosophical attitudes regarding the nature of man and the nature of the universe.

Summing up the relation of theory to behavior, there is more than jest in the conclusion that it is the relation of the chicken to the egg. Each produces the other in an uninterrupted sequence of cause and effect, but the ancient riddle remains unanswered: "Which came first—?" There is another way to illustrate the relation of theory to behavior: Evolution produced Darwin; Darwin proposed the theory of evolution.

Relation of Counselor Training to Theory

In considering the relation of training to theory, it is evident that a person generally does what his nature and training have prepared him to do. A lawyer practices law, a surgeon operates, a psychometrist gives tests. This means that a counselor trained as a clinical psychologist will tend to treat pupils as patients and turn the school into a hospital. Having been alerted to the manifestations of disturbed people, he tends to see them everywhere— and they are not hard to find (in temporary state) among a population of volatile youngsters. On the other hand, a counselor with less training in psychology but with more training in the social and biological sciences and the humanities (not to mention the school situation) will tend to look on the student body as normal and counsel them accordingly, in the faith that they are going through a period where "disturbance" and, in fact, "turbulence" are the rule rather than the exception and that almost all of them "grow out of it" thanks to no other therapy than time.

In any event the training of the two counselors mentioned above has pointed them toward different theories of counseling.

It should be stressed that because of the gap between the theory and the practice of counseling and because of faulty communication between educators and secondary school administrators, too many counselors are being trained to perform one set of tasks and hired to perform another. Herr (1969) found there is *not* a high degree of interlocking relationship between what is appropriate for the counselor to do, what he actually does, and what he is prepared to do. In other words he is performing some functions for which he received no training, and not performing others for which he was especially trained.

The decisive element in both practice and theory, all else considered, is the counselor himself. Course work is important in counselor education; personality is vital. No amount of "right" courses can change the wrong personality for counseling. The head may be furnished with knowledge, but empathy has to come from the heart. There is growing conviction, however discouraging or encouraging it may be to educators and to counselors in training, that counselors are born, not made.

Psychotherapy in High School

As mentioned previously the young person commonly shows many pseudo-pathological symptoms that generally disappear as he gropes toward adulthood, but during this period there is the ever-present danger than he might be triggered into an emotional blowup by counseling techniques not recommended in a school situation. The use of free association, for instance, may possibly draw out primary-process-dominated problems that school counselors are not normally trained to handle. Pointing out that the emphasis during the decade or two around the mid-century on psychology as the core of counselor education has been a mixed blessing, C. Gilbert Wrenn (1962) maintains that one crucial decision regarding counseling goals must be made by every school counselor: "Am I a specialist for a few who are in trouble, or am I a specialist for many with normal growth problems?"

An answer to the above question inevitably leads away from some theories of counseling while leading toward others.

Limitations of Client-centered Counseling in Schools

Counselors have been asked to reevaluate their ideas about the client-centered approach in counseling. They are urged to be semicorrective because lack of direction may put the responsibility on the shoulders of a youngster who lacks the experience or emotional maturity to handle his problem. In other words, let the pupil drive the car toward becoming what he is to be, but put up enough warning signs along the road so that he cannot go too far wrong. As a professional man every counselor has to pass judgments and make decisions regarding such matters. A Lincolnian formula applies here: "You can be nondirective with some of the pupils all of the time, and you can be nondirective with all of the pupils some of the time, but you can't be nondirective with all of the pupils all of the time."

Relation of Counselors' Training to Client-centered Theory

Most school counselors begin their training by joining the Rogerian disciples with enthusiasm. They are enchanted with "client-centered" counseling largely because Rogers gives them a tool and a rationale—acceptance of the other person clears a way to problem-solving—that seems, in the first flush of discovery, easy to learn and easy to apply. The Rogerian system with its faith in the fundamental goodness of man and in the democratic process appeals to counselors in contrast to the systems of the classic psychoanalysts who demean man's basic nature and appear Teutonically authoritative. There is also the possibility that school counselors in training, many of whom have had experience as teachers, seize nondirective counseling as part of a short-lived rebellion against the directive educational procedures with which they have been rather forcefully acquainted.

The honeymoon with the Rogerian ideal seldom ends abruptly, but it cools, and in certain cases a divorce results. As school counselors acquire more sophistication, they tend to develop doubts about nondirective counseling. During NDEA Institutes and other phases of their graduate program, they gain insight into other systems, and they hear counselor educators raise such questions as, "Realistically, how nondirective can you be? Doesn't every counselor affect the atmosphere with his personality and sense of values, and therefore even his presence is directive, right?" To which many counselors who have been so struck with the Rogerian way may now reply, "Roger!"

Reaction of High School Counselees to Client-centered Theory

There are even objections from pupils about client-centered counselors. In most of their classrooms they have been told what to do, and they want to continue to be told. Some students greet the Rogerian approach with wonder, then with delight, and take up the implied challenge to think for themselves. Others may decide that the counselor has no interest in them, that he is incapable, and they display sharp irritation at the lack of direction. They may feel rejected. They may get the idea that this kind of counseling not only is negligible but also is negligent, as indeed it may be, depending on the art of the counselor.

At a national science institute for high school juniors, participants were invited to receive counseling from graduate students taking their supervised practicum course in the counseling laboratory. As I observed most of the adolescents were pleased at the attention they received, comparing this process with what they called the "fast shuffle" that they had experienced with their own school counselors, but a strong minority reacted against the nondirective treatment. This minority obviously wanted nothing from the counselors except test interpretation and occupational information. They showed resentment against the permissive atmosphere, which struck them as dawdling and incompetent or as pressure to elicit personal problems. There seems reason to believe that the counselees in the minority here are more representative of the realistic school situation, whereas the counselees in the majority were responding to an amount of attention possible under the relatively ideal conditions of a campus practicum but not workable (or equitable) in the time-bound public schools. Whatever interpretation may be made of this, one conclusion appears clear: The attitude and the reaction of counselees will tend to shape counseling theory. The psychotherapist tends to attract certain types of patients (problems), and they, in turn, are attracted to him because of his specialization in their kind of troubles. This choice of selection, present to a limited degree in larger high schools, is virtually nonexistent in the smaller schools. The educational setting in general seems to demand a compromise rather than a position toward either extreme of the counseling continuum.

Practicum Surveys of Counseling Theory

Across a period of several years, I have made informal studies of supervised counseling practicum groups on campus to get an idea of how students taking the course intended to relate theory to practice, that is, how they would use the knowledge and understanding gained in graduate work in an actual on-the-job situation.

Results of these investigations showed that although most of the prospective counselors paid lip service to client-centered counseling, they saw themselves as not using this very much (or at least not as much as they thought the counselor educators thought they should!). The majority stressed conviction that different pupils required the application of different theories.

There were counselors in training who felt that many pupils were so limited in basic abilities or backgrounds that the interview had to be structured rigidly if any communication was to take place. There were those who claimed that pupils who "let off steam" and used the counselor as a "sounding board" had to be restrained because the self-indulgence in talk became a luxury neither the counselor nor the school could afford since it robbed other pupils of the right to equal time.

Several of the counselors felt that a client-centered approach should be used only in the case of personal problems. The average run of responses indicated a prevailing confusion which seemed to regard a *direct* answer to a *direct* question as constituting a *directive* answer.

Two significant conclusions seem to stand out: (1) general agreement that counseling theory should be suited to the pupil and (2) that it should not clash with the counselor's personality, i.e., the counselor who remains himself and does not try to put on an act is more convincing and effective than the counselor who tries to use a theory which is not characteristic of him.

Client-centered Counseling in a Junior High School

Notable among programs designed to put a particular theory into practice in the schools is the one initiated by Izaacson while he was director of pupil personnel services at Lexington, Massachusetts. As reported by Boy (1963) and Pine (1963, 1967), who were then staff counselors, ecological conditions in this small-city school system favored such a development; i.e., the administration encouraged new ideas, and the community had proved its willingness to finance whatever services might seem necessary to meet student needs.

With a counselor-student ratio of 1 to 260, in grades seven to nine at Muzzey Junior High School, the counselors worked out a job description broad enough to accommodate a wide range of professional counseling. The fully functioning counselor spends the major portion of his day counseling individuals and groups of students who have learning problems of any kind. He provides informational services but avoids the authoritarian image of a know-it-all who fosters dependency relations with his clients; instead he tends to sound out the personal-social feelings inherent in occupational-educational choices and to encourage total-school cooperation in giving students information about the complicated multiplicity of the world of work.

The counselor functions as a resource consultant; assists in the placing and grouping of students to provide a maximal learning situation for each; provides in-service training for teachers to help them become better acquainted with the philosophical and practical considerations which influence his counseling; and assists in providing testing services but avoids administering tests, especially to his own clientele, because he wants to project a nonjudgmental image focused on the client's self-concept rather than his test profile.

The counselor is *not* a generalist, performing a host of guidance chores, quasi-administrative assignments, and clerical tasks. He *counsels* students in regard to transferring courses, but he neither approves nor disapproves any transfer. He has nothing to do with the scheduling of classes or the arrangement of academic programs. He does not register new students or carry out routine interviews with failing students.

Some of the early acceptors of the *invitation* to come and be counseled used the session to test the nonauthoritative image. The image held firm in the acceptant atmosphere free of moralizing or value judgments, the atmosphere was charged with empathy and confidence in the client's having within himself the power to become a well-integrated and self-actualizing person.

According to criteria initially established, the program worked. During the first year of operation, about half the student body voluntarily sought counseling. During the second year, the self-initiated referrals rose to 70 percent. About half the number of counseling sessions each year were in the *personal* area, with the larger and smaller number of the remainder in the educational and occupational areas, respectively.

Different types of students, regardless of school ability or sex, patronized the service, and a corollary held true; the sex of the counselor made no significant difference in preference. Counselor commitment to Rogerian research based on tape recordings resulted in scores of fruitful sessions later utilized to measure client growth and counselor skills; and no request for permission ever was denied, indicating that trust—part and parcel of the counselor image—prevailed.

Evaluation of the program is limited and awaits more sophisticated analysis; nevertheless it seems clear that, given optimal ecological conditions—administrative backing, community support, and release from inappropriate roles—professionally competent counselors can carry theory into practice. Given similar conditions and competence, a number of theories other than client-centered should prove operable, if for no other reason than that gratified reaction to special attentions appears crucial in all human relationships, including counseling.

An informal follow-up in 1969 by an administrator at Muzzey Junior High School reported: "No erosion. The counseling program is very much alive, functioning well, and still based on the same theoretical rationale."

At the close of the sixties at least four other programs, *one at the elementary level,* based on the Rogerian model and operational mode akin to the "pilot program," had emerged in New England and Canada, while others were in process of meeting the original's criteria. Although difficult to identify on the national scene, there undoubtedly are still other programs in progress, perhaps with different theoretical approaches but expressing school counseling's main conviction: that the major responsibility of the counselor is to counsel pupils and students (with a welcome mat out for teachers and parents as well).

Counseling in the Middle School

A new setting for school counseling developed when educators became sensitive about the special needs of boys in grades six to nine and girls in five to eight; the grades in which the largest percentage of children mature into pubescence, undergoing the excitement of profound psychological and physiological changes, including the unique experience of reaching physical genital maturity. To meet the developmental needs of these preadolescents, the controversial concept of the middle school originated.

Key issues revolve around structure and environment. Middle school advocates feel that fifth and sixth graders have more in common with seventh and eighth graders than they do with children in kindergarten through the fourth grade. Junior high school proponents favor the traditional settings and feel that the middle school is simply a transplant of grades from other school settings that have proved effective.

It is pertinent here to repeat that this chapter is concerned with the effect of the total ecology upon shaping the theoretical approach of the counselor. This includes the developmental stage of both counselor and client, and the needs of each.

One of the characteristics of most developmental tasks (Havighurst, 1953) is that there are special times in life for their achievement—moments when learning circumstances are exactly right. This is true of learning to walk, to talk, to accept toilet training, and to choose a vocation; but there are other tasks that move from one phase to another throughout life.

Learning to get along with one's age-mates, learning to get along with age-mates of both sexes, learning a masculine or feminine social role, learning to participate responsibly as a citizen, these are never-ending tasks from early childhood to old age. According to Havighurst, "Success with a recurring task in its earliest phases probably augurs well for success in the later phases. Consequently, the crucial period for the learning of the task is when it first appears. But new learning must be added as the task changes during later life."

Counselors who move into middle school settings must be prepared to meet the developmental needs of pubescence, needs which are primarily social in nature. Many of these needs will recur at other stages of life, and some of them have occurred previously, but this is a crucial point in time for the learning of personal-social identity and of developing satisfactory heterosexual relationships. As in various stages of life, however, these developmental tasks take place in a matrix of personality patterns established in earlier years; therefore the counselor, as ever, must also be prepared to offer remedial in addition to preventive (developmental) assistance.

Brod (1967) pictured middle school children as going through their stormiest stage of development and called upon a need to review counselor

education programs for the preparation of effective counselors for the new
setting. I believe programs are needed that offer training for the development of effective counselors capable of functioning as counseling specialists
in a variety of work settings. whether it be an elementary school. a vocational rehabilitation office. or wherever. There should be a core program.
common for all counseling candidates. with specialized course work and
supervised experience to prepare each counselor for his preferred job setting, the one that suits his developmental stage.

Elementary School Counseling Prelude: Down the Up Staircase

Among early entries in the trend toward elementary school counseling were
concerned counselors at the secondary level who. to reverse the title of
Kaufman's novel (1964). trudged *down the up staircase* to the lower grades
with the conviction that effective counseling of students in high school
depended on reaching children before inappropriate behavior patterns had
crystallized. These counselors were frustrated by daily confrontations with
learning problems that. if detected soon enough and treated or referred
properly, perhaps could have been (to use the old schoolmaster phrase)
"nipped in the bud."

In scattered school districts across the nation. counselors borrowed
time from their own secondary programs or spent extra hours to travel
down the up staircase in order to counsel pupils. consult with teachers.
confer with parents. and report to administrators. These counselors helped
teachers help children with reading and perceptual problems; they wrote up
federal programs designed to create learning improvement in the aggressive.
the withdrawn, the underprivileged, the "whatever" child; they did their
best to answer the teacher's age-old cry, "Am I pushing this one too far;
this one not far enough"?

Counselors held various kinds of in*tra*views, including social-personal-
occupational, with elementary children. The children were hardly different
in responsiveness from their big brothers and sisters in high school. However, they revealed unexpected gifts of creativity and originality. and often a
startling sense of identity and individuality when compared with their older
brethren who tended to become disillusioned or conditioned ("hardened")
as they climbed up the educational staircase.

Counselors showed teachers how to observe signals of emotional disorders in their classrooms and on the playground; they gave informal work-
shops on such crippling disabilities as dyslexia and cerebral dysfunctioning
(the hyperkinetic syndrome); and through quicker identification and proper
referrals, they sought to help channel the misunderstood drives of children

who once "drove teachers up the walls" and turned homes into emotional shambles.

While urging the administration to hire elementary counselors, the secondary counselors did anything and everything they could to fill the breach below. They were sensitive to the fact that neurological signs of learning disabilities often disappeared by early adolescence. Yet in almost all the children who came up the down staircase with unresolved learning problems, the signs of low self-esteem or hostility built up over years of frustration and failure prevailed. Goodlad's statement (1969) went to the heart of the matter: "Learning disabilities evidenced in the primary grades often go undiagnosed, persisting throughout life and seriously limiting human relations participation."

Even when properly diagnosed, learning disabilities commonly went without attention (treatment) for lack of a professional trained to help the teacher handle Johnny's problem in the classroom situation. In Kaufman's novel the scene recalled by Miss Barrett with the adolescent boy Ferone illustrates the anguish and yearning that sometimes break through years of stumbling through school without the necessary guidance: " 'What makes you think you're so special? Just because you're a teacher?' What he was really saying was: You are so special. You are my teacher. Then teach me, help. Hey, teach, I'm lost—which way do I go? I'm tired of going up the down staircase."

Secondary counselors went down the up staircase to give what aid they could to elementary teachers in relating to boys like Ferone and others. The counselors hoped to reach the children at a time in their growth when learning conditions were optimal, when teachers were closer to their pupils, when parents were more directly concerned with their children; when the total educational enterprise was child-centered rather than subject-matter directed, and when counseling could offer its initial services to clientele whose need for developmental help stretched lifelong ahead.

Enter the Elementary School Counselor

When the new breed of counselor stepped into the elementary school setting, he found a relatively clean slate on which to write and work out his own job description. Fears were voiced that secondary school guidance concepts might be forced on the elementary school. However, fears were allayed when the new counselor, although agreeing that his program differed mainly from the secondary counselor's in developmental steps, types of problems, and techniques rather than in philosophy and goals, acted out his own set of roles in his own setting.

During the later sixties, counselors in growing numbers both read and contributed to journals especially suited to their interests and needs, *The*

School Counselor and the trailblazing *Elementary School Guidance and Counseling.* In addition to the journals, the counselors agreed with what they found in Dinkmeyer (1967, 1968, 1970) and others; that, as in every other kind of counseling, school practice must be suited to the nature of the client and the total environment. In the elementary situation, the counselor operates in a setting where he has to meet the sometimes conflicting demands of children, parents, teachers, administrators, and the community image. Adults often pressure a counselor to "straighten that kid out!", and such unrealistic demands present roadblocks to formal theory.

Most counselors soon learn that, regardless of theory or how they *expected* to practice, they must work within the limits of the philosophy, objectives, and job habits of the specific school from which they get their paychecks. At the same time, they must "learn by heart" the pupils they counsel, dealing with the child's confused and ambivalent attitude about self and significant adults. With heightening awareness of the school as a social organization, many counselors found the "social position," or Adlerian approach, useful in elementary school settings, as Dinkmeyer had suggested (1964).

Adler's practical experience with school children led him to place significant importance on the individual child's striving in his social setting, including the family constellation. Early recollections of childhood were considered clues to present behavior: "My mother always fixed my shoelaces. I never learned to tie a bow."

Adler believed that every act has a purpose, whether understood by the actor or not, and that everyone has the creative power to make biased interpretations of all his experience. An intuitive counselor may hazard a hunch as to the real purpose behind a child's unacceptable behavior and await Dreikur's "recognition reflex," a twinkling eye, sly smile, or other automatic response even when accompanied by a denial: "Could it be that you're not doing your work because you expect the teacher to *tie up all your loose strings,* like your mother?"

Adler gave counselors a framework, concerned largely with interpersonal relationships, for dealing with children in a learning process. Studying the causation of behavior can be important, but beyond that lies the discovery of the child's purposes for his behavior, a discovery that once made by the counselor may be transmitted to the child as a reeducative bridge to better self-understanding and social relationships.

Adlerian or behavioral or even client-centered in formal approach, elementary school counselors were generally agreed that the *three C's* covered the functions of the jobholder: *c*onsulting and *c*oordinating and *c*ounseling. Some saw themselves as Faust's (1968) counselor-consultant with a grasp of survival theory. Many accepted another set of *three C's* added to the original by Costar (1966): *c*ollecting data about pupils, *c*ollaborating with parents, and *c*onducting research studies. Some figured they would reach more children by working mainly through teachers rather than in individual or small-group counseling. Others wondered when there would be time for consultations with teachers so often boxed into self-contained classrooms for most of the day. Perhaps the smallest percentage, but a growing number of these professionals, perceived themselves as a "counselor is a counselor is a counselor," and the availability of specialized pupil personnel services in each particular school system and the semantics of "counseling" would be only two of the variables in this perception of self in job behavior.

Whatever the original opinion of the counselor might be, he had to submit it to proof in practice. He worked out his own professional destination along with helping children toward their own destinies. For instance, there had been doubts that younger pupils would refer themselves for counseling, and further doubts about counselors' ability to relate to this age group.

Experience showed that, provided the counselors were identified as working in their school system and seen doing an effective job with children, even kindergartners would refer themselves; whereas the fragmented counselor, forced to divide his loyalties between schools, faced inevitable criticism, particularly from teachers and administrators, and had little visibility to children.

As far as counselors having difficulty in relating to elementary school children, it was found that the latter—in accordance with discoveries in educational theory and practice during the past few decades—have been "ready" to relate much sooner than adults gave them credit for. True, they are absorbed with the present, their sense of time is primitive, their recital of coming events may amount to fantasy, but they are trying out roles, the same as boys and girls in senior high school. Elementary school children are on different developmental steps but often on the identical lifeline as high school students, as is evident in the passages below:

A girl from kindergarten stepped down the hall to the counselor's office and peeked in at the play therapy session which had been established in accordance with the Ginott (1961) statement: "The child's play is his talk and the toys are his world." Then she began the interview:

> **CL:** I've brought you a problem of mine.
> **CO:** Um-hum.
> **CL:** I've got a boyfriend.
> **CO:** Would you like to tell me about it?
> **CL:** We're going to be married.
> **CO:** Oh?
> **CL:** In ten weeks. There's only one trouble.
> **CO:** Yes?

CL: He wants to have six children. And that's too many.
CO: Um-hum.
CL: Well, goodbye now, I have to go color.
CO: Okay, thanks for coming.

In the same school system, a tenth-grade girl whirled excitedly into the counselor's office:

CL: My boyfriend drove up to see me this weekend, all the way from State. We're going to get married.
CO: Oh. Uh-huh.
CL: Of course he's only a junior in college and he's going to get his law degree and he wants to fulfill his military obligation first.
CO: I guess you're saying it'll be quite awhile before those wedding bells ring out.
CL: It's like a dream.
CO: And you're not sure but you both might wake up and find yourself going with somebody else.
CL: Well. . . . Yes, that's right, and we know it. But we're pretending like it's for real, and maybe it will turn out to be that way, but even if it doesn't, then we've had a lot of fun practicing.
CO: Uh-huh. Rehearsing for coming events.

Not to labor the obvious, the high school counselor interprets the situation because his client has reached a developmental stage near the threshold of reality along the marriage-family lifeline. However, the elementary school counselor avoids any intrusion into the make-believe world of the child who is at a normal developmental stage where she recognizes her own fantasy or will outgrow it quickly and would resent any adult intervention or participation other than acceptance of her story. *Nor would the counselor demean his client by playing a false role.*

In company with their colleagues up the down staircase, elementary school counselors regarded all counseling as concerned with the complete person and thus inevitably personal and psychological in nature. They were determined not to perform tasks inconsistent with their professional roles as counselors, and this determination was reinforced by three prime factors: the collective bargaining surge toward teacher rights and liberties starting in the middle sixties, the hiring of paraprofessionals to handle routine matters, and the appearance of the "computerized counselor," or to reverse the phrase, the "counseling computer."

Now, in the ecology-alerted decade of the seventies, most elementary school counselors are agreed that *both* unconditional positive regard and positive behavioral conditioning ("That's great!") may work wonders *in the same context at the same time.* While they try out a variety of styles and approaches, including the existential stance of Beck (1963) and the reality therapy of Glasser (1965), they are firmly based in learning theory and keenly aware of the developmental processes unfolding childhood before their eyes. Although prepared to take necessary measures before an appropriate referral can be made, counselors are not crisis-oriented but are geared to practice prevention rather than cure, agreeing with Lifton (1961) that the *ultimate* goal of any therapeutic situation is *not* the resolution of the problem but rather an attempt to teach problem-solving techniques. Counselors realize that any time a teacher refers a child to them, they had better set up a more *immediate* goal as well.

Teachers are intensely practical people. They tend to bristle at mention of "theory" or "psychology" or "diagnosis." They have been "diagnosed to death." When they refer a child, they already have made a diagnosis: "This kid needs help and so do I, to help him in my classroom." Counselors realize that *another* explanation of the cause of Johnny's behavior is the last thing teachers want; they want action, here and now.

Armed with Krumboltz's (1965) definition of counseling, many elementary school counselors initiate whatever ethical activities they can imagine in order to enhance the child's image of himself and restore him to the classroom with an *observable* behavior change for the teacher to reinforce. A glance through the professional journals previously mentioned reveals an astonishing variety of devices and situations dreamed up by practitioners operating as "activist counselors." They are not, as certain critics might charge, practicing cookbook counseling or prescribing patent-medicine solutions; they are contriving ingenious ways to free a child from learning disabilities so that he may grow up in proper developmental fashion.

Sensitive to the fact that behavior occurs within a social context, elementary counselors often use small-group counseling methods to observe behavior because of the influence social interactions have upon the child at this age. Many pupils feel more comfortable in a small group of peers who offer support to one another; they benefit from side-learning; they are relieved to find out that others have problems similar to their own; and they often become very directive counselors toward one of the group, challenging his behavior, "telling him off and setting him straight."

When counselors first enter the elementary school setting, they are generally impressed by the most important person in the building, the child himself. There is nothing to equal the experience of watching the enchanted world of knowledge dawn in children's eyes. All wonderful possibilities lie ahead: mysteries to be unveiled, treasures to be found, and miracles to be performed. But the reverse of this magic mirror may also be seen, as evidenced not long ago in an extension class of veteran teachers I taught. The class was discussing "psychological problems of the classroom," volunteering numerous incidents of disruptive behavior in school situations. Finally, one woman, tears in her eyes, stood up and cried indignantly: "I'm in kindergarten. What in the world do the rest of you people do to children after they leave us."

Many counselors remember a similar remark made by a professional at another station along the developmental way, a retired psychiatrist who attended the APGA-ASCA Convention in San Francisco to lend his support to the elementary guidance movement in the "early days." In addressing the group, he explained: "All my life I have been pulling people out of the river, and in my old age I thought I'd like to wander upstream and see who is throwing them in."

The elementary school counselor, who is about as far upstream as anyone can get, is dedicated to keeping young ones from being thrown in the stream. The counselor is also determined to give children their first lessons in navigating the river of life from one landing to the next where other guides are standing by to give the additional instructions and encouragement needed to continue the voyage to safe harbor. He takes pride in his position as the *initiator* of developmental counseling services in the schools and feels that one of his primary functions is "to start them coming" so that from childhood to old age they will be aware of the "place to go" when they need the help of a specialized counselor.

The Great Behavioral Debate

During the late sixties and into the seventies, Patterson and Krumboltz replaced Rogers and Williamson (Skinner) as spokesmen in active dialogue along the nondirective-directive continuum. School counselors welcomed the clarification of issues by these counselor educators. Even those who were, indeed, client-centered could subscribe to Krumboltz's (1965) statement that, since all counseling is designed to affect the behavior of the client, all counseling is behavioral counseling. However, they might strongly disagree with his more explicit definition:

"Counseling consists of whatever ethical activities a counselor undertakes in an effort to help the client engage in those types of behavior which will lead to a resolution of the client's problems."

To the client-centered counselor who asked: "Are you saying that counselors have been wrong all these years in stating goals of counseling like self-actualization, self-fulfillment, self-understanding and self-acceptance?" Krumboltz would answer:

"Not at all. These would be fine goals if each were accompanied by a list of illustrative behaviors to define what it might mean for different clients. These abstract goals are not wrong; they are just not as useful as more specific statements would be."

"But don't people act the way they do because of their feelings, insights, and self-perceptions?"

"It seems more plausible that positive feelings are the by-product, not the cause, of competent behavior and the rewards it brings. Hence, if we succeed in helping people to act more competently, they will receive more positive feedback from their friends, relatives and employers; then their feelings about themselves will improve as a matter of course."

The "social engineering," epitomized by Krumboltz, received a flat dismissal from Patterson (1969) who assumed that human relationships are more important than mechanical methods of behavior modification:

"I think we have evidence for this, while we have no good evidence for the effectiveness of techniques of behavior modification apart from a good human relationship. We will realize soon, as has been the case with every other new method or technique in psychiatry and psychotherapy, that it is the basic human relationship which is curative, or facilitative of positive personality and behavior change, and that it is this factor—call it the Hawthorne effect if you will—which is the effective factor in techniques of behavior modification."

The irony in the situation above is that school counselors in the field and doctoral candidates (Hoppock, 1968) were impressed with the warm, human responsiveness of the behavioral researcher, thus apparently at least helping to prove a point for his opponent.

Some school counselors chose sides in the dichotomy, selecting either the *um-hum—you feel* school or the *that's-good—try this*. Perhaps what most working school counselors continued to say through the roles they played and the functions they carried out was "What we need is a more behavioristic humanism and a more humanistic behaviorism, and I'm working it out the best way I know how, in my own setting."

Tradition of Directive Counseling in High School

The strong tradition toward directive counseling in the schools, based on the didactic method of instruction and the protective principle of custodial care, has been carried forward by the fact that typical school counselors have emerged from the teaching ranks. In their role as teachers they become accustomed to telling pupils what to do, and in their role as counselors they continue to tell pupils, convinced that this is probably best and certainly quicker. There seems little argument that in a school setting the directive counselor can operate with greater *efficiency* than the nondirective counselor, but the vital issue depends on which one can operate more *effectively*. The question the strongly directive counselor has to answer in the watches of the night when self-doubts take the place of dreams, is:

"How would you like it if everybody you ever gave advice to had gone on to take it?"

Eclectic Theory in High School Counseling

Much confusion exists among high school counselors as to what constitutes an eclectic theory of counseling. Is it the weaving of odds and ends of other theories into a crazy quilt? Or is it being Adlerian at nine in the morning and Rogerian at three in the afternoon, with role-playing of Ellis, Sullivan, Mowrer, Williamson, Bordin and others sandwiched in between to suit other pupils of the day?

Eclecticism is as much in tune with the American way of life as pragmatism. The former has been called "the bane of our national life and either responsible for, or a rationalization of, the contradictions, inconsistencies, illogicalities, and opportunistic compromises that figure so prominently in our personal and institutional behavior" (Hartmann, 1942). The spirit of compromise *is* strong in America. Complete ideas and extreme opinions (except in matters that become labeled "national interests") are repellent to the prevailing philosophy. When this republic was a young upstart among nations, de Tocqueville observed the American disposition to form associations on any pretext and for whatever purpose; and in this century Sinclair Lewis (himself a would-be joiner) rose up to satirize the national habit. Perhaps in the light of this history an association of counseling theories is inevitable in the public schools and other settings.

Analysis of Counseling Theories

In considering the suitability of counseling theories at any level, there are four crucial variables that must be balanced in reaching any decision: the nature of the counselor, the nature of the student, the nature of the problem, and the nature of the school situation. Little differentiation need be made among the various theories of counseling. They have a variety of styles but interchangeable parts, most of which can be made to operate in any of the systems once the semantics are overhauled.

Counseling theories are more striking for their similarities than for their differences. Jung is on record as being an early "Rogerian":

> The psychologist has come to see that nothing is achieved by telling, persuading, admonishing, giving "good" advice. He has to relate to the individuality of the sufferer. . . . The deeper the doctor's understanding penetrates the patient, the weaker become the meanings of the principles based on general experience that the doctor first applied (1957).

Freud himself could be nondirective. While a student of Freud, Theo-
dor Reik (1948) bumped into the master on his daily walk along the Ring-
strasse in Vienna and walked home with him. Freud inquired about Reik's
plans, and Reik told him of his problems, about choosing a profession and a
marriage mate. Freud counseled:

> I can only tell you of my personal experience. When making a decision of
> minor importance, I have always found it advantageous to consider all the pros
> and cons. In vital matters, however, such as the choice of a mate or a profes-
> sion, the decision should come from the unconscious, from somewhere within
> ourselves. In the important decisions of our personal life, we should be gov-
> erned, I think, by the deep inner needs of our nature.

Art Related to Counseling Theory

The arts, particularly the art of writing, always have been close to counseling. Psychoanalysis has followed the example of the great playrights and
novelists in attempting to reach the depths of behavior rather than the
superficial layers. A story has to have a beginning, a middle, and an end; so
does counseling. A novel predicates character change; so does counseling.
All artists study the methods and the formats of the masters. Just as an
artist has to learn the principles of perspective before being able to create
an effective illusion, so would it appear that a counselor must learn conformity to certain systems of counseling before being able to encourage freedom of expression in a way of his own. All art earns liberty through discipline.
Not until the rules have been learned does the artist gain the insight to
understand when and how they may be altered or avoided to suit his
purposes. The very restrictions of the sonnet form encourage greater ultimate freedom of expression than the unrestricted license of free verse. Free
verse is permissive; the sonnet is a challenge that calls upon the poet's
ultimate resources. When a poet cannot contain his ideas within the framework of a sonnet, however, he does not break the framework or sacrifice his
inspiration; he moves toward another form of expression. There seem to be
guidelines here for counselors in quest of theory.

Flexibility of Counseling Theory

As far as holding fast to one system of counseling and forcing the counselee
to fit into the framework of that system, it may be recalled that Freud
deprecated all "systems" including his own in the words, *"Moi, je ne suis pas
un Freudiste."* Jung (1957) has been more explicit, declaring that since there
is no nag that cannot be ridden to death, all theories of neurosis and

methods of treatment are a dubious affair. He always found it amusing when businesslike doctors and fashionable consultants would claim that they treated patients along the lines of Adler, Kunkel, Freud, or Jung. He said there simply was not and could not be any such treatment.

> When I treat Mr. X, I have of necessity to use method X, just as with Mrs. Z, I have to use method Z. This means that the real and effective treatment of neurosis is always individual. If it has become evident anywhere that there are not so much illnesses as ill people, this is manifestly the case in neurosis. . . . I myself have long discarded any uniform theory of neurosis.

Summary Statement of Counseling Theory in Schools

The school counselor works in a setting where the primary goal is not rehabilitation but education. He is trained to refer seriously disturbed pupils, not to treat them. The problems brought to him are largely developmental, vocational and educational. Counseling theory at any school level rests on a basic idea in counseling and in educational philosophy, the idea of individual differences. No one theory of counseling is suitable because no single theory can allow for individual differences, not only of the pupil but of the counselor himself.

What can never be repeated too often is that counseling is vitally influenced by the counselor's total ecology. The process of moving into any workable theory involves much more than the professional preparation and job expectancies of the counselor. Within each unique setting, theory and practice create each other indissolubly. Counseling is a growth process, essentially creative in nature, shared by two people and shaped by many peripheral forces including the student body, the peer group, the administration, the faculty, the community at large, the national image, the world *Zeitgeist,* the cosmological eye, and the clock on the wall. In short, school counselors, influenced by a variety of factors including the state of the weather, work out their own personal theories within the limitations of the educational environment (Ratigan, 1967).

A theory of counseling suitable for application in schools must conform to principles laid down by artists and top level leaders in all walks of life. It must be flexible rather than rigid and, like the democratic process itself, adaptable. Call this eclecticism or call it a compromise (synthesis), the fact remains that every life, and every theory in life, faces a continuing adjustment between a world of possibilities and the world of reality.

The beginner in the field of secondary school counseling either tends to become erratically eclectic, piecing together remnants of theory, or he allies himself with a particular theory and clings to it, whether suited to himself and pupil needs or not. Instead of bending his theory or moving along the continuum, he inclines toward breaking the pupil into the mold.

An effective counselor usually begins practice by selecting a theory of counseling that attracts him as being suited to his personality and concept of counseling. As time goes on in his school situation, he discovers that this favorite theory has to be revised constantly to accommodate individual differences in pupils and also the changes within himself. In due course the initial theory may become so altered as to defy analysis of its origin.

In effect, a skillful counselor works out a theory of his own, but he does not start from scratch; he starts from Tyler or Krumboltz or Rogers or Dinkmeyer or someone else with whom he can identify, until in the fullness of experience he becomes his own man, thus fulfilling the ancient inscription said to have been inscribed on the temple of Apollo at Delphi—γνῶθι σεαυτόν—which is the goal of all counselors and of all counseling: *Know thyself.*

Or as that very directive counselor Polonius told his son:

This above all: to thine own self be true,
And it must follow, as the night the day,
Thou canst not then be false to any man.

Bibliography

Allport, G. W. *Pattern and growth in personality.* New York: Holt, 1965.

Arbuckle, D. S. Counselor, social worker, psychologist: Let's ecumenicalize. *Personnel guid. J.,* 1967, **45** (6).

Aubrey, R. F. (Brookline, Mass., Public Schools) Misapplication of therapy models to school counseling. *Personnel guid. J.,* 1969, **48** (4), 273-278.

Bancroft, G. (As quoted by Joseph L. Blau) *Social theories of Jacksonian democracy.* New York: Liberal Arts, 1954. Pp. 271 and 272.

Beck, C. E. *Philosophical foundations of guidance.* Englewood Cliffs, N.J.: Prentice-Hall, 1963.

Benjamin, H. (author's introduction to) Brubacher, J. S. *Modern philosophies of education.* New York: McGraw-Hill, 1939. P. xiii.

Bentley, J. C. (Ed.) *The counselor's role, commentary and readings.* Boston: Houghton Mifflin, 1968. Pp. vii, 70-84.

Boy, A. V., & Pine, G. J. *Client-centered counseling in secondary school.* Boston: Houghton Mifflin, 1963.

Brammer, L. M. The counselor is a psychologist. *Personnel guid. J.,* 1968, **47** (1), 8.

Brod, P. (New York City Board of Higher Education) The counselor in the middle school. *Counselor education and Supervision,* 1967, **6** (4), 349-351.

Costar, J. W. The counselor in the elementary school. *The Michigan elementary Principal,* 1966, **30** (5), 19.

Cottingham, H. F. Personal communication, 1969; Counseling in elementary schools—An overview. *Encyclopedia of educational research,* 1969; *Guidance in elementary schools.* Bloomington, Ill.: McKnight, 1956.

Darley, J. G. *Counseling in the high school.* Chicago: Science Research, 1943.

Dinkmeyer, D. A theory of child counseling at the elementary school level. American personnel and guidance association convention speech, Minneapolis, April, 1955.

Dinkmeyer, D. Conceptual foundations of counseling: Adlerian theory and practice. *The school counselor,* Mar. 1964. *Guidance and counseling in the elementary school: Readings in theory and practice.* New York: Holt, 1968. Counseling theory and practice in the elementary school. *Elementary School Guidance and Counseling,* ASCA, 1968.

Dinkmeyer, D., & Caldwell, C. C. *Developmental counseling and guidance: A comprehensive school approach.* New York: McGraw-Hill, 1970.

Faust, V. *The counselor-consultant in the elementary school.* Boston: Houghton Mifflin, 1968.

Felix, J. L. (Cincinnati Public Schools) Who decided that? *Personnel guid. J.,* 1968, **47** (1), 11.

Gammons, H. P. (Westfield, Mass, High School) *Common sense in guidance.* West Nyack, N.Y.: Parker Publication Co., 1969. P. 14.

Getzels, J. W. Conflict and role behavior in the educational setting. in W. W. Charters, Jr., & N. L. Gage (Eds.), *Readings in the social psychology of education.* Boston: Allyn and Bacon, 1963. Pp. 309-318.

Ginott, H. G. *Psychotherapy with children.* New York: McGraw-Hill.

Glasser, W. *Reality therapy, a new approach to psychiatry.* New York: Harper, 1965.

Goodlad, J. L. Schooling and education. In *Great ideas today.* New York: Great books division of Encyclopedia Britannica, 1969.

Hartmann, G. W. *NSEE 41st yearbook, part II.* Chicago: University of Chicago Press, 1942. P. 180.

Havighurst, R. J. *Human development and education.* New York: Longmans, Green and Co., 1953. Pp. 27-28.

Herr, E. L. The perceptions of state supervisors of guidance, of guidance of appropriateness of counselor function, the function of counselors, and counselor preparation. *Counselor education and Supervision,* 1969, **8** (4), 241-257.

Hoppock, R. Krumboltz by telephone. *Counselor Education and Supervision,* 1968, **7** (3), 319-318.

Ivey, A. E. & Robin, S. S. Role theory, role conflict and counseling. *J. counsel. Psychol.,* 1966, **13**, 31-32.

Jung, C. G. *The undiscovered self.* Boston: Little, Brown, 1957.

Kahn, R. *et al. Organizational stress.* New York: Wiley, 1964. P. 30.

Kaufman, B. *Up the down staircase.* Englewood Cliffs, N.J.: Prentice-Hall, 1964. P. 313.

Krumboltz, J. D. Behavioral counseling: Rationale and research. *Personnel guid. J.,* 1955, 383-384. Personal communication (1969). Behavioral goals for counseling. *J. counsel. Psychol,* 1966, **13** (?), 158.

Krumboltz, J. D., & Hosford. R. E. Behavioral counseling in the elementary school. *Elementary school guidance and Counseling.* 1966 (3), 11-19.

Lifton, W. M. *Working with groups.* New York: Wiley, 1961.

Patterson, C. H. What is counseling psychology? *J. counsel. Psychol.*, 1969, **16** (1), 28.

Paulson, B. B. (Chicago Public Schools) Riposte. *Personnel guid. J.*, 1967, **45** (6).

Peters, D. L. ASCA Newsletter, Dec. 7, 1970, p. 2.

Pierson, G. A. Results and achievements to date: The failures and successes of current guidance practices. *J. N.Y. Acad. Sciences.*, Fall 1961. *Counselor education in regular sessions institutes.* Washington, D.C.: U.S. Department of Health, Education, and Welfare, Office of Education, 1965. P. 39.

Pine, G. J. The effectiveness of client-centered counseling in a junior high school: Some general findings. *The Guidance Journal* (The Ohio State University), Winter 1967, **5** (3), 91-98.

Ratigan, W. School counseling: Relation of theory to practice. In Alfred Stiller (Ed.), *School counseling, 1967, a view from within.* First American School Counselor Association Yearbook, 1967. *Conflicts within counseling and guidance.* Ann Arbor, Mich.: University Microfilms, 1964.

Ratigan, W. & Johnson, W. F. Do guidance and discipline mix? *NEA Journal,* December 1961, 47-49.

Reik, T. *Listening with the third ear.* New York: Farrar, Strauss & Cudahy, 1948.

Roeber, E. C. Roles and functions of professionally trained counselors. In John F. McGowan (Ed.), *Counselor development in American society.* Washington: U.S. Department of Labor and U.S. Office of Education, 1965. Pp. 193-210.

Schorer, M. *Sinclair Lewis: An American life.* New York: McGraw-Hill, 1961.

Shertzer, B., & Stone, S. C. *Fundamentals of counseling.* Boston: Houghton Mifflin, 1968.

Stiller, A. Personal communication, 1969.

Testing, testing, testing. Washington: Joint Commission on Testing, American Association of School Administrators, Council of Chief State School Officers, National Association of Secondary School Principals, 1962.

Walz, G., & Miller, J. School climates and student behavior: Implications for counselor role. *Personnel guid. J.*, 1969, **47** (9), 859-867.

Willower, D. J., Hoy, W. K., & Eidell, T. L. The counselor and the school as a social organization. *Personnel guid. J.*, 1967, **46** (3), 228-233.

Wrenn, C. G. *The counselor in a changing world.* Washington: American Personnel and Guidance Association, 1962.

3

Client-centered Theory

DONALD L. GRUMMON

Client-centered theory or nondirective theory, as it is sometimes called, is derived from the work of Carl R. Rogers, his students and colleagues. As it has developed over the years, it has come to encompass many areas including personality development, group leadership, education and learning, creativity, interpersonal relations, and the nature of the fully functioning person. But the theory began with Rogers's attempts to understand the events occurring in his psychotherapeutic and counseling interviews, and psychotherapy has remained the core of the theory to the present time.

Rogers has become widely recognized as a distinguished teacher, researcher, and writer, but he began his career as a practicing clinician in a community child guidance clinic, and he has maintained his extensive practice of counseling and psychotherapy throughout his professional life. While one of his primary goals is theory development and validation, he believes that for himself the best way to reach this objective is to remain close to the actual source of his theories, the counselor's interaction with his clients. The firsthand experience of the interview—the interviewer's experience as well as the client's—becomes the breeding ground for the insights and hypotheses about the nature of the helping relationship. He believes that the methods of science—rigorous thinking and research validation—are needed to avoid self-deception, but, categorically, for Rogers the *subjective* nature of the client-counselor interaction is one of the fundamental characteristics of the interview and no scientific theory can fully capture its meaning:

> I let myself go into the immediacy of the relationship where it is my total organism which takes over and is sensitive to the relationship, not simply my consciousness. I am not consciously responding in a planful or analytic way, but simply react in an unreflective way to the other individual, my reaction being based (but not consciously) on my total organismic sensitivity to this other person. I live the relationship on this basis.

The essence of some of the deepest parts of therapy seems to be a unity of experiencing. ... In these moments there is, to borrow Buber's phrase, a real and 'I-thou' relationship, a timeless living in the experience which is *between* the client and me. It is the opposite pole from seeing the client, or myself, as an object. It is the height of personal subjectivity (Rogers, 1955, pp. 267-268).

In this chapter client-centered theory will be presented on the intellectual or conceptual level, an approach which of necessity largely ignores the subjective nature of the counseling interview. While the theory can be understood on this conceptual level, one cannot learn to use it effectively in the counseling situation without attending to his own subjective experience. The very nature of the theory prohibits learning a set of rules and procedures and then applying them mechanically and objectively in the counseling interview.

Learning to use client-centered theory, or any counseling theory for that matter, involves discovering for oneself what the theory builder originally discovered for himself. The theory can serve as a map along the route to discovery, but it cannot by itself teach anyone to become an effective counselor. Thus, the application of counseling theory is quite different from the application of, for example, physical theories, which can be applied with little regard for human interaction; counseling theory, being applied in the subjectively-oriented give-and-take between two persons, must be integrated into the counselor's personality. To apply it as we customarily apply theory in physics or chemistry would be to view oneself and the client as objects and would thereby result in the loss of the subjective element that Rogers and many others see as essential. It is in this sense, perhaps, that counseling and psychotherapy will always remain an art, no matter how refined and sophisticated our theories become.

For reasons of clarity and simplicity, Rogers's theory will be presented in a declarative style, which will tend to give the reader the impression that Rogers views his theory as established fact. Nothing could be further from the truth. Rogers has repeatedly emphasized that his theory cannot be taken as dogma, and can best be used as an impetus to new discovery. His theorizing has changed in the past, and he fully expects it to change in the future as new clinical insights are discovered and as new research evidence becomes available. Rogers (1959a) noted that even mature theories contain an unknown amount of error and mistaken inference, and counseling theory which has advanced little beyond the stage of hypothesis development and crude discovery, is especially vulnerable to change.

Rogers (1959a) also points out that a theory is a more dependable guide when it is applied to the events out of which it grew because less inference is needed to apply it and unknown errors are apt to be less consequential. The theory becomes a less dependable guide as it is used to explain more remote events; that is, more inference is required, and slight errors may be magnified.

In following the discussion below, the reader should keep in mind that client-centered theory was developed from interviews somewhat different in emphasis and aim from those prominent in this book. In terms of the continuum from guidance through counseling to psychotherapy suggested in Chapter 1, client-centered theory was developed in a context falling somewhere between counseling and psychotherapy. It has been little used in the guidance type of interview—the interview roughly characterized by the imparting of information. However, the theory is so closely related to many counseling situations that it will be presented as Rogers originally formulated it. The presentation draws heavily from his most comprehensive theoretical statement published in 1959, although earlier and later writings will also be considered. After the presentation of the formal theory, some newer and less systematic developments will be noted, and the theory's application to educational-vocational counseling will be examined. Because of space limitations, the theory will be abbreviated and at times tersely stated. For a more comprehensive view the reader is referred to Rogers's main books (1942, 1951, 1961b, 1967) and to his statement of the formal theory (Rogers, 1959a).

Conception of Man

As stated in Chapter 1, all theory development is influenced by the theory builder's beliefs and assumptions. Therefore a brief outline of Rogers's conception of man is a necessary prelude to a presentation of his formal theory.

1. *Belief in the dignity of man*

Rogers believes strongly in the dignity and worth of each individual. He sees man as capable of making his own decisions, and he respects the right of each individual to do so. A corollary belief is that society's needs are served best by social processes and institutions that encourage the individual to be independent and self-directing.[1]

---

[1] Rogers has frequently spoken and written about the need to examine counseling, educational, student personnel, and other procedures in the light of democratic values. He fears that unknowingly we often act on contrary assumptions. He is suspicious of the "approach of the expert" in which one individual sets himself up, so to speak, as the person who best can select the goals and decide on the most appropriate behavior of another individual. Rogers thinks that too frequently counselors and educators proceed on the assumption that they know best what the *real* needs of clients and students are and, in so doing, they reduce the opportunity for the client or student to develop into a mature, self-directing individual. He is particularly concerned by the prevalent tendency of counselors and educators to urge the democratic ideal, while at the same time, apparently unaware of any contradiction, they develop more effective and more subtle ways of controlling students and clients. See Rogers (1948) and his new book on education (1969).

2. *Fundamental predominance of the subjective*

The significance of the subjective elements in a client-counselor inter-action has already been mentioned, but Rogers's belief in the fundamental predominance of the subjective extends beyond the practice of counseling to most of man's behavior. "Man lives essentially in his own personal and subjective world, and even his most objective functioning, in science, mathematics, and the like, is the result of subjective purpose and subjective choice" (Rogers, 1959a, p. 191). Rogers would say that the reader's act of reading this chapter can ultimately be traced to a subjective choice.

Rogers believes that developments in the behavioral sciences will some-day enable us to understand man's behavior objectively, much as we now understand events in the physical world. However, he also holds

> . . . a very different view, a paradox which does not deny the objective view, but which exists as co-equal with it.
>
> No matter how completely man comes to understand himself as a deter-mined phenomenon, the products of past elements and forces, and the deter-mined cause of future events and behaviors, he can never *live* as an object. He can only *live* subjectively. . . .
>
> The person who is developing his full potential is able to accept the subjective aspect of himself, and to *live* subjectively. When he is angry he is *angry,* not merely an exhibition of the effects of adrenalin. When he loves he is loving, not merely "cathected towards a love object." He moves in self-selected directions, he chooses responsibly, he is a person who thinks and feels and experiences; he is not merely an object in whom these events occur. He plays a part in a universe which may be determined, but he lives himself subjectively, thus fulfilling his own need to be a person (1961e, pp. 20-21).

3. *Tendency toward actualization*

Rogers's early writings emphasized that the client's natural capacity for growth and development is an important human characteristic on which counseling and psychotherapeutic procedures should rely. Over the years, his conviction has grown stronger that the *inherent* tendency of man is to move in directions that can be roughly described as growth, health, adjust-ment, socialization, self-realization, independence, and autonomy. This di-rectional tendency is now labeled the *actualizing tendency* and is defined as "the inherent tendency of the organism to develop all its capacities in ways which serve to maintain or enhance the organism" (1959a, p. 196).

This conception is simple and all-inclusive. In fact, it is the fundament-al characteristic of all life and applies not only to man but to a protozoan, a starfish, a daisy, and a lion. The essential nature of life is that it is an active, not a passive, process, in which the organism interacts with its environment in ways designed to maintain, to enhance, and to reproduce itself. The actualizing tendency is expressed differently in different species. An acorn develops into an oak tree, tall and sturdy in favorable soil and climate, scrubby and gnarled under unfavorable conditions, but a live oak tree nonetheless, maintaining, enhancing, and reproducing itself as its environment allows.

In man the actualizing tendency expresses itself in varied ways. Consider, for example, the child learning to walk. Because of the forward direction of growth and development which are inherent, he learns to walk only if the proper conditions are present. He need not be taught to walk. This directional process is not, of course, smooth and unfaltering. The child takes a few steps, falls, and experiences pain. For a time he may revert to crawling. But in spite of the bumps and the pain and even though walking at first is a less efficient means of locomotion than crawling, the child tries again and again. The process is a painful struggle, but because of his nature, the child continues his efforts until he learns to walk and eventually to run and to skip and to jump.

The life-force can be observed in many areas. At the physiological level the organism's tendency to maintain itself is revealed in the assimilation of food, the maintenance of body heat, and the regulation of body chemistry. At another level the child strives to feed himself rather than be fed, to dress himself rather than be dressed, and to read to himself rather than be read to. Studies show that man shares with other animals a spontaneous curiosity, a tendency to explore and to produce changes in the stimulus field. Man tends to actualize himself by learning to use tools and verbal concepts and to maintain himself by building a shelter against heat and cold. Man builds theories to improve his understanding and control of his world. Man also tends to strive for meaningful interpersonal contacts and toward socialization, broadly defined.

Rogers's thinking has been influenced by many theorists who have observed and emphasized different aspects of this forward moving characteristic of the organism. Maslow (1954) spoke of a hierarchy of motives and needs. As the organism satisfies the needs lower in the hierarchy, such as the needs for food, water, and safety, it then is motivated by higher needs such as those for belonging and love and self-actualization. Goldstein (1940) also used the term "self-actualization" for this basic striving. Mowrer and Kluckhohn spoke of "the basic propensity of living things to preserve and increase integration" (1944, p. 74). But Rogers was particularly influenced by Angyal, who stressed that a fundamental characteristic of life is to move in the direction of increasing independence, self-regulation, and autonomy, and away from external control. Angyal said, "Life is an autonomous dynamic event which takes place between the organism and the environment. Life processes do not merely tend to preserve life but transcend the momen tary status quo of the organism, expanding itself continually and imposing its autonomous determination upon an ever increasing realm of events" (1941, p. 48).[2]

In stressing this actualizing tendency, Rogers wishes to emphasize several ideas.

1. The actualizing tendency is the primary motivating force of the human organism.
2. It is a function of the whole organism, not just some part of it. Needs and motives can be, and characteristically have been, thought of as more specific. While men do seek such specific things as food, sex, and self-esteem, Rogers has some doubts about whether these more specific conceptions of motivation may not have obscured more truth than they have encouraged. In any event, he wishes to emphasize that the organism responds as a whole. Even though at one moment in time the organism may seek food or sex, it characteristically seeks them in ways that enhance rather than diminish its self-esteem and other strivings. Maslow's hierarchy of needs is similar, although not identical, to Rogers's conception.
3. The actualizing tendency is a broad conception of motivation that includes the usual needs and motives such as physiological needs for food and water, those aspects of motivation often termed *tension reduction* or *need reduction*, curiosity, and the search for pleasurable activity. However, more than some theories of motivation, Rogers emphasizes man's tendency to physical growth, maturation (as illustrated by the infant's learning to walk), the need for close interpersonal relationships ("man is incurably social"), and his tendency to impose himself on his environment—to move toward autonomy and away from external control.
4. Life is an active and not a passive process. Rogers sees the organism as an "active, directional initiator," and he rejects the "empty organism" concept of life in which nothing intervenes between stimulus and response. He rejects Freud's thinking that the nervous system would, if it could, maintain itself in an altogether unstimulated condition.
5. Man has the capacity as well as the tendency or motivation to actualize himself. These capacities, often more latent than evident, are released under the proper conditions. Counseling is aimed not at doing something *to* or *for* the individual; but at freeing his capacities for normal growth and development. Counseling theory attempts to specify the conditions that allow growth and development to occur.

[2] Butler and Rice (1963) theorized that self-actualization and drive-reduction theories do not necessarily conflict with one another. They marshal evidence that stimulus hunger or adient motivation is a primary drive and serves as the basis for self-actualizing behavior.

4. *Man is trustworthy*

Closely related to these ideas is Rogers's confident view of man as basically good and trustworthy. Words such as "trustworthy," "reliable," "constructive," or "good" describe characteristics that seem inherent in man.

Rogers of course is fully aware that man frequently behaves in untrustworthy, even "evil" ways. Man is certainly capable of deceit, hate, cruelty, and stupidity. But Rogers views these unsavory characteristics as arising out of a defensiveness that alienates man from his own nature. As defensiveness diminishes and he is more sensitively open to all his experiences, man tends to move in ways we think of as socialized and trustworthy. He strives for meaningful and constructive relationships with his fellow men in ways that enhance his own development and also that of the species.

Rogers's conception contrasts sharply with the view of many psychoanalysts who see man as innately destructive and antisocial: Man is born with instinctual urges that must be controlled if healthy personality development is to occur. To this Rogers answers:

> I have little sympathy with the rather prevalent concept that man is basically irrational, and that his impulses, if not controlled, will lead to destruction of others and self. Man's behavior is exquisitely rational, moving with subtle and ordered complexity toward the goals his organism is endeavoring to achieve. The tragedy for most of us is that our defenses keep us from being aware of this rationality, so that consciously we are moving in one direction, while organismically we are moving in another. But in the person who is living the process of the good life, there would be a decreasing number of such barriers, and he would be increasingly a participant in the rationality of his organism. The only control of impulses which would exist, or which would prove necessary, is the natural and internal balancing of one need against another, and the discovery of behaviors which follow the vector most closely approximating the satisfaction of all needs. The experience of extreme satisfaction of one need (for aggression, or sex, etc.) in such a way as to do violence to the satisfaction of other needs (for companionship, tender relationships, etc.)— an experience very common in the defensively organized person—would be greatly decreased. He would participate in the vastly complex self-regulatory activities of his organism—the psychological as well as physiological thermostatic controls—in such a fashion as to live in increasing harmony with himself and with others (1961f, pp. 299-300).

5. *Man is wiser than his intellect*

Closely related to the foregoing is Rogers's belief that man is wiser than his intellect, wiser than his conscious thought. When man is functioning nondefensively and well, he trusts his total organismic reaction, which often results in better although more intuitive judgments than conscious thinking alone.

Rogers (1963) has puzzled about the function of consciousness or awareness. He sees awareness as one of the latest evolutionary developments, as a "... tiny peak of awareness, of symbolizing capacity, based upon a vast pyramid of nonconscious organismic functioning" (1963, p. 17). When the organism functions freely and effectively, awareness is only a small part of the total activity and "... tends to be reflexive rather than the sharp spotlight of focused attention" (1963, p. 17.) Awareness is sharpened and focused when the organism encounters some difficulty in functioning.

Rogers was stimulated by Whyte who says, "The main purpose of conscious thought, its neobiological function, may be first to identify, and then to eliminate, the factors which evoke it" (1960, p. 37). If Rogers's and Whyte's views about how man functions best are correct, why are man's conscious thinking and functioning so often at odds with his organismic functioning? This problem is considered in the next section on personality theory.

Personality Theory

Of Rogers's theories of personality and therapy, the theory of therapy was developed first and has been more refined as the result of research. However, it is essentially descriptive and contains little explanation of why the client should change with successful counseling. The explanatory concepts are contained in the personality theory, and to it we now turn before considering Rogers's more important contribution in therapeutic theory.

Although still tentative and mainly an outline, client-centered personality theory has been elaborated into a series of interlocking, formal propositions (Rogers, 1951, 1959a). Others have contributed to the theory: Raimy (1943, 1948) to the self theory, Snygg and Combs (1949) to its phenomenological emphasis, and Standal (1954) to the theory of childhood development. Because the account below is considerably abbreviated, these sources should be consulted by the reader wishing to examine the theory for inconsistencies and major omissions.

1. *Every individual exists in a continually changing world of experience of which he is the center (Rogers, 1951, p. 483)*

This is the private world of each individual's experience and is sometimes called the *phenomenal field* or the *experiential field*. It includes all that goes on within the organism that might reach consciousness, although only a small part of the organism's experiences are ever conscious at any given time.[3] For example, I can be deeply engrossed in a game or a conversation and not be consciously aware of the physiological accompaniments of hunger which are being experienced by my organism.

Rogers wishes to emphasize in this proposition that only the individual himself can know this world of experience in any genuine and complete way. We can never know the full experience of another as he fails an examination or goes to a job interview. We can observe another individual, measure his reactions to various stimuli, have him record his thoughts and reactions on psychometric tests, etc., but we can never know fully and vividly how he experiences and perceives any given situation.

Of course, many of the individual's experiences are not readily available to his awareness and thus are not a part of his phenomenal field. If he becomes aware of them, he will do so only under certain conditions, which are discussed more fully in a later section.

2. *The organism reacts to the field as it is experienced and perceived. This perceptual field is, for the individual, "reality" (Rogers, 1951, p. 84)*

3. *Behavior is basically the goal-directed attempt of the organism to satisfy its need as experienced, in the field as perceived (Rogers, 1951, p. 484)*

These two propositions emphasize that we do not react to some absolute reality but to our perceptions of that reality. Rogers has observed that a man dying of thirst in a desert will struggle as hard toward a mirage as to reach a real body of water. Snygg and Combs (1949) cite a personal example to emphasize this point. One of the authors was riding as a passenger in a friend's automobile on a lonely Western highway at night. Suddenly the headlights illuminated a large object in the middle of the road. The driver appeared unconcerned, but the passenger feared a serious accident. Finally he grabbed the steering wheel and guided the car around the object. The driver, a native of the West, had seen the object as a harmless tumbleweed, whereas the passenger, who lived in a landslide area of the East, had seen it as a boulder. Each reacted according to his own perceptual reality. Knowing the "perceptual reality" of each, we can understand and even predict the behavior of both persons without knowing the objective reality of whether the object was actually a rock or tumbleweed.

---

[3]Awareness and consciousness are used synonymously in client-centered theory. Consciousness is the symbolization, although not necessarily the verbal symbolization, of experience. This symbolic representation of experience may have varying degrees of vividness and clarity and, in the figure-ground terminology of Gestalt psychology, may be in the center of awareness as figure or in the background of awareness as ground.

Rogers notes that man is continually checking his perceptions against one another in order to make them a more reliable guide to reality. Each perception is like a hypothesis to be checked against further perceptions: A material first seen as salt is found to taste sweet, and the perception changes to regard it as sugar. While man's perceptions tend to become accurate representations of reality as he interacts with his environment in attempts to satisfy his needs, many remain unconfirmed or only partially confirmed. The important psychological fact to remember is that reality for any given individual is his perceptions of reality, regardless of whether or not those perceptions have been tested and confirmed.

4. *The best vantage point for understanding behavior is from the internal frame of reference of the individual himself*[4] *(Rogers, 1951, p. 494)*

Rogers defines the *internal frame of reference* as "all of the realm of experience which is available to the awareness of the individual at a given moment. It includes the full range of sensations, perceptions, meanings, and memories, which are available to consciousness" (1959a, p. 210). Understanding another individual from the internal frame of reference is to concentrate on the *subjective reality* that exists in that individual's experience at any given time. Empathy is needed to achieve this understanding. By contrast, understanding another individual from the *external frame of reference* is to view him, without empathy, as an object, usually with the intent of emphasizing *objective reality*. Objects such as a stone or an electron have no experience with which we can empathize. Persons become objects in this sense when we make no empathic inferences about their subjective experiences.

Rogers sees the internal and external frames of reference as two different ways of knowing, each of which has its usefulness. His theory of therapy is built on understanding the client's internal frame of reference, but hypotheses of that theory can be verified only by adopting the external frame of reference. Nevertheless, understanding another person from the external frame of reference is to view him from our own internal frame of reference. The counselor's internal frame of reference may more closely approximate objective reality than the client's, but it is still only the counselor's *perception* of objective reality; and it tends to ignore the client's subjective experience of reality.

---

[4] See Snygg and Combs (1949) for a discussion of an assumption that seems to be inherent in this and the preceding propositions, namely, that a meaningful and complete psychological theory of behavior can be based on an examination of behavior from the internal frame of reference.

5. *Most of the ways of behaving which are adopted by the organism are those which are consistent with the concept of self (Rogers, 1951, p. 507)*

The *self-concept* or *self-structure* is an important construct in the client-centered theoretical system. For Rogers it is an organized conceptual gestalt consisting of the individual's perception of himself alone and of himself in relation to other persons and objects in his environment, together with the values attached to these perceptions. The self-concept is not always in awareness, but it is always available to awareness. That is, the self-concept by definition excludes unconscious self-attitudes that are not available to consciousness. The self-concept is considered fluid, a process rather than an entity, but at any given moment it is a fixed entity.

Stated more informally, the self-concept is the picture an individual has of himself along with his evaluation of this picture. For example, the client may perceive of himself as above average in intelligence, as a good student except in mathematics, as unattractive to members of the opposite sex, as liking to work with his hands, as loving his parents, as afraid of the future, etc. And he may value any of these characteristics either positively or negatively.

The importance of the self as a regulator of behavior was one of the earliest ideas emphasized by the client-centered group, and it assumed considerable importance in their counseling long before most other parts of the personality theory were developed. Of course, many theorists have been interested in the self, but attention was first drawn to the importance of the self in client-centered counseling because clients continually talked about their "selves" once they became deeply involved in counseling. Expressions such as the following were common: "I just cannot see myself as capable of directing a bunch of unruly kids in a classroom." "I am good at jokes and making small talk, but I am really a very shy person underneath." "I have always been a loving and dutiful son, and I owe it to my father to consider carefully his wishes about my schooling." "I am capable of doing the work when I study, but I am really more the socializing type." "I try to hide the real me." "I'm just no good underneath this false front."

Over the years clinical observation and considerable research made it apparent that attitudes toward the self were an important determiner of behavior. Changes in the client's behavior and attitudes toward others seemed to follow changes in attitudes about himself. As the evidence accumulated, the self-concept evolved into the central construct of client-centered theory.

Needs, of course, are also important determinants of behavior. But needs can usually be satisfied in a wide variety of ways, and the particular behavior selected to meet a need is usually consistent with the self-concept. For example, the need for food or physical activity is satisfied by behaviors consistent with the person's self-concept: "I need food, but I also consider myself an honest person and therefore do not steal from the local supermarket." Similarly, a person who does not view himself as aggressive, does not react with anger and violence when some need is frustrated by another person. Instead, he may cajole or flatter or withdraw, in an attempt to meet his need elsewhere in ways more consistent with his self-concept.

The reader should note that this part of client-centered theory states that most of the behavior adopted by a person is consistent with his self-concept. However, maintaining this consistency is often difficult, particularly, for example, if the satisfaction of a strong need necessitates behavior that objectively would be contrary to the individual's self-concept. In such situations the individual can employ various defensive maneuvers in an attempt to keep his perception of his behavior consistent with his self-concept. This kind of situation forms the basis for Rogers's view of maladjustment and will be considered in the next sections presenting the client-centered theory of childhood development and the theory of threat and defense.

6. *Early childhood development and the basic estrangement of man*

How does it happen that man is so often at war with himself? Rogers calls this the problem of incongruence or dissociation, a problem repeatedly encountered by those who study the dynamics of human behavior. A clarifying example would be the student who consciously wishes to succeed in school but who repeatedly engages in behavior that diverts him from his studies and ensures his failure.

In general terms Rogers's answer is that an incongruence or rift develops between the individual's self-concept and his organismic experience because love from his parents and significant others is made conditional upon his introjecting certain constructs and values as if they were his own. The constructs and values that are incorporated into his self-concept are often rigid and static and prevent the child's normal process of evaluating his experiences. Therefore the child develops and attempts to actualize a self that is contradictory or incongruent with organismic processes based on the actualizing tendency.

a. The organismic valuing process.   As the human infant begins life, he evaluates his experiences against the criterion of his basic *actualizing tendency,* which as noted earlier is the only motive postulated by the theoretical system. The infant values and seeks those activities that further the aim of the actualizing tendency, and those negating this aim he values negatively and avoids. This way of regulating behavior is known as the *organismic valuing process.* It involves a feedback mechanism that ensures that the infant's behavior will meet his motivational needs.

b. The development of the self-concept. Some of the infant's experiences are differentiated and crudely symbolized as an awareness of being. They are termed *self-experiences* and eventually become elaborated into the *self-concept.* A part of the actualizing tendency becomes differentiated as a tendency toward self-actualization.

c. The development of the need for positive regard. As his awareness of self is emerging, the infant is also developing a *need for positive regard* which can be viewed roughly as the need for warmth and love from his mother. According to Rogers, this is a persistent and pervasive need and is universally present in all human beings.[5]

The infant must infer from his mother's tone of voice, gestures, and other ambiguous stimuli whether or not he is receiving positive regard. Partly because of this ambiguity, the child develops a total gestalt about how his mother regards him, and he tends to generalize each new experience of approval or disapproval in the context of his total experience of being loved or unloved. In addition, because of the strength of the need for love, the infant can at times become more responsive to his mother's approval than to experiences that actualize the organism.

d. The development of the need for positive self-regard. The experiences of being loved or not loved become attached to self-experiences and thus to the developing self-concept. The result is the development of a learned need for *positive self-regard.*

e. The development of the conditions of worth. The development of the need for positive regard sets the stage for the child to seek experiences, not because they satisfy his actualizing tendency, but because they satisfy his need for his mother's love. When these sought-after experiences are self-experiences, they also satisfy his learned need for positive self-regard. In this way the need for positive self-regard also becomes selective.

We now come to an important characteristic of the need for positive self-regard, namely, that it can be satisfied or frustrated in the absence of interaction with the mother or other significant persons in the child's life. In time, therefore, the child comes to seek (or avoid) self-experiences solely because they satisfy (or frustrate) the need for positive self-regard. In other words, the child learns to discriminate the conditions under which his need for his mother's love and his own self-esteem are more apt to be satisfied than frustrated. When the infant seeks or avoids self-experiences on this basis, he is, in Rogers's terminology, living by the *conditions of worth* or, in Rogers's older terminology, by values introjected from others. Thus, a sec-

---

[5] It seems to me that this idea comes close to postulating a second motive in the theoretical system, especially since the need for positive regard is seen as universally present in infancy and since it sometimes acts in opposition to the actualizing tendency. However, Standal (1954), who refined this portion of the theory in his dissertation, presents a rationale that this need is learned and arises out of the infant's developmental situation.

ond regulatory system of behavior comes into existence, and it can conflict with the organismic valuing process where the actualizing tendency is the criterion. [6]

f. The development of incongruence between self and experience.   Incongruence, or inconsistency, between the self-concept and experience is a key concept in client-centered theory. A state of *incongruence* exists when an individual's self-concept is different from the actual experience of his organism. A child is incongruent if he thinks of himself as loving and wishing to take care of his younger sister when he is organismically experiencing anger and jealousy over having to share his mother's love and attention with her.

We can now return to our account of childhood development and explain how an incongruence between self and experience is brought about. As noted earlier, self-experiences are the raw material out of which the self-concept develops. Self-experiences that are consistent with both the organismic valuing process and the conditions of worth present no problems, of course. They are accurately perceived and symbolized in awareness and become incorporated into the self-concept. However, self-experiences that contradict the conditions of worth would, if accurately perceived and assimilated, frustrate the child's need for positive self-regard. Thus, they tend to be selectively perceived and distorted in awareness, or even completely denied to awareness, in an attempt to make them consistent with the conditions of worth. This maneuver allows the child to act in terms of his actualizing tendency and still meet his need for self-esteem. These denied or distortedly perceived self-experiences cannot, however, be accurately integrated into the developing self-concept. It is in this manner that the self-concept becomes partially incongruent with organismic experiences based on the actualizing tendency.

g. The basic estrangement of man.   In short, the child learns to need love and to avoid the behavior that he anticipates might bring disapproval. Soon he learns to view himself and his behavior as he thinks his mother views him, even though his mother is absent. In this way, he seeks some behaviors that are not organismically satisfying, and, when they are also self-experiences, they may become incorporated into the developing self-concept. Other behaviors that are organismically satisfying are distorted in awareness in an attempt to maintain his mother's love and his own self-esteem. Nor can these experiences be satisfactorily integrated into the developing self-concept. The end result is an incongruence between self and experience.

The basic tendency of the organism is to fulfill itself according to the actualizing tendency; however, as the self-concept develops, this same inher-

---

[6] The reader will probably observe here some similarity with the Freudian conception of opposition between the id and the superego. However, closer examination will show many differences. Rogers's actualizing tendency, for example, is quite different from Freud's concept of the id.

ent characteristic is also expressed as a tendency to actualize the self. As long as the self-concept and organismic experience are congruent, man remains whole and integrated. But when incongruence develops between self and experience, man is in conflict, torn between the basic actualizing tendency and the actualization of his self-concept. He is now vulnerable to psychological maladjustment. He can no longer live as a whole, integrated person. He becomes a person divided against himself, with one part of him true to the actualizing tendency and one part of him true to the inaccurate self-concept and its incorporated conditions of worth.

Rogers (1963, 1964) sees this situation as the basic estrangement in man. Because of the natural but tragic developments in early life resulting in specific types of social learning, man has become untrue to himself. This concept is central to all of Rogers's thinking. Man avoids this war within himself when his self-concept is a changing gestalt based upon his organismic experience. Man needs to be more open to his experience rather than trying to defend a rigidly organized self-concept based upon the conditions of worth, i.e., the values introjected from others. The self must be loosely organized and viewed as a continuing process of becoming. Instead of being rigidly defended as a static entity, the self-concept needs to be a process of continual change and expansion as the individual opens to each new experience.

Rogers's main theoretical interests about personality and psychotherapy are centered on this process of change and becoming. This interest helps to explain why the developmental aspect of the personality theory has been so little expanded. Rogers is interested primarily in how people change and become, not in how they got the way they are. Nonetheless, the theory of childhood development is logically important to Rogers's main interest, and it has implications for child-rearing practices.

h. Illustration and application to child rearing. Consider the young child who has just discovered his mother's china tea cups. Young children are naturally interested in the world around them, and the child will use all his senses to examine the tea cups. He notices their shape and color; he feels them to see if they are rough or smooth; he puts them in his mouth to see how they taste; he swings them in the air to experience their weight; and he bangs them against something to hear how they sound. Only the unusual mother is not emotionally upset to discover her child among the wreckage. She roughly grabs the remaining cups away, plunks him (not too gently or lovingly) into his playpen, and calls him a naughty, bad child. In short, an experience that was organismically satisfying is now associated with loss of love and diminished self-esteem.

The child experiences an almost endless repetition of this general situation. The child experiences loss of love if he touches this or that, if he asks too persistently for help when his parents are engaged in other activities, if he fights with his brother over a toy, if he hits his sister when he is jealous and angry with her, if he wanders away from home and frightens his mother about his safety, if he shows too much interest in his sexual organs, if he urinates out-of-doors, and so on. It is small wonder that the child develops a self-concept incongruent with many organismic experiences based on his actualizing tendency.

In theory, the incongruence between self and experience would not develop if the child were unable to discriminate any of his self-experiences as being more or less worthy of love than any other self-experience. In practice, this never happens. However, less incongruence will develop as more of his self-experiences are met with love and acceptance.

In practice, the mother values her tea cups and naturally is frustrated and angry when they are broken. The more this anger violates a rigidly held self-image of what she thinks a good mother should be (her conditions of worth), the more likely she is to externalize the cause of the anger as her child's "bad" behavior. The more she is open to her experience, the more she can own the anger *as hers* and assume responsibility for it *as hers.* She might feel, for example, "I love my child, but I like my tea cups too, and I am hurt and angry that they are broken." If these feelings can be owned and communicated as *her* feelings because she values both the tea cups and the child, then a somewhat different learning situation is possible. The potential is present for the child to discriminate between his and his mother's experience: "I enjoy playing with the tea cups" (versus, "I am a bad boy, unworthy of mother's love if I play with the tea cups"), "but mother is hurt and angry when her tea cups are broken." This learning helps to socialize the child without establishing, at least so strongly and rigidly, the conditions of worth. Haime Ginott (1965) makes excellent use of this principle in his book on parent-child interactions.

The essence of the matter as seen by this writer is simply this. If parents can be *open* and *nondefensive* to both their own and their child's experience, can *value* both their own and their child's experience, can *differentiate* between the two, and can *communicate* this valuing and understanding to the child, then the child is less likely to grow into an adult who is at war within himself. In the language of the theory, the conditions of worth are less likely to develop.

7. *Threat and the process of defense*

"The essential nature of threat is that if the experience (which is incongruent with the self-concept) were accurately symbolized in awareness, the self-concept would no longer be a consistent gestalt, the conditions of worth (incorporated within the self) would be violated, and the need for self-regard would be frustrated. A state of anxiety would exist" (Rogers, 1959a, p. 227).

When an individual is incongruent, he is also *vulnerable:* An accurate perception of his organismic experience would threaten a disruption of his self-concept. If, in addition, he is aware, even dimly aware, of this threat, a state of tension or *anxiety* exists. The threat need not be clearly perceived. It is sufficient that it be *subceived,* a term Rogers borrows from experimental studies of perception. To be subceived means to be discriminated just below the level of conscious awareness. *Anxiety* is thus the response of the organism when a discrepancy between the self-concept and experience threatens to enter awareness, thus forcing a possible disruption of the self-concept.

The individual defends himself against threat and the accompanying anxiety by denying the experience, or more frequently by misperceiving the experience to make it more consistent with the self-concept. By this maneuver, the individual maintains the consistency of his self-structure and reduces both the awareness of threat and the anxiety. The actual threat, of course, remains (he is still vulnerable), but the person has defended himself against it. He pays the price for this gain, however, in a rigidity of perception and a distortion of reality.

In response to strong and unsatisfied needs of the organism, behavior sometimes occurs that is inconsistent with the self-concept in a context where it cannot be easily denied or distorted. In such instances the person typically disowns the behavior with reactions like "I didn't know what I was doing"; "I was very upset and not myself"; or "If the evidence wasn't right in front of me, I wouldn't believe it. It's just not like me at all."

The probability of this kind of reaction increases with the severity of emotional disturbance. Neurotic behavior is often incomprehensible to the individual himself, since "it is at variance with what he consciously 'wants' to do, which is to actualize a self no longer congruent with experience" (Rogers, 1959a, p. 203). Statements like the following are frequent in the counseling interviews of neurotic clients: "I didn't want to do it, but I did. I just can't understand why." Or, "I just have no control over this feeling. It doesn't even seem a part of me but is like some intruder."

The usual defensive behaviors so frequently discussed in the literature (such as projection, rationalization, wish-fulfilling fantasy, and the like) can, according to Rogers, be fitted into the client-centered scheme of threat and defense, but we shall not take the time to illustrate this here.[7]

8. *The process of change*

To change the process of threat and defense, the self-concept must become more congruent with the individual's actual organismic experiences. But changes in the self-structure are resisted because these tend to violate

---

[7]Psychotic behavior is accounted for by a different part of the theory and results when a failure of the defenses is accompanied by a serious disorganization and a breaking down of the self-structure.

the conditions of worth and the learned need for positive self-regard. The avenue to change, therefore, involves creating the conditions where there is less threat and less need to resist. According to the theory, this calls for a corrective relationship with another person which will decrease the necessity to act upon the conditions of worth and will increase the individual's positive self-regard. That is, there must be a reversal of the conditions described in the section on infant development. The theory of therapy, to be presented shortly, describes the conditions that make this possible. The aim is to relax, little by little, the boundaries of the client's self-concept so that it may assimilate denied and distorted experiences. In this way, the self becomes more congruent with experience.

9. *Optimal adjustment or the fully functioning person*

The ideally adjusted person is completely open to all his experiences. His experiences are not, of course, always in awareness, but they are always available to awareness in accurately symbolized form. That is, he exhibits no defensiveness. There are no conditions of worth, and the individual experiences unconditional positive self-regard. His self-concept is congruent with his experience, and he acts in terms of his basic actualizing tendency which also actualizes the self. Since his experiences change as he meets different life situations, his self-structure becomes a fluid gestalt, always in the process of assimilating new experiences. The individual experiences himself, not as a static being, but as a process of becoming.

This hypothetical, fully functioning person would be

> fully open to his experience [and] would have access to all of the available data in the situation on which to base his behavior: the social demands; his own complex and possibly conflicting needs; his memories of similar situations; his perception of the uniqueness of this situation. The data would be very complex indeed. But he could permit his total organism, his consciousness participating, to consider each stimulus, need and demand, its relative intensity and importance, and out of this complex weighing and balancing, discover that course of action which would come closest to satisfying all his needs in the situation. An analogy which might come close to a description would be to compare this person to a giant electronic computing machine. Since he is open to his experience, all of the data from his sense impressions, from his memory, from previous learning, from his visceral and internal states, are fed into the machine. The machine takes all of these multitudinous pulls and forces which are fed in as data, and quickly computes the course of action which would be the most economical vector of need satisfaction in this existential situation. This is the behavior of our hypothetical person.

The defects which in most of us make this process untrustworthy are the inclusion of information which does *not* belong to this present situation, or the exclusion of information which *does*. It is when memories and previous learning are fed into the computations as if they were *this* reality, and not memories and learning, that erroneous behavioral answers arise. Or when certain threatening experiences are inhibited from awareness, and hence are withheld from the computation or fed into it in distorted form, this too produces error. But our hypothetical person would find his organism thoroughly trustworthy, because all of the available data would be used, and it would be present in accurate rather than distorted form. Hence his behavior would come as close as possible to satisfying all his needs—for enhancement, for affiliation with others, and the like.

In this weighing, balancing and computation, his organism would not by any means be infallible. It would always give the best possible answer for the available data, but sometimes data would be missing. Because of the element of openness to experience, however, any errors, any following of behavior which was not satisfying, would be quickly corrected. The computations, as it were, would always be in process of being corrected, because they would be continually checked against their consequences[8] (Rogers, 1962c, pp. 27-28).

Theory of Therapy and Personality Change

Rogers's theory of therapy and personality changes follows an "if-then" model and consists of three main parts: conditions, process, and outcomes. If certain *conditions* exist, then a definable *process* is set in motion which leads to certain *outcomes* or changes in the client's personality and behavior.

A. Conditions of Therapy

Most schools of therapy emphasize technical psychotherapeutic skills and the specialized training needed to acquire these. Consequently, much has been written about topics such as dream interpretations, free imagery, handling transference, manipulating ambiguity, or the subtle use of positive and negative reinforcement. In contrast, a concern with such topics is conspicuously absent from Rogers's theory of therapy. He has long believed that certain attitudes held and communicated by the therapist are the important ingredients which promote change in the client.

Rogers's early writings discussed these therapist attitudes in quite general terms, but beginning in 1957 Rogers and others have developed more precise formulations. These therapist attitudes have come to be known as the *therapist condition variables,* or simply as the *facilitative conditions.*

In 1957 Rogers set forth the conditions which are both *necessary* and *sufficient* to get the process of therapeutic personality change under way;

---

[8] Rogers's theory of creativity is closely related to his theory of the fully functioning person.

that is, the process will commence only if the stated conditions are present and will not commence unless they are present. Other conditions which might be helpful in getting the process under way were not included in the formal theory. Since then (Rogers, et al., 1967, p. 98), he has agreed that it is difficult, if not impossible, to establish the necessary and sufficient conditions of therapy, but he still believes that therapist attitudes can account for much of the constructive change which occurs in counseling and psychotherapy. That the more precise formulation of the therapist condition variables had heuristic value has been clearly demonstrated by the flood of research which followed Rogers's 1957 paper.

As paraphrased from Rogers (1957, 1959a, and Rogers, et al., 1967), the theory states that the amount of process movement and the amount of constructive personality change occurring in therapy are dependent upon the degree to which:

1. The therapist is *congruent* or *genuine* in the relationship.
2. The therapist experiences *unconditional positive regard* or *warm acceptance* for the client.
3. The therapist exhibits *accurate* and *empathic understanding* of the client's *internal frame of reference*.

Three other condition variables not dealing with therapist attitudes are added for the sake of completeness and clarity.

4. The client and the therapist are in *contact* with one another.
5. The client is in a state of *incongruence,* being *vulnerable* and preferably *anxious.*
6. The client perceives, at least to a minimal degree, the therapist's *genuineness, unconditional positive regard,* and *empathic understanding.*

The fourth proposition merely calls attention to the logical necessity that there must be at least a minimal relationship between the client and the counselor. Two persons are in *contact* if each makes a difference in the experience of the other. This condition will most certainly be met in most counseling situations, although Rogers points out that it often appears necessary for the contact to be of some duration before the therapeutic process begins. The condition might be very difficult to meet in working with extremely withdrawn psychotics. See Gendlin (Chapter 16, and Rogers, et al., 1967) for a fascinating account of the client-centered approach with withdrawn schizophrenics.

The reader will recall from the section on personality theory that the client is *incongruent* and, therefore, *vulnerable* when his self-concept is different from the actual experience of his organism. Although Rogers theorizes that the process can get under way if the client is merely vulnerable, he believes that the process is more likely to begin if the client is also *anxious,* that is, if he is also aware of the threat to his self-concept. Most self-referred clients are, of course, anxious.

The first three propositions dealing with genuineness, warm acceptance, and accurate empathy are the important part of the theory. The therapist holding and acting in terms of these attitudes builds a therapeutic climate which results in what Rogers sometimes refers to as the client's experience of being fully accepted or fully received.

The early formulations of the client-centered view stressed the importance of the counselor's basic acceptance of the client and respect for his integrity as an independent, autonomous individual. The relationship was to be free of any type of pressure or subtle coercion. Not only was the counselor to refrain from intruding his own values and biases into the counseling relationship, but he was to forego such commonly used procedures as setting goals, giving advice, persuading, making interpretations, and delineating topics for discussion. The counselor did not play a passive role as has sometimes erroneously been stated. Great emphasis was placed on an active warmth and responsiveness to the client, a sensitivity to his feelings, and a genuine acceptance of the client as a person. The counselor's aim was an active and sensitive understanding of the client as he experienced and revealed himself during the interviews. The counselor concentrated on creating a permissive atmosphere, free of threat to the client's self, so that he felt free to express the doubts, the unspoken attitudes, and the unwanted impulses which complicated his life. It was this atmosphere which released the growth potential of the client and enabled him to effect constructive changes in his personality and way of living.

The foregoing generally describes the attitudes of the client-centered counselor. However, the modern formulation speaks less, either directly or implicitly, about prohibitions upon the therapist and frees him to become a more active participant in the relationship. The emphasis is upon creating the conditions whereby the client feels fully received—no matter how this may be achieved by a particular counselor.

Neither does the current theory speak of the nondirective techniques which were frequently discussed in the earliest literature. In finding ways to implement the counselor's basic orientation to the client, the early writings stressed such techniques as structuring the interview, silence, simple acceptance, and reflection of feelings versus responding to intellectual content. Therapeutic techniques have gradually been de-emphasized in favor of attitudes which facilitate the interpersonal relationship. Some counselors with only a superficial understanding of client-centered counseling fail to comprehend this shift of emphasis. Frequently, they use so-called nondirective techniques to implement attitudes quite different from those advocated by the theory. The client-centered counselor does, of course, still use many of the nondirective techniques (particularly reflection of underlying feeling), but he does not feel bound by them nor does he employ them as planfully and deliberately as he once did. In his reaction against technique-oriented counselors, Rogers goes so far as to declare "reflection of feeling" a misnomer which contributes to misunderstanding. "When it plays a real function, this kind of response is not a reflection of feeling, but an honest, groping attempt on the part of the therapist to understand fully, sensitively, and accurately the internal feeling of his client" (Rogers, et al., 1967, p. 515).

CONGRUENCE OR GENUINENESS. Of the three condition variables, congruence is first in importance. Unless the counselor is genuine in the relationship, his warm acceptance and empathic understanding become unreal and lose much of their significance.

In the formal language of the personality theory, congruence means that all aspects of the counselor's organismic experience during the interview are freely admissible to his awareness and that his self-concept is congruent with these experiences. The counselor trusts his experience and is free to act in terms of it. In more familiar language, the counselor is a genuine, integrated person in the counseling relationship. He is freely and deeply himself with no front or facade, even unknowingly. In everyday life, we readily sense this quality in a person. And we tend to trust such persons because we sense they are being what they are in an open, transparent way. We also sense the person who plays a role and relates to us from behind a facade, and we tend to be cautious about what we reveal of ourselves to such persons. The genuine counselor is spontaneous and is openly being the feelings and attitudes which flow in him. He is open to both pleasant and hurtful feelings. If negative feelings are present, the counselor can employ these constructively, not destructively, to facilitate honest communication between himself and his client. The genuine counselor comes into direct personal encounter with his client.

Since counselors are human beings and cannot be expected to achieve the ideal of perfect adjustment, let us note immediately that the theory does not say that the counselor must be a completely congruent person. It states that if the counselor is congruent *in this relationship with this client,* then the process of therapy will get under way. It is sufficient that the counselor be accurately himself during the counseling hour. In addition, this proposition, like the others, should be understood as existing on a continuum rather than on an all-or-none basis.

The aim of counseling is not, of course, for the counselor to continually discuss his own feelings with his client. At one level this part of the theory stresses the therapeutic value of a nonexploitive, authentic interpersonal encounter; the potential value of open, honest feedback when meaningful exploration or communication is being blocked; and the facilitative encouragement to nondefensive self-exploration which genuineness provides. At another level the theory stresses that counseling will be inhibited if the counselor feels one way about the interview and the client but acts, even though subtly, in a different way.

On occasion, genuineness will allow feelings which inhibit the other facilitative conditions. If I am bored or irritated with what my client is saying to me, I cannot be congruent with this feeling and at the same time be experiencing unconditional positive regard for my client and an empathic understanding of his internal frame of reference. In contrast to his earlier writings, Rogers now gives priority to genuineness. Although, as stated above, the aim is not for the counselor to continually impose his own thoughts and feelings on the client, the counselor does bring his feelings openly into the interview when these are persisting feelings that interfere with his warm acceptance and his empathic understanding of the client. This helps to keep the counselor genuine in the relationship, and even where the counselor's feelings pose a problem for the client, the difficulty is now at least out in the open where the client has the opportunity to deal with it.

As previously noted in the section on personality theory, it is important that the counselor both recognize and express the feeling as his own and not as something for which the client is to blame. It is, after all, the counselor's and not the client's feeling. To be sure, the feeling arose in the client-counselor interaction, but another counselor might react quite differently.

UNCONDITIONAL POSITIVE REGARD OR WARM ACCEPTANCE. The essence of this facilitative condition is that the therapist experiences a deep and genuine caring for the client as a person, and that this caring is uncontaminated by evaluation of the client's feelings, thoughts, and behavior as good or bad. The therapist values and warmly accepts the client, but this concept goes still further and states that no conditions are placed upon this valuing and warm acceptance. Rogers began using the technical, although more awkward, term *unconditional positive regard* to emphasize this absence of conditionality. The therapist genuinely accepts and cares for the client and experiences none of the client's self-experiences as being more or less worthy of positive regard. The new term also places more emphasis, than did early conceptions, upon liking or caring for the client which clinical and research evidence indicates accompanies successful therapy. Rogers carefully points out, however, that this is not a possessive caring which arises out of the counselor's own needs.

Butler (1952) resurrected Dewey's terms *prizing* and *appraising* to help define this concept. To prize another person means to value or esteem him. Appraising, on the other hand, implies an ongoing discriminating, comparing, and selecting process in which different values are assigned to the various aspects of the person thus discriminated. Thus, the concept of unconditional positive regard implies that the counselor is not appraising the client but rather is prizing him no matter what feelings and motivations the client experiences during the interview. The client is prized as much when he experiences "bad" feelings such as hate, selfish desire, confusion, or self-pity as when he experiences "good" feelings such as friendliness, accomplishment, mature self-confidence, or tender affection.

Some persons become disturbed and think that this concept implies approval of all the client's behavior. It does not. None of the client's behaviors are judged as making the client more or less worthy of being prized as a person.

The term unconditional positive regard is an unfortunate choice in that it implies an absolute, all-or-none characteristic, whereas it should be thought of as a matter of degree. The counselor can experience more or less unconditional positive regard for the client, but the complete experience of this, as the term seems to make mandatory, is not a practical possibility (although Rogers does think there are brief periods in counseling when the counselor experiences a complete and unconditional positive regard for his client).

It should be noted that the theory states that the counselor must *experience* unconditional positive regard for the client. The word "experience" means that the counselor actually *feels* a prizing for the client. It is not enough that the counselor hold abstract attitudes of respect and acceptance of the dignity and worth of other persons. This abstract or intellectual attitude may help the counselor to develop feelings of unconditional positive regard for his client, but the crucial condition is that the counselor experience such feelings as he relates to his client. Obviously this experience cannot exist until there is a basis for it in the client-counselor interaction. In this sense there is always an element of uncertainty and risk in each new counseling case.

Although client-centered counselors have written much about unconditional positive regard and the related concepts of acceptance, respect for the client's separateness, prizing, and even love for the client, it is difficult to convey the precise meaning of the concept. It is a deep and pervasive experience on the part of the counselor; yet it is not blind, maudlin, intense, or possessive. Perhaps it involves basically a deep feeling and respect for life, for what *is*, for *being* and a willingness to experience this fully, without reservation, as it is revealed through the client.

Most theories have concepts similar to the client-centered concept of positive regard, so in this sense Rogers offers nothing unique. Yet client-centered theory goes further than other theories. Rogers has defined the concept more precisely, has articulated theories about the influence of positive regard on the process and outcome of therapy, and has stimulated research to test these propositions. Also, client-centered counselors think that other theoretical orientations employ additional concepts which contradict at least to a degree the full meaning of unconditional positive regard. For example, counseling approaches which call for considerable diagnostic activity on the part of the counselor must introduce situations in which the client will experience that some of his self-experiences are being more or less prized by the counselor.

ACCURATE EMPATHY. The main "work" of the therapist is to understand sensitively and accurately the client's experiences and feelings and their meaning to him as these are revealed during the moment-by-moment interaction of the therapy hour. The therapist strives to sense accurately and fully the inner world of the client's subjective experience. The emphasis is upon the "here and now" of the immediate present. By his empathic understanding, the therapist hopes to help the client get closer to himself, to experience more of his deeper feelings, and thus to encourage recognition and resolution of the incongruences between self and organismic experience.

The concept of accurate empathy, like the other facilitative condition concepts, has evolved over the years in the direction of freeing the therapist to be a more active participant in the therapeutic encounter. High levels of accurate empathy go beyond recognition of obvious feelings to a sensing of the less obvious and less clearly experienced feelings of the client. The client's apparent feelings are, of course, recognized and understood, but the therapist also strives to understand those aspects of feeling which are present but which the client less clearly perceives and communicates. The therapist helps the client to expand his awareness of these feelings. High levels of accurate empathy often involve using subtle cues to help the client get closer to implicitly meaningful aspects of his experience which are still preconceptual and thus difficult to understand and express. This newer concept of accurate empathy is similar to the psychoanalyst's attempt to help his patient deal with preconscious material. This comparison is misleading, however, to the extent that the reader may understand the psychoanalyst's interpretation as cognitively clarifying the patient's preconscience experience according to some conceptual schema. The client-centered therapist (and perhaps many psychoanalysts as well) hopes to further the client's experiential involvement with and expansion of those "hinted at" and felt aspects of "preconscious" subjective experience. Too much emphasis upon conceptual clarification often intellectualizes the process and diverts the client from his inner experience.

Rogers defines the state of being empathic as perceiving

> . . . the internal frame of reference of another with accuracy, and with the emotional components and meanings which pertain thereto, as if one were the other person, but without ever losing the "as if" condition. Thus it means to sense the hurt or pleasure of another as he senses it, and to perceive the causes thereof as he perceives them, but without ever losing the recognition that it is *as if* I were hurt or pleased, etc. If this "as if" quality is lost, then the state is one of identification (1959a, pp. 210-211).

From the section on personality theory, the reader will recall that to concentrate on the client's internal frame of reference is to concentrate on the client's *experience* of reality as contrasted with objective reality. One of the difficulties in mastering the client-centered approach to counseling is that in the main we are not accustomed to concentrating on the internal frame of reference of another individual but instead view that individual and his situation from our own internal frame of reference, that is, from our own view of what objective reality is for the individual and his situation. The client-centered approach thus requires that the counselor unlearn familiar ways of relating to others.

COMMUNICATION OF THERAPIST CONDITIONS. The final condition listed by Rogers in the formal theory is that the client himself must perceive the counselor's genuineness, his experience of unconditional positive regard, and his empathic understanding. Obviously the client will not unless the counselor successfully communicates his experiences to the client. The counselor, therefore, strives to relate to the client in such a way that his basic attitudes are implicit in everything he says and does. Bodily posture, facial expression, tone of voice, comments made, comments not made, etc., are all important. When these arise naturally and spontaneously out of the counselor's experience of unconditional positive regard and empathic understanding of the client's internal frame of reference, much of the problem of communication is solved.

Genuineness, respect or warm acceptance, and accurate empathy are the attitudes or facilitative conditions which in Rogers's opinion are basic to bringing about personality change. How useful and how accurate has this formulation been?

Rogers's impact upon counseling and psychotherapy is the result of his talent for studying the complex and often confusing events of therapy, and then identifying essential elements in comparatively precise and testable language. The heuristic value of this talent is amply demonstrated by the flood of research and productive thinking which followed his original paper on the conditions of therapy.

The facilitative conditions are constructs involving considerable subjectivity, yet it has been possible to develop operational definitions and measuring instruments which have been used to test the theoretical propositions.

Over the years a number of well-designed studies have provided research support for that part of the theory dealing with the counselor-determined conditions deemed necessary to getting the process of counseling under way, that is, the counselor's genuineness or congruence, his unconditional positive regard, and his empathic understanding of the client's internal frame of reference.

One method of researching the theory has been to employ a relationship inventory in which both the client and the counselor can make after-interview ratings of the counselor's congruence, empathy, and unconditional positive regard. Findings with this method support the theory (Barrett-Lennard, 1962).

Another method has been to have judges rate sections of interviews on reliable rating scales which were built to measure the three therapeutic conditions. Halkides (1958), as reported by Rogers (1961c), compared "most successful" with "least successful" counseling center cases and found that high levels on each of the three conditions were associated with successful outcomes at the .001 level of confidence.

Following these pioneering studies, Rogers, Gendlin, Truax, Kiesler, and others (1967) used essentially these same measurement procedures in their extensive Wisconsin studies with hospitalized schizophrenics. The findings of these studies are too voluminous and complex to review in this chapter, but some of the highlights can be noted. Recall that the theory of therapy states that if the therapeutic conditions are fulfilled, then a definable process is set in motion which results in favorable outcome.

Although it was not true on all outcome measures, the Wisconsin studies definitely show a positive relationship between high levels of facilitative conditions and favorable outcomes. The data are more ambiguous about the relationship between conditions and process. Condition variables were not associated with positive *movement* on the process variables over therapy, and this finding may in part result from the fact that very little process movement occurred in these hospitalized schizophrenic subjects.

Although the measures of genuineness, warm acceptance, and accurate empathy correlated with each other, the correlations were low which indicates they tap different dimensions of the therapeutic interaction. That is, the three condition measures are not just different ways of viewing what might be thought of as a good therapeutic relationship. In fact, some evidence suggests that neurotic and counseling center populations may react differently to each of the conditions as compared to schizophrenics. Neurotics perceive primarily genuineness and empathic understanding, whereas the schizophrenics perceive genuineness and warm acceptance. One interpretation of this finding is that relationship formation is more important to the schizophrenic, whereas self-exploration is more important to the neurotic.

Another finding of interest was that the patients and the independent raters of the interviews agreed in their judgments about the level of facilitative conditions, and there were positive correlations between these ratings and outcomes. Therapists' ratings of the facilitative conditions, however, were discrepant from those of independent raters and patients, and the therapists' ratings correlated negatively with outcomes except in the more successful cases. It would seem that therapist ratings of condition levels are not always to be trusted.

In another finding, the amount of genuineness, warm acceptance, and accurate empathy extended by the therapist was partly a function of the patient as well as a function of the therapist himself. This is an important finding demanding further research. It suggests that at least some therapists can offer high facilitation conditions to some types of clients and not to others. Working with counseling center populations, Hampton (1968) found a trend for counselors to extend lower levels to clients with high needs for social approval (and therefore less open to exploring self), and Farkas (1969) found a similar trend with clients who externalized their problems. Clients with these characteristics tend to be less successful in psychotherapy, and this may be because counselors offer them lower facilitative conditions.

Carkhuff and Alexik (1967) found that very high-level functioning counselors were not changed when an "actor" client experimentally reduced her level of self-exploration, whereas moderate-level functioning counselors under this same situation decreased their levels of facilitative conditions. In short, available evidence suggests complex interactions between client and therapist variables which are important to research further, for they presumably influence outcome in significant ways.

The Wisconsin research found that the level of the facilitative conditions stabilized early in therapy (about the eighth interview) and remained rather consistent thereafter, even though many cases continued several years. Truax and Carkhuff (1967, p. 89) report that several other studies confirm this finding and Truax believes (personal communication) that ratings made at the fourth or fifth interview for typical cases can predict the average level of conditions throughout the therapy. Since the level of facilitative conditions predicts outcome, this possibility, if confirmed, could have important practical implications. We might be able to determine whether it is worthwhile for a particular client-therapist pair to continue with therapy.

Since the end of the Wisconsin data collection in 1963, a substantial and still growing research literature has appeared on the therapist condition variables. This literature is too extensive and complex for this chapter, and the reader is referred to Truax and Carkhuff (1967) who devote a substantial portion of their book to this undertaking. However, a few broad themes will be noted and discussed.

1. The evidence is extensive and compelling that high levels of facilitative conditions predict favorable case outcomes in spite of the crudeness of measuring instruments. On the other hand, considerable outcome variance is still unaccounted for, indicating that other factors are also important. Carkhuff and Berenson (1967) estimate that we can account for about 20 percent of the variance of typical outcome indexes and 33 to 50 percent of quasi-outcome indexes such as insight scales. Presumably more accurate measuring instruments would account for more, but not all, of the outcome variance.

2. This body of theory and research is especially important because it represents the first comprehensive and systematic attempt to study empirical cause and effect in psychotherapy. The theory originally proposed by Rogers and the studies which followed have been successful in isolating and measuring fundamental change-producing influences in counseling and psychotherapy.

3. Additional therapist condition variables have been proposed and are gradually being researched, such as appropriate self-disclosure, openness, flexibility, intimacy of interpersonal contact, spontaneity, commitment, and so forth. Little is yet known about these facilitative conditions with the exception of *personally relevant concreteness,* which defines a dimension ranging from the therapist encouraging vagueness and abstractness in the client to helping the client discuss feelings and experiences in specific and concrete terms (see Carkhuff and Berenson, 1967).

4. That the facilitative conditions are related to case outcome provides a compelling reason that counselors should be trained to offer higher levels of these conditions. Fortunately, this has proved relatively easy to do in 25 to 100 hours when the conditions are taught directly. The various rating scales developed for research have proved quite useful when used in reverse for training purposes (see Truax and Carkhuff, 1967; Carkhuff and Berenson, 1967; and Carkhuff, 1969). It is especially noteworthy that the facilitative conditions can be taught to nonprofessionals who can apply them in a variety of interpersonal and quasi-counseling situations. For example, Gendlin (Chapter 20 in Rogers et al., 1967) argues that it is not only economically impossible to provide individual psychotherapy to all hospi-

talized patients, but that it is of doubtful usefulness as well. Since
hospital personnel spend many hours of personal contact per week
with the patient compared with only one or two individual therapy
hours, it is more economical and probably more productive to train
all hospital personnel to offer the facilitative conditions. Persons
from outside the hospital who might be interested in visiting one or
two patients regularly might also be trained.

5. Rogers, along with others, views in general the therapeutic relationship as a special instance of interpersonal relationships. He also sees
growth and personal development in psychotherapy as a special
instance of growth and change which may occur in many settings.
Therefore, he believes his theory of therapy and personality change
should be applicable to other forms of counseling and psychotherapy and beyond that to such settings as group encounters, to teacher-student and parent-child interactions, to friendships which produce personal growth, to husband-wife relations, etc.

Some evidence now exists, although more confirming research
is needed, that the facilitative conditions affect outcome in other
forms of psychotherapy (Truax and Carkhuff, 1967, especially
Chapter 2).

Gordon (1955) applied client-centered principles to group leadership, including industrial settings, and Rogers is now devoting
considerable attention to their application in the classroom (1951,
1959, 1967c, 1967d, 1969).

Only a trickle of hard research evidence is available about the
significance of the facilitative dimensions to other-than-counseling
situations, but more should be forthcoming since Carkhuff has developed scales that can be applied to interpersonal processes. Aspy
(1967) found that high-level functioning teachers elicited, over a
school year, significantly higher gains on four of five achievement
tests as compared with low-level functioning teachers. Only the spelling test revealed nonsignificant differences. In another study Aspy
and Hadlock (1967) found that students of the highest-level functioning teacher gained an average of two and one-half academic years
during the school year, while students of the lowest-level teacher
gained only six achievement months. Shapiro and Thérèse (1969)
found that college students with high-level functioning roommates
earn higher grade point averages than do students with low-level
functioning roommates.

6. Research evidence is accumulating which shows that high levels of
genuineness, warm acceptance, and accurate empathy result in therapeutic gain, whereas low levels result in no gain or client deterio-
ration on outcome measures. This finding was first noted in the
Wisconsin data and has since been confirmed in other studies

(Truax and Carkhuff, 1967, especially Chapters 1 and 3; Bergin, 1963 and 1966). It appears that psychotherapy and other interpersonal relationships can be for better or for worse (Carkhuff, 1967). This finding is so important and has such far-reaching implications that it requires further replication and study in depth. If generally true, the finding carries compelling suggestions for training and for who should and who should not be allowed to practice counseling and psychotherapy.

The finding also has important implication for outcome research. Although considerable controversy exists about interpretation, most studies of psychotherapy show little difference in outcomes between the experimental or therapy group and a control group or some established base line of the spontaneous remission rate (Eysenck, 1952; Levitt, 1957). But such comparisons involve the average gain for the experimental group. If some clients get better and some get worse as the evidence strongly suggests, then we cannot conclude that therapy is ineffective, because it has been effective for some of the experimental group. The facts support this reasoning because, as Bergin (1963) has pointed out, the experimental group as compared to the control group increases in variability on the posttherapy measures. When we put this finding together with the discovery that clients offered low-facilitative conditions show no gain or get worse and those offered high conditions get better, then we have strong support for Rogers's general theory of therapeutic change, or at least for that portion of the theory dealing with the therapist condition variables.

7. Carkhuff and his colleagues have extended this portion of Rogerian theory beyond individual and group counseling. Making use of learning principles, Carkhuff advocates direct skill training in the facilitative conditions as the preferred mode of treatment for a wide variety of helpee populations. He sees this approach to treatment as more useful and economical whenever disturbed interpersonal relations are a fundamental source of the difficulty. To date, Pierce and Drasgow (1969) have taught facilitative interpersonal functioning to psychiatric inpatients, and Carkhuff and Bierman (1970) have done the same for the parents of emotionally disturbed children. A stimulating account of this approach to treatment can be found in Carkhuff's two-volume work (1969).

B. The Process of Therapy

Client-centered counselors have devoted considerable effort to discover *order* in the process of counseling and psychotherapy. Does a characteristic sequence of events occur during a series of successful counseling interviews? And more importantly, are there particular events or client experiences during the course of counseling which are responsible for bringing about changes in the client's personality and behavior? These questions, particularly the latter, are difficult but crucial to understanding counseling and psychotherapy. The answers, when available, will define the nature of psychotherapy and will set forth the laws governing therapeutic change. Without the answers, we cannot even know for sure whether the client has been involved in an on-going psychotherapy process. Without the answers, outcome studies cannot be interpreted accurately, nor can we learn the basic facts about what conditions make the therapeutic process possible.

Insight was long assumed to be at least one essential element of the process leading to change, but this view is now questioned. Not only is insight seen as resulting from other events, an end product so to speak, but it also is evident that change occurs in the absence of insight (see Hobbs, 1962).

Over the years, these questions about process have been approached in many different ways. At times, the search has emphasized naturalistic description; at other times, an attempt to specify the essential change producing variables. A considerable body of knowledge about process has been generated, but dependable answers are still elusive. As a result, there is no *one* client-centered position about process, and it is in this area more than others that research has forced modifications in the theory.

1. EARLY FORMULATION. In the earliest formulation Rogers (1942) described the process as proceeding through successive but overlapping stages of release and exploration of feeling, through seeing relationships and the achievement of insight, followed by decision making and positive action. This description was confirmed when Snyder (1945) and later Seeman (1949) studied case protocols and found that the release of negative feelings was followed by the expression of positive feelings and that successful counseling tended to move from statements of problems, to insight, to discussing and planning of activity.

2. CHARACTERISTIC CHANGES IN THE SELF. Another approach has been to describe the process in terms of changes in the self-concept and attitudes toward the self. Many studies examining electrically recorded and transcribed cases have shown that there is a movement from negative to positive feelings about the self over successful client-centered counseling and that this movement fails to occur or is much less pronounced in unsuccessful cases (Raimy, 1948; Seeman, 1949; Sheerer, 1949; Stock, 1949). It should not be supposed, however, that there is an even progression over the series of counseling interviews. Frequently negative feelings increase during the counseling before the trend to positive feelings is seen. Wide swings between positive and negative feelings are fairly common.

These shifts in self-attitudes are seen as an important part of the process which may account for other kinds of changes taking place in the client. For example, Sheerer (1949) has shown that increased acceptance of self is accompanied by an increased acceptance of other persons.

Raskin (1952) investigated the hypothesis that a significant part of the counseling process is that the reference point for valuations shifts from others to the self during the course of successful counseling. He found that there was a significant tendency over counseling for the client to place greater emphasis on himself as the evaluator of experience.

3. THE FORMAL THEORY OF PROCESS. Rogers developed a formal theory of therapeutic process in 1953, although it was not published until six years later (Rogers, 1959a). This theory spelled out a series of propositions which are abbreviated and summarized below. Following the "if-then" model, the theory states that if the conditions of therapy presented earlier are established and maintained over a period of time, then the following process is set into motion:

1. The client gradually becomes freer in expressing his feelings in verbal and motor channels, and these feelings increasingly have references to the self rather than to the nonself.
2. "He increasingly differentiates and discriminates the objects of his feelings and perceptions, including his environment, other persons, his self, his experiences, and the interrelationships of these" (Rogers, 1959a, p. 216). In so doing, the client's experiences become more accurately symbolized in his awareness, and he gradually becomes aware of experiences which he has previously denied or distorted.
3. "His expressed feelings increasingly have reference to the incongruity between certain of his experiences and his concept of self" (Rogers, 1959a, p. 216). Because of this the client experiences threat and anxiety. The defensive process presented in the theory of personality would prevent this overt experience of threat were it not for the "... continued unconditional positive regard of the therapist which is extended to incongruence as much as to congruence, to anxiety as much as to the absence of anxiety" (Rogers, 1959a, p. 216).
4. The self-concept gradually becomes reorganized to include experiences which were previously denied or distorted in awareness. Thus there is an increasing congruence between self and experience with less need for defensiveness.
5. The client increasingly feels positive self-regard and reacts to his experiences less in terms of the conditions of worth based on the values introjected from others and more in terms of the organismic valuing process based on the actualizing tendency.

4. THE ROLE OF IMMEDIATE EXPERIENCE IN PSYCHOTHERAPY. It should be noted that the formal theory outlined above does not attempt to explain why this process should lead to constructive changes in the client. The theory restricts itself to describing the fundamental nature of the process which occurs once the appropriate conditions are established and maintained. The explanation of why this leads to successful outcomes is contained in the basic assumptions and in the theory of personality. For Rogers, the "neurotic" aspects of personality are those fashioned from the attitudes and values of others which develop a self-concept that is at odds with the individual's own organismic experience. During therapy, a healthier personality develops as the client becomes ever more open to his immediate feelings and concretely experienced personal meanings.

The next step was taken by Gendlin and Zimering (1955) and by Gendlin (1961a) when they proposed that the concrete, ongoing feeling process itself was the crucial change-producing element in psychotherapy. They introduced the term *experiencing* to convey their views that the personality is not made up of contents ("experiences") but is an ongoing, ever-changing feeling process which is always meaningful to the person even when it cannot be conceptualized and communicated in words. In an important book, Gendlin (1962b) treated the concept of experiencing systematically, and attempted to show its explanatory power for many other concepts in personality and psychotherapy (see also Gendlin, 1967).

The concept of experiencing, although not entirely new, is difficult to convey in words because it deals with a contentless process which is ongoing and ever-changing. It is similar to what is often thought of as emotional versus intellectual insight; as working through, feeling through, as being completely involved; as experiencing affect versus talking about affect; as experiencing one's self versus talking about one's self as an object; as dealing with concrete personal reality versus thinking logically and deductively, etc.

Experiencing in a special sense is seen as the essence of therapeutic change. Experiencing always occurs in the immediate present. If attended to, it is always implicitly meaningful to the person and "can be directly referred to by the individual as a felt datum in his own phenomenal field" (Gendlin, 1962b). The experiencing process may or may not be verbally conceptualized by the individual, but experiencing is always something different from the conceptualization. Experiencing is also always made up of many elements which no conceptualization can capture fully. Much of the client's experiencing in successful therapy may be preconceptual. It is a common occurrence in interviews for clients to refer to their experiential meanings without being able to label them or even to describe them very adequately. Instead, the client may point to his experiencing with phrases like "this all tied up feeling" or "this thing I sense . . . I don't know, but it is really something." Not infrequently, client and counselor will communicate meaningfully about the experience for some considerable time, and yet each has only the vaguest idea in logical and conceptual terms what the experience actually is. It is implicitly meaningful but still preconceptual.

To illustrate that experiencing is always implicitly meaningful, even when it cannot be conceptualized in words, Gendlin cites an everyday experience. Suppose you are listening to a discussion and are now about to say something which you feel is relevant and important. But as you wait your turn to speak, you are distracted and lose what you are about to say. You never had conceptualized your thoughts in words. You had a "felt sense" of what you wanted to say, and that felt sense was meaningful to you. You search for that again, and the experience of recapturing it, if indeed you do, is distinct and unambiguous. There is a physically-felt release, a change in bodily-felt condition, and you now "know" what you are about to say even though you do not yet "know" it in words. In this illustration Gendlin notes that a person can have, lose, and regain "a felt meaning" which never was in the form of words.

Gendlin gives the term *direct referent* to this felt meaning in experience. Experiential *focusing* (Gendlin, 1969) is the directing of one's attention to these felt meanings. When the client guides his verbalization and interactions with the therapist by these direct referents, there is a carrying forward of experience which Gendlin calls *referent movement.* The direct referent changes; different facets of it emerge into prominence; different meanings are felt. The direct referent in experience always consists of many things that are potentially separable but not really separate. They function together in this feeling in a physically-felt, ongoing process. If the client allows the "wholeness" of such meanings to guide his verbalizations, rather than some imposed logic or value system, Gendlin believes that *referent movement* will occur. There will be an unfolding which has its own organismic sense and value direction. The experiencing *process* which produces change in the client is under way. Gendlin sees man not as one made of preset "content," ideas, or emotions which can be manipulated by logic; but as one who has an experiencing process which changes as he responds to it in words or actions. The client's attempts to verbalize his experience, as well as his interactions with the therapist, carry the process forward in ways which were previously blocked or constricted. A sensed fear of the boss becomes a feeling of hurt when he disapproves of me, which involves feelings of helplessness, which involves feelings of deprivation and loneliness, etc.

Oversimplifying, the essence of therapy for Gendlin is the unfolding of the experiencing process. Client and therapist grope to conceptualize implicit, felt meanings without intellectualizing and diverting the experiencing

process. He sees a direct interpersonal encounter between client and therapist, the empathic reflection of feeling traditionally associated with the client-
centered method, or the properly timed interpretations of other approaches,
as capable of achieving this objective.

Rogers cites the following example as illustrating what he calls a
"molecule of change."

> In the thirty-first interview she is trying to discover what it is that she is
> experiencing. It is a strong emotion. She thinks it is not guilt. She weeps for a
> time. Then:
>
> **Client:** *It's just being terribly hurt!* . . . and then of course I've come to see
> and to feel that over this . . . see, I've covered it up.
> A moment later she puts it slightly differently.
> **Client:** You know, it's almost a physical thing. It's . . . It's sort of as though
> I were looking at myself at all kinds of . . . nerve endings and-and
> bits of . . . things that have been sort of mashed. (Weeping)
> **Therapist:** As though some of the most delicate aspects of you—physically
> almost—have been crushed or hurt.
> **Client:** Yes. And you know, I do get the feeling, Oh, you poor thing.
> (Pause)
> **Therapist:** You just can't help but feel very deeply sorry for the person that is
> you (Rogers, 1959b, p. 52).

Rogers thinks that repeated experiences such as these are the essence of
psychotherapy and have the following characteristics:

1. It occurs in the existential moment. It is not "thinking about" but
   "an experience of something in this instant."
2. There are no barriers to the experiencing, no holding back.
3. The experience is complete in that all elements are freely present in
   awareness. Often the experience is not really new; it may have been
   experienced before but not experienced completely. It has a new
   intensity.
4. It has a quality of being acceptable to the client. The feeling *is,* it
   exists, and it is found acceptable on this basis. The client in the
   example above "*is* the self-pity she feels—entering fully and accept-
   ingly into it—and this is integration at that moment" (Rogers,
   1959b).

During the middle 1950s, Rogers immersed himself in naturalistic observation and spent many hours listening to recorded interviews in an attempt to identify the essential change-producing elements of psychotherapy.
The result was a new paper on therapeutic process (Rogers, 1958 and
1961d) and a scale for measuring that process (Rogers and Rablen, 1958;
and Rogers, 1959c). Rogers and Gendlin, who worked together during this

period, were thinking along similar lines. Rogers defined seven parallel variables: (1) feelings and personal meanings, (2) manner of experiencing, (3) degree of incongruence, (4) communication of self, (5) manner in which experience is construed, (6) the relationship to problems, and (7) the manner of relating to others. Each variable was rated along a continuum which ranged from rigidity and fixity of perceptions, feelings, and experience at one end to "flowingness" and "changingness" at the other end. A brief summary of one part of the process scale should give the reader an idea of how Rogers attempted to conceptualize and study the essential nature of personality change:

> The process involves a change in the manner of experiencing. The continuum begins with a fixity in which the individual is very remote from his experiencing and unable to draw upon or symbolize its implicit meaning. Experiencing must be safely in the past before a meaning can be drawn from it and the present is interpreted in terms of these past meanings. From this remoteness in relation to his experiencing, the individual moves toward the recognition of experiencing as a troubling process going on within him. Experiencing gradually becomes a more accepted inner referent to which he can turn for increasingly accurate meanings. Finally he becomes able to live freely and acceptingly in a fluid process of experiencing, using it comfortably as a major reference for his behavior (1961d, pp. 156-157).

By rating samples of the client's behavior throughout a series of interviews, it is possible to relate process level and movement during therapy to condition and outcome variables. Rogers and Gendlin both theorize that process movement should be greater in successful cases rather than in unsuccessful cases; and some preliminary research indicated that this was in fact true (Rogers, 1961d). However, further research with counseling center clients at the University of Chicago and schizophrenics at the University of Wisconsin produced some unexpected findings (see Gendlin, et al., 1968; Rogers, et al., 1967).

The research findings show that higher levels on the experiencing scale, and on the other closely related process scales, do in fact differentiate successful from unsuccessful cases; however, the successful cases are high on the experiencing variables even at the start of therapy. Clients who enter therapy with the ability to engage in experiential focusing become the success cases, while those low in this ability become the failure cases. This was true for both the neurotic and schizophrenic subjects. It appears that experiential focusing is an important behavior leading to change, and that its level is a good index of ongoing effective therapy. In this sense Rogers's and Gendlin's theorizing was confirmed. But it was also predicted that this mode of behavior would increase over the course of therapy; that is, the therapist could create the conditions that would encourage the growth and development of this behavior. Some studies found upward movement on the process scales, but others did not. And even where the upward movement was statistically significant (which it was for all cases combined), the increase was so small for most cases that it could hardly account for the difference between success and failure. Very few cases increased more than half a scale point.

Thus, process level rather than process movement accounts for success; the client-centered counselor was doing little, in most cases at least, to improve the client's experiential focusing ability. Nor is openness to one's ongoing experiential process equivalent to psychological health, because many clients were high in this ability when they entered therapy even though they were also quite maladjusted.[9] Instead of defining psychological health, experiencing and the other process scale variables seem to measure behaviors which enable a person to profit from psychotherapy.

The implications of these findings for theory and professional practice will be discussed in a later section.

C. Outcomes of Counseling and Psychotherapy

It is difficult to distinguish clearly between process and outcomes.[10] When we study outcomes directly, we examine the differences between two sets of observations made at the beginning and end of the interview series. Many process studies make successive observations over a series of counseling interviews and, in a sense, are miniature outcome measures which establish a trend line for the case. Many of the process studies referred to in the previous section are in one sense as much outcome studies as they are process studies. Consider, for example, the studies showing an increased acceptance of self and others between the beginning and end of counseling.[11]

Nor does the formal theory make a clear distinction between process and outcomes. The main proposition in Rogers's theoretical statement about outcome is, "The client is more congruent, more open to his experience, less defensive" (1959a, p. 218), but we note that the process theory has already stated that these same conditions are gradually developing throughout the interviews. The outcome theory does go on to spell out some of the theoretical implications of this main outcome, but these could be

---

[9] The schizophrenics did, however, score considerably lower on the process scale variables than did the neurotics.
[10] For a detailed discussion about the relationship between process and outcomes see Cartwright (1956) and Gendlin (1956).
[11] Process studies which attempt to isolate the actual events which produce change are in a somewhat different category.

considered logical deductions within the framework of the personality theory rather than main propositions in their own right. For example, the theory states that the client's psychological adjustment improves, that he experiences more acceptance of others, that he becomes more realistic and objective, that his self-ideal becomes more realistic, that his behavior is seen by others as more socialized and mature, etc.

More readers will probably be interested in the concomitants in everyday behavior than in the more general outcomes just presented. As the result of client-centered counseling, does the client earn better grades, make more intelligent vocational choices, maintain better relations with his peer group, improve his leadership capacities, show greater originality, less frequently drop out of school, etc?

In a moment we shall list a number of areas in which research studies have shown change to take place, but before doing this, we wish to interject a note of caution.

There are almost an unlimited number of specific behaviors which might be investigated in outcome studies. Which ones of these should be investigated?

One approach is to select for study those behaviors that we especially value. Most educational communities, for example, value good grades, and many school counselors may wish to establish that their work helps students achieve this desired result. We can study the effect of counseling on school dropouts. Or some might wish to determine whether counseling results in better school citizenship. And sometimes college professors want to know whether counseling results in more students' choosing to major in their particular field of study.

We immediately see a problem in this approach to outcome studies, namely, that different people value different things. That more good students elect to study journalism as the result of counseling may be valued by the journalism faculty and be devalued by the liberal arts faculty. This problem appears to be circumvented when there is more general agreement about the value, as in the case of good grades in the educational community, but even this can present problems. On occasion, poorer grades could be the concomitant of successful counseling. We might argue for this (although some would not) in the case of an "overachieving" student who, before counseling, spent all his time anxiously striving for academic perfection to the exclusion of all social life, school activities, and even friendly relations with his fellow students.

There is still another problem when the value orientation is used to select the criterion to be studied. If we are going to rest our case about the effectiveness of counseling on whether or not it promotes this or that desirable behavior, we must also consider whether some other procedure might not produce the result more economically and to an even greater degree. We might grant that improved grades are a desirable result but find that counseling is far less effective in promoting this than, for example, better audio-visual aids or a study methods course. Ideally, counseling methods should be varied systematically and examined in relation to client types and specific outcome measures. However, this research strategy involves controlling for so many complex variables that it is not practicable in most settings. Gordon Paul's (1966) comparison of insight therapy, systematic desensitization, and placebo therapy for public speaking anxieties is an excellent example of research following this model, but it is only a beginning and leaves many variables unaccounted for.

The value problem cannot, of course, be avoided in considering the outcomes of counseling. What can be avoided is letting the value orientation deter us from learning more about what specific events in counseling lead to what specific kinds and amounts of behavior changes. We need much more of this kind of information before we can make intelligent value judgments about the usefulness of particular kinds of counseling.

Another possible answer is to avoid the specifics of behavior and investigate more general characteristics which, on theoretical or research grounds, are thought to bear a relationship to quite a number of specifics. This at least simplifies the task, although not as much as one might think. For example, we can determine through personality tests whether adjustment improves, on the assumption that general adjustment changes will have far-reaching effects. Or we can study perceptual rigidity in problem solving and infer that any changes noted would also operate in a wide variety of everyday life situations. The difficulty with this approach is that personality and behavior theory is still filled with uncertainties. In one sense the investigations are as much personality research as they are counseling outcomes research.

If one is willy-nilly going to become involved in personality research, it seems only logical that the outcomes to be studied should be relevant to the personality theory on which the counseling is based. The outcome study results can then be fed back into the main theory, and in so doing, we not only improve the theory, but we also promote insights into why particular outcomes occur or fail to occur. This approach to outcome studies has frequently, but not always, been used by the client-centered group. There is more frequent study of constructs, such as the self, which are more important to client-centered theory than to trait-and-factor or psychoanalytic behavior theory. This is as it should be if the investigator is to get the most explanatory mileage from his efforts.

The strategy of outcome research is complicated and full of pitfalls, but we cannot dwell further on these here, except to say that results must be interpreted with caution. We shall move on to listing some of the outcomes not mentioned in the previous section on process which, on the evidence available, seem to be associated with successful client-centered counseling.

1. There is an improvement in psychological adjustment as shown on the Rorschach, the Thematic Apperception Test, and personality inventories of the self-report type (Dymond, 1954a; Dymond, 1954b; Grummon and John, 1954; Haimowitz & Haimowitz, 1952; Mosak, 1950; Muench, 1947; etc.).
2. There is less physiological tension and greater adaptive capacity in response to frustration as evidenced by autonomic nervous system reactivity (Thetford, 1952).
3. There is a decrease in psychological tension (or an increase in personal comfort) as measured by the Discomfort-Relief Quotient (Assum and Levy, 1948; Cofer and Chance, 1950; N. Rogers, 1948).
4. There is a decrease in defensiveness (Grummon and John, 1954).
5. There is a greater degree of correspondence between the client's description of his self-picture and his description of his wanted or ideal self. Among other things, this is sometimes viewed as an index of self-esteem (Butler and Haigh, 1954; Hartley, 1951).
6. Friends tend to rate the client's behavior as more emotionally mature (Rogers, 1954b).
7. There is an improvement in overall adjustment in the vocational training setting (Bartlett, 1949, in Seeman and Raskin, 1953). This study is perhaps of special interest to the general counselor since the outcome measure was training officers' observations over a six-month period of such things as interpersonal factors, academic achievement, efficiency in study and work habits, tendency to worry, and commitment to goals.
8. Axline's (1947) research suggests that client-centered play methods with elementary school children may result in accelerated reading improvement even though no special reading instruction has been given.

The one comprehensive study examining the effectiveness of client-centered therapy with hospitalized schizophrenics reveals less favorable outcomes (Rogers, et al., 1967). The results varied somewhat depending upon the specific outcome measure under investigation, but in many respects the therapy group as a whole showed no greater evidence of positive change than did the matched control group of patients. This result is qualified by the finding that both groups improved; and with the exception of individual therapy, the control group received all the best treatment that a modern hospital can afford, including in some instances group therapy. The therapy group did show some advantages over the control group, such as a slightly better release rate from the hospital and statistically significant improvements in personal and interpersonal functioning as judged from Thematic Apperception Test records.

New Developments

A significant contribution of client-centered therapy has been its emphasis on testing theoretical propositions by empirical research. Considerable data are now available to examine the theory just presented, and revisions in both theory and practice seem to be occuring even though these are not yet cast in formal terms.

For years Rogers and his colleagues believed that the client-centered approach was suitable for all clients, and this position was incorporated into formal theory when Rogers proposed that his therapist condition variables were both the necessary and sufficient conditions for therapeutic change. Rogers did not set up one set of conditions and therapy process for one type of client and another set of conditions and process for other types of clients. The early research and clinical observation provided considerable support for this position. Client-centered counselors, particularly highly skilled counselors, obtained good results with many types of clients, and the pattern of successes and failures did not coincide with the usual diagnostic categories of pathology and personality type.

However, in presenting the research on the therapist condition variables we noted that these variables accounted for much but not all of the outcome variance, even when we made allowance for the crude measuring instruments. The empirical findings suggest that Rogers's theory is valid but incomplete. That is, other therapist variables or procedures influence outcome, as well as client variables and context variables. The best estimate available is probably that of Carkhuff and Berenson (1967) who find that genuineness, empathy, and warmth account for between 20 and 50 percent of outcome variance depending upon the therapeutic situation and the outcome measures employed. These estimates are for the entire research sample being studied, not for an individual subject.

Other research found that some clients failed to respond at all to the client-centered approach. Kirtner and Cartwright (1958) found a lower incidence of success among clients who accept little self-responsibility for their problems and who see the source of their problems as residing outside of themselves, and this finding has been replicated by Farkas (1969). The accumulating evidence caused Rogers (1961d) to suggest that all psychotherapists, not just the client-centered therapist, have not yet learned much about how to create effective therapeutic conditions for clients showing such characteristics as the following:

Communicates only about externals and is unwilling or unable to communicate self.

Neither recognizes nor owns feelings and personal meanings.

Has rigid personal constructs and thinks of them as fact rather than as constructs.

Avoids close and personally communicative relationships which are constructed as dangerous.

Either does not recognize problems or perceives them as external to the self.

This description is basically the process variable of experiencing which Gendlin and Rogers both theorize is the essential element of the change process itself. The process research reported earlier revealed that:

1. Process level rather than process movement is associated with outcome. Persons who early in therapy show low-process levels tend to remain low and are failures, whereas persons rated high initially tend to remain high and are successes.
2. High-process level is a good index of ongoing, effective therapy.
3. The therapist condition variables, in most instances at least, fail to increase process level.
4. The client's level on the process scales is not a good index of adjustment or maladjustment.

These and related findings, although still tentative, seem to have important implications for client-centered theory and practice. Rogers's openness to organismic experience does, under the proper conditions at least, help to promote personal effectiveness and psychological health. However, by itself this does not always produce psychological health as the main thrust of the personality theory applies. Client-centered therapeutic procedures are of demonstrated effectiveness in that the condition variables account for a substantial portion of outcome variance. Nevertheless, they fail to develop the level of experiencing behavior which the theory and research findings indicate is necessary for change.

This state of affairs has caused some persons to believe that the theory is obsolete, but this conclusion seems premature for a theory that is still stimulating much research. Also, much of the theory which was once unique and controversial has now been absorbed by the profession; therefore, it can hardly be considered obsolete. For example, the emphasis upon the ongoing interaction between therapist and client as a crucial ingredient of effective therapy, the emphasis on empathic understanding, the equalitarian nature of the relationship, and the focus on the experiential process and the current psychological situation of the client versus a concern with past intrapsychic events are elements of the theory which the profession has incorporated. It seems more plausible to believe that both theory and practice will continue to evolve, although this may mean that some of the theory's distinctive features will become blurred in the process.

This seems to be happening already. The modifications in the therapist's approach to withdrawn schizophrenics is one illustration of this (see Chapters 16 through 19 in Rogers, et al., 1967). Another example is Gendlin's (1968, 1969) concern with how experiential focusing can be taught in therapy and elsewhere. Some of his most recent therapist methods are at times quite active and directive, although they are still used in conjunction with more traditional Rogerian methods.

Although avoiding the client-centered label, Carkhuff and Berenson (1967) place the Rogerian therapist condition variables (empathy, respect, and genuineness) among their primary core dimensions of interpersonal process, which they see as serving an essential, dynamic function for all counseling and psychotherapy of whatever variety. Their model is more comprehensive in that they also believe tnat client-centered methods must be supplemented in many instances by other procedures, such as confrontation, interpretation, behavior modification, and information giving. Carkhuff (1969) also introduces new elements into the theory when he advocates employing different levels of the facilitative conditions at different stages of the therapy; and when his preferred mode of treatment is to teach the client directly those interpersonal behaviors advocated by client-centered theory.

Although stated with a much different emphasis, Patterson (1969) seems to take a similar position, except that he chooses, perhaps too arbitrarily, to define psychotherapy as a "specific remedy for a specific obstacle to self-actualization—that is, the absence or inadequacy of the interpersonal relationships necessary for self-actualization. Thus, *counseling or psychotherapy is a method of behavior change in which the core conditions (or the relationship) are the sufficient conditions for change to occur*" (p. 20). He then agrees that many things other than defective interpersonal relationships can stunt self-actualization. These "stunting" conditions call for other types of interventions, such as information giving, teaching, or behavior modification. Thus, Patterson advocates procedures which go beyond Rogerian theory with the proviso that these supplementary or alternative procedures be called something other than either counseling or psychotherapy.

Truax and Carkhuff (1967) borrow heavily from Rogerian process variables, especially with their depth of self-exploration and therapist condition variables. However, they also believe Rogerian theory is incomplete and therefore make use of learning theory, add other therapist variables, and advocate "ancillary" therapeutic ingredients.

I am personally acquainted with many persons who studied with Rogers and who still make extensive use of Rogerian concepts. However, the overwhelming majority of these persons, including myself, have become more eclectic in their thinking and professional practice. The direction of this change is that the counselor or therapist usually becomes more active with his client in one way or another. Obviously, different counselors have different reasons and different goals for becoming more active; but the overall picture is that most client-centered counselors decide after a time that they can be more helpful to the clients by supplementary procedures not covered in Rogerian theory. Information-giving, direct teaching, and helping the client cope with his current life situation are frequently the main departures from traditional practice. A more significant departure, however, involves some form of direct interpersonal encounter, or some other procedure which encourages an experiential interaction between therapist and client. The client must deal with this in the here and now, and the therapist helps him deal with it in ways which promote growth. We can, of course, see forerunners of this in Rogers's increasing emphasis on therapist genuineness; but this new development seems to be a quantum change. Many client-centered therapists are expressing themselves much more freely during their interviews and are actively reaching out to their clients in diverse ways. A new emphasis, and intent, underlies this activity which differs from the older emphasis upon responding receptively. The therapist is now more apt to stir things up, and then to respond receptively to the meanings and feelings this brings forth. The theoretical underpinning for this type of therapist activity has not yet been formulated, but Gendlin (1969) seems to be moving in this direction by noting that interpersonal interactions can be more powerful than focusing for producing "referent movement" in the experiencing process. Carkhuff's theorizing about confrontation is also a step in this direction.

Since the middle 1960s, Rogers's (1967b) main interest has been working with basic encounter groups which are a variant of the currently popular sensitivity groups or T groups. He has not yet written extensively about this work, and I have little first-hand knowledge about his current thinking; therefore, no systematic account of Rogers's latest theorizing has been attempted in this chapter. However, some changes are evident in the direction of "stirring things up." The very term Rogers has selected, the "basic encounter group," suggests this change. He believes that the intense and often stormy interpersonal encounter which he encourages in these groups has the potential for bringing about considerable change in the participants, usually for better although sometimes for worse. He seems to have broadened rather than abandoned his previous theoretical position. The focus is still on self theory, on process, and on the importance of openness to immediate feelings and experience. The shift, as I see it from a distance, expands the nature of the therapeutic conditions which can bring about change. The greater activity of the therapist, or the group leader's encouragement of the uncensored expression of personal feelings by members of the group, is being used more and more as a way of getting the experiencing process under way, a process which Gendlin and Rogers believe is basic to personality change.

Application of the Theory to General Counseling

As noted earlier, Rogers states that his theory, like all theories, is a more reliable guide when it is applied to those events which the theory was developed to explain. Like other psychodynamic theories, client-centered theory developed from counseling and psychotherapeutic interviews aimed at personality change. When personality change is the counselor's goal for his client, there is no need to discuss the theory further. The counselor may wish to base his work on some other psychodynamic theory, but there is no question about the direct relevance of the client-centered approach. For many counselors, client-centered theory will offer distinct advantages over competing theories. Its major concepts do not arise primarily from the study of psychopathology; its major aim is not to cure "sick" people but to help people live more satisfying and creative lives regardless of the level at which they enter counseling. One of client-centered theory's major tenets is that the counselee has the capacity to direct his own life. The theory is perhaps more broadly appreciable than many theories because the client does not have to view himself as sick or disturbed in order to seek help with personal problems.

The work of the general counselor, however, does not always emphasize underlying personality change, and this poses special problems for client-centered theory to which we now turn our attention. Many clients seek help from the general counselor for concretely defined problems that often appear more cognitive than emotional in nature. The client is not seeking deep self-exploration and extensive personality reorganization. Many requests for help in making educational and vocational choices fall into this category, and the discussion which follows will focus on this area; but other problems brought to the general counselor might be included as well.

Before discussing the application of client-centered theory to education-al and vocational counseling, I wish to note, and then set aside, an impor-tant theoretical issue which the behavior modifications adherents have placed on center stage. The extreme position of this group rejects categori-cally that change in the underlying personality is ever an appropriate goal of counseling. They advocate that the counselor should help the client to specify his problems in concrete, behavioral terms and that all counseling should aim *directly* at altering the troublesome behaviors. Psychodynamic theories of personality and behavior of whatever variety are simply mis-guided and false, and thus irrelevant to the work of the counselor. The central issue here, of course, is the truth or falsity of competing families of theories, and this chapter is not the appropriate place to consider this raging dispute. Counselors who view all psychodynamic theories of behavior as mistaken will not be interested in the application of client-centered theory to the work of the general counselor.

The Goals of Counseling

Reorganization of the self is the primary goal of client-centered counseling. The theory states that successful counseling will dissolve the conditions of worth, increase openness to organismic experience, and thereby increase the degree of congruence between the self-concept and experience. In this way the client becomes a more fully functioning person. The client-centered counselor does not ask how he can solve a particular problem, or promote this or that specific behavior change. He asks how he can provide a rela-tionship which the client can use for his own personal growth. Within this emphasis there is, of course, the expectation that the client will discover better ways of meeting his life problems and that he will solve specific problems; however, the counselor does not set forth specific problem solu-tions or specific behavior changes as the goal of counseling. He is primarily concerned with changes in the self.

A weakness of client-centered theory for the general counselor is that the successful resolution of many educational and vocational problems (as well as other presenting problems) does not require a reorganization of self. It is, of course, true that fundamental personality change is needed for resolving some educational and vocational problems, that attitudes and values are always involved to a greater or lesser extent, and that vocational decisions are intimately related in most instances to the establishment of personal identity. Nonetheless, it is just plain silly for the general counselor to proceed as if the reorganization of self should be the main objective for all his clients. Frequently, more conservative objectives will suffice and better meet the client's expectations. This means that there are instances when the general counselor should supplement the client-centered approach by other counseling theories and methods.

Rogers's theoretical statements are not inconsistent with this view. One of his necessary conditions for therapy is that the client should be incongruent as well as anxious. For the general counselor we should modify this proposition to state that the client should be incongruent in those areas of his personality that are significantly related to his problem. If this condition does not hold, client-centered theory is only partially relevant. To illustrate, at Michigan State University, first- and second-year students wishing to change their majors customarily come to the Counseling Center for assistance. That such students may have marked incongruence in the sexual area of their lives or in their relationships with their parents may be irrelevant to resolving the immediate problem. If we assume no incongruence of any consequence in areas relating to their choice of major (an assumption which seems justified in many instances), then counseling as conceived of by Rogers would not get under way with the immediate problem at hand. Of course, counseling might get under way in other areas where the student is incongruent; but desirable as this might be, it still leaves both student and counselor with the issue of selecting an appropriate major.

It should be added that even under these conditions much, although not all, of client-centered theory is still relevant. The counselor's genuineness, his empathic understanding of the student and his situation, and his liking and respect for the student as a person help to create an effective working relationship that is beneficial for diverse counseling objectives.

A concern often expressed by others about the client-centered view of goals deserves consideration. It is asserted that the counselor cannot, as a responsible member of society, accept all goals that the client might conceivably set for himself. Suppose, it is argued, that the client elects to settle his financial problem by stealing, or his conflict with a roommate by physical violence. And what about suicide? Do not examples of this nature prove, it is argued, that the counselor must set at least some goals for the client?

The specific setting in which many counselors work imposes similar, although not always such obvious questions. The teacher who refers a student because of persistent disruptive behavior in the classroom expects some improvement in this behavior, and by accepting the student for counseling, does not the counselor commit himself to a particular goal? If we work with students experiencing academic failure, may not the nature of the counselor's job require setting the goal of academic improvement or alternatively, dropping school for some more appropriate objective?

The client-centered counselor has many answers for these and related questions which space does not allow us to consider here; however, the fundamental basis of these answers lies in the truth or falsity of the theory itself. If the theory is correct, allowing the client to set goals will not result in the socially unacceptable consequences which the questions are intended to imply. A paradox in client-centered theory is that more constructive personality and behavioral changes occur when the counselor refrains from setting goals (no matter how desirable these goals may be) and concentrates instead on creating the proper conditions for change. Rogers would add that even though the theory is not proved, it rests on considerable research support, and that research in other areas supports conclusions similar to the client-centered view (for an account of some of these, see Rogers, 1951, pp. 56-64).

There are, however, practical problems in leaving the goals of counseling to the client. Whether it is desirable or not, the counselor in accepting his job frequently does commit himself to certain goals for his clients. High school counselors may have administrative responsibility for determining the student's course of study. We have previously mentioned that at the writer's institution students in the first two years of college are required to confer with a counselor before changing their major area of study. For many of their cases, Veterans Administration counselors are required by law to certify the feasibility of the client's training objective.

An important characteristic of these and similar situations is that the goal is imposed on both client and counselor. In the case of the Veterans Administration counseling, for example, the goal is imposed on the counselor because of terms of his employment and on the veteran because he wishes to qualify for training benefits which are offered by the government only under certain conditions. Such externally imposed goals are not uncommon in counseling. They create a special case for client-centered counseling, but they need not seriously interfere with the establishment of an effective counseling relationship so long as the nature of the situation is understood and accepted by both client and counselor. Sometimes the client does not accept the externally imposed conditions, and the counselor must be alert to this possibility. The counselor deals with this as he would with any other issue arising in counseling: He attempts to understand and clarify the meaning which the situation has for the client.

An externally imposed goal often means that counseling is not voluntary with the client; it is a hurdle to be got over. This can cause severe complications which are best avoided whenever possible. Sometimes the counselor can work with and change the client's feelings about undergoing counseling, but unless he can, counseling is usually unsuccessful.

Most counselors of whatever persuasion agree that the desirable outcome of counseling is self-realization and self-direction. However, in many settings the limits imposed on the counselor's time with any one counselee will prevent the full realization of this objective. All theories, not just the client-centered theory, have difficulty coping with this reality limitation. The most frequent answer when a case threatens to be long is to circumscribe the problem area to be dealt with, that is, to set a more limited goal. Client-centered counselors, perhaps more than most counselors, are reluctant to do this because of their emphasis on letting the client set goals and because of their great concern with self-actualization. However, short-term counseling can be done. Useful assistance in limited areas of the client's life is not infrequently reported even in one-interview cases. Bartlett's (1949) research (see section on *Outcomes*) reporting on the postcounseling adjustment of veterans in training situations was done on cases with only a limited number of interviews.

The problem of time is most acute with clients presenting frankly emotional problems, and usually these clients require quite a number of interviews before we see significant change. When practical considerations do not allow a lengthy series of interviews, it is possible as suggested above to set limited goals for the counseling; however, an alternative approach more congenial to the client-centered counselor is to set limits on time and still leave the client free to use the allowed time as he wishes (Lewis, Rogers, & Shlien, 1959; Shlien, 1957). The writer with some success has told clients that because of the waiting list, they could have only a limited number of appointments. The client may be disappointed, and less change can be expected; but usually the client can use the remaining time constructively.

Giving Information

A serious weakness of client-centered theory for general counseling is that it says little about the role of information in assisting clients, or, if we confine ourselves to the terminology of the theory, the role of information in self-actualization. [12] The theory does, of course, assume that the individual is continually interacting with his environment and is differentiating new aspects of the environment in an attempt to meet his needs. The theory's deficiency is that it says little about the influence of the stimulus situation in this interaction between person and environment. Instead, the theory stresses that it is the individual's perception of the environment (or of the information, if you wish) which determines his behavior.

There is much value in Rogers's reminding us that reality for the individual is his perception of that reality. In psychology generally and in counseling in particular, we often slide over this truth too quickly. Just giving the client information about an occupation or a course of study does

[12]Actually Rogers has written about the use of information in educational and vocational counseling in a little book jointly authored with Wallen (1946). The book is rather practical in its approach and was written before the present theory was fully developed, but it is still of considerable interest to the general counselor.

not mean that he perceives this as we intended. It is also valid and useful to call attention to the role of the self and the defensive process in determining what is actually perceived. However, it is equally valid and useful to recognize how perception is influenced by information and the stimulus situation generally. The theory's failure to elaborate how the environment influences perception and behavior is for the writer a significant omission which has special relevance for many counseling situations.[13]

Information can alter perception and behavior, and it is appropriate that educational and occupational information is a time-honored tool of the counselor. Consider the preengineering student who has his heart set on engineering but is having difficulty with mathematics. Counseling reveals that his perception of "an engineer" more accurately fits the role of a technician in a mechanical field. When presented with a realistic job description of the two occupations, he cheerfully makes plans to enter a technical school where he can get training to do what he wanted to do all along.

Since client-centered counselors do in fact give information to their clients, the question arises as to how information giving can be integrated into the theory as it is currently formulated.

To be maximally useful, information must be accurately assimilated and used by the client in an integrative manner. We can infer from client-centered theory that if the information is theatening to the self, it will be distorted and resisted in some way. Under these circumstances the counselor can profitably play down the need for information and concentrate instead on creating the conditions which reduce the threat and allow the self to change. On the other hand, if the information is not threatening but can be perceived by the client as providing ways to maintain and enhance the self, then the information should be provided. In other words, appropriate information can be assimilated when it helps the client to meet his perceived needs and to achieve or to formulate his goals. Sometimes it is also given to change a perceived goal to a more suitable goal, but this is apt to be effective only when the information is perceived as nonthreatening to the self and when it points to a new goal which is perceived as self-enhancing.

In the illustration of the preengineering student cited above, the information given was nonthreatening and pointed to a new but self-enhancing goal. It was assimilated and used in integrative fashion. Slightly altering our example might produce a quite different result. Suppose that the student were under considerable pressure from his parents to enter the university and qualify in engineering, and further suppose that the student's need for

---

[13] In one sense this is an unfair criticism. The essential point underlying the writer's criticism is that counseling practice needs to be based on a complete theory of behavior, and Rogers makes no pretense that his personality theory and therapeutic theory achieve this objective.

self-esteem was perceived by him to be dependent on meeting the expectations of his parents. The information supplied by the counselor would be threatening and would tend not to be accurately assimilated and appropriately used. While we might all agree that the information is of great potential value to the client, the counselor is still faced with the problem of how the client can assimilate and use the information.

This suggested modification of the theory provides a guide to the use of information in general counseling, but on logical grounds the theory is still vulnerable since in practice the counselor cannot always know in advance whether relevant information will threaten the client's self-concept. Thus the counselor in providing information will sometimes violate the conditions of reduced threat which client-centered theory postulates as necessary for therapeutic change. Fortunately, most clients are not as delicate as we sometimes think. Even when the counselor supplies information which proves threatening to the client's self-concept, little damage is done if the conditions for the therapeutic relationship have been established and are being generally maintained and if the information is communicated with warmth, understanding, and a readiness to receive fully the responses of the client. The counselor must, of course, be alert to any threat created by the information and attempt to deal with this constructively. He should not force the issue and attempt to convince the client that the information provided is both correct and relevant. If even subtle resistance is met, the counselor can profitably concentrate on trying to understand the personal meaning that the new information has for the client. If the client has a different perception of the information from that intended by the counselor, the client's perception must be recognized and explored. Denying the validity of the client's perception and attempting to prove it unfounded will not change the fact of the client's feelings about the matter. Too frequently counselors become ego-involved and defensive once they have committed themselves to a particular view of the situation.

This discussion would not be complete without mentioning some additional factors which the client-centered counselor considers before too quickly supplying information to his client. First, the presenting problem frequently is not the real problem that the client wishes to bring to counseling. He may be "testing the situation out" with a superficial problem which appears to lend itself to a cognitive-informational approach. Empathic listening and getting to know the client often allows the real problem to emerge.

Second, most problems the client brings to the counselor are not basically problems of lack of information. Students have ample opportunities to pick up information about courses of study, financial aids, occupations, employment opportunities, and the like. If they do not have the information, it is usually readily available. Therefore, there is presumptive evidence that the essential nature of the problem is not lack of information but blocks to the effective gathering and use of the information. Information will not be particularly helpful until these blocks have been explored and resolved.

Third, too much emphasis on information and external reality can divert the client from significant self-problems. Too often the client gets the impression that his subjective feelings and attitudes about the problem are not appropriate to the counseling situation. He feels that he is expected to be rational and objective about the matter. In any case, the subjective self-elements are at least mildly threatening and often only dimly perceived by the client. The client can readily be diverted, and the counselor's approach therefore needs to make it easy for the client to bring self-elements into the interview.

In brief, the attitude of nonevaluative listening and empathic understanding can help avoid many pitfalls surrounding the use of information in counseling. It allows the more personal and threatening self-elements to emerge, and it helps the counselor to know what, if any, information may be pertinent and how it can best be communicated.

Because beginning client-centered counselors are sometimes overly cautious about providing information, it need also be said that the counselor's failure to give information under some circumstances can be perceived by the client as rejecting, while the giving of information can be experienced as a sign of caring and acceptance. For example, the repeated parrying and avoiding the client's questions can defeat the central aim of the client-centered approach.

Using Tests

Although Rogers (1946) has written one article about the use of tests in counseling, the current theory makes no mention of their use, and for many counselors this will be a significant omission.

It is immediately apparent that using tests as a source of information for the client is essentially the problem of information giving discussed in the preceding section. The chief difference is that tests, by their very nature, provide information of great relevance to the self, and because of this, test information is more likely to instigate the process of threat and perceptual defense. The client is seldom indifferent or neutral to what tests may reveal about him.

Many client-centered counselors find it easiest to use tests infrequently. They see educational and vocational problems, where tests are traditionally used, as just another variety of personal problem. And as in other kinds of counseling, the counselor is interested in the person, not merely in the initial problem which he presents. This does not mean that the presenting problem is ignored. On the contrary, as with other presenting problems, the counselor is interested in how the client views his problem and himself in relation to it, and the counseling relationship develops on this basis. It is perfectly possible for the client to clarify, reformulate, and reach decisions about an educational or vocational problem by considering himself in relation to any number of issues, e.g., to work and school experiences, to family relationships, or to social values. Test information is not essential and at times may even divert the client from more significant issues.

The client-centered counselor preferring this approach will not automatically exclude the use of tests. "The client may, in exploring his situation, reach the point where, facing his situation squarely and realistically, he wishes to compare his aptitudes and abilities with those of others for a specific purpose. When tests come as a real desire from the client, they may enter into the situation" (Rogers, 1946, p. 142). According to this principle, however, tests will be used infrequently, and when they are used, it is likely to be in the later stages of counseling.

One of the special problems about tests arises because so many clients come to counseling expecting them. Often this seems to reflect the client's interest in having someone else make a decision for him. He, of course, wants the decision to be made in his own interests, and this requires that he be known and understood. Tests, he thinks, will provide this understanding. No doubt tests can be used, and too often are used to make the client's decisions for him; however, for the writer this is not a function of counseling. It is far better to put the tests and other information into a computer and grind out a result. If counseling is to justify itself, it must offer something more than this, for it appears that before too long computers will supercede counselors as processors of information. This "something more" for the client-centered approach is that counseling is a learning experience involving the functioning and organization of the self. Tests can be useful in this process, provided that the information they supply is integrated into the self-concept.

This does not, of course, entirely dismiss the problem of the dependent client who seeks magical answers in test information. Not infrequently, withholding tests from these clients is experienced as rejection, and they merely go elsewhere for help. Although this issue has not been studied extensively by the client-centered group, some suggestions can be made.

Giving tests to dependent clients may help them to discover that tests do not provide the satisfying answers they had anticipated, and at this point it may be possible for client and counselor to embark on a more fruitful counseling experience. But this will not happen if the counselor uses the test information to make the client's decision for him.

The problem of dependence, at least mild dependence, is extremely common, and most counselors would agree that counseling should help the client move in the direction of independence and self-direction. Rogers (1946), Bordin and Bixler (1946) and others have pointed out that the traditional use of tests in educational and vocational counseling does little to foster independence. Bordin and Bixler note that students coming to the Counseling and Testing Bureau at the University of Minnesota typically project responsibility for their problem onto the counselor or the referring agent. The counselor may reinforce this when he asks the many questions needed for an appraisal, when he selects and assigns tests, etc.

To help meet this problem and also to facilitate the client's assimilation and use of test information, Bordin and Bixler (1946) developed a procedure for client self-selection of tests.[14] The counselor states in nontechnical language the type of judgment the test can make, and it is then left to the client to decide whether the information would be useful in considering his particular problem. The authors report that this is often a struggle for the client. He usually explores his feelings and doubts about the self-relevance of the appraisal under consideration and often brings forth a wealth of significant material. This helps the client develop a deeper understanding of his problem which sometimes results in a radical restatement of the problem. The approach also encourages active participation by the client and a coming to terms with self-responsibility. The authors think a further advantage of this approach is that the client is better motivated to take a long test battery and that in taking the tests he is keenly aware of the significance of his own performance.

Seeman (1948) investigated the effectiveness of client self-selection of tests and reports evidence that the client's selections are relevant to their situations. He also reports that the self-selection situation is unstructured enough to allow the client to explore many areas unique to his situation.

How the process works can be illustrated by a recorded interview excerpt from Seeman's research.

C: This math test would give you an indication of your background in math and also help predict how a person is likely to do in our College of Engineering.

S: I'm a little scared of math. But (pause) that would give me an idea of where I stand now in my math background. Right?

C: That's right.

S: Well, I think I've got an idea of where I stand now in my math background; it's one of my weaker points. But I've always been told that if I work at it, I could do well in it. But I don't know.

C: It's hard for you to know about what others say concerning your potentialities.

S: That's right. At times in math, I've done very well when I applied myself a little more. But then at other times I didn't do so well and it just seeme like I hated it. And as a result, well, I got mighty low marks.

[14] Shostrom and Brammer (1952) report a similar procedure using a printed test selection guide. Bordin (1968) also discusses this approach in his more recent work entitled *Psychological Counseling*.

C: You really had some ups and downs in math.

S: Yes, that's sure. Well, it seemed to make a lot of difference as to the instructor I had. Some would tell me that I—well, in junior high school I was told that I was quite hopeless with it, and that sort of discouraged me. So I let it go for a year and then went to summer school to—well, to do what I'm doing now, to find if I could do it or not. Well, I got a B in it. So my math background now, I don't think, I know just about where I stand in that, I think.

C: You feel that the test wouldn't be necessary because you can size it up for yourself.

S: I can size it up pretty well for myself, that I'm not very high in math.

C: Umhum.

S: Well, on the other hand, maybe it wouldn't be a bad idea to take it.

C: You're a little undecided on that one, aren't you?

S: Yes . . . so I'd know actually just how bad off I am.

C: So even though you don't think you're going to do well on it, you'd like to take it.

S: Even though I don't think I'll do well on it at all (1948, p. 340).

The interpretation of test results in educational and vocational counseling often introduces a crucial phase of the counseling in which the client either integrates test predictions into his thinking and planning or distorts and rejects them. Bixler and Bixler (1946) describe a client-centered approach which encourages the client to participate in test interpretation and to relate test results to other relevant material. They recommend that test results be reported factually with a minimum of the counselor's opinion as to their implications for the client. The counselor does not say, "This result indicates you will not do well in college." Instead he says, "Ten out of one hundred students with scores like yours will succeed in college," and leaves the interpretation of this fact for the client to decide for himself. "When the counselor allows the client to make his own interpretation, he is free to express these attitudes which so frequently interfere with his use of test data. As he expresses them to an accepting counselor, there is a greater opportunity for them to dissipate and the client will gain a better insight into his motivation. It is only as the client can understand and accept himself that he can make actual use of tests" (Bixler and Bixler, 1946, p. 154).

The following excerpt illustrates the Bixlers' approach to test interpretation. The counselor has just pointed out that fifteen to twenty students of each one hundred with scores like hers succeed in college:

S: (looks stunned, then confused)

C: This is awfully disappointing.

S: Yes, it is. I had hoped I'd find something I could succeed in.

C: It seems to leave you without anything to go into.

S: Yes, but I can do the work. I have trouble concentrating, my study habits are poor, I never studied in high school and I don't know how.

C: You feel the reason for your trouble is your poor study habits, not a lack of ability.

S: Yes, I didn't get good grades in high school, but I didn't study either. Now when I want to study I worry and get tense. My mind goes blank when I take tests.

C: You're pretty worried about your school work and that seems to make it harder to succeed. (Pause).

S: It's my last hope. (Head sinks on chest, lips quiver.)

C: You're so upset about this you feel like crying.

S: (Does) I feel so silly. (C recognizes her embarrassment, and she continues to cry and discuss various elements of her anxiety about school.) I've got to make good. I'm not as smart as most kids, that's true. There are some subjects that go over me, but I think I can make it. I don't know what to do.

C: You have to make good and yet you'.e afraid you can't. It leaves you pretty badly mixed up.

S: Decides to continue seeing C until she can work out a solution (1946, p. 153).

This excerpt illustrates the main features of how the client-centered counselor handles the introduction of test or other kinds of information into the counseling interview. The information is presented as factually and objectively as possible. The client is not urged to accept any particular implication the information has for his situation. Instead the counselor concentrates on empathically understanding what the information means to the client and by this assists the client to explore further and to assimilate and use the information.

Summary

The usual goal of the client-centered counselor is to produce changes in the functioning and organization of the client's self, and thus the theory is directly relevant to the work of the general counselor whenever this is his appropriate objective. Nevertheless client-centered theory is deficient for some aspects of the general counselor's work. The two most important of these are: (1) The functioning and organization of the self may not be a crucial aspect of all the problems brought to the general counselor, and (2) the cognitive-informational approach is a useful counseling procedure with many clients.

A fundamental weakness of client-centered theory is that it fails to take sufficient note of how behavior is influenced by the stimulus situation and the nature of the environment generally, and perhaps this omission is far more important to the general counselor than to the therapeutic counselor. In the final analysis, general counseling needs to be based on a complete theory of behavior. However, the present state of knowledge in the behavioral sciences offers no complete theory of behavior which can guide all the counselor's activities, and in practice all counselors, knowingly or unknowingly, tend to draw upon several theories. If the counselor uses tests or other information which allow for predictions about the client's future performance in an academic program or a vocation, he is drawing upon a body of knowledge often called trait-and-factor theory. Similarly, if the counselor agrees that test or other information may sometimes be resisted by the client, he is drawing upon self-theory, some other dynamic theory, or perhaps learning theory.

Many of the counseling situations not covered adequately by client-centered theory can be handled quite successfully in actual practice, although some originality and adaptability is called for from the counselor. This concluding section has suggested some possible adaptations for educational and vocational counseling which are consistent with the client-centered approach.

As a final point, it should be emphasized that all counseling takes place in an interpersonal relationship, and that client-centered theory deals more than anything else with the *nature of the interpersonal relationship* in which constructive personality growth and change can occur. In this sense client-centered theory is directly relevant to any helping relationship. Even though the practice of the general counselor may call for adaptations of the formal theory and departures from some of the usual procedures employed in client-centered therapeutic counseling, the counselor will be maintaining the essence of the client-centered approach if he succeeds in creating a counseling relationship in which his client has the experience of being fully received.

Bibliography

Angyal, A. *Foundations for a science of personality.* New York: Commonwealth Fund, 1941.

Aspy, D. The differential effect of high and low functioning teachers upon student achievement (abstract). In R. R. Carkhuff & B. G. Berenson (Eds.), *Beyond counseling and psychotherapy.* New York: Holt, 1967. Pp. 296-297.

Aspy, D., & Hadlock, W. The effects of high and low functioning teachers upon student performance (abstract). In R. R. Carkhuff & B. G. Berenson (Eds.), *Beyond counseling and psychotherapy.* New York: Holt, 1967. P. 297.

Assum, A. L., & Levy, S. J. Analysis of a non-directive case with followup interview. *J. abnorm. soc. Psychol.*, 1948, **43**, 78-89.

Axline, V. M. Nondirective therapy for poor readers. *J. consult. Psychol.*, 1947, **11**, 61-69.

Barrett-Lennard, G. T. Dimensions of therapist response as causal factors in therapeutic change. *Psychol. Monogr.*, 1962, **76** (43, Whole No. 562).

Bartlett, M. R., & staff. Data on the personal adjustment counseling program for veterans. Personal Adjustment Counseling Division. Advisement and Guidance Service. Office of Vocational Rehabilitation and Education. Washington, D.C., 1949.

Bergin, A. E. The effects of psychotherapy: Negative results revisited. *J. counsel. Psychol.*, 1963, **10**, 244-255.

Bergin, A. E. Some implications of psychotherapy research for therapeutic practice. *J. abnorm. Psychol.*, 1966, **71**, 235-246.

Bixler, R. H., & Bixler, V. M. Test interpretation in vocational counseling. *Educ. psychol. Measmt.*, 1946, **6**, 145-155.

Bordin, E. S. *Psychological counseling.* New York: Appleton Century Crofts, 1968.

Bordin, E. S., & Bixler, R. H. Test selection: A process of counseling. *Educ. psychol. Measmt.*, 1946, **6**, 361-374.

Butler, J. M. The evaluative attitude of the client-centered counselor: A linguistic-behavioral formulation. Dittoed paper, Counseling Center, University of Chicago, about 1952.

Butler, J. M. Client-centered counseling and psychotherapy. In D. Brower & L. E. Abt (Eds.), *Progress in clinical psychology.* Vol. 3. *Changing conceptions in psychotherapy.* New York: Grune & Stratton, 1958.

Butler, J. M., & Haigh, G. V. Changes in the relation between self-concepts and ideal concepts consequent upon client-centered counseling. In C. R. Rogers & R. F. Dymond (Eds.), *Psychotherapy and personality change.* Chicago: University of Chicago Press, 1954. Chap. 4.

Butler, J. M., & Rice, L. Adience, self-actualization, and drive theory. In J. M. Wepman & R. W. Heine (Eds.), *Concepts of personality.* Chicago: Aldine, 1963.

Carkhuff, R. R. An integration of practice and training. In G. Berenson, & R. Carkhuff (Eds.), *Sources of gain in counseling and psychotherapy.* New York: Holt, 1967. Pp. 423-436.

Carkhuff, R. R. *The counselors contribution to facilitative processes.* Urbana, Ill.: Parkinson, 1967. (a)

Carkhuff, R. R. *Helping and human relations.* Vols. I and II. New York: Holt, 1969.

Carkhuff, R., & Alexik, M. Effect of client depth of self-exploration upon high- and low-functioning counselors. *J. counsel. Psychol.*, 1967, **14**, 350-355.

Carkhuff, R. R., & Berenson, B. G. *Beyond counseling and psychotherapy.* New York: Holt, 1967.

Carkhuff, R. R., & Bierman, R. Training as the preferred mode of treatment of parents of emotionally disturbed children. *J. counsel. Psychol.*, 1970, **17**, 157-161.

Cartwright, D. S. A synthesis of process and outcome research. *Discussion papers*, Counseling Center, University of Chicago, Vol. 2, No. 19, 1956.

Cofer, C. N., & Chance, J. The discomfort-relief quotient in published cases of counseling and psychotherapy. *J. Psychol.*, 1950, **29**, 219-224.

Dymond, R. F. Adjustment changes over therapy from Thematic Apperception Test ratings. In C. R. Rogers & R. F. Dymond (Eds.), *Psychotherapy and personality change.* Chicago: University of Chicago Press, 1954. Chap. 8. (a)

Dymond, R. F. Adjustment changes over therapy from self sorts. In C. R. Rogers & R. F. Dymond (Eds.), *Psychotherapy and personality change.* Chicago: University of Chicago Press, 1954. Chap. 5. (b)

Eyserck, H. J. The effects of psychotherapy: An evaluation. *J. consul. Psychol.,* 1952, **16**, 319–324.

Farkas, A. The internal-external dimension of experience in relation to process and outcome of psychotherapy. Unpublished master's thesis, Michigan State University, 1969.

Gendlin, E. T. Outcome and process. *Discussion papers,* Counseling Center, University of Chicago, Vol. 2, No. 21, 1956.

Gendlin, E. T. Experiencing: A variable in the process of therapeutic change. *Amer. J. Psychother.,* 1960, **15**, 233–245. (a)

Gendlin, E. T. Sub-verbal communication and therapist expressivity: Trends in client-centered psychotherapy with schizophrenics. *Discussion papers,* Wisconsin Psychiatric Institute, University of Wisconsin, No. 17, 1961. (b)

Gendlin, E. T. Client-centered developments and work with schizophrenics. *J. counsel. Psychol.,* 1962, **9**, 205–212. (a)

Gendlin, E. T. *Experiencing and the creation of meaning.* New York: Free Press, 1962. (b)

Gendlin, E. T. Values and the process of experiencing. In A. R. Mahner (Ed.), *The goals of psychotherapy.* New York: Appleton Century Crofts, 1967.

Gendlin, E. T. Focusing. *Psychotherapy: Theory, research and practice,* 1969, **6**, 4–15.

Gendlin, E. T., Beebe, J., Cassens, M., & Oberlander, M. Focusing ability in psychotherapy, personality, and creativity. In J. M. Shlien (Ed.), *Research in psychotherapy.* Washington, D.C.: American Psychological Association. 1968, Vol. III, Pp. 217–241.

Gendlin, E. T., & Zimiring, F. The qualities or dimensions of experiencing and their change. *Discussion papers.* Counseling Center, University of Chicago, Vol. 1, No. 3, 1955.

Ginott, H. G. *Between parent and child.* New York: Macmillan, 1965.

Goldstein, J. *Human nature in the light of psychopathology.* Cambridge, Mass.: Harvard, 1940.

Gordon, T. A. *Group-centered leadership.* Boston: Houghton Mifflin, 1955.

Grummon, D. L., & John, E. S. Changes over client-centered therapy evaluated on psychoanalytically based Thematic Apperception Test scales. In C. R. Rogers & R. F. Dymond (Eds.), *Psychotherapy and personality change.* Chicago: University of Chicago Press, 1954. Chap. 11.

Hahn, M. E., & Kendall, W. E. Some comments in defense of non-nondirective counseling. *J. consult. Psychol.,* 1947, **11**, 74–81.

Hahn, M. E., & MacLean, M. S. *Counseling psychology.* (2nd ed.) New York: McGraw-Hill, 1955.

Haimowitz, N. R., & Haimowitz, M. L. Personality changes in client-centered therapy. In W. Wolff (Ed.), *Success in psychotherapy.* New York: Grune & Stratton, 1952.

Halkides, G. An investigation of therapeutic success as a function of four variables. Unpublished doctoral dissertation, University of Chicago, 1958.

Hampton, P. T. Client's need for approval as a factor affecting process and outcome of psychotherapy. Unpublished master's thesis, Michigan State University, 1968.

Hart, J. T. The evolution of client-centered psychotherapy. *Psychiatric Institute Bulletin*, University of Wisconsin, 1961, **1** (2).

Hartley, M. Changes in the self-concept during psychotherapy. Unpublished doctoral dissertation, University of Chicago, 1951.

Hobbs, N. Sources of gain in psychotherapy. *Amer. Psychologist,* 1962, **17,** 741-747.

Kirtner, W. L., & Cartwright, D. S. Success and failure in client-centered therapy as a function of initial in-therapy behavior. *J. consult. Psychol.,* 1958, **22,** 329-333.

Levitt, E. E. The results of psychotherapy with children. *J. consult. Psychol.,* 1957, **21,** 189-196.

Lewis, M., Rogers, C. R., & Shlien, J. M. Time-limited, client-centered psychotherapy: Two cases. In A. Burton (Ed.), *Case studies in counseling and psychotherapy.* Englewood Cliffs, N.J.: Prentice-Hall, 1959. Chap. 12.

Maslow, A. H. *Motivation and personality.* New York: Harper, 1954.

Mosak, H. Evaluation in psychotherapy: A study of some current measures. Unpublished doctoral dissertation, University of Chicago, 1950.

Mowrer, O. H., & Kluckhohn, C. A dynamic theory of personality. In J. McV. Hunt, *Personality and the behavior disorders.* New York: Ronald, 1944.

Muench, G. A. An evaluation of non-directive psychotherapy by means of the Rorschach and other tests. *Psychol. Monogr.,* 1947 (13) 1-163.

Patterson, C. H. A current view of client-centered or relationship therapy. *The Counseling Psychologist,* 1969, **1,** 2-27. Rejoinder and Commentary, Pp. 63-68.

Paul, G. L. *Insight vs. desensitization in psychotherapy,* Stanford, Calif.: Stanford, 1966.

Pierce, R. M., & Drasgow, J. Teaching facilitative interpersonal functioning to psychiatric inpatients. *J. counsel. Psychol.,* 1969, **16,** 295-298.

Raimy, V. C. The self-concept as a factor in counseling and personality organization. Doctoral thesis, Ohio State University, 1943.

Raimy, V. C. Self references in counseling interviews. *J. appl. Psychol.,* 1948, **12,** 153-163.

Raskin, N. J. An objective study of the locus of evaluation factor in psychotherapy. In W. Wolff (Ed.), *Success in psychotherapy.* New York: Grune & Stratton, 1952. Chap. 6.

Rogers, C. R. *Counseling and psychotherapy.* Boston: Houghton Mifflin, 1942.

Rogers, C. R. Psychometric tests and client-centered counseling. *Educ. psychol. Measmt.,* 1946, **6,** 139-144.

Rogers, C. R. Some implications of client-centered counseling for college personnel work. *Educ. psychol. Measmt.,* 1948, **8,** 540-549.

Rogers, C. R. *Client-centered therapy: Its current practice, implications, and theory.* Boston: Houghton Mifflin, 1951.

Rogers, C. R. Changes in the maturity of behavior as related to therapy. In C. R. Rogers & R. F. Dymond (Eds.), *Psychotherapy and personality change.* Chicago: University of Chicago Press, 1954. Chap. 13.

Rogers, C. R. Persons or science? A philosophical question. *Amer. Psychologist,* 1955, **10**, 267–278.

Rogers, C. R. The necessary and sufficient conditions of therapeutic personality change. *J. consult. Psychol.,* 1957, **21**, 95–103.

Rogers, C. R. A Process conception of psychotherapy. *Amer. Psychologist,* 1958, **13**, 142–149.

Rogers, C. R. Significant Learning: In therapy and in education. *Educ. Leadership,* 1959, **16**, 232–242.

Rogers, C. R. A theory of therapy, personality, and interpersonal relationships, as developed in the client-centered framework. In S. Koch (Ed.), *Psychology: A study of a science.* Vol. III. *Formulations of the person and the social context.* New York: McGraw-Hill, 1959. Pp. 184–258. (a)

Rogers, C. R. A tentative scale for the measurement of process in psychotherapy. In E. A. Rubinstein, & M. B. Parloff (Eds.), *Research in psychotherapy.* Washington, D.C.: American Psychological Association, 1959. Pp. 96–107. (c)

Rogers, C. R. The essence of psychotherapy: A client-centered view. *Annals of Psychotherapy,* 1959, **1**, 51–57. (b)

Rogers, C. R. The process equation of psychotherapy. *Amer. J. Psychother.,* 1961, **15**, 27–45. (a)

Rogers, C. R. *On becoming a person.* Boston: Houghton Mifflin, 1961. (b)

Rogers, C. R. The characteristics of a helping relationship. In C. R. Rogers (Ed.), *On becoming a person.* Boston: Houghton Mifflin, 1961. (c). Chap. 3.

Rogers, C. R. A process conception of psychotherapy. In C. R. Rogers (Ed.), *On becoming a person.* Boston: Houghton Mifflin, 1961. (d). Chap. 7.

Rogers, C. R. The potential of the human individual: The capacity for becoming fully functioning. (Mimeographed paper, University of Wisconsin), Madison, Wis.: 1961. (e)

Rogers, C. R. A therapist's view of the good life: The fully functioning person. In C. R. Rogers (Ed.), *On becoming a person.* Boston: Houghton Mifflin, 1961. Chap. 9. (f)

Rogers, C. R. The interpersonal relationship: The core of guidance. *Harv. educ. Rev.,* 1962, **32**, 416–429. (a)

Rogers, C. R. Some learnings from a study of psychotherapy with schizophrenics. *Discussion papers,* Wisconsin Psychiatric Institute, No. 27, University of Wisconsin, 1962. (b)

Rogers, C. R. Toward becoming a fully functioning person. In *Perceiving, behaving, becoming.* 1962 Yearbook Association for Supervision and Curriculum Development, National Education Association. (c)

Rogers, C. R. The actualizing tendency in relation to "motives" and to consciousness. *Nebraska symposium on motivation.* Lincoln: University of Nebraska Press, 1963.

Rogers, C. R. Toward a modern approach to values: The valuing process in the mature person. *J. abnorm. soc. Psychol.,* 1964, **68**, 160–167.

Rogers, C. R. The process of the basic encounter group. In J. F. T. Bugental (Ed.), *Challenges of humanistic psychology.* New York: McGraw-Hill, 1967. Chap. 28. (b)

Rogers, C. R. The facilitation of significant learning. In L. Siegel (Ed.), *Instruction: Some contemporary viewpoints.* San Francisco: Chandler, 1967. Chap. 3. (c)

Rogers, C. R. The interpersonal relationship in the facilitation of learning. In R. Leeper (Ed.), *Humanizing education.* Association for Supervision and Curriculum Development, NEA, 1967. (d)

Rogers, C. R. *Freedom to learn: A view of what education might become.* Columbus, Ohio: Merrill, 1969.

Rogers, C. R., & Dymond, R. F. (Eds.), *Psychotherapy and personality change.* Chicago: University of Chicago Press, 1954.

Rogers, C. R., Gendlin, E. T., Kiesler, D. J., & Truax, C. B. (Eds.), *The therapeutic relationship and its impact.* Madison, Wis.: University of Wisconsin Press, 1967.

Rogers, C. R., & Rablen, R. A. A scale of process in psychotherapy. Madison, Wis.: University of Wisconsin Press, 1958.

Rogers, C. R., & Wallen, J. L. *Counseling with returned servicemen.* New York: McGraw-Hill, 1946.

Rogers, N. Measuring psychological tension in nondirective counseling. *Personal Counselor,* 1948, **3,** 237-264.

Seeman, J. A study of client self-selection of tests in vocational counseling. *Educ. psychol. Measmt.,* 1948, **8,** 327-346.

Seeman, J. A study of the process of nondirective therapy. *J. consult. Psychol.,* 1949, **13,** 157-168.

Seeman, J., & Raskin, N. J. Research perspective in client-centered therapy. In O. H. Mowrer (Ed.), *Psychotherapy theory and research.* New York: Ronald, 1953. Chap. 9.

Seeman, J. Client-centered therapy. In D. Brower & L. E. Abt (Eds.), *Progress in clinical psychology.* Vol. V. New York: Grune & Stratton, 1956.

Shapiro, J. G., & Therese, Voog. Effect of the inherently helpful person on student academic achievement. *J. Counsel. Psychol.,* 1969, **16,** 505-509.

Sheerer, E. T. The relationship between acceptance of self and acceptance of others. *Journal consult. Psychol.,* 1959, **13,** 169-175.

Shlien, J. M. Time-limited psychotherapy: An experimental investigation of practical values and theoretical implications. *J. counsel. Psychol.,* 1957, **4,** 318-322.

Shostrom, E. L., & Brammer, L. M. *The dynamics of the counseling process.* New York: McGraw-Hill, 1952.

Snyder, W. U. An investigation of the nature of nondirective psychotherapy. *J. gen. Psychol.,* 1945, **33,** 193-223.

Snygg, D., & Combs, A. W. *Individual behavior: A new frame of reference for psychology.* New York: Harper, 1949 (now Combs & Snygg, 1959).

Standal, S. The need for positive regard: A contribution to client-centered theory. Unpublished doctoral dissertation, University of Chicago, 1954.

Stock, D. The self-concept and feelings toward others. *J. consult. Psychol.,* 1949, **13,** 176-180.

Thetford, W. N. An objective measure of frustration tolerance in evaluating psychotherapy. In W. Wolff (Ed.), *Success in psychotherapy.* New York: Grune & Stratton, 1952.

Truax, C. B. Elements of psychotherapy. *Discussion papers.* Wisconsin Psychiatric Institute, No. 38, University of Wisconsin, 1962.

Truax, C. B., & Carkhuff, R. R. *Towards effective counseling and psychotherapy.* Chicago: Aldine, 1967.

Whyte, L. L. *The unconscious before Freud.* London: Tavistock Publications, 1960.

4

Trait-factor Theory and Individual Differences[1,2]

E. G. WILLIAMSON

The forms of counseling involving trait-factor or individuality theory of human nature are based upon the postulates that aptitudes, or potentiality for the performance of specified types of work or activities, are identifiable prior to training (including education at any given level but with different levels of emergence). The aptitudes are also visible prior to performance in employment or activity which requires a given type of aptitude reinforced by motivation. Moreover, another basic assumption is held by these advocates; namely, that effective performance of developmental activities or vocation which requires these given aptitudes yields maximum intrinsic satisfaction to the student-in-training (education) as well as to one who is, or is to be, regularly employed (Weiss, Davis, England, & Lofquist, 1967). Hence the practice has evolved of administering aptitude and interest tests prior to enrollment in school or employment itself. Other underlying assumptions will be detailed in a moment. And we shall discuss in a later section two modifications, or supplements, of traditional aptitude testing of employed workers: (1) the use of training-on-the-job as an aptitude test in the case of culturally deprived individuals with deficient formal education, and (2) the use of nonfinancial incentives to induce optimum use of possessed aptitudes to yield satisfaction in employment. The latter assumption has its parallel in the use of incentives to induce optimum effort to learn in school.

[1] I am indebted to Drs. Ralph Berdie and Donald Biggs for their critical assistance in preparing this revision. Dr. Donald Hoyt kindly permitted me to use part of one of his counseling interviews conducted when he was at the University of Minnesota.
[2] The reader is, of course, urged to explore many other facets of man's work as more than employment for economic support in Henry Borow (ed.), *Man in a World at Work*, Boston: Houghton Mifflin Company, 1964.

While subscribing to the wholeness of the individual (as contrasted with fragmentation into aptitude, affect, etc.), the major application of theory in this chapter will be to counseling which emphasizes choice of school or work (Solem, 1968). This is not restricted to the initial choice of a career but to successive stages of development of the individual, including the intangible problem of value commitments. The best source of research on vocational choice by Tiedeman, Super, and Crites is Crites (1969), Part II. The counseling of clients who experience affective or emotional disturbances is the subject of other chapters of this book.

Historical Evolution

Francis Galton (1883) was one of the early behavioral scientists who studied empirically and systematically the measurable differences in capacities and aptitudes among individuals. Such differences, of course, had been observed (by estimation or judgment) and practically utilized, but Galton emphasized the possibility of measuring differences in behavior and relating these to patterns of development. The German psychologists, while concentrating on problems of measuring behavior, had given little attention to individual differences. In contrast, Binét and Henri (1895) in France and J. M. Cattell (1890) in the United States concentrated their behavior measurement efforts on individual differences. They were among the first to introduce the study of individual differences as they worked on problems of behavior prediction and differential prediction. Hugo Münsterberg (1913 and earlier), a German psychologist who transferred to Harvard University, called attention to and demonstrated the implications of such differences not only for education but also for industry and government. This in turn gave a new impetus to these developments in American psychology. Frank Parsons, a man of diverse talents, initiated the use of some of the available aptitude and capacity tests to youth in search of vocational choices (1909, his first and only book).

Although some psychological research and theorizing continues to minimize the importance of individual differences, a large part of contemporary psychology is devoted (1) to the study and evaluation of differences in individual behavior and (2) to observations directed toward the relevance and significance of such differences. A collection of historically relevant papers is found in the volume edited by Jenkins and Paterson (1961). Detailed descriptions of the recent status of this research can be found in the texts by Anastasi (1958) and Tyler (1961, 1965) and the *Annual Review of Psychology* (1950 to 1957, 1959 to 1960, and 1969).

The empirical study of differential psychology continued for several decades before it was anchored in a theoretical base. The theory of evolution provided some stimulus for English scientists interested in human diversity and variation; but, for the most part, these early observers were concerned primarily with refining their methods of observation, developing their techniques of statistical analysis, and systematically ordering their observations and conclusions. What has been inadequately labeled "trait-and-factor theory" had its formal origin in the early statistical work of Galton (1883) and Pearson (1937). Spearman (1927) and Burt (1941) extended the statistical and logical foundations for this theory, and Clark Hull (1928) and L. L. Thurstone (1931, 1935) provided further extensions.

For not-fully-informed counselors, differential psychology has more effectively provided methods and data rather than a psychological theory. A theory of personality organization has evolved and has had some significance, but the fact that so many counselors have been much more aware of the research and methods than of the theory raises a question about the role of theory in counseling.

In psychology, behavior is the raw material. The psychologist observes behavior; in processing his observations, the psychologist makes use of concepts and constructs, or ideas, which are the substance of theories. When the psychologist observes an individual's behavior, he applies (usually silently but at times overtly, e.g., T group) adjectives and adverbs to the individual and to the behavior. For instance, he watches an athlete run and describes the person as a fast or slow runner. From such observations and words arise the concept of "speed," which relates the distance the man has run to the time required. Speed is measurable and the concept is convenient for purposes of communication.

Concepts used by psychologists also arise in part from their assumptions about the basic organization of human nature; in part from methods and procedures, in part from the social setting; and in part from the language, thought habits, and other personal idiosyncrasies of the scientist. The basic concepts of some personality theories are related to the clinical or occupational context and operations in which their originators were involved. Similarly, the concepts of some learning theories are related to the animal laboratories in which the psychologists work. The concepts of the differential psychologists are closely tied to empirical research. These concepts should lead to a mature theory if one accepts the criterion stated by R. B. Cattell (1959, p. 257):

> The maturity of theoretical developments may be tested by two touchstones. First, a scientific system is generally more mature when its concepts arise from specially developed operations and techniques other than those available to everyday observation and to the layman. Secondly, theory is more mature if we can point to ensuing predictive and controlling powers which are real enough to have led to potent technologies, recognizable in specially developed social institutions.

In 1931, G. W. Allport published one of the earliest theoretical analyses of traits of personality (as contrasted with aptitudes or capacities of personalities of earlier days). He proposed that traits had more than nominal existence, that they were more generalized than habits, that they were dynamic, that they could be established empirically, that they were only relatively independent from one another, that they were different from moral or social judgments, and that they could be viewed in terms of other traits within the individual or in terms of distributions of single traits within the population. About the same time, he was coauthor of the "Allport-Vernon Study of Values," an early and relatively sophisticated attempt to assess personality traits. A few years later (1936) he published a monograph identifying thousands of trait names and labels used in describing personality and behavior.

In 1966, in a cogent and interesting paper labeled "Traits Revisited," Allport reviewed the use of the concept of traits in personality theory, examined the criticisms that have been made of this concept, and labeled his epistemological position as *heuristic realism*. He said:

> Heuristic realism, as applied to our problem, holds that the person who confronts us possesses inside his skin generalized action tendencies (or traits) and that it is our job scientifically to discover what they are. Any form of realism assumes the existence of an external structure ("out there") regardless of our shortcomings in comprehending it. Since traits, like all intervening variables, are never directly observed but only inferred, we must expect difficulties and errors in the process of discovering their nature. (p. 3)

He concludes his paper with this paragraph:

> As a safeguard I propose the restraints of "heuristic realism" which accepts the common-sense assumption that persons are real beings, that each has a real neuropsychic organization, and that our job is to comprehend this organization as well as we can. At the same time our profession uniquely demands that we go beyond common-sense data and either establish their validity or else—more frequently—correct their errors. To do so requires that we be guided by theory in selecting our trait slices for study, that we employ rationally relevant methods, and be strictly bound by empirical verification. In the end we return to fit our findings to an improved view of the person. Along the way we regard him as an objectively real being whose tendencies we can succeed in knowing at least in part beyond the level of unaided common-sense. In some respects this recommended procedure resembles what Cronbach and Meehl (1955) call "construct validation," with perhaps a dash more stress on external validation.
>
> I have also learned that while the major foci of organization in a life may be few in number, the network of organization, which includes both minor and contradictory tendencies, is still elusively complex. (pp. 8-9)

Concepts of traits and factors are useful to psychologists who approach personality (including aptitudes) either analytically or synthetically. In both instances the psychologist conceives of behavior in terms of both small, relatively simple behavioral units and patterns or combinations of these units. The analytically-minded psychologist observes the behavioral employees. Still later, he tries to break these into their component units. On the other hand, the synthetically-minded psychologist starts with the behavioral units and looks for the patterns they form. Both are dealing with behavioral bundles of varying size and complexity.

Adaptations of the Theory

The trait-factor theory of counseling originated historically in adaptations of laboratory exercises; later, theories were applied to the selection of employees. Still later, the assignment of World War I army recruits to army tasks and occupations employed this methodology of classification. The army used psychological tests which had been perfected in America under the leadership of Cattell, Münsterberg, Thorndike, Otis, and others. Dvorak much later developed occupational ability patterns for use in the U. S. Employment Service (Dvorak, 1956). Similar developments occurred in the British Employment Service. The basic logic and methodology of matching the requirements of work with measured aptitudes of men, in terms of work potential, proved to be adaptable as an underpinning technology for counseling individuals in regard to some aspects of their lives including cognitive, noncognitive behavior, and goal-oriented behavior. The method is based upon comparing an individual with external reference norms or validity groups of known individuals.

One of the adaptations of the trait-factor methodology was the use of personality tests as is illustrated by the Minnesota Multiphasic Inventory. The tests were standardized first on inmates in psychiatric hospitals and "normal" nonhospitalized adults and adolescents. Later, other external criterion (reference) groups of known traits, including those diagnosed by psychiatric and clinical psychologists, were characterized by the categories of therapy (Welsh & Dahlstrom, 1956). This personality test has been used to identify differences in categories of student leaders: fraternal, religious, political, and editorial (Williamson & Hoyt, 1952).

As in the case of matching methodology with adults and later with adolescents, one of the essential characteristics of the trait-factor-theory was its use of external criteria against which to check or compare or validate the tested (measured) characteristics of an individual being counseled or considered for employment. That is, measures and judgments of the qualifications (Weiss, Davis, England, & Lofquist, 1967) of an individual in counseling before choice of work or of vocation necessitates an external criterion group of individuals of known characteristics. For example, when one examines the vocational interests test formulated by E. K. Strong, Jr., one sees that the scores yielded by this instrument provide a comparison of an individual (before he engages in work) with a known criterion group classified in terms of a given vocation practiced. As stated above, a similar use of external criterion groups was used in the case of the Multiphasic so that one may read the score to mean that an individual on an "elevated" score answers the questions and therefore resembles, in these respects, the criterion group of individuals as diagnosed by psychiatric methods.

Value Commitments

In a later section I will discuss value commitments as sources of behavior. Here I note that a number of instruments have been developed in the past several decades which seek to identify an individual's general value commitments. Examples are the Allport-Vernon Test (Allport, Vernon, & Lindzey, 1960) and the Pace and Stern instruments (Pace, 1963; Stern, 1958). The latter are designed to identify students' perceptions of the values inherent in the academic institution as the students experience and observe them. In the case of these types of personality tests of values, external criterion groups for validation are less readily identified in our sociological organization of American culture. That is, certain value commitments of criterion groups do not stand out and are not easily identified, as is the case of one's occupation. Nevertheless, the contribution of the trait-factor-logic and methodology is clearly evident. There is an attempt to identify not only an individual's internal appraisal of himself but also some externalization (reference or comparison) of these observations so that they may be dealt with psychometrically and clinically in the counseling relationship.

At the present time this method is the best we can do. However, many factors that are not fully identified are involved in the individual's utilization of his aptitude or predicted success or failure and in the actual obtained results as judged by the external criterion of the employer or by a teacher's examination.

Without such test instruments (imperfect as they are), we would be at a loss to help the individual clarify his chances for success or failure before he attempted tasks of a classroom or of an occupation. This aspect of the trait-factor theory has been a substantial contribution, making counseling more than guesswork. The individual is able to identify his aspirations and judge whether he possesses the means to apply successfully his aptitudes and aspirations to a given task. As I have said elsewhere (Williamson, 1965), the deficiency of the method was that it made certain naïve assumptions about the factor of motivations (affect) of the individual in the utilization of his aptitudes in the task confronting him. Because of the recent fusing of certain aspects of psychotherapy (Phillips, 1968; Sanderson, 1954), with a more sophisticated understanding and appraisal of motivational factors, and vocational counseling based upon trait-factor analysis, we are coming closer to an approximation of an adequate technological foundation of counseling.

For me, still another example of adaptability and relevance of the trait-factor logic and methodology is to be found in that little-discussed topic which I prefer to call disciplinary counseling (Parker & Gometz, 1968; Williamson & Foley, 1949). Discipline can be viewed as a forced-choice type of decision making in which the individual's value commitments, or the objectives of his misconduct or misbehavior, provide a hazy decision-making choice which might have become so habituated as a life style that the individual no longer is able to trace out its logic or its psychology (Biggs, 1968; Williamson, 1968; Boren, 1968). All he knows is that he finds himself in trouble with organized society and organized institutions such as the school (criterion or reference groups) if he behaves one way rather than another. Unhappily, such individuals spend so much time resenting and resisting conformity to the external criteria of behavior in the form of rules and regulations that they have little time and almost no desire to understand themselves. More importantly, these individuals do not realize the price that they are paying when they choose to behave in a manner which leads them into conflict with organized society.

In this case, as in the above examples, there is evidence of societal or local institutional external criteria, confused, conflicting, and complex though they be. These criteria together with the fact that enforced regulations have historical roots are usually little appreciated and understood by the individual who rejects them and tries to go alone (autonomy), while wishing to retain his privileges of membership in organized society. The counselor can usually aid the client to see that these external criteria imposed by group membership (conformity to group norms) are a price that may be worth paying so that he can achieve his objectives, or his value commitments, and still avoid open conflict. Perhaps then he may go through the rational process of internalizing these external forms of control so that he approximates self-regulation avoiding open conflict with the group. For me, the logic and the methodology are adaptations of the trait-factor theory originally forged in employment practices and in vocational counseling. The relevancy of this theory to value commitments will be clear in a later section.

Other Forms of Behavior

Concepts of motor and manual behavior have not been as systematically organized as cognitive behavior; but a considerable amount of research, extending back to that of the Minnesota Employment Stabilization Research Institute (Paterson & Darley, 1936), has proved useful to counselors. The testing program of the United States Employment Office, the General Aptitude Test Battery, provides the most useful source of information (Dvorak, 1956).

The work of Thurstone (1931), Strong (1943), and Guilford (1954) provide evidence concerning useful concepts and constructs related to vocational interests. Many interest inventories now used by counselors are to some extent based on this research; and interests can be conceived in terms of factors with labels such as science, theory, mechanical, verbal-linguistic, social service and welfare, salesmanship, and business. In an extensive analysis of interest, Guilford, et al., (1954) identified twenty-eight interpretable factors, six of which he regarded as definitely directed toward vocational stereotypes or occupational classes. Some of the remaining interest factors had vocational implications of a broad nature. They concluded that

> The structure of the domain of interests, therefore, seems to include a limited number of vocationally oriented variables superimposed upon or differentiated from a broader base of general interest variables that have nonvocational implications as well. (p. 36)

Guilford recognized the correspondence between scoring categories of current interest inventories and interest factors but emphasized the need for greater correspondence. The Minnesota Vocational Interest Inventory and the 1969 Revised Strong Vocational Interest Inventory incorporate in their structures the concept of interest factors.

The most extensive analysis of personality and temperament has been reported by R. Cattell and Warburton (1967), whose work suggests that somewhat the same concepts can be applied usefully regardless of the methods used in observing behavior that reflects personality characteristics. Ratings of persons by others, objective tests, and personality inventory scores provide data that fit into a consistent system of personality concepts. They describe 412 different tests which provide 2,366 scores, and present the factor loadings of each score for which these are available. Counseling use of the Cattell Personality Inventories has been limited by the rather esoteric vocabulary and limited external validation used in identifying and labeling concepts.

Many personality inventories used in counseling are based on empirical standardization construction as opposed to factor analytic construction. A recent comparison by Crewe (1967) suggests that with the same pool of inventory items, factor analytic scales, and empirically developed scales tend to provide the counselor with essentially the same information.

External Criteria Are Relevant in Evaluating Many Forms of Behavior

The improvement of one's self in one's work, for example, is a desirable product of counseling. But to this criterion of self-improvement I would add that the counselor should find ways of helping the individual to become aware of other possible selves, including vocations. This leads to his moral right to choose which self he wishes to become, provided of course that he understands the consequences (prices) that he must pay for his choice; and the rewards and satisfactions he may anticipate. I do not see these two outcomes of counseling as being in opposition, although there may be some therapeutic counselors who feel that the counselors should not suggest anything "new" to the individual. To me this is nonsense, because in education we are all in the business of helping to modify each other's becoming the best of possible selves; that is, aspiring to become that kind of an individual which I choose to characterize as humane and happily productive.

This brings me to my next point, that the individual is not the only criterion (autonomy à la Rousseau) of the "good life." Indeed, there are external criteria of the good life which sometimes are improvements over the individual's aspirations. Frequently a change of view toward one's possible selves occurs during the growing-up process; frequently it is the result of an injury, a new experience, a trauma such as grief, or some other startling experience (including some forms of discipline!) which causes the individual to stand off and look at himself. Then he sees whether or not he has become (or is striving to become) the best of all possible selves. Again, the qualifying adjective "best" (*areté* excellence) refers to the fact of life that no one "is an island unto himself" and that we interpenetrate and influence each other. If this were not so, then the schools and the home life would be a mockery, and disorganized society as a whole would be an anarchy. The fact that we will continue to argue about what are the criteria of the good life, as externally judged by ourselves and others, does not negate the assumption that there *are* external criteria. In all our activities we are evaluated by someone else, which means that someone else's criteria of the good life are applied to us. According to that person's criteria we may be found to be short of the possible or adequate. This is as true of social behavior and morality as it is of one's vocation.

I am not arguing against the validity and relevancy of internal criteria which the individual sets for himself (including the criterion of vocation choice and other sources of satisfactions). However, I am saying that the individual grows up with a conception of what he wants to become which is modified, often as a result of initially modeling himself after an adult whom he admires. The individual is, without doubt, the product of the influence of many external criteria; he does not grow without reference to others' perception and evaluation of him. This type of reasoning leads me to reject the concept of human development characterized by that phrase, "Hands off— let the bud unfold." I am certainly in favor of letting the bud unfold in all its richness, although I find many buds to be rather lean and stunted (deprived) when they are uninfluenced by the enrichment which comes from some forms of external forces. What we are trying to do in counseling, vocational as well as other forms, is to help the individual select from among his internal impulses and aspirations, and also those perceived in others or in the history of the human race, which ones he wishes to internalize and make his own. In this sense the external become the internalized aspirations. But the bud does not unfold without reference to, or uninfluenced by, the external ecological conditions.

One of the forms of modern counseling in the schools has evolved as a dyadic relationship between an older person and a younger one who is in the process of maturing through vocation and other forms of living. The older person sometimes is perceived and accepted, at least temporarily, as a role model of what the individual wishes to become. But at other times he (the elder) is rejected just as parents (and the Establishment) are sometimes rejected as role models. Nevertheless, it is characteristic of human development in our Western culture that the individual possesses *not* the inalienable right to become whatever he wishes to become but the option of becoming whatever he wishes to become *in awareness of alternative roles (and prices),* that is, an awareness of an anticipated variety of adult objectives as perceived during childhood and adolescence.

Unfortunately, the concept of permissiveness, that is, "letting the bud unfold as it wishes," or choosing whatever vocation the unaided individual desires, is often perceived by the growing individual at various stages of life as being thwarted and restricted by others, sometimes by his own peers and sometimes by an older person or even by counselors. All these influencing individuals are referred to as "authority figures," or often even perceived as "authoritarian" figures, threatening and restricting the individual's becoming what he wishes to become. This is an unhappy and unfortunate perception because many of the other perceived selves do not wish to dominate the individual but merely to open him to new vistas or possibilities of choice of role. To be sure, there are indeed many authoritarian adult role figures, but sometimes they are not quite as repressive as those to be found among one's peers, who sometimes serve as thwarting external influences. And I think it is one of the unsolved problems of all types of counseling to aid the individual student to modify through direct influence and experiencing these perceived authoritarian figures so that they will be perceived as benign figures.

While all counselors seek not to be perceived as authoritarian or even as authority figures, they are never certain how they will be perceived by the student being counseled. I have written elsewhere about power, authority, and the counseling relationship in terms of this uncontrolled perception (Williamson, 1968). Perhaps this is one of the reasons why so many counselors shy away from discipline, which is of course at the heart of authority, but not as authoritarianism, as is foolishly and simple-mindedly assumed by some counselors and counselor educators. It is largely an unsolved problem. it seems to me, how we will create the perception that counselors are friendly authorities, being older and therefore in the authority relationship of possessing professional knowledge of possible use to the student. Just separating ourselves from school authorities in the school, who are unfortunately often perceived as using authority in an authoritarian manner, does not satisfy me as being necessarily the only, or the most effective, way of creating a kind of perception and acceptance of counselors that we seek to maintain to achieve our desired results. I suggest that this is an unsolved problem, and that we had better face it frankly rather than run away from authority to the Shangri-la of the supposed authorityless office of the vocational or therapist counselor.

Another aspect of all forms of counseling theory which concerns me is that counseling should be an initiating stage directed toward self-managed development, although *not* toward complete autonomy which I think is less than full humaneness. That is, I believe that the fullness of human development is achieved through interrelationship with other individuals. Unfortunately we may have created the expectation on the part of many of our students that we alone are "miracle" men or women and that we can tell them what to become, vocationally and in other dimensions, in one easy stage and easy lesson. Actually, what we are doing is helping the individual to *initiate* a style of work and living which, hopefully, will continue the rest of his life so that he will become self-counseling to a certain degree, particularly since obsolescence of work, morals, and mores will force him to make many changes in his styles of living (*Daedalus,* Summer 1967). But the self-counseling student must perceive his own deficiencies as a person and therefore recognize that he needs help which he has learned is to be exploited through the counselor's efforts. Moreover, he has learned some of the methods of counseling such as the search for objectivity, for self-understanding, and for alternative ways of the good life. This is the reason that, for me, counseling is the initial stage of a long continuing process of human development; hopefully, the individual will participate by helping and wanting to become *all* that he can become.

With this form of self-management continuing throughout life, the counselor must introduce the individual student to the concept that he will change and that his work requirements as well as societal demands on him will change. Perception and anticipation of change are areas of counseling that essentially we have left untilled. Planned change or controlled change that can be initiated by the individual in anticipation—years ahead, perhaps—is my notion of a maturing process of interrupted stages of development of a life. Life does not stretch out into the future as more of the same. There are interruptions of various sorts—automobile accidents, wars, obsolescence of tools and skills, and changes in public demands, mores, morals, and so on. We have left largely untouched how to introduce a youth to anticipate and welcome change in work and living rather than to think of life as being one continuing evolvement of more of the same. We do not want to frighten the individual who rigidly or naïvely expects a life of certainty, but we certainly want him to face the reality that he will change and so will his society. However, we do not yet know how to introduce this concept of change into the counseling relationship.

The lack of anticipation of change by our clientele is the handicap that we have created for ourselves by organizing and creating expectation that counseling is available to deal with problem crises of initial choice of career objective or with something "gone wrong" with one's life. It is as though we sold ourselves as a "fix-it-up" (repair) type of profession. And once an individual has fixed himself up or been fixed up, then counseling is thought to be completed until the next crisis occurs. So much of the literature of counseling is built around this concept that one must rail against it. In actual fact, life does proceed from crisis to crisis or problem to problem and from anxiety to anxiety. But there are underlying developmental stages which call for recounseling within self-management counseling, a learned process applied to self which goes on continuously. It is as though there were a curve of upward development, which is the life span and life development of a human being, with little jagged peaks and valleys which indicate deviations from the dominant upward curve. We should center our attention and effort, and that of the students, upon the long-range developmental upward curve and not exclusively upon temporary but often painful and immediate peaks and valleys of a minor sort.

These are a summarization of my conceptions of the role of counseling in human development. It should be clear why I reject letting the bud unfold itself without regard to ecology or environmental influence, and why I find it difficult to believe that the bud has within itself all the resources necessary to become a full human being characterized by humaneness. We are an interdependent society, or, to put it another way, we are interdependent individuals even though our relationships with others often become quite impersonal or depersonalized with a perceived subordination of the individual.

Role Expectancies as Factors In Choices

One peculiar requirement of society, school, or vocation has often been referred to as "role expectancy." No such data are included in the counselor's repertoire except that one may assume that the "criterion" group of "successful" persons has perceived and attained the expected "standards of performance" (roles). Many experimentalists and authors have made different references to this elusive variable, and perhaps it is integral to our discussion of value commitments as sources of behavior or as reference groups.

Perhaps Festinger (1954) had in mind goal-directed motivation as a source of one's evaluation of one's behavior; he used the term "social comparison."

In a study of one occupation (the school superintendent), Gross, Mason, and McEachern (1958) refer to the subject's behavior with reference to role expectation as he perceives it.

Merton (1957) uses the term self-assessment with other persons with whom the subject may or may not have direct contact.

Feldman and Newcomb (1969, Vol. I) report an elaborate research project in which the Allport-Vernon-Lindzey Test was used with different college populations for more than a decade to discover differences among the groups and within the groups (as reference groups). They were using the value inventory to determine the impact of the college years (experiences) upon changes or persistence of role expectancies or reference groups as value commitments of the individual student. Religious commitments declined, but aesthetic sophistication increased from freshmen to seniors. There was an increased and intensive commitment to tribalism or provincialism of "privatism" (family and work associates) during the college years. One recalls the political doctrine of isolationism that erupted after World War I. What are the implications for counselors as students adopt such limited reference groups to determine their role expectancy?

I assert that in future years counselors may need to assist students to orient themselves to unperceived but clearly anticipated role expectancy, many of which may not be clearly understood or accepted until the student experiences the school roles directly, or in the case of a worker in a vocation, role expectancies may be defined and redefined from time to time in the work experience. But what of roles beyond family and vocation? Is not the student or client to become a participatory citizen in our republic, à la Jefferson?

Value Commitments as Sources of Behavior

In a previous section I discussed the trait-factor theory of counseling as it originated and developed in relationship to the identification of work capabilities prior to (education) job training and employment. But man consists not of aptitudes alone or even of measured work interests; his life adjustments and satisfactions also affect the behavior and strivings arising from his value commitment, or internalized (subjective?) criteria of what he considers to be the "good life." His behavior arises out of matters he considers to be important as forces in determining his style of living, his daily behavior, and his aspirations which serve to "pull" (*teleology*) him into the future. Field refers to this factor as "progress in goal directed activity" and as the "pleasure of successful pursuit" (Field, 1967). Counseling therefore, at least within the context of school, college, and societal missions, can be viewed as one possible means of cultivating the individual's striving for and understanding of alternative value commitments in the good life preparatory to rational choice of personal goals.

This is not indoctrination or instruction in what is the "right" value commitment. but rather it is a rational process of helping each individual to identify the alternative ways of living (reference norms) which are open to him. In this sense, counselors are special agents of possible change in the individual's progressively chosen goals in life. Counselors who work in the school setting are as dedicated as the school is to aiding students to develop with due regard for certain, often conflicting but always complex, motions of what the good life consists of (in a multiplicity of forms for different individuals). A mature individual learns to live reasonably happily within culture conflicts and to avoid warfare with organized society's value hierarchies and restraints upon his freedom of choice.

In the absence of objective data about life commitments, counselors must infer an individual's values from behavior manifestations, observed or heard within and outside the interview.

As I indicated earlier, in at least one instance, some objective indications about chosen values are indicated in the case of juvenile delinquents who persist in clinging to antisocial (antinorm) impulses and attitudes. Monachesi and Hathaway (1963) reported that some of the MMPI scales of ninth grade boys and girls were related to ratings of delinquency proneness. Perhaps more data on this type of research will be available in the future for counselors' use as indicators of values which the student considers as relevant for him. At the present time, a counselor would be less than effective and perceptive if he neglected to give consideration to such traces or indicators as are currently available to him.

If value commitments as defined by the philosopher Whitehead are "matters of importance," then they undoubtedly, in complicated ways, serve as sources of behavior. And in the absence of other indicators, one may seek to read backward from observable behavior to infer the values in many instances. However, more research and clinical observations of a hardheaded sort are needed as contrasted with the simple-minded use of the printed data on any instrument as though the data were definitive and adequate for categorizing individuals. In this connection, I recall the early days when I was first reading abnormal psychology. We had learned enough about Freudian psychology to use glibly the term "inferiority complex," as though it were an already validated, externalized category of a criterion group of known characteristic. And in the simple-minded way that most of us used to categorize persons with a label such as that one, we seemed to think that we had disposed of the case, diagnostically and even therapeutically, by casting the individual into a category bin as though we were sorting potatoes of different sizes and textures.

To return to my main point, let me illustrate what I mean by alternative forms of values of the good life by stating a few that are clearly evident in our own culture. Let me stress again that no individual is forced (for a price!) to choose any one of these forms of the good life, but at least a counselor, even sometimes by the very way he relates to the student in an educational setting, is perceived as the role model, among others, in explicating and demonstrating some of these forms of good life.

It seems evident to me that counseling, at least that within education, is grounded not only on tested (measured) aptitudes and interests but also on a complex of internalized values. One of the principal values consists of efforts to aid each student to achieve the good life, which is characterized, among other dimensions, as humane. It is explicated within counseling, when appropriate to the student, in stages of development as the individual pursues his adopted style of living. I mention five stages merely for illustration since there are many other values enjoyed in the pursuit of the good life.

First, every teacher and certainly every counselor hopes that every student will seek that form of maturity which is characterized by *openness to change.* This is particularly relevant with respect to the accelerated tempo of change in our American culture today. Each individual must learn to anticipate and manage changes within himself and to cope with demands which society and his vocation make of him. Indeed, for example, with respect to the problem of vocation we are told that in the future decades every individual must expect to change his type of work several times in his occupational career. Counselors thus face problems of how to introduce to a student at an early age, before the individual has emotionally fixated upon one kind of work, this concept of anticipated and controlled change. This must be accomplished sometimes without reference to his own capabilities to receive training and to succeed in that type of work.

Second, clearly the school in our tradition, cultivated from ancient Greece through Rome, is dedicated to teaching *thoughtfulness* (rationality) as a style of living. That is, we try in counseling to aid the individual to use his rational capacities in seeking to understand and to formulate evaluative judgments about the complex, unsolved issues of our urban culture. For example, racial discrimination and cultural deprivation are only two currently demanding solutions. The counseling relationship is indeed an experience in rational thinking about oneself in relationship to others and to one's society.

Third, schools in Western culture are dedicated to teaching every individual that he should develop *compassion* for those less fortunate, for example, those of the minority groups, the culturally and economically deprived, and the physically and mentally handicapped. Ours is a culture, at least partially, dedicated to help those who have not attained the full happiness and satisfaction which we consider in our moral commitments to be attainable and necessary in the great society. To make the point relevant to counseling, for example, the counselor will be performing a civilizing service if he introduces the client at the point of choosing a business career to John Dewey's concept that everyone should expect to do "some social good." The contemporary businessman, especially those employed within corporations, is soon inducted into the tribal ritual of adopting a favorite charity and joining a "service" organization which contributes to the betterment of the lot of the needy and deprived.

Fourth, counselors have a rich opportunity in education to help the individual learn *respect* as well as *understanding* of other cultures as alternative forms of the good life (see *privatism*). Because of our modern intercontinental communication, business, and industrial systems, class distinctions and barriers are gradually being eroded to replace the concept of a monolithic (tribalism) form of the good life, a form long linked with Western religion and morality.

Fifth, clearly as a result of education and counseling within education, an individual student should be committed to some self-chosen *social or moral cause or value* which serves as a source of and a guideline for his living. And the force of counseling within education should be to reduce the number of socially noninvolved individuals who are selfishly committed only to their own development (again see *privatism*). The trait-factor theory of counseling, like other theories, is geared to the Western concept of *freedom of choice*. This freedom of choice applies to these and many other values, as a modern societal theory for the full utilization of available manpower (D. G. Paterson in Wolfle, 1969) both with regard to personal development and with regard to the evolvement of organized society. Indeed, today we are slowly and painstakingly reconstructing Western culture so that minority groups and other neglected ones may have freedom of choice long denied to their ancestors, even within "civilized" Western culture.

Subjective (internal) versus Objective (external) Data

In our efforts to measure, or at least identify, internalized value commitments as sources of motivated behavior, that is, motivated and striving to achieve certain desired end goals or stages of development (the ancient concept of *teleology*), we are in effect seeking to objectify, or to quantify, the subjective data of human experience which each individual perceives in a highly individualized manner.

Perhaps this urge to quantify all experiences is one of the most clear cut differences between the psychological tradition and experimental methodologies of Münsterberg, for example, and Freudian therapy which also deals with subjective experiences but usually in a nonquantitative approach and methodology. We all hold that all human experience is subjective as perceived by each individual. But in the last century the tradition in Western psychology of individual differences and educational and industrial placement has been to objectify subjective experience in the sense of registering it on some kind of "meter," or psychological test, so that it may be dealt with not only as an individual datum, but also through scientific ways of manipulating quantified data.

We can perhaps understand the trait-factor theory and methodology of counseling in terms of this age-old problem of attempting to reconcile subjective and objective data or experience of each individual. A case in point is the debate between advocates of the Rorschach versus the MMPI as *adequate* descriptions of an individual's personality. Another illustration of this opposition of quantified data versus qualitative reports is the contrast between E. K. Strong Jr.'s measured interests and Kitson's method of self-analysis and self report of occupational interests.

We can understand the complexity of the counselor's problems and therefore be more enlightened about our use of different theories of counseling, and their supporting methodologies, if we consider the advantages and disadvantages of objectification of human experience in contrast with other methods of dealing with subjective experience. Let me cite four advantages of quantification:

First, since the writing of Bacon's *Novum Organum*, the mathematical analysis of objective and observable data has been characteristic of the scientific method as applied to different kinds of human experiences in Western civilization. Such mathematical analyses are not possible if one deals only with subjectively experienced data without attempts of objectification as introduced first by Bacon and then by German psychologists a century ago.

Second, a marked approximation of precision or accuracy in measurement or identification of experience is possible through such quantification. For example, in the use of psychological testing, test scores may be manipulated mathematically to yield a probable error of estimate which serves as a guideline or restraint on the counselor's use of those scores in his efforts to aid the client to understand himself in comparison with others and with known external criterion groups in school and vocation. This analysis is not as precise if one deals with nonquantified data.

Third, objectification of data, or quantification, makes possible a great-er degree of *clarity of communication* among different individuals, and par-ticularly among those who study scientifically such quantified data. This closer approximation to clarity is in contrast with the ambiguity of subjective-ly reported data which suffers from the lack of precision of terms descrip-tive of the data. For example, two people who are judging the "brightness" (scholastic aptitude) of a particular student will not know whether they are reporting the same type or dimension of "brightness" (intelligence) if each reports only his judgment, instead of comparing his findings with a com-monly reported objective score on the same, or comparable, test of "brightness."

Fourth, quantification of subjective experience also permits *massed data* so that one can characterize more than one individual at a time. We do not fully appreciate the historical significance of using massed data to char-acterize groups or classes rather than isolated individuals. Such description of groups of individuals is certainly less precise, and sometimes meaningless or ambiguous if qualitative or subjective descriptive categories are employed. For example, until we had available measured massed data about southern Negroes or immigrants from southern Europe, we necessar-ily employed descriptive adjectives that proved to be less precise or some-times misleading and inaccurate when compared with measured verbal apti-tudes or what was then called intelligence.

What I refer to as subjective data, in contrast with quantified or objec-tive data, is characteristic of the qualitative report of an individual who has experienced something individually and in isolation in many instances. Per-haps one of the most clear-cut illustrations of this kind of limitation is *revelation* as a source of "knowing," as reported by those who experience, in Zen Buddhism for example, what is referred to as "satori," a mystical, highly individualized report of "insight" into the meaning of the universe. The American psychologist William James in his book *Varieties of Religious Experience* included a chapter on the *mystic,* whose individualized expe-rience yields "private" knowledge that is not communicable to anyone else because he is unable to describe to others his experiences in words which possess universal meaning among other individuals.

Quantification or measurement, when appropriate and possible, does yield closer approximation in the precision of universal meaning. In this connection, a modern therapist's concept of insight, with regard to one's self, seems to have some similarity to the revelation reported by the mystics and is, therefore, sometimes difficult to communicate from the experiencing individual to the therapist.

But we must recognize that in objectifying and quantifying data descrip-tive of the experience of an individual alone, or in masses, we may have

unknowingly discarded or not fully utilized some of the subtle individualized subjective experiences that may have valid relevancy to "knowing" an
individual. This poses a problem that is very prominent in the experience
and operations of a counselor as he listens and tries to perceive and understand his client's internal frame of reference, his subjective experience with
all its complexity of conflict, contradictions, and even vagaries. Each counselor must continuously make up his own mind, based upon tested and
explicit assumptions, about whether the so-called objective data available
about a client are the *only* (or most relevant available) data that yield some
or an adequate understanding of the individual client or whether he, the
counselor, needs to seek some degree of insight into uncommunicated data,
even data not as mathematically precise as are yielded by the use of psychometric instruments such as psychological tests.

To a very substantial extent the trait-factor theory underlying counseling is based upon the assumption that significant data, although not necessarily *all* the relevant data, are yielded by objective instruments and *verified
case history studies* as well as reported observations by other counselors,
teachers, parents, and associates. (The latter often of unknown reliability
and validity!) Without a great deal of sophisticated research yet to be done
on the strengths and limitations of using subjectively reported data versus
quantified data, a counselor needs to supplement one kind of data with the
other (in awareness of the limitations of each) in order to make more
certain that the counselor is identifying the "true" picture or a "true" understanding of the individual with all his complex motivations and experiences. This is to argue that counselors should not blindly and passionately
adopt one category of theory, each with its peculiar type of supporting data,
as being exclusively advantageous over another in our present state of
limited knowledge.

Still another fact relevant to counseling in the use of external criteria,
such as work units, quality of product of effort, reported judgments of
excellence, and the like, is that we are able to discover that the categories
into which we classify individuals by race, color, sex, political commitment,
personality types, and the like, are not discrete but are rather continuous,
quantitatively, even with respect to what we loosely call qualitative data.
Even the category "student" is not homogeneous but yields a large standard
deviation of every measured characteristic. And, indeed, we can observe
that such an experience as perceived color is quantifiable. For example,
every student of elementary physics knows that the subjective (individualized) experience which we call color has long since been scientifically reduced to quantified continuous data in terms of molecular vibrations and
when one passes from the subjective experience of red to green, one has

traversed not only from one qualitative category of experience to a second, but also over a section or band of a range of continuous vibrations.

Similarly, we need to remind ourselves that the use of objective data in classifying and understanding persons highlights (etches) the individuality of each client, who does not lose his uniqueness, even in the process of computerized mass data. In the history of quantified measurement of individuality, this old problem of the individual versus the group emerges once more for argumentation and debate as though it were an either-or proposition, a one or the other. But the adequate counselor is trained to perceive the uniqueness of each individual even *within* the context of comparisons with other individuals or within massed data. Indeed, he perceives a heightening of individuality by comparison with other individuals or with the entire group or class of which this client is a member.

Using Objective Data to Predict an Individual's Criterion Standing

The crucial problem of predicting an external criterion is complex, and every counselor should adjust his expectations with regard to the accuracy of his efforts to identify the individual's potentiality to meet the requirements of external criteria in work and school, in interpersonal relationships, and in personal adjustments within society. For the psychologically trained and oriented counselor any percentage of increase in accuracy of prediction is an improvement over chance or "guesses" or even expectations, by students, parents, or prospective employers. But 100 percent accuracy of prediction is not yet attainable. This evaluative conclusion is at variance with the earlier criticisms, for example, by Brewer of Münsterberg's aptitude testing. Brewer called the tests "invalid" (Brewer, 1942); and by invalid apparently he meant less than fully accurate. But an experimentally trained counselor knows that whatever accuracy we have attained today is better than what we have had in the past, and that is the best we can do at present, even after centuries of research. Contrary to followers of Kitson, we do not return to self-analysis just because we have not achieved 100 percent accuracy (Kitson, 1931). We, rather, continue to strive to improve accuracy through patient, painstaking, hardheaded research, which will be illustrated by means of the prediction tables included in this chapter.

Counseling Use of Data Predicting External Criteria

The matching of work requirements and school requirements with the identified capabilities, aspirations, or value commitments of an individual is not a mere matching process of mechanical computer style. Rather, counseling

consists of assisting the individual to identify his full capacities and potentialities and to utilize them in choosing and in preparing for a mature adult
life in which his internal satisfactions are as important as external criterion
of work production or other requirements for meeting the demands of the
job or of the school or of social adjustments.

The complexity of this type of counseling is illustrated by the following
case study:

Eloise

Eloise came to her school counselor saying she thought she would like to
attend either Moorhead State College or Carleton. She and the counselor
discussed courses of study, requirements for admission, expenses, and activities,
and then Eloise raised the question of likelihood of success at each of these
colleges. To help answer this question, the counselor turned to the expectancy
tables.

Eloise had a High School Class Rank of 58 and a Minnesota Scholastic Aptitude Test (raw) score of 70 which placed her at the 99th percentile on general
college freshman norms. The counselor noted that Eloise's HSR fell in the
middle group on the HSR tables while her MSAT score placed her in the top
group. Turning to the tables for these two schools, the counselor indicated the
parts of the tables for these groups.

	D or higher average	C or higher average	B or higher average	Size of group
Carleton				
HSR 99	99	75		Less than 10
MSAT 99	99	89	24	Over 100
Moorhead				
HSR 91	91	32	2	20-50
MSAT 99	99	94	48	50-100

He explained to Eloise that the numbers indicated the chances in 100 that she
would earn a grade point average of at least D, C, and B, respectively.

In helping Eloise understand these figures the counselor pointed out that the
HSR figures for Carleton are based on less than 10 people and might not be a
very good indication of her likelihood of success. The counselor showed Eloise
that according to the HSR part of the Moorhead table her chances of being at
least a "C" average student were not high (32 out of 100). The counselor and
Eloise knew that illness had kept her from earning high grades in high school.
The illness that had caused her to miss so much school was over and she was
making excellent grades during her senior year. The counselor suggested that
they consider the figures from the MSAT tables. The predictions here were

that Eloise would be able to do at least "C" work and possibly "B" work, or better, at either college, with some indication that she might earn slightly higher grades at Moorhead.

Using the information from the tables in conjunction with other information about Eloise's goal for attending college, probable causes of her high school record, and also admission requirements, Eloise may decide she ought to look into any one of [sic] number of possible considerations, some of which may involve the use of the expectancy tables for other Minnesota colleges.

Counselors should recognize that the personal meaning of the probability figures in these tables will vary for different students. For a student who wants very much to attend a certain college, a 50-50 chance of being at least a "C" student may be encouraging. For the student who is looking for more assurance, a 50-50 chance of being at least a "B" student may be seen as too large a gamble. The decision to make application for a specific college must, of course, rest with the student whose aspirations, motivation, and willingness to assume various levels of risk will temper the probability figures.

There is nothing in these tables that can be used legitimately as a basis for informing any student that he *cannot* achieve a given grade level in any specific college nor for informing him that he *will* achieve at least at a specified level. These tables provide counselors and their students with a summary of the grade-getting experiences of previous Minnesota high school graduates who have attended Minnesota colleges. That such information can be misunderstood or misinterpreted cannot be too strongly emphasized.

The person in the school who works with students about post-high school plans in a professional manner will study these tables until he understands both the value of the information provided and its limitations. The person who cannot find or take time for such study of these tables should refrain from their use. (Research Bulletin, University of Minnesota, Student Counseling Bureau, 1963.)

The following statistical tables are further illustrations of the counselor's use of probability tables, based on expectancy of success in school grades, using the records of actual grades obtained by students previously enrolled in the indicated schools. In Table 4-1 (Jex, 1966) the predictive data are available for all colleges and technical institutes in the state of Utah. The table may be entered in terms of the rank in high school class of a given student being counseled, and the general probability is indicated for the achievement of a given grade point average.

Table 4-2 is a similar probability expectancy table derived from the College Entrance Examination Board (part scores) combined with high school grades for students in the Georgia Institute of Technology (Berdie, et al., 1963).

TABLE 4-1

Predicted Freshman Grade Point Averages for Students from Three Different Levels of High School Performance

Curriculum Predicted	Predicted GPA for:			
	Student at 15th %ile rank	Average High School Student	Student at 85th %ile rank	Standard Error of Estimate
Brigham Young University (Overall)	1.31	1.95	2.59	.60
University of Utah (Overall)	1.11	1.80	2.49	.63
Utah State University (Overall)	1.37	2.02	2.67	.60
College of Eastern Utah (Academic Only)	1.77	2.31	2.85	.69
College of Southern Utah (Overall)	1.77	2.41	3.04	.61
Dixie College (Overall)	1.77	2.35	2.93	.66
Snow College (Overall)	1.59	2.20	2.81	.61
Westminster College (Overall)	1.60	2.16	2.71	.55
Weber State College (Overall)	1.69	2.28	2.86	.62
Weber State College (Nursing)	2.06	2.37	2.68	.45
Weber State College (Technological)	1.69	2.32	2.94	.73
Weber State College (Trades)	2.29	2.99	3.69	.74
*L.D.S. Business College (Overall Business)	2.02	2.61	3.21	.57
Stevens Henager College (Overall Business)	1.89	2.48	3.07	.61
S.L. Trade Tech. Inst. (Business Practice)	2.22	3.01	3.80	.57
S.L. Trade Tech. Inst. (Practical Nursing)	2.37	2.97	3.57	.56
S.L. Trade Tech. Inst. (Technological)	2.28	2.89	3.50	.80
S.L. Trade Tech. Inst. (Trades)	2.22	2.92	3.60	.64
Utah Trade Tech. Inst. (Bus. & Sec. Science)	2.33	2.95	3.57	.51
Utah Trade Tech. Inst. (Practical Nursing)	1.89	2.61	3.34	.53
Utah Trade Tech. Inst. (Technological)	2.42	3.11	3.80	.59
Utah Trade Tech. Inst. (Trades)	2.48	3.31	4.15	.60

*Students must have grade-point average of at least 2.50 for graduation.
SOURCE: Jex, F. B., *Predicting Academic Success beyond High School*. Salt Lake City: Frank B. Jex, 1966, p. 13.

TABLE 4-2

Expectancy Table for Georgia Institute of Technology. Proportions of students with various index scores (based on formulas using college board scores and high school averages) who will make an average college grade of C or better, B or better, and A their first year. Sex: Male.

All Students, N = 1,744

Index V + 2 M + 33 HSA	Student Will Get Average of		
	C	B	A
3,800		.74	.09
3,600	.99	.58	.04
3,400	.96	.41	.01
3,200	.91	.25	
3,000	.81	.13	
2,800	.67	.06	
2,600	.50	.02	
2,400	.33	.01	
2,200	.19		
2,000	.09		
1,800	.04		
1,600	.01		

SOURCE: Berdie, R. F., Layton, W. L., Swanson, E. O., & Hagenah, T., *Testing in Guidance and Counseling.* New York: McGraw-Hill, 1963, p. 130.

These tables of probability may be taken (within a reasonable time period from the original date of data collection) as the most accurate, available basis on which to assist students to anticipate their own chances of the indicated success in meeting the requirements of the external criterion of teachers' grades in the named colleges. Obviously, as was noted in the case of Eloise, other case data, e.g., illness, need to be given some consideration in applying these probabilities to a given student since the tables of expectancy are derived in general from the indicated group of students, i.e., those not known to be atypical or abnormal.

Another table will indicate one of the several methods of determining the stability of test data used in comparing a given student with a criterion vocational group. Campbell (1966) reported research on the stability of measured (tested) interests over a period of thirty years. In this study the subjects tested were forty-eight bankers. The stability of interests is indicated in Table 4-3.

Employment and School Training as Substitutes for Aptitude Tests

Within the past few years the societal and political pressure for improvement in education and employment of the culturally deprived and minority groups has produced changes of major importance for counselors at all

TABLE 4-3

Test-Retest Results over Thirty Years from Forty-eight Bankers

Scales	Test M	S.D.	Retest M	S.D.	r_{xx}	5 10 15 20 25 30 35 40 45 50 55 60
Artist	16	7.2	18	10.0	52	
Psychologist	7	9.0	10●	10.3	67	
Architect	17	10.0	19	9.7	71	
Physician (Rev)	10	9.8	15★	10.3	65	
Osteopath	20	8.2	20	8.4	56	
Dentist	21	9.8	22	8.2	73	
Veterinarian	19	8.7	23★	10.8	58	
Mathematician	14	8.9	19★	10.8	74	
Physicist	8	10.2	11●	12.1	77	
Engineer	24	13.2	25	10.5	76	
Chemist	15	11.3	16	10.2	76	
Production Manager	35	8.6	32●	7.1	65	
Farmer	36	9.0	34	9.2	60	
Aviator	22	13.4	19	9.6	66	
Carpenter	22	13.2	21	10.9	72	
Printer	26	11.5	24	10.2	58	
Math Phys Sc Tchr	26	12.9	24	12.9	41	
Ind Arts Teacher	10	13.8	10	13.4	66	
Voc Agric Teacher	19	12.8	22	13.4	52	
Policeman	29	9.6	26	9.5	43	
Forest Service Man	23	12.2	19●	12.2	51	
YMCA Physical Dir	19	11.1	16	11.8	39	
Personnel Director	21	9.5	18	13.6	51	
Public Administrator	28	8.9	27	11.0	39	
YMCA Secretary	21	12.1	19	13.1	36	
Soc Sc HS Teacher	27	10.5	25	12.4	40	
City School Supt	21	10.8	20	10.7	41	
Social Worker	15	9.3	15	11.8	49	
Minister	12	13.5	12	12.7	47	
Musician (Performer)	16	10.7	18	10.4	74	
C.P.A.	28	11.7	30	10.4	69	
Senior C.P.A.	31	10.5	31	12.6	36	
Accountant	37	9.8	34	11.2	45	
Office Man	41	8.2	38●	9.6	51	
Purchasing Agent	40	9.2	37●	9.4	64	
Banker	51	9.7	50	8.8	70	
Mortician	32	8.2	35★	9.5	63	
Pharmacist	23	8.0	27★	8.2	47	
Sales Manager	33	9.1	32	9.5	62	
Real Estate Salesman	40	9.4	40	9.2	57	
Life Insurance	32	9.9	33	8.7	59	
Advertising Man	25	8.6	26	8.7	51	
Lawyer	29	8.8	32	8.5	50	
Author-Journalist	26	7.3	28	8.7	40	
President-Mfg Conc	36	10.3	38	9.8	39	
Specializ. Level	31	7.0	30	9.4	44	
Interest Maturity	52	6.0	49	8.4	27	
Occupational Level	58	7.2	58	8.3	47	
Masculin-Feminin	48	8.7	45●	7.0	53	

● Mean difference significant at .05 level.   —— = Test profile.
★ Mean difference significant at .01 level.   ---- = Retest profile.

SOURCE: Campbell, D. P., "Stability of interests within an occupation over thirty years," *J. Appl. Psychol.*, 1966, *50*, (1), Pp. 51–56.

levels of schools. Unfortunately, research data in process are not yet in print and available. Look for publications by Dr. Robert L. Kahn, Dr. Margaret S. Gordon, and Dr. Daniel E. Diamond.

For decades some psychologists and anthropologists have contended that psychological aptitude tests, particularly those used for employment or admissions to colleges, are "unfair" to culturally deprived minority individuals who are not "test broken" or skilled in test-taking. The child-rearing practices and deficient or intermittent schooling in elementary grades have ill-prepared these children to compete with middle-class students who have benefitted from the usual experiences in accredited schools. Indeed, in one study (Plaut, 1957; Clark & Plotkin, 1966) Negro students with low admissions test scores, but who were admitted experimentally, succeeded within the first year of college in overcoming their initial handicap. In some colleges it is now regular admissions policy to admit a given percentage (usually 2 or 3 percent) of black applicants who do not meet the faculty-established admission requirements on such national tests as those of the College Entrance Examination Board.

In these instances the first year's performance on course (teachers') examinations is accepted as a more accurate prediction of subsequent performance than are the regularly standardized scholastic aptitude tests.

A parallel shift has taken place in a large number of industries from the use of employment aptitude tests to the evaluation of work competence by means of systematic initial training on the job for a varying number of months. The U.S. Department of Labor relates efforts of separate industries, alone or in cooperation through the National Alliance of Businessmen, to employ "hard core" unemployed persons from the economically deprived living in slums, ghettos, or "inner cities" (*Employment Service Review,* 1968). Similar efforts are reported in the case of unemployed American Indians (*Employment Service Review,* 1967).

Wolfbein (1967) summarized a number of industrial experiences using substitutes for employing qualifying tests in the cases of hard-core unemployed adults. He reported the innovation of employing workers by means of the "utilization of nonverbal testing [and no testing at all] in selection of trainees." A second illustration is summarized in the following:

> In the Chicago Job Opportunity Through Better Skills (JOBS) project, experience with clients led to the rejection of tests in the trainee selection process in dealing with the culturally disadvantaged youth ...
> ... The only valid question that a training program should ask of so-called 'hard core' youth is whether they want training.

In another city the agency reported that:

> Supplying food to trainees who had not had breakfast, eye glasses to trainees who cannot focus on a printed page, or carfare to those who would otherwise

have to walk considerable distances to the training site turn out to be almost dramatically effective in remedying lateness, absences, and dropping out from ongoing programs.

As was the case of the admission of students to college with low admissions test scores, the justification for tryout employment of the hard-core adults is that the low level of education handicaps the applicants in the taking of paper-and-pencil aptitude tests. In some cases systematic training on the job becomes a substitute source of evaluation of competence.

Kempton (1967) reported, in satirical evaluation, the experiences of Dr. Kenneth Clark in "preparing" applicants to the Sheet Metal Workers Union, New York City, to take an aptitude test required for membership in Local 281 preparatory to employment. The nature of the preparation is not discussed, but high test scores were achieved by most of those tested. Every counselor knows that "coaching" for tests does make a great difference in the cases of many test scores. But presumably Clark was seeking to achieve for his applicants still another established fact, namely, that it is assumed in all psychological testing that those tested have had approximately equal opportunity to learn the materials being tested. Thus Clark's findings can be and should be interpreted as corroborating other evidence that many hard core unemployed persons and culturally deprived students have had unequal and deprived opportunity in comparison with those middle-class persons who experience the "normal" expectations of preparation for aptitude and other types of tests.

This preliminary conclusion has great significance for counselors in the test interpretation for all culturally deprived persons and indicates the necessity of great caution in interpreting any test scores.

A comprehensive and critical study on testing, counseling, and training of disadvantaged youth for work has been reported by the staffs of a number of different city services manning projects for the employment of school drop-outs. Various reprint reports from the Employment Service Review are collated in one monograph (U.S. Department of Labor, 1964).

Still another current substitute for traditional aptitude testing is the U.S. Employment Service's experimental tryout of BIB (Bibliographical Information—nonstatistical data) as reported by Mathis as follows:

An example of the dedication to R-R methodology is the widespread use of weighted application blanks and biographical information blanks.

The United States Employment Service (USES) has been conducting a nationwide test-validation study for the Occupation, Volkswagen Mechanic. A major experimental variable in this research is a biographic information blank (BIB). Examples of items from the USES study are:

2. How old were you when you were married?
8. How much life insurance did you have when you took your present job?

13. How much education did your mother have?

16. How many times did your family move before you were 18 years of age?

19. How well off was your family?

Invasions of privacy notwithstanding, by statistically comparing the BIB responses of good workers against those of poor workers, a set of right answers can be specified which will increase the proportion of good workers in future selection." (1964).

Nonfinancial Incentives in School and Vocation

In the opening paragraph of this chapter, I referred to two basic modifications in the use of trait-factor theory. The substitution of training experience for aptitude tests was one. A second has to do with that often mentioned factor of motivation in one's work. Clearly the mere possession of aptitudes does not in itself guarantee that the possessor will be highly motivated to use them at the tasks assigned to him in school or in vocation. Much has been written and spoken about the necessity of cultivating the *urge* to do what one is able to do.

In schools we assign grades on examinations as "rewards" for effort to learn the content of books and classrooms. In industry various comparable external forms of incentives have been used to induce individuals to want to do what they are expected to do. In industry these following motivational methods have been used with some degree of effectiveness: supervision (strict or relaxed), relationships with supervisors, working conditions (noise, temperature, etc.), salary (with bonuses), security of work, and a host of other methods and techniques.

In the case of motivating students, one may conclude, at least tentatively, with Field (1967) that the students' perception of progress in self-selected (interiorized external) requirements is a most important factor in inducing motivation of effort. To be sure, much remains to be learned as to how to reward progress in learning so as to result in further effort.

With respect to motivating workers in industry, Herzberg concludes that the most important factor in inducing workers' efforts at the job has to do with creating employee attitudes through "organizational climate" of a high morale type. To give the employee "challenging work in which he can assume responsibility" (Herzberg, 1968) is most crucial. Darr (1968) argues for "participative management" as one of the most effective ways of maintaining high morale among workers. Possible implications for "unrest" in schools and colleges are legion and leads one to the conclusion that a massive reappraisal of the age-old delineation of student and teacher (and those in authority) is surely needed at the present day. This is a topic I have discussed elsewhere.

Thus it seems that both in school and at work each individual must perceive that he is considered important as a person and that his tasks are meaningful to him as expressions of his interests and capabilities. The terms "climate" and "ecology" are now being used to describe the totality of the environment or the human relationships within which the individual derives satisfaction and dignity of self through his efforts to use his capabilities. The counselor can play a most significant role in creating such climate if he does not restrict his efforts to the one-to-one interview relationship. In an innovative experiment Brown (1968) reports relevant experiences in manipulation of the environment of a college residence hall. Numerous other research studies in school and vocation indicate the possibilities of reorganizing environmental climate to induce motivation in order to increase effort at assigned work tasks.

The Role of the Counselor

The purpose of the counselor is to help students change their behavior by learning. First, the students need to learn more about their own characteristics: their abilities, their interests, their temperaments. Next, they must learn what their implications are for the total behavior of the person. Perhaps here is where this type of counseling differs most from the more elemental form proposed decades ago by Frank Parsons. Parsons thought that if the person learned enough about his own characteristics, and about his job opportunities, he could fit the two together. In a sense, we now hold that the student-client must become something of a psychologist, or a behavioral scientist, and perceive himself as his subject.

The counselee also must learn about the alternative opportunities available to him. He must know what society offers, the conditions society imposes, the rewards offered, and the probabilities of attainment. Then, he must learn more about ways of relating himself to society. He must consider the kind of person he is in relation to the social and personal goals he adopts. In a sense, he must learn what decisions he should make, how decisions are made, and how decision making must become a continuing process rather than a single event.

The purpose of the counselor is to help the student modify his behavior by helping him to learn. In this sense, the counselor is a teacher. Good teaching in the counseling office, as in the classroom, is *much more than* "telling the 'right' answer." To help a student learn one must do much more than provide him with information. The basis of much of what is to be learned is often provided by the student. Effective counseling and effective teaching both depend on a *personal* relationship between the teacher and the learner, and adequate consideration of the emotional dynamics of each.

In approaching teaching and learning in counseling, for convenience we can do what is done in other teaching situations and think in terms of *content*, or what behavior is to be changed, and *method*, or what the teacher, here the counselor, and the learner do. In counseling, the content too frequently is quite limited and may initially include a single item or a very few items of behavior. One or several hours may be devoted to producing productive learning. The content also may consist of a broad repertoire of behavior of varying degrees of interdependence. The content differs from person to person and within the same person it differs from time to time.

Together the counselor and counselee decide what behavior is to be changed and what the appropriate content is. They may decide that the changed behavior centers around an educational or vocational decision; a choice of means for establishing relationships with others; or a definition, clarification, and choice of values or even life styles. Counseling then provides an opportunity for the participants to identify gaps in the counselee's knowledge and behavior repertoire, with the hope that appropriate learning can occur.

This approach suggests that if the counselee is to learn more about himself, such learning will be facilitated if the person working with him also knows something about him.

The content of such counseling instruction also consists of knowledge about the counselee's social setting, or environment. What alternatives in style of living are available to the counselee, how accessible are they, how does one take advantage of them, what information about them is useful in making selections and choices? Many counselors make considerable use of educational or occupational information for these purposes, and knowledge regarding community resources is essential.

Thus, the counselor and the counselee assemble and examine information about both the counselee and his surroundings. They consider the significance of such information and its implications, reject some, follow up others, and incorporate some (relevant) in their apperceptive mass. Each item of information may be the source of a number of hypotheses. Each item of information may serve as evidence that increases or decreases the probability that should be attached to one or more of the hypotheses. For example, a low course grade in mathematics class suggests the hypothesis that a person's mathematical ability is poor. A score on a mathematics test may tend to support that hypothesis or may suggest another hypothesis that in spite of the low grade, the person does have good mathematical ability. Comments made in the interview regarding relationships with friends or families may suggest hypotheses that in turn are examined in light of scores on personality inventories. Expressed vocational goals suggest other hypotheses and relevant evidence concerning these may be obtained from vocational interest inventories, recreational and work histories, and school performance.

The role of the counselor can be demonstrated best by examining what he does. First, he sometimes merely listens attentively. At other times he converses with counselees. He may simply suggest that the counselee start to discourse about whatever concerns him, or he may suggest that the counselee describe occupations he has considered, conditions that exist between him and his family, or his study habits. The general suggestions more often are found in the early stages of counseling, the specific suggestions later on.

When appropriate, the counselor also asks questions. These questions may be designed to provide information so that the counselor has a better understanding of the counselee. Frequently, however, the questions are designed to expedite the counselee's self-understanding. The question, "How do you feel about that?" may be asked so that the counselor can learn more about the counselee's preferences, or the counselor may ask the question because it will facilitate the counselee's attempt to describe that which concerns him. The counselor must use questions carefully and cautiously. The unwise and excessive use of questions, particularly early in an interview, can result in the counselee's perceiving the counseling situation as one in which the counselor asks questions and the counselee answers them, a relationship too similar to some teacher-student relationships.

Counselors also provide information to counselees, information about the counselee, about his social environment, about selected psychological concepts and about the process of decision making. Information about himself may be data the counselee does not at present have at hand. These may be derived from test scores, work or school records, or information obtained from other sources. The new data also may be obtained in the interview and essentially consist of inferences derived from what the counselee has said. The counselor detects feelings, attitudes, and values implicit in what the counselee has said, and feeds this information back to the counselee, who may be not fully aware of what he has expressed.

In addition to presenting new data, the counselor also organizes data of which the counselee is aware. The counselor may note a statement the counselee makes early in an interview, and later in the interview, or perhaps even several interviews later, relate that statement to another one made by the counselee. For example, the counselor might say,

Last week you told me that you didn't think you had much mathematical ability and that you had considerable trouble with math in high school, and today you're saying you seem to be interested primarily in scientific occupations.

In considering hypotheses relevant for the counselee's decisions, the counselor notes information bearing on these hypotheses and at appropriate times assembles the information, calls it to the attention of the counselee, and discusses it with him.

The counselor also interprets to the counselee information about himself. This is closely related to the process of organizing data, but it is somewhat different insofar as it allows for considerably more attention to be paid to the counselee's reactions to the information. The data may be eagerly accepted, violently rejected, or fearfully regarded; and the counselor then discusses with the counselee what the information may come to mean.

The counselor also provides information to the counselee about his social environment: information about jobs, schools, financial resources, community facilities and services, training programs, lines of promotion, or civic responsibilities. The information also may center around prevailing attitudes in the community, social values, changes occurring in attitudes and values, reactions that the counselee's behavior can elicit from peers and others in the community, or even the state of the nation in general.

A considerable amount of the counselor's time may be spent in providing information to counselees regarding concepts of human behavior. Some segments of counseling interviews may sound like *abbreviated* courses in psychology. For example, a counselor may spend considerable time discussing with the student the concepts of traits and factors. He may attempt to help the student distinguish between abilities and interests. He may provide information so that the student has some understanding of the concept of intelligence, academic ability, mechanical aptitude, clerical aptitude, or mechanical comprehension. He may converse with a student about how some of these concepts are identified through the use of psychological tests. He may discuss with him the personal implications, for the counselee, of probability theory.

The counselor also may attempt to provide to the counselee information about the nature of ambivalent behavior. Many students are quite concerned about their inability to select a vocation to which they feel both attracted and repelled. Frequently counselees are concerned because of conflicting feelings directed toward their parents, spouses, or friends. They may be frightened by negative feelings or simply confused by conflicting ones.

Counselors may provide information to counselees about other psychological principles. Man's bisexual nature may not be understood by a person and may be a source of anxiety. The nature of hostility and ways of handling one's own may be sources of distress. Although providing information about such principles may assist a counselee in and of itself, usually we assume that providing such information is only one part of the counselor's task and that such information must be integrated with other available data, interpreted appropriately, and explored in many of its aspects by the counselee and counselor.

The counselor also provides information to the counselee about the decision-making process itself. He may review with the counselee other decisions that the counselee has made. He may stress the tentative nature of most decisions. He may attempt to teach the counselee that usually decisions are made in gradual steps. While providing such information he may reassure the counselee that most decisions are not irreversible, that most can be progressive, and that most can be reviewed and evaluated before the counselee makes a final (tentative!) commitment.

The counselor also may serve as an advisor. He may advise a student to delay a decision, to make a tentative decision, to seek further information, to discuss decisions with others, to obtain exploratory experiences, or to take tests. Such advice is instrumental in aiding the student to make his own decisions. Some counselors feel that providing this type of assistance to counselees may make them increasingly dependent on the counselor. Some, in general, avoid all advising on the assumptions that advice is equivalent to exhortation and that exhortation is ineffective. But I hold that when a counselor advises a counselee, usually he is advising the person to do something instrumental that the person is not reluctant to do and the advice may serve primarily as a stimulus to tentative consideration or even to tentative action, not to finality of commitment.

In addition to conversing with counselees, counselors also converse (confidentially) with other persons as part of their counseling responsibility. They may speak with parents, teachers, employers, or friends, with the purpose of obtaining information that will help them work effectively with the counselee. Of course, here the guidelines provided by a professional code of ethics have to be carefully observed. Such discussion may have the purpose not only of obtaining information about the counselee but also of producing helpful changes in the counselee's environment. For instance, a foreign student working with a counselor may be reluctant to approach a professor because in his home country this simply is not done. The counselor consequently may speak with the teacher about arrangements for the student to have oral examinations rather than the written examinations with which he has difficulty. Possible changes in bringing up children may be discussed with parents, or discussions with roommates may result in changes in living conditions.

In addition to conferring with counselees and with other persons, the counselor is responsible for assembling information about the counselee. He may give psychological tests and inventories, refer the counselee to others who give such tests, or take the initiative to assemble records containing, among other things, scores on tests previously taken. The counselor examines school, health, and work records and other information about the counselee. He then attempts to obtain enough information about the counselee so that he has a well-stocked (tentative-provisional) concept of who the person is.

He also collects information regarding the relevant environment in which the counselee lives and those environments in which he may be living in the future. He will gather information about schools, jobs, and community. If a counselee comes from a neighborhood with which the counselor is unfamiliar, he may attempt to learn more about that neighborhood. He may attempt to learn more about the school from which the counselee comes. He may attempt to learn more about the hospital ward in which the counselee is a patient or the company in which the counselee is an employee. In schools and colleges, he may attempt to gather information about student organizations, school programs, or campus activities of possible relevance for the counselee. For each counselee he does this selectively, but the end result is that after working with hundreds of counselees, the counselor has assembled a fund of such information that may be helpful (with appropriate modifications) with a number of persons from similar backgrounds.

One of the important functions of the counselor is to assemble what we will call normative data. While not by any means limited to test data, this is, for example, illustrated by the way the counselor uses test norms. A test score is meaningless unless it can be compared to scores of other persons of known characteristics. Multiple norms are available for most tests, and the counselor has to decide which norms are most appropriate for comparison purposes when working with a counselee. Sometimes appropriate norms are not available, and then the counselor must decide how such norms can be obtained. Counselors in schools and colleges frequently are responsible for institutional testing programs and these serve to provide norms useful in counseling individuals. The counselor needs normative data not only for tests but also for other behavior indices. Norms are indices of comparison with reference or criterion groups. For example: How many people change jobs how often? How many students at various levels are educationally or vocationally undecided? What are the dating behavior, the religious beliefs, the delinquency records, the predominant values of the groups to which the counselees belong? When a counselee wants to compare himself to his peers in terms of academic achievement, athletic ability, or popularity, the counselor can understand the counselee better if he knows something about the behavior typical of the counselee's peers. These references to external norm groups also highlight the uniqueness of each counselee.

The counselor may gather information informally and unsystematically, or he may carefully and systematically assemble data and process it in a way allowing for rigorous interpretation. One of the more exact ways of handling *some* normative types of data is by making use of regression equations. Usually the data included in regression equations consist of test scores, although not necessarily so. The relationships between different kinds of information are observed and various kinds of information are combined to provide optimum predictions of the behavior that concerns the counselee and counselor. Test scores, high school grades, and family background information may be combined in a regression equation designed to predict grades in college. Such predictions are useful in helping counselees consider varying probabilities related to attendance at different colleges. Most counselors find regression equations difficult to describe meaningfully to counselees, and although they may use the data from such equations in organizing the information they have about the person, they may be reluctant to spend much time in an interview identifying these questions.

An Illustrative Case (Abbreviated)

The following excerpts from three counseling interviews demonstrate how a counselor, working with a university student completing her second year in college, learns about the girl's dilemma. The counselor reviews information already available about the counselee, obtains more data, synthesizes and reviews these with her, and works with her as she makes a decision.

C: And now we can get down to business. Do you want to tell me how you happened to come in?

S: Well, ah, sort of a recent problem. I decided to change my major about two weeks ago when it came time to make admissions for the School of Medical Technology; I'm a sophomore. And ah, now I don't know what I'm going to go into and I'm taking Psychology IX, in which the Professor (_____) discusses the services over here, and I thought I might as well avail myself of them.

C: How did you happen to choose that field?

S: Well, ah, sort of a combination of things. (pause) Well, the first thing ... I think the major reason why I took it was I wanted to have something. .... It's always nice to know what you're going into ... and, ah, medical technology was something ... was a field in which I thought I'd be doing something for other people and, I had liked the sciences in high school and knew I could do well in them, and ah we had a public health nurse ah who came around and showed us movies of medical technologists at work and ... and it was sort of an idealized movie I think.

C: Um hum.

S: And they have cautioned me that while you're going to school you might as well get something which you can fall back on. (pause) But I still wanted to get closer to my interests.

C: Um hum.

S: And I just don't know where that vocation is.

C: ... and that the medical technology program is too narrow to encompass all your interests.

S: That's right.

C: O.K. And that's the primary reason you dropped out?

S: Um hum.

C: Um hum.

Some Implications for Counseling Practice

1. The reader of this chapter should not mistakenly conclude that counselors depend solely upon scores on tests in their efforts to aid young and old in identifying their potential for given tasks at work or in school. The totality of the counselee's life history of varied experiences, efforts, tryout, aspirations, interests, and socializations must enter into the total counseling process and relationship.

2. Moreover, no one should foolishly oversimplify the attainment of vocational and school proficiency as simply a matter of inheriting the requisite genes and then passively letting "nature take its course." Indeed, it is clear that aggressive and persistent effort are needed to utilize (and perhaps fully to develop?) whatever capacities, capabilities, aptitudes, or abilities one possesses (from whatever source or sources). The counseling relationship involves, therefore, the cultivation of interests, desires, or aspirations to attain (develop) one's full potential. Moreover, the familial, neighborhood, and even *Zeitgeist* (historical period) are important determinants of the extent and manner of evolvement of one's potentiality (Wolfle, 1969).

3. Vocational counseling, contrary to Parson's early formulation, is a continuing experience with definable stages (Super) of maturation and, for many (young and old most?), drastic changes of task in school or occupation or both. Counselors need to initiate each counselee into this continuing task and thus aid each to begin the lifelong task of self-counseling.

4. Counselor and counselee need to become mature in appraising and recognizing the degree of accuracy (probable error of estimate) of each item of data which enters into one's appraisal of aptitude, aspiration, or motivation. It follows that there is a wide range in approximation of accuracy and relevancy (forecasting significance) to be found among the myriad of items of case data. Unhappily, too infrequently do counselor and counselee seek to estimate the degree or precision characteristic of each such item. The innovation "tests" yielded a measurable increase in precision of one kind of data but research is needed to improve the accuracy of other relevant data (Anastasi, 1958).

5. Without minimizing the necessity of vocational and other forms of counseling for the individual, one must at the same time stress the strategy for human society of the identification and utilization of all capabilities of all human beings of all races, nationalities, socio-economic strata, beliefs and dispositions. Human talents are society's richest resources and all efforts should be devoted to the full utilization of those resources (D. G. Paterson, in Wolfle, Ed., 1969).

6. No effective counselor utilizes one and only one form of the several categories (styles of counseling) covered in this book. That is, the counselor assisting young and old to identify and utilize possessed aptitudes is not neglectful of emotional assets and liabilities of his client or of his interests, attitudes, and other dimensions of his personality. To be sure, each counselor evolves his own special competency (preference?) with certain aspects of human development, but he is not so foolish as to assume that his client is fragmented into any of the classical categories which characterize the chapters of this or any book on counseling.

7. At an early age each individual should be encouraged and aided in cultivating the perceptual habit of evaluating his experiences (including wide reading) in search of "signs" of potential aptitudes and interests. He should be encouraged to discuss his tentative "findings" periodically with peers, parents, and school counselors; and when he is so inclined, and when school and work require it, he should make his "choice" in the form of tentative hypotheses to be further evaluated by "tryout" experiences. When his evaluation indicates to him that his choice is not a good "fitting" for one such as he, he should reconsider or be aided to search for one that is congruent with the results of his tryout in school or at work.

8. Fundamental in individual psychology that is basic to counseling is the existence of man's freedom to choose what form of development (e.g., choice of vocation, values, cosmological beliefs, etc.) he shall strive to attain or become. But contrary to the anarchist extreme of individualism, there are limits on freedom of choice. Both the individual and the collective but separate subgroups of society are constantly reviewing and changing these limits, sometimes through dialogue and at other times through violence and revolution. At the moment our society is in the throes of forming new freedoms of choice for the long repressed minority groups of blackmen, Indians and Chicanos. Indeed, American culture is also struggling over the age-old issue of the molding of persons that we call child-rearing and youth maturing. We are also continuing to struggle with the depersonalized impact of our industrialized society upon its individual members separately and collectively.

9. Hopefully, man's search for new and productive and satisfying forms of the "good life" will continue for each one, separately and collectively, and that another William H. McNeil of some future century will be able and innovative enough to write a new *Rise of the West* (1963), reporting still more progress in man's efforts to civilize and humanize himself and his fellow men.

10. Counselors should practice the art of consultation with other counselors, parents, therapists, measurement specialists, cultural anthropologists, and other social scientists. In social casework, periodic case (staff) conferences have been well established as a standard means of communication, not of bureaucratic detail, but of comparative interpretation of case data and (loose) agreement as to the role of different individuals in their relationships with clients, young and old. This practice should take place at all ages of clients and in all contexts. The college counselor has the advantage of

availability of the same staff and often in the same building. But the enlarged pupil personnel staff is rapidly becoming established at all school levels. The counselor working in the industrial context is not usually so fortunate in availability. However, this extension of practice will come in time as the need for consultation and enlarged enlightenment becomes clearly an advantage. But at the present time the college counselor enjoys the advantage of range and ready availability of other relevant experts for consultation. This is especially evident in the case of social scientists who enlighten the counselor's sophisticated understanding of complex societal and international forces that bear upon the happiness and success of each individual in different ways. Finally, there are in colleges potentially helpful humanists and philosophers as well as historians who are available to make counseling far more than a mere job-hunting or fix-it-up type of restricted maturing experience. Rather these individuals will aid each client to experience counseling in one or more of its several forms, dyadic, encounter, T group, and others.

Bibliography

Allport, G. W. What is a trait of personality? *J. abnorm. soc. Psychol.,* 1931, **25,** 368-372.

Allport, G. W., & Odbert, H. S., Trait—names: A psycholexical study. *Psychol. Monogr.,* 1936, **47** (1, Whole No. 211).

Allport, G. W. *Personality.* New York: Holt, 1946.

Allport, G. W., Vernon, P. E., & Lindzey, G. *Study of values: A scale for measuring the dominant interests in personality,* (3rd ed.) Boston: Houghton Mifflin 1960.

Allport, G. W. Traits revisited. *Amer. Psychologist,* 1966, **21,** 1-10.

Anastasia, A. *Differential psychology.* (3rd ed.) New York: Macmillan, 1958.

Anastasia, A. (Ed.) *Testing problems in perspective.* American Council on Education, Washington, D.C., 1966.

Aston, A. W. Further validation of the environmental assessment technique. *J. educ. Psychol.,* 1963, **54,** 217-226.

Aston, A. W., & Holland, J. L. The environmental assessment technique: A way to measure college environments. *J. educ. Psychol.,* 1961, **52,** 308-316.

Baxter, B. Job testing and the disadvantaged. *Amer. Psychologist,* 1969, **24,** 637-650.

Berdie, R. F., Layton, W. L., Swanson, E. O., & Hagenah, T. *Testing in guidance and counseling.* New York: McGraw-Hill, 1963. P. 130.

Berdie, R. F. What priority should govern the college admission of students from economically disadvantaged and socially deprived backgrounds when weighted against the goal of excellence? ODS Staff Papers, No. 39, E. G. Williamson, (Ed.) Minneapolis: University of Minnesota, October 1968.

Biggs, D. A. The counselor who teaches decision-making and problem-solving skills. Unpublished, 1968.

Boren, J. E. Permissiveness and guidelines. Unpublished sermon, 1968.

Boring, E. *History of experimental psychology.* New York: Appleton Century Crofts, 1942.

Boring, E. *Psychologist at large,* New York: Basic Books, 1961.

Borow, H. (Ed.) *Man in a world at work,* Boston: Houghton Mifflin, 1964.

Breaking the barriers of isolation, suspicion and unemployment. *Employment service Review,* 1967, **4** (6), 6-9.

Brewer, J. M. *History of vocational guidance: Origins and early development.* New York: Harper, 1942. Pp. 201-202.

Brown, R. D. Manipulation of the environmental press in a college residence hall. *Personnel guid. J.,* 1968, **46** (6), 555-560.

Burt, C. *The factors of the mind.* New York: Macmillan, 1941.

Campbell, D. P. Stability of interests within an occupation over thirty years. *J. appl. Psychol.,* 1966, **50** (1), 51-56.

Cattell, J. M. Mental tests and measurements. *Mind,* 1890, **15,** 378-380.

Cattell, R. B. *Personality traits growing from multi-variant quantitive research in psychology: A study of a science.* Vol. 3. S. Koch (Ed.), New York: McGraw-Hill, 1959. 257-327.

Cattell, R. B., & Warburton, F. W. *Objective personality and motivation tests: A theoretical introduction and practical compendium.* Urbana: University of Illinois Press, 1967.

Clark, K. B., & Plotkin, L. The Negro student at integrated colleges: Summary. In E. W. Gordon & D. A. Wilkerson, *Compensatory education for the disadvantaged.* New York: College Entrance Examination Board, 1966. Pp. 116-124.

Crewe, N. M. Comparison of factor analytic and empirical scales. *Proceedings: 75th annual convention, American Psychological Association,* 1967. Pp. 367-368.

Crites, J. O. *Vocational psychology.* New York: McGraw-Hill, 1969. Part II.

Cronbach, L. J., & Meehl, P. Construct validity in psychological tests. *Psychological Bulletin,* 1955. **52,** 281-302.

Darr, J. W. Motivation and morale—Two keys to participation. *Personnel guid. J.,* 1968, **47** (6), 388-397.

Davis, R. V., England, G. W., & Lofquist, L. H. A theory of vocational behavior, 1963. Revised with David J. Weiss, *Minnesota Studies in Vocational Rehabilitation,* 1968, Bulletin 47, xxiii.

Dvorak, B. The general aptitude test battery. *Personnel guid. J.,* 1956, **35** (3), 145-152.

Feldman, R. A., & Newcomb, T. *The impact of college on students.* Vol. 1. San Francisco: Jossey-Bass, Inc., 1969.

Festinger, L. An experimental investigation of the effect of unstable interpersonal relations in a group. *Research methods in the behavioral sciences.* Minneapolis: University of Minnesota, 1954.

Field, F. Guidance model or conceptual framework for guidance. *Personnel guid. J.,* 1967, **6** (2), 225-228.

Galton, F. *Inquiries into human faculty.* London: Macmillan, 1883.

A government commitment to occupational training in industry. Report of the Task Force on Occupational Training in Industry, August 1968.

Gross, N., Mason, W. S., & McEachern, A. W. *Explorations in role analysis. Studies of the school superintendency role.* New York: 1958.

Group procedures in counseling and guidance. *The School Counselor,* 1968, **15** (5).

Guilford, J. P. *The nature of human intelligence.* New York: McGraw-Hill, 1967.

Guilford, J. P., Christensen, P. R., Bond, N. A., Jr., & Sutton, M. U. S. Factor analysis, study of human interests. *Psychol. Monogr.,* 1954: **68,** 1-38.

Herzberg, F. One more time, how do you motivate employees? *Harv. bus. Rev.,* 1968, 53-62.

Hull, C. *Aptitude testing.* Tarrytown-on-Hudson, N.Y.: World, 1928.

Industry, labor, government: Assault on hard-core jobless problems. *Employment service Review,* 1968, **5** (5 & 6), 2-9.

Jenkins, J. J., & Paterson, D. G. *Studies in individual differences.* New York: Appleton Century Crofts, 1961.

Jex, F. B. *Predicting academic success beyond high school.* Salt Lake City: Frank B. Jex, 1966. P. 13.

Kempton, M. A. Kemptonian view of 'aptitude' testing. *Employment service Review,* 1967, **4** (5).

Kitson, H. D. Analyzing yourself. *I find my vocation.* New York: McGraw-Hill, 1931. Pp. 104-105.

Mathis, H. I. Hope for the disadvantaged and the aptitude barrier. *Personnel guid. J* in press.

Merton, R. K. *Social theory and social structure.* (Rev. ed.) Glencoe, Ill.: Free Press, 1957. Pp. 281-386.

Monachesi, E., & Hathaway, S. R. *Adolescent personality and behavior.* Minneapolis· University of Minnesota Press, 1963.

Münsterberg, H. *Psychology and industrial efficiency.* Boston: Houghton Mifflin, 1913.

Pace, C. R. *Cues: College and university scales.* Princeton, N.J.: Educational Testing Service, 1963.

Pace, C. R. Perspectives on the student and his college. In Lawrence E. Dennis and Joseph E. Kauffman (Eds.), *The college and the student.* Washington, D.C.: American Council on Education, 1966.

Pace, C. R., & Stern, G. C. An approach to the measurement of psychological characteristics of college environments. *J. Educ. Psychol.,* 1958, **49,** Pp. 269-277.

Parker, C. A., & Gometz, L. Disciplinary counseling: A contradiction. *Personnel guid. J.,* 1968, **46** (5), 437-443.

Parsons, F. *Choosing a vocation.* Boston and New York: Houghton Mifflin, 1909.

Paterson, D. G., & Darley, J. G. *Men, women and jobs.* Minneapolis: University of Minnesota Press, 1936.

Pearson, K. *The grammar of science.* London: Dent, 1937.

Phillips, J. Behavior modification in counseling. *Northwest College personnel association Journal,* Winter 1968. 31-34.

Plaut, R. L. *Blueprint for talent searching.* New York: National Scholarship Service and Fund for Negro Students, 1957.

Preparing disadvantaged youth for work. U.S. Department of Labor, Bureau of Employment Security, 1964.

Research Bulletin. Student Counseling Bureau, Office of the Dean of Students, Minneapolis: University of Minnesota Press, 1963, **5** (2).

Sanderson, H. *Basic concepts in vocational guidance.* New York: McGraw-Hill, 1954.

Solem, A. Priorities in manpower research. *Journal of employment Counseling,* 1968, **5** (1), 2.

Spearman, C. *The abilities of man.* New York: Macmillan, 1927.

Stern, G. C. Preliminary manual activities index. *College characteristics index.* Syracuse: Psychological Research Center, Syracuse University, 1958.

Strong, E. K., Jr. *Vocational interests of men and women.* Stanford, Calif.: Stanford, 1943. Pp. xxix, 746.

Thurstone, L. L. A multiple factor study of vocational interests. *Personnel J.,* 1931, **10**, 198-205.

Thurstone, L. L. *The vectors of mind.* Chicago: University of Chicago Press, 1935.

Toward the year 2000: Work in progress. *Daedalus, Journal of the American Academy of Arts and Sciences,* Summer 1967.

Tyler, L. E. *The psychology of human differences.* New York: Appleton Century Crofts, 1965. P. 572.

Tyler, L. E. *The work of the counselor.* (2nd ed.) New York: Appleton Century Crofts, 1961. Pp. xiv and 327.

Welsh, G. S., & Dhalstrom, W. G. Construction. *Basic readings on the MMPI in psychology and medicine.* Minneapolis: University of Minnesota Press, 1956. Pp. 58-123.

Williamson, E.G., & Foley, J. *Counseling and discipline.* New York: McGraw-Hill, 1949.

Williamson, E. G., & Hoyt, D. Measured characteristics of student leaders. *Educational and psychological Measurement.* 1952, **12**, 65-78.

Williamson, E. G. Power, authority and the counseling relationship. In V. F. Calia & B. D. Wall. (Eds.), *Pupil personnel administration, new perspectives and foundations.* Springfield: Charles C Thomas, 1968.

Williamson, E. G. *Vocational counseling.* New York: McGraw-Hill, 1965. P. 125.

Wolfbein, S. L. *Education and training for full employment.* New York: Columbia, 1967. P. 179.

Wolfle, D. (Ed.) *The discovery of talent.* Cambridge: Harvard, 1969.

5

Psychoanalysis and Counseling

PAUL T. KING and KENT F. BENNINGTON

Like many theorists, Sigmund Freud began with a technique and from there generated a theory of psychotherapy and personality. Freud's theoretical formulations of human behavior are perhaps now better known than any other as a result of long-standing literary popularity of psychoanalysis in the United States. Freudian theory has received extensive attention in professional and lay publications, movies, cartoons, and other forms of mass media. Consequently, rather than attempt a further delineation of the theory itself, we shall instead present an application of psychoanalytic thought to counseling practice.

Our intention in rewriting the present chapter has been to focus attention on the actual "stuff" of counseling without attempting to present a comprehensive elaboration of psychoanalytic theory itself. Many highly readable, thoroughgoing accounts of psychoanalytic theory are readily available to the interested student who wishes to pursue the theoretical underpinnings of psychoanalytically oriented psychotherapy (Alexander, 1963; Brill, 1938; Hall, 1954; and Munroe, 1955). In moving from technique to theory and back again, as Freud did, we hope to avoid the difficulty of trying to relate a theoretical stance to the actual practice of counseling. The difficulty is that discussions of theory too often remain at highly abstract levels of description and consequently serve little useful purpose for the student who wishes to apply his learning to realistic counseling and psycho therapeutic relationships. It seems particularly important to elucidate a representative variety of ways in which the practitioner can implement psychoanalytic theory as he counsels persons seeking his help. We shall attempt to identify those basic psychoanalytic tenets which the counselor may utilize in his conceptualization of the counseling process. At the same time we will accentuate the practical application of such basic concepts as ambiguity, anxiety, and transference. A discussion of anxiety appeared in the first edition of this chapter, and we have made an effort in the present edition to include further elaboration of ambiguity and transference as significant variables in the counseling process.

Again, it is not our purpose to redefine or resummarize psychoanalytic theory, nor is it our intention to rehash controversies over the usefulness of psychoanalytic therapy. Perhaps the most fundamental underlying assumption of the chapter is that psychoanalytically derived thinking can be profitably applied to counseling relationships in such a way that counselors can not only develop some dynamic understanding of their clients but can proceed on the basis of those concepts, ideas, and hunches to productive therapeutic interactions. We have used the words counselor and therapist interchangeably throughout the chapter.

The main body of the chapter will be directed primarily toward professionals working in individual, one-to-one helping relationships with clients. Some attempt is made, later in the chapter, to relate psychoanalytically rooted concepts to the general area of student personnel work, treated within the context of promoting institutional change. Regardless of the setting in which one is working, however, certain assumptions regarding the nature of man operate in one's relationships with clients; it is to these assumptions, as they apply to a psychoanalytically derived orientation, that we will now turn our attention.

Motivational Themes and the Fixity of Behavior

It is difficult for the layman to regard Freud's theories without being appalled at the basic content and apparent seaminess of his fundamental concepts. Perhaps an early distinction should be made between the psychoanalytically formulated nature of man as perceived by the layman and what was intended by the psychoanalysts in their tentative formulations. The layman's view of psychoanalysis often seems to be that of a system bent on discovering man's basest self and confronting him and society with his rascality and depravity. Often the dominating aura of psychoanalysis eventuates in a perception of man as a fragile, logical, and moralistic organism easily overthrown by an archaic and mysterious unconscious. People find it hard to be dispassionate about such a theory.

Freud and his followers were aware of the impact that his discoveries were having on his contemporaries in Europe, specifically on the medical students who attended his Vienna lectures during the winter semesters of 1915-1917. Sensing the resistance with which some of his ideas about unconscious motivation were being received, he admonished the interns that by repudiating that which was unfamiliar and distasteful to them, they were repeating the mechanism of the dream structure and were denying his hypotheses a rational and considerate treatment.

Freud and present-day analysts have been subjected to criticism for using this particular type of admonition. The implication that resistance to psychoanalytic theories stems from one's personal resistance to unconscious motivation rather than to empirical resistance to Freud's idea has been a sore spot to scientifically trained psychologists for a long time. While it is true that many psychoanalytic theories are either presently experimentally unverified or are unverifiable by their nature, much resistance to the acceptance of analytic theory appears to stem from the threatening content with which it is concerned. The analytic viewpoint of the nature of man, as it is perceived by the layman, seems more closely linked with the latter type of resistance (resistance to content) than to the former (resistance because of empirical nonverification).

What is the nature of man as seen from a psychoanalytic framework? Semantically oriented analysts point out that there is no nature of man but "natures of men." To the analyst the unique and individual development of each person transcends in importance the common elements that can be ascribed to human beings in general or to a particular culture. His therapy is based on this uniqueness. Also, different schools of analytic thought would regard man's nature from different perspectives with somewhat different "natures" resulting. The classically Freudian school, which gives central importance to the sexual drives, the instinct of aggression, and the significance of biological needs, emerges with a different nature of man than do the nonlibido schools, which emphasize the primary needs of the human self and place the instincts in a secondary position.

Still, certain common denominators about what sort of being man is do arise from the theoretical fabric of psychoanalysis, and these are capable of being delineated.

Man is born with certain structural limitations that are imposed by the genetic union of his parents. There are certain limits—intellectual, physical, maturational—beyond which it is unreasonable to think any individual organism might go. Such structural restrictions preclude the average man from becoming a theoretical physicist or from pole-vaulting 16 feet. Within these restrictions, however, there is great latitude for personal, idiosyncratic development. The ability to discriminate cues afforded by the environment and to base adjustive actions on these discriminations, the severity or munificence of the milieu, and the good fortune one has had in escaping trauma or disease give each person his individuality, but within the structural limits of the organism. Dissension arises between psychoanalytic schools concerning the importance of this environmental molding. The more stringent Freudian position would give preeminence to the biological needs and instincts of the organism.

While man decidedly has been shaped by his environment, he has also modified his environment extensively to meet his demands. As Ruth Munroe points out:

> Man proposes to master his environment rather than adapt his body to it, to create a human world in which temperature is regulated by a thermostat instead of a furry skin, in which food comes so regularly and so neatly packaged that he is scarcely aware that the terms of his body require the unsportsmanlike killing of fellow animals on a grand scale. In general, man's needs as an organism, the terms he presents for tenancy on this planet, have become so confused with the terms he has imposed on his environment that it has become difficult to say where one set of terms leaves off and the other begins (1955, p. 6).

All psychoanalytic schools encompass both concepts of heredity and environment, but differ in the relative importance they attach to each.

Man is seen as being both animalistic and human simultaneously. He shares with animals his activations of behaviors that serve homeostatic ends—the need for nutritional restoration, elimination, etc.—and his needs to reproduce the species and propagate his kind. In addition, man has developed communicative techniques that have liberated him from a more instinctual, animal-like existence. As a result of this liberation and the consequent elaboration of the communicative process, he has developed distinctly human qualities cherished by himself and endearing to society. Courage, honor, devotion, and loyalty are essentially human qualities that will vary in form from culture to culture but are almost universally positively regarded. This approaches the lower boundaries of man's spiritual or religious self. These latter qualities he shares minimally, if at all, with animals. So, then, psychoanalytically, man is animalistic, but with something added. To accept man's human self does not deny his animalistic being.

There is a definite tendency for psychoanalysts to consider personality and character to be relatively "fixed" after the first five or six years. This means that the individual's characteristic ego defenses will have been formed, his manner of interacting with the world and other individuals will have been chosen, and his basic feelings of anxiety or security will have been established. Analysts, of course, do not feel that there is absolutely *no* personality change after the sixth year, but that the core of the personality has been formed. This core is thought to remain with the person throughout his life unless altered by therapeutic intervention or unusual life situations. Consequently, we should not expect an individual who demonstrates an anxious, withdrawn attitude at the end of his formative years to turn into an easy-going, affable extrovert at age twenty.

This assumption of the psychoanalytically oriented psychologist is troublesome to counselors and psychologists who are not of this persuasion. It implies a pessimism about their ability to help individuals to any great extent and seems to lend a final and immutable cast to personality.

Another assumption made by the analysts is that of a motivational theme that runs throughout the life of each individual. These themes might be hidden at times because of ego defensiveness, but continue to lie dormant, waiting to manifest themselves when personal controls are weakened. An example of such a theme is the feeling that one cannot exist without total love and dependency on another, or that if one allows others to become emotionally close to them they will be "absorbed" and lose their feelings of self. These themes, not always observable, reappear under situations that induce regression, such as threat and trauma. Not only do the basic motivations reemerge but the primitivized thinking and early ego defenses are recrudesced.

American and European cultures have had difficulty in seeing psychoanalysis in constructive terms in spite of the increasing publicity it has had over the last several decades as a potent and useful therapeutic tool. The layman often fears that the nobility and sublimity of man will be seriously threatened by an acceptance of the tenets of psychoanalysis. Analysts, on the other hand, feel that an acceptance of man's more primitive self in no way attenuates his good qualities, but that a lack of acceptance of man's primitive self does not tend to ennoble life but instead makes it incomprehensible.

Freud made several comments about the suppression of unpleasurable psychic content in his ninth lecture, which was concerned with dream censorship. The audience was protesting that psychoanalysis was attributing so much of man's behavior to a fundamental, evil predisposition. Freud confronted his audience with their blindness to the egotistical baseness in human nature and man's more or less unreliability in all that concerns sexual life. He further pointed to the war then devastating Europe, hinting that so much destruction could not have been loosed by a few unprincipled, ambitious men if these destructive tendencies were not also present in most men. Freud says: "It is no part of our intention to deny the nobility in human nature, nor have we done anything to disparage its value. On the contrary, I show you not only the evil wishes that are censored but also the censorship which suppresses them and makes them unrecognizable" (Riviere, 1958, p. 154).

Man's behavior is partly determined by unconscious processes that are motivational and goal-directed in nature. He wishes, wants, fears, and abhors things of which he is consciously unaware. These forces strive for expression, but must be disguised because of their nature and content. This results in man's occasional inexplicable behavior, even to himself, and leads to the formation of distorted and censoring operations of the ego. One never has access to his unconscious; one can only see its operation and insistence in terms of symbolism and transference manifestations.

Every human act is considered to have a double meaning. One meaning is its commonplace, realistic meaning that would characteristically be ascribed to the act by a nonpsychological observer. The other meaning, its symbolic meaning, stems from unconscious and repressed urges and can best be understood in terms of analysis and insight.

Persons are most clearly revealed by examining their past and focusing on their specific lines of genetic development. A longitudinal and historical perspective makes the most accurate prediction of how an individual might act in the future and gives the most enriched and comprehensive explanation of his present behavior.

> Psychoanalysts differ as to just how early experiences structure later personality trends and as to the specific role of the infantile unconscious. Adler and Horney tend to think of the problem mainly through a more careful interpretation of the old saw: as the twig is bent so the branch inclines. In their view, early experiences set the pattern for later expectations and later techniques of adaptations. Freudians, however, tend to think of a relatively separate history for the various aspects of development, of the actual freezing of some aims at the infantile level by the mechanism of repression, while other aims develop more or less in accordance with the requirements of the social milieu and are only influenced by the persistence of the repressed aims (Munroe, 1955, p. 33).

Whatever the school, all psychoanalysts make use of and respect the genetic approach to understanding human behavior.

There is some tendency for psychoanalysts to wonder if certain, maybe all, ego defense mechanisms are inherited. They would not oppose the idea that the "selection" of ego defenses are *largely* learned, but many would contend that biological predilections toward certain types of defenses are probable. Along this same line, many analysts feel that neurotic conditions are inheritable to a degree, and that definite predispositions exist. Two personal communications in the past several months from geneticists, one of whom is also a psychologist, have plainly stated the case for the genetic transmission of neurotic conditions in both humans and experimental animals.

For analysts the importance of understanding the modeling influences of childhood is paramount. Childhood is a time when behavior is most open, flexible, and tractable. It is also a time when emotional experiences tend to be the strongest, and traumas and early learning experiences consequently tend to be overlearned and are instrumental in shaping the character structure of the child.

Psychoanalytic theory has never emphasized the learned component of behavior, although there are many references to habits being formed and certain behaviors resulting in satisfaction. One gets the feeling that psychoanalysts are not oblivious to the effects of the environment, but that they are overly preoccupied with the biological, inherited, unfolding structure of the psyche.

Client Commitment to Behavioral Change, and the Purpose of Interpretation

One of the most frequent questions asked by persons who are in the initial stages of psychological counseling is "How is just talking about my problem going to help?" Often this is followed by the explanation by the client that he has discussed it before, perhaps with friends or relatives, and has experienced little relief. The prospective client may see little that can be accomplished by talking and is frequently suspicious that the sessions will be an inconvenient waste of time. This attitude is often typical of persons who have sought therapy of their own volition as well as of those who have been urged by friends and relatives who are concerned for the client.

This question needs to be resolved by the beginning client before he is able to make any sort of substantial commitment to psychotherapy or counseling. Many therapists will try to answer this question in a supportive and nontechnical way. This has the effect of reassuring the client that he has come for a definite purpose, and that he can expect a sincere and conscientious effort on the part of the therapist. Because it is implied by the client's question, the therapist may interpret the initial resistance the client has as uneasiness about beginning work on his problems. Frequently the analytically oriented therapist will choose to minimize such support and reassurance by immediately responding to the person's obvious ambivalence and uncertainty about initiating therapy. Such a position would depend on the therapist's estimate of the client's ego strength, the maladjustment with which he is suffering, and assessments of his anxiety and maturity. In general, reassurance would seem more appropriate with narcissistically regressed clients or with those who would defect in therapy without early indications of authoritative help on the part of the therapist.

It is also perhaps necessary to acknowledge the underlying conviction that therapeutic change is biologically, and even psychologically, limited. Personality change, as conceptualized here, is limited by heredity, the severity of early childhood trauma, intellectual or cognitive ability (the ability to manipulate symbols—a highly important skill in psychoanalysis), and the client's motivation to change.

Without sufficient desire to change on the part of the client, then it may be, and usually is, virtually impossible to facilitate significant personality changes. The motivation to change is generally considered by most counseling theorists as a fundamental prerequisite to personal growth. The client who is forced into the counseling relationship by others, or by extenuating circumstances, is less likely than the highly motivated client to benefit from the counseling experience. Many counselors, whether in secondary school settings, colleges, industry, or the military, will undoubtedly be faced with the difficult, highly undesirable situation of having to counsel a student or client who has been required by the administration or courts to enter counseling. This is a particularly familiar situation to psychologists who have worked with prison or mental hospital populations, where many clients enter counseling in compliance with institutional regulations.

In addition to a desire to change, psychotherapeutic progress or change depends to a great extent on the condition of the client's ego. An ego that is badly damaged, as for example that which has suffered the trauma of early childhood abandonment by the mother or mother-surrogate, does not give the counselor much to work with in therapy. The counselor needs a fairly well-formed ego to work with if counseling is to be successful, otherwise he may find himself investing considerable time with virtually no progress. The only, or one of the only, reason counselors sometimes find themselves working at length with a client whose ego is so malformed that there is little if any chance for therapeutic improvement, is the counselor's unwillingness to acknowledge the hopelessness of change within the client, whom he has come to know as a person. With the increased demands for counseling services and with the relative shortage of counselors, it seems increasingly important for counselors and psychotherapists to evaluate realistically the client in terms of ego formation and the potentiality for growth or personality change.

Interpretation of behavior and its underlying dynamics also has much to do with process of therapeutic change. Interpretation is one of the basic methods of psychoanalysis which is considered instrumental to changing client behavior. Psychoanalysis is very much an insight-oriented approach to counseling and as such assumes that increased awareness of one's own dynamics will increase one's ability to change to a more productive, more spontaneous style of life. Consequently, interpretation plays an important role in the therapeutic process. It is not a cure in itself and must be understood carefully if one is to use it effectively. Freud himself recognized that interpretation of the client's experience would not in itself facilitate the necessary changes in behavior; and, as a result of this, he stressed the importance of timing in interpretation. The timing of interpretation should be carefully integrated with the client's thinking and should not, as Ford and Urban (1965) point out in their summary of psychoanalytic therapy, run parallel to the client's thinking, providing him with the impression that the interpretations are relevant, but without enabling him to use them productively. The point here is that the counselor or therapist must have a real sense of the client's thinking in order to successfully carry out the process of interpretation. Within the context of psychoanalytic thinking, then, interpretation is one of the essential ingredients of psychological change in counseling.

The Function of Anxiety, Some Cited Research

Brenner (1955), in speaking of research, mentions several psychoanalytic principles which he feels must be accepted as valid from the outset. These principles seem to be equally applicable to analytically oriented counseling. On the basis of these assumptions, the counselor will apply his therapeutic vigor with the expectation that the client will be improved by this process. Let us take a look at these assumptions.

The therapist will assume the existence of unconscious mental processes, such as urges, wishes, and fears, of which the client is unaware. He will also accept as valid certain characteristics of the operation of the primary process, including symbolism. He will regard the primary process as placing continuous demands on the ego to find outlets for gratification; and he will regard the content of the primary process as timeless, that is, repressed material which, when discharged, appears as fresh and as real as at the time of the original repression.

He would also accept as valid the separation of the functions of the mind into ego, superego, and id. He would tend to concentrate particularly on the concept of conflict between impulses of the id and the defenses of the ego and on the relation of such conflicts to anxiety and pain.

The attitude toward anxiety is of central importance in psychoanalytic thinking, although the explanations of how it emerges and what functions it performs for the organism are varied and contested. Whatever anxiety is, it seems to be something to which the organism is extremely sensitive and, when it occurs in large doses, can find intolerable.

Because of anxiety's central position in psychoanalytic theory, it seems necessary to avoid an oversimplification of the concept and to give the reader some feeling for its complexity. The following discussion of anxiety has this as its purpose.

Freud, while not overlooking the importance of environmental influences, related anxiety to instinctual sources—in keeping with his consistent biological position. The culturally oriented analysts (Fromm, Horney, Sullivan) believe inner impulses arise through the mediation of cultural pressures, which, if repressed, are perceived as a frustration of the person's potentialities with consequent hostility, renewed repression, and anxiety. Baura (1955, p. 95) reports in summarizing Horney's position on anxiety, "The development of anxiety would not be seen as the expression of the ego's fear of being overwhelmed by instincts or by being punished by the superego but as a failure of specific safety devices erected against external dangers."

Zetzel (1955) points out two sets of variables in connection with anxiety: (1) anxiety as an exaggerated response to minimal external danger and (2) anxiety as identical with normal fear but arising in response to an internal subjective threat. She also says that unrelieved external dangers from which flight is impossible produces reactions indistinguishable from pathological anxiety.

Zetzel (1955) and Rangell (1955) both differentiate between primary anxiety and secondary, or signal, anxiety. Anxiety seems likely to occur when the ego is confronted by threat from within which it can neither bind nor discharge. This primary anxiety is a reaction to danger, the danger being a continuance or worsening of the helpless state in which the ego is threatened with overthrow or extinction. It is traumatic in nature.

Signal anxiety operates in a different manner. It, too, is a response to danger, but the anxiety, being less intense, is welcomed by the organism as a warning of impending trouble that can now be avoided. The person is able to make some constructive use of the warning message. Under conditions in which the ego is weakened or regressed, the discharge of anxiety becomes more diffuse and explosive; the use of anxiety as a signal degenerates, with a consequent loss of effective action. Rangell sees anxiety, signal or traumatic, as a physiological reaction to danger perceived by the person and suffered, not produced, by the ego.

There is some speculation that the early mother-child relationship determines the ability of the ego to handle situations and manifest anxiety of the signal type, which implies the ability to withstand tension. Zetzel (1955) feels that the ability to tolerate anxiety and to avoid denying it is a vital prerequisite for healthy character development.

I have taken the liberty of going beyond the concept of anxiety and including other negative states of the organism in order to point out two unique and appealing positions taken by Lilly (1960) and Jacobson (1953).

Jacobson reconciles tension and discharge theories of affects (anxiety could be included here) by suggesting that affects are better understood in terms of energic flux on either side of a median line. This seems to imply, according to Kaywin (1960), that beyond a certain intensity, biological and physiological processes will always be perceived unpleasurably (anxiety?) or painfully and, in the extreme, lead to shock and death. Pleasurable perception is confined within conditioning limits. Kaywin states, "Whether it will or will not be pleasurable will be relatively determined, depending upon factors which may simply be described as the state of the organism relative to a particular reaction pattern at the moment" (1960, p. 638). It seems plausible that mild stimuli can be perceived as pleasurable, but when these stimuli are intensified, they are capable of arousing anxiety.

Lilly (1960) discusses reward and punishment systems in the brain; one subserves pleasurable sensations and activities, the other subserves punishments, as well as painful and angry kinds of sensations, activities, and reactions.

In discussing a psychophysiological basis for two kinds of instincts, Lilly lists several points in sequence that support his hypothesis: (1) When spots of extreme neuronal activity are introduced into these systems by implanted electrodes, fully developed affects, emotions, and instincts are observed behaviorally. (2) Research has indicated that there are two-way connections between these reward and punishment systems and the cortex, as well as with systems lower down within the brain stem and spinal cord. (3) It is possible that sufficiently strong stimuli applied elsewhere in the brain will overflow into these reward or punishment systems to render them active in the same sense that weak electrical stimuli would. For example, it would be possible for a loud noise, by overflow into a punishment system, to create the feeling of fear.

In experiments with monkeys, death seemed imminent when negative systems of the brain were stimulated for too long a period of time, but behavioral reversal could be induced by stimulating a reward system. Lilly says, "One cannot conceive of any ego functions without some sort of rewarding and punishing going on concomitantly and continuously. ... These rewarding and punishing systems must be continuously operative in greatly differentiated detail in all aspects of waking and sleeping life" (1960, p. 663).

This comparatively lengthy, but still insufficient, discussion of anxiety is introduced to stress the enormous complexity of the concept of anxiety. Readers should beware of closing prematurely on a simplified notion of anxiety or of allowing their thinking about it to be circumscribed by the influence of a particular theory.

One of the essential aims, then, of any psychoanalytically oriented therapy is to reduce the anxiety of the client to manageable limits in order for the ego to function in a more discriminating and effective manner. The goals of counseling and the role of the counselor will be taken up in later sections. Now we are concerned with how the analytic process works, how anxiety is reduced, and how the ego is strengthened.

The position taken in this chapter is closer to Freudian psychoanalysis than to any of the other psychoanalytic schools. In terms of understanding how behavioral changes are effected by the use of psychoanalytic methods, it seems appropriate to give the reader an account—although greatly abbreviated and with many omissions—of the process as it would occur in full-scale analysis as opposed to adaptations of psychoanalytic principles.

The primary task of the client in therapy is to talk. Without productivity on the part of the client, the resolution of emotional problems is impossible, and the work of the therapist is effectively thwarted. In most instances, long and pointed silences will be identified as resistance in its most primitive form, with some few exceptions.

This is an outgrowth of one of the basic assumptions of psychoanalysis: the idea of intrapsychic conflict. This conflict is caused by a force or tendency residing in the preconscious that opposes direct and immediate discharge of instinctual energy. This element became manifest clinically in the resistance to recollection and verbalization, and manifest genetically in the tendency to repress or censor thoughts, wishes, or other tendencies derived from the sexual drives.

Arlow says, "Verbalization is perceived as representing the substitutive discharge of quantities of controllable energies for the more massive discharge in action or symptoms of the highly mobile cathexes of the unconscious system" (1961, p. 46). Through speaking, the client weakens repressive forces in his personality and allows for the draining off of pent-up feelings and bound energy.

As the client becomes progressively desensitized to elements within himself that were previously sensed as threatening, less energy is used by the ego to maintain its defenses. Consequently more energy is available for the cognitive and rational processes of the ego which are needed to grapple with reality and to meet the id demands for finding outlets for instinctual expression.

As new insights are formed and new emotional linkages are perceived, there is an increasing relaxation of ego defensiveness during which the person feels on better terms with himself and under less internal strain. The ability of the ego to use realistic and delaying tactics in dealing with unconscious emotional drives is increased as well as the ability to make fine, discriminative judgments. These judgments, generally negative in nature, have the character of indicating to the client that "this is different from that." For example, as therapy progresses and the meaning of the transference is understood, the client is able to tell the differences between a boss who is irritable due to a grueling day and a punitive father on whom his economy of happiness used to depend. Or, that a coquettish young lady who flashes him an obscure smile does not harbor the predatory attitude toward men that he sensed in his mother.

With an expanding capacity to make discriminations of this sort, the client feels a growing ability to master problems that confront him in the real world as well as a lessened intimidation from unconscious urges, which are now emerging and more clearly seen for what they are—childhood residue.

Now more of the total energy of the person is enmeshed with the world outside his skin, he is finding a constructive use for his potentialities, and there is a constant discharge of affect into the real world that makes for a sharpening of the sense of reality, a clearer delineation of the boundaries of the ego (what is me and not me), and diminished feelings of morbidity.

The dislodging of a psychoneurotic condition ultimately requires a total emotional confrontation by the client of his psychoneurotic way of life and the masochism, agony, dulled awareness, predicaments, burning resentment, loneliness, etc., that are a part of it. Also required is a keen awareness of precisely what anticipated or real tragedy this psychoneurotic structure shielded him from. The high point in discrimination is reached when the client is capable of laying the past and present side by side and distinguishing the dead world from the live one.

Although this account of the process by which a client changes from poor to good mental health is short in the telling, the process itself will often require more than one hundred interviews with clients showing expected spurts of progress, backsliding, and lingering on plateaus that are unavoidably a part of therapy but that rarely make good reading. Therapeutic ascent is by no means steady, and the therapist who expects it should be aware of his own regressive and narcissistic anticipations.

Revitalizing the Client

Counselors and counseling psychologists are found in various places such as high schools, university counseling centers, industry, mental hospitals, and community services, to name a few. Although some common counseling goals could be claimed by persons working in all these places, more often the individual setting will influence and delimit what the counselor can hope or expect to accomplish.

The type of problems the counselor is likely to encounter, the freedom with which the counselor may see clients with emotional problems over long periods of time, and the type of counseling that is "acceptable" will often be policy decisions made by the agency for which the counselor works.

Characteristically, high school counselors will not be as free as psychotherapists in university centers to see clients over an extended period of time or for more serious emotional problems.[1] Counseling psychologists working in mental hospitals will find their efforts essentially focused on vocational problems, whereas counselors in community agencies find many opportunities to work with emotional problems as well as vocational. The application of psychoanalytic principles will ordinarily have more relevance where personality factors are involved and where the counselor has the freedom to see certain clients for many interviews. However, psychoanalytic formulations of problems encountered by counselors in other settings and with other than emotional problems would seem to find some use. For example, Bordin et al. (1963) have developed a psychoanalytic framework for vocational development based on the assumptions that work is a sublimation of the *direct* gratification of one's impulses and that the "earliest work of the organism in food getting and mastery of the body and coping with the stimulations of the environment" are developmentally related "to the most highly abstract and complex intellectual and physical activities." Furthermore, they assume that adult and infantile activities share the same instinctual sources of gratification, and that the essential need pattern which will govern later occupational choices is determined during the first six years of life.

This particular frame of reference may be useful to the psychoanalytically oriented counselor in his work with vocational problems. Certainly it will affect his approach to the client in terms of assuming that basic need

---

[1] No distinction is being made here between personal adjustment counseling and psychotherapy, as the author feels that no line between these two concepts could be drawn on a reasonable and meaningful basis, and even if it could, it is beyond the scope of this chapter to attempt to make this distinction.

We feel it is semantic nonsense to ask questions such as, "Where does counseling end and psychotherapy begin?" or "Are psychoanalytic techniques appropriate to counseling?" This implies that we know the limits or boundaries of what constitutes counseling, psychotherapy, or psychoanalysis, and of course there are no such clear delineations. All three concepts might be subsumed under the larger abstract of "helping people." One might facetiously ask, "Where does chemistry end and physics begin?" Both are subordinate to the larger concept of physical science. Few persons would lose sleep over such a problem. For example, at one end of a helping-people scale, a "helper" might be dealing with strong emotionality in the client, using free association or free imagery, interpreting behavior, inducing regression, etc. At the other end of the dimension, a "helper" might be dealing with cognitive reorganization, improving study techniques, providing information about vocational choices, coaching for social poise, etc. We should have little difficulty in labeling the first type of helping behavior, psychotherapy. The latter type we could easily label counseling. Where these two concepts merge somewhere in the middle, we are apt to experience semantic confusion and often try rigidly to define what one class of behavior is in terms of what the other is not. Reality rarely provides the opportunity for a nice fitting of this type of Aristotelian thinking or labeling. The dimension adumbrated above is that of "depth." This depth dimension should not be identified as a significance-nonsignificance dimension, nor should it be identified as a prestige-nonprestige dimension, etc. Dimensions should be evaluated on their own merits and not as integral parts of other dimensions, or adjuncts.

patterns have already been established, and that his role as counselor is to help the client make decisions which are consistent with needs established early in life. The counselor does not, therefore, set about the task of changing the client's need pattern, since he assumes that it remains relatively stable throughout the client's lifetime. The psychoanalytically derived framework of vocational development devised by Bordin and his colleagues, in addition to spelling out basic assumptions and determining the general approach taken by the counselor, also sets forth rather specific occupational categories dependent upon the primary need pattern of the client. In this way, personality development and vocational choice become intimately connected in such a way that the former significantly influences the latter, particularly where vocational satisfaction is concerned. At the theoretical level, job satisfaction is not likely to result from vocational commitments which do not meet basic, primitive need patterns of the individual.

People find their way to counselors' offices because they are unhappy in some respect. The degree of this unhappiness varies from minimal to severe, and the things about which a person can be unhappy are apparently limitless—poor grades, trouble with parents, social awkwardness, sex, feelings of unworthiness, ad infinitum. Counselors, according to their theoretical positions, will choose to help these persons by using techniques with which they are most familiar and secure. A danger arises when counselors tend to perceive client problems in terms of their own special area of interest or capability—for example, the vocational counselor who perceives most of his clients as being unhappy because of vocational maladjustment or, conversely, the analytically trained counselor who feels that trouble on the job is invariably traceable to the client's troubled childhood. The predispositions of both counselors seem likely to do a disservice to the client.

A fundamental goal of counseling is to help a person solve a problem and to feel better after doing it. Analytically trained counselors tend to build up a case load of persons with minor emotional problems. These problems would ordinarily not be severe enough for referral to a psychiatrist and would be ones with which the counselor feels he could be effective within a reasonable time limit. A "reasonable time limit" often depends on the policy of the agency in which the counselor is employed. In some agencies, counselors find considerable leniency in the amount of time they are free to devote to a client, some of whom may receive as many as one hundred interviews or more. These clients are not typical ones, however. The twenty- to fifty-interview range for personal adjustment clients is more common.

The analytically trained counselor would regard his clients in certain fundamental ways on which he would base his constructive action. Principally, he would view his client as having psychological processes of which he is unconscious as well as those of which he is conscious. He would feel that behavior is shaped in every moment of existence by an interaction of conscious and unconscious processes. He would pay particular attention to whether the unconscious factors in the personality were dominating or interfering with the client's behavior. He would feel that behavior could not be materially changed without ascertaining what these factors were. He would anticipate meeting resistances in the client that might require certain techniques to overcome. His aim would be to bring these unconscious conflicts under the domain of conscious control.

Kubie (1950) lists three types of psychotherapy: (1) Simple, nontechnical, nonanalytic psychotherapy which deals with conscious situational problems and conflicts. This will usually involve support, guidance, advice, or assistance in handling life situations. (2) Analytically informed psychotherapy, which may be both palliative and expressive. The therapist is alert to the interplay of unconscious forces and the way in which they affect the person's symptoms. (3) Analysis itself, the crux of which is an effort to share with the client full insight into his unconscious mechanism. A primary tool for this is the interpretation of transference.

Therapists with analytic training will usually operate between levels two and three. Some counselors will aim at bringing about a deep reorganization of the personality, which would require the client to recapture and express strong emotional feeling. This reduces the intensity of the repressed affect, and, if accompanied by emotional insights of sufficient depth, is capable of modifying and restructuring the personality.

Some therapists will aim at the goal of showing the person how to live within the confines of his psychoneurosis with as little discomfort as possible. With such techniques, the counselor ordinarily will not require the client to abreact his most deeply repressed feelings, although some emotional expression by the client is always sought. The length of time required for this type of therapy is shorter. The overt behavior of the client will frequently be interpreted, and the symbolic meaning of his symptoms will be discussed. The counselor tries to give the client more cognitive control over his affect by siding with the ego, as it were, in its effort to handle the partially repressed primary process, rather than allowing the unconscious feelings to be expressed with full intensity. (More about this in a later section.)

In short-term therapy, the client's emotional transference to the counselor does not develop to the extent that it does in therapy that goes on for a longer period of time. Occasionally, the counselor will use techniques such as free imagery, hypnosis, or multiple therapy (discussed in the next section) to bring unconscious material to light that would ordinarily be revealed in transference phenomena. However, the use of these techniques is not excluded when a more complete job of therapy is attempted.

Some university counseling centers and community counseling agencies provide the opportunity for clients to undergo deep, reconstructive psychotherapy in which the maximum therapeutic use of transference can be made.

Evan defines transference ". . . as a regressive discharge mechanism by which repressed impulses are repeated in the therapy situation and shifted via phantasy gratification from unconsciousness to consciousness where they are made accessible to the analytic work of transition from primary to secondary process" (1961, p. 28).

Although the principle goal of counseling is to help the person solve a problem, one of the most important subgoals is the establishment and working through of the emotionally transferred feelings that the client has for the therapist. The nonresolution of transference in the counseling relationship allows the client to maintain his infantile, narcissistic attitudes toward life and to continue his nonsatisfying relationships with people. The relationship between the counselor and client is the essence of psychoanalytic therapy and must be thoroughly understood in all its manifestations before the client can be expected to change fundamentally.

Transference in the counseling relationship never has to be created by the counselor but can be expected to develop spontaneously (Kubie, 1950). It appears to be a compulsive function of the psyche, and transference phenomena are observable even in the best adjusted individuals.

According to Ruesch (1955) transference springs from early childhood situations in which experiences are overly intense and are more related to nonverbal than to verbal cues. It gathers momentum when the possibility of varied contact between individuals is reduced, when the exchange of messages becomes redundant, or when feedback phenomena cannot be relied on to correct distorted impressions.

One of the essential goals of therapy, then, is to improve the ability of the client to communicate and to reduce the inequality in the past development of verbal and nonverbal communication. Ruesch, in discussing some of the goals of therapy, says, "If the therapist's endeavor is directed at improving the patient's ability to communicate, the patient will eventually be able to relate with progressively lessening transference" (1955, p. 39).

The counseling process aims to disrupt the current life theme of the person and to establish a new and more satisfying one (Mullan, 1960). The deeply entrenched, habitual ways of adjusting that are unsatisfying will need to be interrupted and modified if the client is to improve. The therapeutic encounter has this as its purpose. There are several built-in aspects to the therapy process that effectively bring about this end. Although the client brings his history into the interview, the relationship is immediately spontaneous; it has no background. The atmosphere within the therapy hour is timeless: The past, present, and future are telescoped into one. The domain of the interview hour is all embracing (Mullan, 1960). Two persons are present, cloistered within the therapy room, each giving the other his total attention. There is the feeling of a fresh beginning. All of this acts to change the client's typical way of behaving, broadens the scope of his awareness, and gives him more living room.

Another goal of counseling would be the revitalization of the client, increasing his ability to get along with others. Meerloo (1962) says that one characteristic of almost every sort of growth is an alternating forward and backward movement rather than a continuous steady progress. It is seen in all phases of life, from the neurotic person enmeshed with his fixations to the repair of cellular damage due to pathology or disease.

The controlled regression that occurs during the counseling process has a revitalizing effect on the client. Often clients seem goaded to tear themselves down and resurrect themselves in a way that feels looser, more adaptive, and satisfying. Usually, this retrogenesis—this going back and putting things together anew—results in a reacceptance of people and an increased tolerance for their humanness. These effects are more easily seen in spontaneous regression that occurs when people take vacations, forget their cares, and renew their spirits. Human relationships during these times often take a turn for the better.

Ambiguity and the Counselor's Role in Therapy

This section will indicate some of the general tasks of the analytically oriented counselor, showing his role during the interview hour and then demonstrating his functioning in more specific situations.

Before we can fully understand the counselor's role, it will first be helpful to elaborate on the concept of ambiguity. Ambiguity as a therapeutic variable should not be overlooked in any discussion of the application of psychoanalytic theory to counseling and psychotherapy. At least one person (Bordin, 1955) in the area of counseling psychology has attempted to concretize our understanding of ambiguity by pointing out three fundamental ways in which counselors can be ambiguous: (1) appropriate content, (2) the client-counselor relationship, and (3) the therapist's personal life. In terms of content, counselors vary in the extent to which they indicate to the counselee which topics are appropriate for discussion, with the psychoanalytically-oriented counselor being least specific in indicating to the client what he should or should not talk about. From this point of view, "anything goes" where content is concerned. The analytic rule "tell me anything that's on your mind" suggests the ambiguity of structure imposed upon interview content by the counselor. Directly opposite in approach is the active structuring of the "rational-emotive" and behavior modification schools.

The ambiguity of the client-counselor relationship also characterizes psychoanalytically oriented therapy. Unlike the client-centered approach, psychoanalytically-derived counseling does not allow for the counselor to freely communicate his own feelings to the client. In fact, the psychoanalytic emphasis on ambiguity of the counselor seems diametrically opposed to the "transparency" emphasis currently encouraged by such theorists as Rogers (1961) and Jourard (1964) and in the research of Truax and Carkhuff (1967). The psychoanalytic counselor remains a relatively unknown quantity to the client; the counselor is opaque. The client is encouraged to express and reveal himself; the counselor remains undisclosed, so that the counselor is not only a mysterious, smokey figure, but because of his lack of clarity the relationship is ambiguous also.

Ambiguity functions in such a way that as the counselor continues seeing the client, the client becomes more and more deeply engrossed in the problems which need resolution. Ambiguity allows the client to project any number of internally derived characteristics onto the counselor or therapist, which lays the groundwork for the transference phenomena discussed in another part of this chapter. Ambiguity creates anxiety in the client, and sets the stage for "parataxic distortion" and transference. Clients presumably project their own personality and emotional conflicts onto ambiguous stimuli, which means in the face of ambiguous stimuli it becomes nearly impossible for even the most well adjusted person to avoid reading his own conflictual feelings in the stimulus situation. So, what we are saying is first that ambiguity facilitates the transference process and second that it provides a backdrop against which conflictual and irrational feelings are more clearly apparent. And it is the emergence of these irrational and conflictual feelings which give rise to anxiety, which within psychoanalytic theory is seen as a defensive reaction to the feelings themselves. A clearer understanding of ambiguity and anxiety is essential to any counselor who wants to work effectively with his clients. As Bordin (1955) noted some time ago, there appears to be an optimal level of anxiety for each client, which, if exceeded, only impedes therapeutic progress. "Thus, it becomes necessary for the therapist to relate the degree of ambiguity to the level of anxiety which will be optimal for a particular client" (Bordin, 1955).

The counselor-therapist may with certain clients want to limit the ambiguity he imposes on the counseling relationship depending upon the intensity of the conflicts involved and the defensive capabilities of the client. The client with a low tolerance of ambiguity, loosely organized thoughts, weak defenses, etc., may be a poor candidate for an extremely ambiguous counseling relationship and counselor; whereas a highly realistic client with many strong defenses and highly organized thinking processes (rationality) might without the ambiguity of the therapy situation remain misunderstood by the counselor. The ambiguity allows the counselor in the latter case to go beneath rational, well defended surface and more quickly penetrate to levels of conflict.

Ambiguity produces another effect. We have already discussed psychoanalytically derived counseling from the standpoint of one-upmanship, and can speculate with some certainty that ambiguity defines the counseling relationship in such a way that the counselor is one-up on the client. The counselor's mystique along with his invitation to the client to disclose himself clearly implies the dependent position of the client, assuming the client accepts the invitation. Ambiguity in counseling places the counselee in the position of needing protection, and from this point of view one would wonder whether transference is not more of a response to the vulnerable position the client is placed in, than it is a distortion of the therapist figure. Perhaps the healthy client is the one who could reject the therapist's invitation in the beginning; or perhaps, as Haley (1963) suggests, a cure is evidenced in the patient's unwillingness to try to become one-up on the therapist any longer, that is with his lack of caring about the power dimension of their relationship.

One of the functions served by transference in an ambiguous situation such as a therapy interview is that of meeting the safety needs of the client in such a way that he is assured of protection from this nebulous, basically unpredictable human being sitting across from him. Transference in this sense perhaps is the client's way of making his immediate environment more predictable and thereby reducing threat. Bordin (1955) at least suggests the possibility that transference does decrease in direct proportion to the ambiguity of the therapist. Transference may persist because of the tendency of psychoanalytically-oriented therapists to maintain an optimal level of anxiety in the client which is often accomplished through a maintenance of the ambiguous therapist-client relationship. Or perhaps the ambiguous stimulus shifts gradually during the therapeutic process from therapist to client, that is, as the client's feelings become clearer to him, his behavior becomes actually less predictable. So it may well be that ambiguity in the latter sense, i.e., in terms of unpredictability of the client's behavior, predominates during middle and latter phases of therapy.

But ambiguity, as such, has limits beyond which it becomes unproductive, if not clearly debilitating, for the client. Consequently, it is the further responsibility of the counselor to engender an atmosphere of security, in which the client is able to discuss the most intimate matters with feelings of trust and confidence. The counselor should appear professional in manner without being formal or stiff. Although frequent expressions of empathic understanding are used by the counselor, it should not be perceived by the client or counselor as the mothering of a lonely child.

The task of the counselor is to keep the client at the job of producing material and actively attempting to uncover repressed or conflictful content. This does not mean that the counselor demands incessant conversation from the client, because many occasions will occur when the client appears to "run dry" and is unable to produce anything relevant. These temporary lapses are understood by the counselor but are not allowed to continue for too long or to occur too frequently. The responsibility for the production of the material rests on the client, although when particularly strong resistances are met, the counselor may use special techniques to assist the client. In short, the client should never get the feeling that the burden for his improvement rests solely with the counselor.

The counselor will make initial judgments whether the individual client is suitable for the particular type of therapy that he offers. Certain types of character structures are not suitable for analytically oriented counseling, and it is up to the counselor to protect his clients from long therapeutic encounters in which the client cannot be aided.

Nacht (1955) feels that clients whose anxiety is not too acute and has not been structuralized into phobic or obsessional symptoms are most amenable to therapy. However, analytically oriented counseling could be considered effective with clients who present mild free anxiety, phobic symptoms, or symptoms of an obsessive-compulsive nature. Depressed clients and those with moderately severe marital problems in which the possibility of divorce is remote seem to respond well to therapy.

Therapy is contraindicated for clients who show schizoid personalities, paranoid states, or severe hypochondriasis; and the prognosis is guarded for persons with marked conversion symptoms. Sometimes persons in this latter group respond to more directive, supportive therapy, but results are often impermanent because of the plasticity of the ego. Treatment is rarely indicated for persons who have a history of habitual delinquency or drug addiction.

As we mentioned before, the counselor is warm, sincere, and understanding in his encounter with the client; but he also maintains a therapeutic atmosphere that is, at the same time, depriving and nongratifying of some of the client's most basic aims. The counselor, in denying the direct gratification of these aims, becomes a loved but frustrating object. This lack of gratification for the client facilitates regression which is necessary for the reduplication of infantile conflicts within the therapy situation (Fleming, 1961). The client struggles for the fulfillment of his passive dependency needs with the therapist, and when these needs are not gratified, the client's urge to know himself and to communicate this to the counselor takes precedence. This need to know and communicate would seem to be an essential condition if the therapeutic process is to achieve its purpose.

The counselor will often have to make judgments about the use of special techniques and methods to facilitate the therapeutic work. Clients frequently encounter hard-shelled resistances that delay the course of treatment for extended periods. Although some clients simply need additional time for further exploration of these blockages for them to dissolve, others will require the use of special means to penetrate them. Free imagery, multiple therapy, and the setting of termination dates are techniques which help the client through resistant periods in his therapy.

Free imagery[2] is a technique that asks the client to relax as completely as possible and to report to the counselor the visual images that occur. The technique has the effect of reducing contact with reality, which diminishes the controlling functions of the ego and allows unconscious material to be expressed.

Multiple therapy employs two counselors with one client. In this situation the dynamic complexity of the therapy relationship is enormously increased in such a way that the client finds it difficult to gear his old defenses to the new situation. Also, as the client usually accords superior status to the counselor, the original family constellation of mother and father is effectively reduplicated.

The setting of a specific termination date sometimes puts an end to the resistance to certain transference and countertransference phenomena with the result that the relationship gathers new meaning, and new insights are gained.

The counselor who uses such techniques will need to familiarize himself with indications and contraindications for their employment.

The counselor who does therapy has a paramount obligation to understand his own feelings throughout the therapeutic process as well as the feelings of his client. Colm (1955) feels that the essential part of therapy comes when the therapist is able to contact the center area of the field of experiences of the client, as opposed to contact with the client's defensive circumference. This center-to-center contact can only be established if the therapist is aware of his own feelings about the client. If center-to-center contact has been established, decidedly negative attitudes may be expressed by the therapist or the client without damaging the relationship.

After the therapist has reached a point where the client is fully involved in the transference relationship, failure of therapy from that point on is usually traceable to the therapist rather than to some inability on the part of the client. Such failures often arise from the counselor's unawareness of and inability to handle his countertransference. Siegman (1955) points out that the client's perception of the counselor as an omnipotent person or magician exacerbates the counselor's guilt-laden Oedipal wish to displace the awesome rival parent, which can thus become a significant source of countertransference.

Positive transference can be more difficult for the counselor to handle than its negative counterpart because of the guilt that it produces in the counselor. Such guilt will tend to make the counselor disturb the positive transference by ill-timed interpretations and to look overly hard for signs of negative transference. He might also divest himself too early of the powers

---

[2] The pioneering work in free imagery has been done by Joe Reyher, Michigan State University.

granted to him by the client, with an interruption of the therapy relationship. In psychoanalytically oriented counseling, the resolution of the emotional transference seen in the therapy relationship is crucial.

The role of the counselor demands that he be aware of his function and responsibility within the therapy hour. He should understand the way in which he may be used within the interview to be of the most service to the client—his therapeutic participation, in other words.

The counselor needs to devote all his attention to understanding the productions of the client. To understand the client, he must have access to his own unconscious but still fall short of regressive daydreaming to meet his own unfulfilled needs. His ego processes must be available for use by the client, performing the function of subjecting to reality the associations and productions of the person in therapy (Fleming, 1961). Fleming says, "The therapist, then, must function in two worlds simultaneously, the client's world and his own, a real world and an unreal one, the past as well as the present. He must perform this function while maintaining his own integrated position" (1961, p. 705).

Transference—the Essence of Therapy

Whatever psychoanalytic theory has accomplished, it has demonstrated that all behavior is not guided by the rationality of the conscious mind. Some writers assert that even if consciousness could be somehow extirpated or held in abeyance for a period of time, intact motivational systems would then still operate within the organism and action would still be carried out. In other words, consciousness, per se, is not thought to be required for organized, purposive behavior.

Psychoanalysis has also made it clear that the mental purview of consciousness makes up only a small part of the total activity of the mind. A clear analogy is that of a spot light (consciousness) on a dark night (unconscious and preconscious activity) in which the rays from the light illuminate only a small part of the landscape. The focus of the light may be changed, or objects within the light's beam may influence a new direction of illumination, but still the lighted area remains a small fraction of the total landscape (Wepman and Heine, 1963).

One does not have direct access to his unconscious. The activities of the unconscious become visible through its effect on the preconscious and the conscious. Freud made it indisputably plain that slips of the tongue, the dream content, and erroneously carried out actions, betrayed the deeper impulses and wishes of the individual, and were not simply ordinary mistakes. These mistakes, thought Freud, were caused by the leakage of unconscious material into the ego processes, and they were labeled *transference*

(Allport, 1961). The basic meaning of the term, then, is the amalgamation of primary and secondary process material which is caused by a weakening of the repressive barrier (unconscious defenses) that separates the preconscious from the unconscious.

"In ordinary usage however the term has come to have a more circumscribed meaning and now implies the special persistent tendency the client has to misinterpret and to misperceive his therapist" (Wepman and Heine, 1963). Several conditions obtain within psychoanalytic therapy which facilitate the formation of transference. The analyst sits behind the client offering an ambiguous figure with minimal reality cues for the client to perceive. The analyst ordinarily refuses to establish a friendly relationship with the client, which makes it difficult for the client to validate his subjective impressions of the analyst, thereby making these impressions vulnerable to the intrusion of unconscious material. The therapist generally does not provide realistic gratification for the client. This forcing of abstinence on the client militates for regression, making it all the more likely that id material will be infused into the therapeutic relationship.

Stern (1957) says transference can be defined as a fixation to a previous situation displaced onto a substitute object which symbolizes the previous situation. Anna Freud regards transference as a fixation upon infantile libidinal impulses, along with the defenses against them.

Freud spoke of the traumatic effects of transference and specified its positive and negative qualities. He pointed out that the individual attempts to relive the original trauma so that it may be mastered and the anxiety reduced (positive). The negative aim of the ego, however, is to repress all, so that no trace of the original trauma is recognizable.

Psychic trauma may be set off by any sort of stimuli that imply to the person that the original trauma may be anticipated in all its original freshness. These threats are intense and trigger the individual's primary defenses, signifying the failure of internal homeostatic regulators. When threat is extreme for the individual, hallucinations, perceptual distortions, and other types of primary defenses may be elicited. Stern (1957) considers transference and primitive defenses as a basic survival mechanism, stating that, "We may conceive of the human mental apparatus as a grandiose extension of the processes that safeguard equilibrium and the survival of the individual."

The threat of the return of the original trauma must not be underestimated; it creates a vague apprehension in the person when the impinging stimuli are similar to those experienced by the child in the original situation. When the child is mothered, it provides a relief from the somatic tension, however it creates in the child a sense of dependency and a feeling that danger may be circumvented only when mother is present. The closeness of the mother also provides the opportunity for libidinal gratification (hugging, stroking, etc.). Some authors posit that the child's ability to visualize the image of the mother reproduces the subjective feeling of physical closeness and consequently restores a feeling of homeostatic balance in the mental economy of the child (Stern, 1957). Transference, therefore, takes on a dual meaning signifying the libidinal closeness of the mother as well as the protection she affords in shielding the child from danger. Any cue in the environment that elicits a need for protection or libidinal gratification is capable of setting the transference process in motion (King and Neal, 1968).

King and Neal (1968) say:

Transference is most easily observed in psychotherapy. The client finds in the therapist an acceptable substitute which symbolizes his lost dependence object. The original object is most often the mother or father of the client as they are remembered in childhood. The first manifestations of the transference are usually tension provoking for the individual in therapy. The therapist is often ambivalently, perceived as a person who provides protection from hovering disaster, but also as a person who may fail to satisfy the client's strong dependency needs, and one who might desert him in a crisis. This is particularly apt to be so if the same parental figure was perceived as providing safety, but also one in whom psychic trauma might originate. During the initial stages of therapy, especially in the case of clients who are frightened and regressed because of situational stress, the therapist may encounter a diffuse transferability that later becomes more specific as the child-like ego develops the capacity to maintain cathexes to specific love objects (Stern, 1957).

And further:

Confusing to clients and therapists alike is the side-by-side existence of reality syntonic and transference attitudes, when, in one moment, the client will regard the therapist as a father, demonstrating identical attitudes which were characteristic of him as a child, and later, within the same interview, will see the therapist in realistic, objective ways. As a general rule the stronger the experienced anxiety, the greater is the urge that reparative mastery over the trauma prevails. However, at the same time, it is more likely that the reality syntonic attitude will be overthrown by the individual's need to revert to libidinal dependency on the transference object (Stern, 1957). This is why during the terminal phases of psychotherapy, it is common for the client to show stronger transference attitudes, as his anxiety is exacerbated because of the approaching separation from the therapist and the interruption of this dependent object relationship.

Psychoanalysts feel that before any deep personality change can be effected that the transference must be understood in all its intricacy and thoroughly worked through. The client then sees how the residue of his past is affecting his present-day relationships and is able to discontinue his childish anticipations of how adults will treat him and how he should act around them. Anxiety is drained from his personal interactions because his secondary processes, his ego functions, have been able to discriminate the past from the present; there is less eruption of repressed id material into the preconscious and conscious; and his ego feels strengthened because of a sense of increasing mastery over his environment. Above all, the essential thing that the resolution of transference accomplishes is the return of affect to the client. His feelings are now his own. Rather than being a puppet dangled on the vagaries of fortune, he becomes aware of his potency as a person and a purposeful manipulator of objects (in the kindest sense of the term) in his life space.

The Link between Counseling and Psychoanalysis: Fits and Misfits

The application of psychoanalytic techniques to counseling practice is greatly restricted when the counseling is done in an educational setting. In a high school the restriction is even greater than in a college.

One may consider the application of psychoanalytic theory from two points of view. The first view would be that of therapeutic intervention, or the modification of the life adjustment of the individual by psychotherapy. To the extent that psychoanalysis attempts to deal with unconscious motives and conflicts that shape the person's behavior, many therapeutic interviews over prolonged periods of time are usually required. For example, a masochistic or self-defeating life orientation in a high school student will not be undone in a few interviews. As was mentioned before, some college counseling centers allow students to be seen for as many interviews as are required, but even these centers tend, in general, to discourage prolonged therapy. Consequently, if one looks for the application of psychoanalytic theory from the therapeutic intervention point of view—the doing of therapy—in education settings, especially in high schools, he will find it an inconvenient and unsought-after technique.

If one considers psychoanalytic theory from a second point of view, that of providing a frame of reference for evaluating the behavior and personality structure of clients, then, even in educational settings, psychoanalytic theory can be useful.

Much seemingly inexplicable behavior in a student's interaction with teachers and school officials can take on new meaning when seen in the light of transferred attitudes carried over from the student's home life. A child who repeatedly displaces his original hostility toward his mother onto a teacher may enter a vicious downward spiral of rejection, bewilderment, and increased acting-out behavior unless the displaced and unconscious aspects of his conflict are explained, if only to the teacher. Of course, the counselor must have additional outside information on which to base his interpretation and must avoid the absurdity of labeling *all* hostile behavior as displaced and unconscious.

Inappropriate dependency or love attachments may be viewed in a similar manner—as expressing impulses whose original aims and objects have been unconsciously inhibited by the student for security reasons. When a counselor, sure of his information on the basis of repeated observations of such behavior and with test data and knowledge of the student's external environment, is able to interpret this behavior to the educator, a great deal of confusion may be eliminated.

Tactful discussions and cautious interpretations to the parents can often be helpful in easing the student's problem by giving them an understanding of his behavior. Counselors, acting as consultants, are often able to restore emotional equanimity to educators who have become involved in transference situations with students when these educators are able to perceive the possible substitute character of their participation. The anxiety and feelings of loss of control provoked by being intimately entangled in a relationship that they do not understand is thereby reduced. The counselor or school psychologist may wish to work with the student himself by nonanalytic techniques, but the help he can give significant persons in the student's environment may be considerable.

An understanding of personality or character structure can be useful in evaluating the constructive action that needs to be taken with certain clients, and the range of hit-or-miss remediation can be narrowed. It is not implied that *only* psychoanalytic theory can supply this understanding.

Suppose that a young high school student is unable to engage in activities that involve direct competition, any avenue of participation that remotely involved failure is scrupulously avoided, and mild obsessive-compulsive symptoms are evident. The counselor *tentatively* hypothesizes an early wound to the student's narcissism—an interaction with a person that prevented him from being able to continue to love himself—and he also senses the hostile undergirdings of the student's personality. He would be aware of the effectiveness of the student's obsessive-compulsive ego defenses and consequently would not expect to relate to the student easily and quickly. The counselor might arrive at a tentative dynamic formulation of the problem: The student seems to have equated opportunity for failure with loss of his parents' love and his own self-love along with consequent fury at this anticipated deprivation. His meticulousness and compulsivity represent safety for him, as he uses them to bind back his aggressiveness toward others and toward himself. These defenses are therefore self-corrective in nature.

The counselor might then wish to set up some situations in real life where the student could risk competition with fear of failure minimized. Or the counselor might wish to set up a role-playing situation with several students in which the client may experience failure in a protected situation and thereby begin to reassess his attitudes about failing. There would be no attempt here to get the student to reexperience the original traumas or to reclaim the original affect.

The point of view that psychoanalysis provides a way of thinking about motivation, a framework in which troublesome behavior or feelings may be understood, would seem to be compatible with the aims of counseling psychology.

The authors wish to underscore that analytically oriented therapy is not the most appropriate one for high school counselors or college student personnel workers. Many other theories are assimilated and used more comfortably, and those ways of talking about people and their behavior seems more natural. Phenomenology, learning theory, general semantics, and other theories will seem more usable to school counselors and personnel workers.

When one attempts to apply psychoanalytic theory to "general" counseling and personnel work, it becomes immediately apparent that the theory is operating on the fringe of its "range of convenience," to use a term of the late George Kelly. The "focus of convenience," still borrowing from Kelly (1955), for psychoanalysis, of course, was the one-to-one relationship with hysterics reared in mid-Victorian Europe. Through the writings of Freud and his followers, the theory has become applicable to a wider range of situations and disciplines. Its range of convenience has been increased. Psychoanalysis has much more to say about the personal adjustment counseling that occurs in therapeutically inclined counseling centers or community mental health centers than it does about the wider spectrum of student personnel work, with which counseling has become increasingly concerned in the past five years. Perhaps, we should not hastily conclude that analytic theory has nothing to contribute to the development of students in their traffic with the extra-academic affairs of the schools and, for that matter, with development in their postcollege vocational life.

The theory of psychoanalysis can make a contribution in helping us conceptualize what happens to people between the ages of seventeen and seventy-two, especially concerning their ego development. For a long time, this time span has been sadly neglected in terms of both clinical interest and research. Psychoanalysis has contributed knowledge about personality growth during the early years, child development disciplines and the psychologies of youth and adolescence have provided information about the teenage years, and geriatrics in recent times has furthered our knowledge about old persons. Sanford (1966) points out that when an individual enters his twenties, there seems to be an implicit assumption that nothing much happens to him until he "breaks through" again about sixty or sixty-five. Obviously, people continue to live, become afraid, see their hopes shattered, exult over triumphs, and, unless pathology intervenes, continue to develop. Some of the fastest development goes on during the years the individual is attending a university, while he is being continuously confronted with broadening experiences, is having his value systems purposely and seriously challenged, and being exposed to new role models that urge him to experiment with new behaviors.

Ego psychology, an offshoot of psychoanalytic theory, along with analytic theory itself, may provide some workable hypotheses for understanding the intellectual and emotional development of college students.

One of us, several years ago while working in a counseling center of a large university, tallied all the problems which he was able to collect which were reported by freshmen who came to the counseling center. Within a year, several hundred separate and identifiable problems had been accumulated. In listening to many of these problems being subsequently discussed in counseling interviews, several themes sifted out that stood in a superordinate position to the more commonplace problems the freshmen originally presented.

This is clearly a matter of interpretation, but if the themes were abstracted and interpreted correctly, they seemed to signify that many freshmen perceived (our wording) coming to the university as:

The first significant emancipation from their parents with attendant separation anxiety.

A situation which might lead to a diminution of control of their impulses, and which might lead to acting-out behavior, which had previously been prevented by the parent's capacity to reinforce the student's superego.

A place, because of its enormous complexity, which sorely taxed the capacity of their egos to assimilate, organize, and execute coping behaviors that were appropriate to the new situation.

Symbolizing the crossing of the boundary from the limbo of teenage dependency into adult responsibility, along with feelings of nostalgia, which prompted many wistful "backward" glances.

The first serious opportunity (now taking a developmental point of view) for them to grow up, confront themselves about their potential, limitations, and impact as an adult social being.

A time to delineate the boundaries of their ego from the general culture as well as to explore and reassess their values against the background of a vast amount of up-ending stimulation.

We doubt if anyone can make a case for students not changing during the time they are in college. There is evidence and speculation that many developmental changes occur from the freshman to the senior year. White (1952) mentions four growth trends that occur in late adolescence during the college years. He sees the stabilization of ego identity occurring during this period, the development of the "self one feels one's self to be." It implies a more permanent self concept less subject to the vagaries of external evaluation. As Sanford (1966) says, "... anything that increases the likelihood that the sense of self will be based on personal experience rather than on outside judgments favors the stabilization of ego identity." It is a time when one is adequately tuned to the world of reality, but at the same time one is able to sort out one's values and preferences. This enables one to know what one feels about the issues in one's life, but also permits one to feel a sense of separateness from others.

White also mentions the college age adolescents experience a deepening of interests and a more purposeful outlook on life. It is at these times that quite often the student finds a vocational aim to which he may devote the rest of his life. Some students find they have the capacity for serious scholarship and apply real industry to their field of interest. With this solidifying interest may come a change in, or crystallization of, the individual's identity. It is as if the individual understands how he is to behave and what he is to do with his enthusiasm and energy. He feels more secure and self-contained.

There is an increase in the freedom with which one relates to others. College provides the opportunity for intimate and varied friendships. There is the possibility of experimenting with new roles of behavior; there is a sense of risk-taking in interpersonal encounters. Many upper classmen especially are allowed to flout tradition and maintain their personal values or loyalties, sometimes in the face of strong pressure to do otherwise. Genuineness as a person and openness with others are not strangers to today's well-adjusted college youth.

As a corollary of the increase in freedom in personal relations is a decided surge in the humanizing of one's values. Things are perceived in terms of what they mean to social purposes and goals. Students find it easier to adopt the frame of reference of another person and consequently are more able to understand how they feel in a given situation. Many of the values they brought with them from high school may have undergone a serious revision under the onslaught of opportunities for sexual experimentation, new ideas they have learned in the classroom, and just being exposed to persons who are vastly different from those back home. Their concept of what a human being may be is drastically widened, and many students, not all, adopt a more tolerant attitude toward others, and are capable of delaying some of the signal reactions to the personal foibles of others, which were so easily triggered in the past.

Obviously, many schools are designed to promote growth and development in their students. These schools have a minimum of teachers who foster dependency in their pupils, and, in general, students are treated with respect and accorded a considerable measure of adult independence and responsibility. Unfortunately, there are too many schools which still have curricula saturated with "mickey mouse" courses which students find almost totally unrelated to the crucial concerns in their lives. Lecture methods still may kill off ardor for studying, and methods of evaluation may result in the student's being so apprehensive about examinations that test-taking becomes a farcical measure of the student's ability to endure anxiety rather than to demonstrate what he knows about the course content.

The administration's preoccupation with the rules and regulations by which students should live tends to have an infantilizing and frustrating effect on college populations. Overly harsh regulations about dormitory hours, conditions for intervisitations between sexes in the dorms, or the use of alcohol at social gatherings have become focuses of conflict between students who feel unduly oppressed and administrators who feel their controls slipping, and who consequently take firmer stands to reassure themselves. The student's sense of identity as an adult and his ego functioning may suffer a retarded acceleration under such circumstances.

In the well-known Vassar study, Sanford (1966) found indications of a changing identity for women during the college years. As this study was done on women, its relevance to college students in general must be circumscribed. However, Sanford found that seniors showed more disturbance with respect to identity than freshmen, feeling more dissatisfaction and vacillation than their younger schoolmates. Seniors also tended to be less authoritarian in their outlook, more variable in their relations with adults, and to make fewer categorical distinctions between youths and adults, or between males and females. Seniors, compared to freshmen, tended to be more flexible, less compulsive, and more unconventional. There seems to be a "loosening up" of one's emotional life and values as one moves up the educational ladder. Freshmen are seen as holding on to the values they brought with them from high school, partly for security reasons, accounting for some of their rigid and conventional attitudes. Seniors, knowing more who they are as individuals, have permitted themselves a greater freedom in experiencing and perceiving the world.

The college years do not seem to be static and marked by an absence of developmental change. Much appears to be happening. It is a time for continued ego development and stabilization (Sanford, 1966).

Initial Therapeutic Contact

The first therapy interview is perhaps the most important one. The initial interview will occur after the counselor has made a decision on the basis of a screening interview or test data about the client's suitability for counseling. It is somewhat analogous to first dreams in therapy, in that it allows the therapist to see the basic elements of the emotional problem more clearly than they may be viewed for a long time to come. It is quite common for dreams to be reported during the first interview, as the client's knowledge of the approaching encounter with the therapist may understandably stimulate the dream.

At the outset of the counseling, when the impact of the fresh relationship with the therapist is extremely potent, the client will often reveal the basic roots of the problem before he is able to organize his defenses and ward off the unique and unaccustomed relationship that is forming with the therapist.

The first hour can make a deep impression upon some clients. For one thing, it is the beginning of hope for a new and better life. Symbolically, it can have a stronger, more primitive meaning. It may symbolize a deep wish to surrender all responsibility for coping with the world to the therapist, in a hope that the client may sustain nurturance, love and protection. Harbored in this magical wish is not the need to get well, but to continue the gratification of the infantile pattern of adjustment by dependency on the therapist. This rather complete dependency, easily observable in some clients, indicates a regression to the oral stage of development and may represent a wish to become one with the first cathected object, the breast.

The counselor is seen as offering hope, comfort, and the capability of solving the client's problems. In this guise, the therapist may represent the pre-Oedipal mother, a person who is omnipotent, all-reassuring, and provident of total security as long as separation does not occur. This may partly explain the deep sigh of relief and freedom that some beginners in therapy give when the first therapy hour has terminated, although, in reality, their pain at facing themselves is just beginning.

The initial contact also allows the counselor to get some sort of therapeutic commitment from the client. The counselor may even remark that there is a lot of work to be done and that the road ahead will not be easy, but that he (the therapist) will do everything he can to help, if the client feels that he can make the same sort of investment.

Clients often come to counseling sessions expressing the wish to get well, or to be "cured." This frequently means that they want freedom from anxiety or the symptoms that have been bothering them, but they show little inclination to deal with the problems that are causing the anxiety or the symptoms. Structurally this implies that the ego defenses in the preconscious are not functioning effectively and that primitive id impulses and wishes are coming threateningly close to awareness giving rise to symptoms and anxiety. Many clients will feel guilty about experiencing such "abnormalities," which further increases the pain and discomfort of the client. In initial interviews, the therapist may say something to reassure the client that his odd feelings and behavior will be dealt with in the future, and that they are indications of problems the client has which may be worked through and alleviated. Often, an acknowledgment by the therapist of the symptoms in an attitude that seems unalarmed is enough to make the client feel better about his unreasonable feelings or behavior.

During the first interview, the therapist has several things that, for the future course of therapy, he must accomplish. He must indicate to the client that he is a warm, human being, although the therapist must not appear gushy, seductive, or false in the creation of this impression.

The therapist by his manner will ordinarily insinuate that anything goes, that the client may talk about anything without fear of eliciting an alarm or evaluative reaction on the part of the therapist.

The therapist ideally will communicate to the client that he is a genuine person and is sincerely interested in what he has to say, and that he is not attending simply because of an obligation.

Some clients will remark that the therapist is getting paid for the job and that he really is not interested in them. Some therapists, to reassure the client if this is in order, will state that they believe in their capacity to help with problems such as the one the client has brought to him. This word of encouragement (if the therapist is honest about it) can be particularly helpful to clients who are unduly distraught or uncertain whether the process of therapy will really do them any good.

To be helpful, the therapist should not be seen as a person who automatically takes over the cares and burdens of the client, although neither should he appear so professional as to be inhuman or noncompassionate.

Counseling Style—Strategies for Change

To some extent the style and technique that is used depends on the individual counselor. Also, the attitude of the client will influence the counseling style to some degree. Some talkative clients will allow the therapist to adopt a more passive attitude, while the silent client will demand a more active intervention from him.

The prevailing atmosphere of the interview is one of alert listening, the counselor conveying to the client that he is totally absorbed in his verbal productions. He may have the client sitting vis-à-vis, or he may have the client turn his back to him in order to minimize the social carryover of a face-to-face relationship. The client must have the feeling that the main responsibility for progress in the interview lies with him, although he senses that the counselor is fully engaged in the helping process.

Most interviews begin with the client's recounting the significant experiences that have occurred since the last meeting and his feelings about them. Clients well along in therapy at this point will move into a relating of their dreams since the last session. If the client is not able to understand the meaning of the dream, and the counselor feels he knows the meaning of the dream symbolism, he may wish to interpret (tentatively) what he thinks the dream means. Parts of the dream that are still unexplained and that seem significant may require free association or free imagery in order to discover what is being expressed. Frequently during this process the meaning of a dream the client was unable to grasp previously will become clear in the associative process of trying to understand the current one.

Some therapists will use the nonverbal cues offered by the client as a means of understanding his present emotional state. Such cues as pallor, sweating, posturing, preening, and undue relaxation can often furnish opportunities to tap some pocket of strong affect that would remain undetected if attention were focused solely on the verbal output. Care is required in interpreting these physiological reactions and defenses (they can be both), for the meaning of these preverbal reactions (reactions that were present before the child learned speech) can be far beyond the ability of the client to assimilate them when offered in an interpretation. Occasionally calling attention to the physiological reaction is enough to uncover the real feeling that lies behind it.

As the client relates the routine events that have occurred over the past several days, the counselor will listen for patterns of reaction that are similar to the early patterns revolving around significant happenings in the early years. For example, the counselor might sense the similarity between the feelings of shame followed by strangulated anger recently experienced by the client and an early episode with his mother which served as the prototype. This insight alone will rarely suffice to change his behavior very much unless he also understands the operations of this emotional sequence in his present life—the constant repetition of feeling furious because he has been made to feel guilty. There is a present-day trend in most traditional therapies toward an increased therapeutic use of interpreting patterns of reaction to the client rather than having him focus on dredging up forgotten traumas.

During the middle and later stages of therapy when the transference is strong, the therapist will expend the main part of his therapeutic effort in helping the client see the transference relationship for what it is: a recapitulation of attitudes and feelings that were unresolved with early figures in the client's past. During the efforts of the client to resolve his feelings about the therapist as a duplication of someone in his past life, the therapist will attempt to side with the client's ego as well as present himself in as realistic a light as possible. This helps the client make the discrimination between the therapist and the person whom he symbolizes. This frees the client's energy, which was absorbed in defending and maintaining this distorted relationship, for use by the client's ego in coping with the world. To effect this resolution, the counselor might set a termination date to bring to light some of the passive aspects of the transference that have lingered because of the client's faint hope that the relationship will never end.

Particularly strong resistances in therapy might have to be overcome by special techniques mentioned earlier, such as free imagery or an interruption of counseling for a period of time. Sometimes counselors will deliberately set a schedule of irregular appointments in order to upset the timing of the client's resistances, or perhaps he will schedule an early morning appointment (eight o'clock), hoping to arrive at some fresh material before the client's customary defenses are established for the day.

When the therapist senses that the end of therapy is approaching, he may wish to search in two areas of the client's life for lingering manifestations of the client's emotional troubles: (1) the client's terminating relationship with the therapist and (2) the client's ability to translate his newly found self into action in the world of reality. Some clients resolve one of these areas and fail to resolve the other. To feel that a "complete" job has been done, the client must be relating freely with the therapist, with transference at a minimum, and also must be putting into action in the real world parts of himself (id derivatives) previously rendered inactive by repression.

Ego Psychology: Some Special Techniques

As psychoanalysis has evolved, it has developed offshoots and variations, many of which have swollen in size and importance until they have developed into major systems themselves. One of these variations is ego psychology, which is much more closely related to the generally accepted aims of counseling psychology than the parent system, psychoanalysis. In general, ego psychology tries to augment the client's assets rather than requiring him to dredge up repressed id material, with its unavoidable appalling effect upon the person in therapy.

Certain writers are important in the development of ego psychology, and many of these men had strong psychoanalytic backgrounds. Notable examples are Hartmann (1964), Federn (1952), Kris (1951), Lowenstein (1950), and Shapiro (1962). These men have written extensively and have given the field a cohesiveness that makes it stand out as different from standard psychoanalysis.

Freud in some ways might be labeled the first ego psychologist, although students of Freud contend that he died before he had a chance to develop thoroughly his position. Freud, at the time of his death, appeared to be commencing to wrestle with some of the philosophical issues that have confronted ego psychologists for the past twenty-five years.

The ego develops out of the id, thought Freud. He theorized that the energy used by the ego in its task of coping with the world was really provided by the unconscious mind. Freud originally thought of the ego as a class of instincts in its own right, but later changed his mind and subsumed ego instincts under a larger class of sexual instincts.

Freud first thought that the ego was an ever-strengthening ruler who proceeded from perceiving instincts to controlling them, and from obeying instincts to curbing them. His subsequent position was that of seeing the ego as an arbitrator of disputes between the demands of the id and those of reality. Freud considered the ego's main function to be that of mental organization. But the ego had other important mental tasks to accomplish. It had to synthesize the demands made on it from within the body and from outside reality. It was faced with preserving both the organism and the species. The sense organs fell under its domain, as well as voluntary movement. It also had to adapt to stimulation—withdrawing from overstimulation and adapting when stimulation was within manageable limits. Above all, the charge to the ego was the control of the instincts, deciding when and how they could be expressed.

A fresh and attractive approach to ego psychology has been followed by White (1963) of Harvard University. White posits that the ego does not get energy from the id, never has, never will, but has independent energies of its own. This eliminates the id as the father of the ego system. White's documentation of his position by citing selected research is impressive.

To White, ego energies are those that pertain to adaptation and coping—energies that are governed by and attuned to reality. According to him the ego strives for two things: effectance, the tendency to put forth effort so that the environment may be influenced; and competence, the feeling that what one has tried to do has been done well. There is a joy for the ego in mastering, controlling, and wresting satisfaction from a world that is a potential depriver. These things are their own reward since they imply that the organism is capable of ultimately providing for its own security and delight.

King and Neal (1968) in contrasting ego therapy and traditional analytic therapy, say that ego therapy tends to focus on one or two ego defects rather than undertaking to remold the entire personality.

> The boundaries of the emotional problems are more sharply circumscribed. Both the therapist and the client realize they are looking for specific, maladaptive behaviors, along with its point of origin and the environmental nutriment that keeps such behavior alive. This obviates the endless looking for an evanescent childhood trauma that may result in interminable therapeutic interviews, because neither the client nor the therapist is apt to know when he has found

"it". In shorter terms, this may be labelled a therapeutic attitude of specific purpose, and it is communicable from the therapist to the client, because quite often the client will not have it.

The ego psychologist has as his main aim the strengthening of a weakened ego. In such cases, the ego is considered to be spending too much of its energy in maintaining its defenses and too little energy coping with the demands of reality. The ego apparently has a knack of acting out both sides of an internalized conflict. The result is that much energy is used within the psychic apparatus in maintaining this struggle, in fantasy, and in dead-center ambivalence. New methods are coming along that are designed to strengthen the ego and make a person feel less at the mercy of his impulses and conflicts.

Some of the new ego therapies do not seem to be very different from one another, and in some cases one has to strain to separate the overlap. All ego therapies attempt to recharge the ego, to reinforce the individual's feeling of mastery over his situation, and to induce him to view his impulses as manageable and with less alarm.

A type of ego therapy, known as the echoing approach, focuses upon the ego's pattern of self-attack. The therapist consistently confronts the client with his low regard for himself and may even overstate this situation on occasions. The therapist communicates throughout his continuous confrontation with the client that he is close to the client and will not desert him regardless of what direction his aggression takes. An attempt is made with this approach to reverse the pernicious circumstances under which the ego was formed. The infantile ego was unable to express hostility toward the original objects (parents) because the object was perceived as too distant or needed too badly to risk separation by becoming angry at the object. The object (therapist) now emotionally within reach becomes an appropriate target for hostility rather than the ego itself, and this time the hostility does not drive the object away, result in loss of support, nor terminate the relationship. The client has learned a new method of dealing with his aggression, and this makes the sensing of aggression within himself a much less dangerous percept (Nagelberg and Spotnitz, 1958).

Another method of strengthening the ego is brought about by the therapist devaluating himself, but with a definite purpose in mind. This is known as "devaluating the object." The therapist implies to the client that he (the therapist) is inadequate, that he probably has adjustment problems himself, and that he is not the paragon of strength that the client wishes him to be. Rather than being omnipotent, the therapist presents himself to the client as ineffectual. This technique attempts to reverse the process of faulty ego formation. Because the original object (a parent, a loved one, etc.) was seen as being too valuable and elevated to be a proper target for hostility, the client now watches his security object, the therapist, reduced in status until he seems to be the equal of the client. This lowering of the therapist to the client's level induces the client to feel there no longer is a justifiable reason for holding back his hostility toward the therapist, so a release of aggression occurs. This has a strengthening effect on the client's ego by convincing the client that released hostility does not always have the effect of terminating relationships (Nagelberg and Spotnitz, 1958).

Ego therapy attempts to do several things, one of which is to provide for a budgeted release of hostility and to allow the client to feel more capable of putting into action some of his hostile impulses without feeling so intimidated by them. Another goal of ego therapy is to induce the client to feel stronger, to be in greater control of his fate, and to have more "positive regard" for himself. This is Rogers's term, but it expresses it so beautifully. A distinct difference emerges between ego therapy and other approaches. In ego therapy, the therapist attempts to take over the function of one side of the ego conflict, thus permitting the ego to unify itself against what the therapist represents. Heretofore, both sides of the conflict had been symbolized within the ego itself. The ego was on a dead-center balance, so to speak. When the therapist assumes his unilateral position, it allows the ego to see more clearly the internal war which was going on within, and to express feelings (usually hostility) toward someone other than itself.

Grossman (1964) has identified a specifiable type of ego therapy called hyperbolic therapy. The therapist attempts to overexaggerate or caricature certain parts of the client, such as his defensive perfectionism, the immediate indulgence of his oral dependency needs, etc. This naturally requires a good relationship between client and therapist, and should be avoided during the early part of the therapeutic encounter.

Self-defeating attitudes may be brought to light by this method. It enables the client to see parts of himself in bold relief and externalized. King and Neal (1968) say:

> The client is able to see the area of the self that is being criticized, as well as the internal standards against which the defective self is being measured. Gradually the criticizing part of the self may take on human characteristics of someone in the client's past with such clarity that the critical self is identifiable. A client may say, 'You know, I have been treating myself exactly as my father used to treat me when I failed to accomplish something!' The therapist attempts to re-externalize the attitudes of the parents that were originally introjected by the client by his over-accentuation of his resistances. It is as if the therapist lends his weight to a part of the client's structural system, freeing ego functions for a closer, re-evaluative look at reality.

One type of ego therapy needs special mention. It is one of the more exciting types of ego therapy to us. It seems to have applicability to individual psychotherapy and—here's the exciting part—to some of the new types of group activity presently so visible. Shapiro has done the major work in this area, has elaborated upon his position, and has indicated the practical importance of his work.

Shapiro questions whether it is possible for anyone to "be himself." This has been a common aim for clients and therapists alike—to be natural, to be one's self. Shapiro says there is no single psychological self, but many subselves tied together by a superordinate personal identity. Shapiro puts emphasis upon uncontrived self-disclosure in personal interactions, both in and out of therapy. The ability to communicate, according to Shapiro, comes from a system of intracommunicative subselves. Some of the different types of subselves which may exist within a client are the hurt child who pouts; the remote onlooker, passive and uninvolved; mother, father, or judge; the omnipotent subself that secretly feels it is superior to the therapist; and the internal saboteur which tries to wreck all efforts of the ego to achieve satisfaction and tranquility.

From this theoretical position, Shapiro has developed an ego therapy model that is analogous to family group therapy. It is the task of the therapist to implement communication among the various subselves of the client. Through this process of communication, various subselves become increasingly delineated, and the boundaries between subselves become sharper.

Subselves interact with each other much on the same order that individuals do in everyday life. For example, one subself may have a punitive relationship with another subself, an analog being a critical father berating the inadequate child. The dominance hierarchy of subselves will vary, and the frequency with which subselves preponderate will change over time. Subselves, according to Shapiro, have a tendency to link themselves with external figures in the daily milieu of the client, when, for example, psychology trainees imitate their supervisors in posture and speech in interview situations.

In this theoretical vein, the client becomes "pathological," when there is inadequate communication between subselves, when one subself does not accept another subself, or when there is a war over which of two subselves will dominate. One subself may try to withdraw from the subself system, or a subself may try to obliterate or destroy another subself. When such things occur, psychological symptoms often eventuate.

When warring subselves are activated, there is a tendency for individuals to externalize these conflicts and find symbolic representation for them in the real world. This is a paradox, because it is the reverse of this process early in childhood which accounts for the internalization of conflictful real-life situations, enabling the child to manipulate traumatic events "inside his skin" without being exposed to the dangers of "living it." The inclination of the client to externalize his conflicted subselves on persons in his environment, of course, worsens his interpersonal relationships, as persons then become actors in his personal drama, and his personal correspondence with the world is one step further removed.

Therapy attempts to delineate the different subselves so that they are identifiable and have unity, to promote the acceptance of one subself by another, and to reverse the process of defensive externalization of subselves so that the subselves are seen as a part of the ego, thus obviating the need to find symbolic representation for them. Behavioral change comes from the reinforcing acceptance one subself has for another, rather than reinforcements doled out by the therapist.

The therapist tries to be aware of the subself that the client is experiencing at the moment. This is possible only when the therapist and the client are familiar with the subselves that exist within the ego system. The therapist may attempt to show how one of the subselves is aligned with individuals in the life of the client—e.g., a maternal, perfectionistic subself is projected onto the person of the therapist, who is then rejected. It is also crucial for both therapist and client to understand how therapy is perceived in relation to the subselves. Does the client see therapy as supportive of the injured, helpless child subself, or is it war between a suppressed, masculine, independent subself and a dominating therapist? Therapists pay special attention to the client's need to manipulate them into a position which gratifies the client's neurotic need to remain disturbed and dependent. Several years ago, one of us had a client who conceptualized his relief from neuroticism when his deserted-little-boy subself truly forgave a mother subself which ruled by guilt and withdrawal of love.

Making the Therapist Nervous—Special Problems

a. The client who won't talk. A great deal of therapist sweat and irritability has been engendered by the client who comes in and, after a quick relating of his troubles, refuses to go on in the discussion of his problem. This may happen on the initial interview, but it can also happen after several interviews when good rapport has apparently been established. Zeligs points out that therapists are too quick to conceptualize this silence as resistance, when it can have various other meanings. He states, "When the patient's speech is inhibited and silence prevails, the . . . analytic aim is not merely to get the patient to speak, but to try to make meaningful for him the unconscious reasons for his inability to speak" (1961, p. 11). In his analysis of a young woman, Zeligs points out the different ways that silence was used by her during therapy. According to him, silence may be used as re-repression of thought, as a means of retreating from reality, as a struggle for power with the therapist, revenge against a parent, a wish to die, etc.

Loomie (1961) sees silence occurring with the greatest frequency in connection with resistance to verbalizing feelings about the transference, and he stresses the oral and sadistic impulses that are important ingredients in these transferences feelings. He also notes that their self-punitive life behavior is paralleled by the analytic propensity for negative therapeutic reaction and the continuation of spiral patterns of provocativeness and atonement.

Arlow (1961) points out the resistance aspects of silence, but also feels that silence can be an invitation to the therapist to participate in an acting out of primitive fantasies. In this instance, silence is used in the service of discharge rather than resistance. Silence here points at joint repetition, rather than recollection.

Silence always needs to be understood in some light, and chronically silent clients may be considered delinquent to a basic rule of analytically oriented therapy: The client must communicate his feelings.

b. The client who acts out. The acting-out client is usually a source of concern to the counselor. For one thing, there is the possible danger or trouble that will accrue to the client as a result of one of his acting-out episodes. Also, the counselor knows that such behavior is gratifying to the client, yet defensive in nature, making emotional insights difficult for him to achieve. It is this very acting-out that protects him from the insights that are so painful.

Most practitioners of psychoanalytic therapy forbid and discourage acting-out, but Silverberg (1955) feels that such a procedure can have relevance only when the acting-out is occurring in the therapy hour. He cautions against the therapist's prohibiting acting-out, assuming a disciplinary role and thereby encouraging the client to react to him as an actual authority figure, rather than as an authority figure by way of transference. This change in attitude on the part of the client can make the interpretation of the transference difficult and confusing to the client, for he has evidence that the therapist, in actually becoming authoritarian, is the sort of person he judged him to be. The emotional insight that could come from an interpretation of the client's distorted perception of the therapist is obscured by the real-life behavior of the therapist.

Acting-out may be understood as an overt and dramatized manifestation of the transference. It signifies the lingering on of a traumatic bygone experience, the memory of which is unverbalized. The acting-out is seen as repeated efforts on the part of the client to rectify the helplessness of the original traumatic experience. Silverberg also points out that at stake for the client are his current claims to omnipotence as well as a test of the effective-

Paul T. King and Kent F. Bennington

ness of his aggression and the establishment of his self-esteem. The simple prohibition of acting-out behavior has the effect of heightening anxiety and creating conditions under which emotional insights may be expected, but it can also create a perception of the therapist that is unfavorable for the effective resolution of the transference.

    c. Teen-age vicissitudes. The teen-age years in this culture are marked by a definite instability in mood and an alternation of attitudes and behaviors. There will be shifts in interests, inconsistent progress toward goals, and many general indications of the state of flux and transition that is going on within the adolescent. Although teen-agers are pronouncedly egotistical, they seem to be capable at the same time of extreme self-sacrifice and devotion (Strean, 1961).

    Fountain (1961) says that adolescence is a time when psychic forces are disturbed and that new harmony is achieved as the adolescent gradually becomes an adult. He indicates that this restoration is accomplished by two processes: (1) the formation of new defenses, primarily against Oedipal and pre-Oedipal impulses and (2) the practice of continuously trying out these defenses, during which the ego learns which defenses are better and how and when to apply them.

    The strain upon the adolescent psyche is partially traceable to the reactivation of Oedipal fantasies and impulses. At the same time, the adolescent is experiencing heightened physiological urges and changes which are disrupting the solidity and stability of his ego that he knew during latency. Mother, brothers, sisters, and father are imbued with these Oedipal colorings, and he is faced with the necessity of making nonincestuous object choices and integrating himself into the social order of others his own age.

    The threat of reliving the Oedipal anxiety induces a partial regression that eases the discomfort for a while, but does not last long because of the deeper fear of emotional surrender and dissolution of the ego that would occur if regression were to continue (Geleerd, 1961). This situation makes for a constant alertness on the part of the ego, a forerunner of anxiety, in case the defenses are inadequate.

    Geleerd emphasizes the constructive effect of this partial regression, feeling that the ego needs to withdraw from its various anchors of cathexis in order to prepare itself for adult object relationships.

    With all these demands on the adolescent ego, it is still a time of growth and differentiation. The teen-ager wishes to be grown up, to have new experiences, and he is filled with anticipation of a better life awaiting him. There is heightened interest in artistic and scientific activities. The intellect appears more perceptive and grasping. Many ego functions receive a boost. It is a time for irreversible change.

    Fountain (1961) points out the impairment of the synthetic functions of the ego due to the adolescent's increased narcissistic attitude and regression to earlier stages of development. He pays particular attention to the adolescent's need for immediate gratification, his inability to accept life's subtleties, and his intolerance of frustration. He says, in showing the linkage between castration anxiety and frustrations in the early life of a child, "To experience anxiety or to be frustrated in expected gratification represents to such children castration. The similar quality of adolescents is due to the same cause. Castration fears have a resurgence in puberty" (1961, p. 33).

To Fountain, the adolescent's need for quick gratification and his intolerance of frustration represents castration, abandonment, engulfment, or other misfortune depending on the nature of his pre-Oedipal experiences.

Some analytically oriented counselors feel that deep therapy for the teen-ager is contraindicated as the ego already has so many demands on it and so much change and conflict to harmonize.

Strean (1961) mentions the similarity between the adolescent and the adult schizophrenic, in that both manifest pronounced narcissism, mood shifts, extreme negativism, weak defenses, and hindering functions of the ego. Many adolescents see the therapist as a threat and are hesitant to seek treatment on their own.

Strean notes the suspicions that some adolescents have of friendly support on the part of the counselor. He mentions a paradigmatic technique sometimes successful with adolescents in which the therapist tries to mirror the personality of the client, feeling that many adolescents cannot tolerate a more serious therapeutic intervention because of the irrationality of their egos. The client, sensing that the therapist is a kindred spirit, becomes more interested in him, whereupon the therapist then strategically selects certain types of roles and offers himself as a likeness of introjection and identification by the client. The therapist might join in the client's fantasies by telling wild and fanciful tales about himself, as the client does, or by allowing the client to project his impulses and wishes upon the therapist, while the therapist remains nondefensive about it all, indicating by his attitude that these attributes are not too dangerous to live with. Such procedures increase the self-confidence of the client until, hopefully, the client's own problems and the transference can be dealt with directly.

Scholastic achievement will occasionally take a turn for the worse when adolescents encounter counseling and therapy, and the counselor may often have to face the accusations of the referrer or the parent that the client made better marks before counseling began. This can usually be explained on the basis of the client's increasing preoccupation with material that had previously been repressed, with time consequently being taken away from his studies. Often, after therapy is over, the client's marks will get worse while holding up throughout therapy. Such clients will have been working beyond a limit that is comfortable for them and, with more freedom to be themselves, will set more comfortable goals.

Dependency on the therapist can be troublesome for both the client and the therapist. Extreme dependency can be intolerable for some teenagers and will lead them to terminate therapy prematurely. Counselors will want to be alert to such "flights into health" and search the transference relationship for new meaning. The client may unconsciously see the therapist as demanding total allegiance and self-sacrifice in return for allowing the client to depend on him, resulting in the client's fear of a complete loss of self—regression to a phase of undifferentiated object relationship in which the client confuses his own ego boundaries with those of the therapist.

The loss of ego boundaries in the disturbed adolescent client is more likely—though still rare—than in the adult client, because of the changing, taxed, unstable state of the ego.

In general, the counselor may rely on a strong need of the adolescent to grow up, master his problems, fulfill his destiny, and become an adult.

d. The client who "thinks" all the time. Experienced counselors, particularly those working in an academic setting, have often been confronted with clients who operated at highly abstract levels of thinking, and who in so doing prevented themselves from experiencing much in the way of feelings. In the intellectualized client, there is a separation between thought and feeling, just as there is in the dependent client, which we shall talk more about in a moment. The intellectualized person lives, so to speak, at the level of thinking. He cogitates. He searches for intellectual understandings of himself and the world about him. He tries to find all manner of experience and meaning at cognitive levels. While all of us are conceptualizers, we do not live at highly conceptual levels every moment of every day. We sense the world about us, we "know" it, if you will, at very low levels of abstraction; we taste, we smell, see, hear, feel, etc. And here emerges one of the important distinctions between intellectualizing and so-called normally functioning clients. The intellectualized client confines his "experience" to the realm of words and ideas, and, in that sense, he has become cut off from an integral part of himself, a part which was extremely important in his childhood.

One of the difficulties college counselors frequently experience with intellectualized clients is that of being strongly attracted to the ideas being expressed by the client. Another way of saying this is to point out the pitfall of being caught up in the "content" of the client's verbalizations and thereby losing awareness of the client's style of expression. Intellectualized clients, also, are typically well-defended at rational, cognitive levels and easily field counselor responses and reactions which are also at that level.

One problem to avoid with this particular kind of client is that of reinforcing verbally defensive behavior through concentrating on understanding and encouraging intellectual insights. Insights may be the very thing which the intellectualized client is seeking. In fact, you can almost bet on it. Part of the reason behind this is related to the fact that, if he is dealt with by the counselor at this level, he will never be forced into the position of changing his behavior significantly. He can continue in the same intellectual mold with his new self-understandings without having to modify his conduct or behavior. A further elaboration appears in another of the "Special Problems" entitled *A Time for Decision*, which seems directly related to the dynamics of the intellectualized client.

It should be pointed out also, while we are on the topic, that because of the attractiveness which psychoanalytically oriented counseling and psychotherapy holds for intellectualized clients, the counselor who practices within a psychoanalytically derived framework can expect to deal with this kind of problem relatively often. This does not mean, however, that psychoanalytically oriented counseling is intellectualized or devoid of affect, since, for Freud, the entire treatment process involved dredging up deeply repressed affects.

It has already been pointed out that an underlying assumption guiding our thinking in the writing of this chapter is that reality is an ever-changing, process-oriented phenomenon. In this sense, to experience the joy of living one must be able to experience the vicissitudes of changing, growing, and developing, and it is precisely this kind of experiencing which the client cannot do well. Moreover, it is this type of experiencing which traditional psychoanalysis, with its dismal picture of pleasure as tension-reduction, does not fully acknowledge. In the most fundamental sense, our experience occurs at very low, nonverbal levels of abstraction. Consequently, the person who allocated importance solely to high levels of abstraction, a common pitfall of this type of client in psychoanalytic therapy, may be trying to live in an unchanging universe, where it is virtually impossible to experience the "ordeal of change," for better or for worse. In this sense, the intellectualized life is the "safe" life.

Traditionally, the intellectualized client has been treated no differently than any other category of clients seeking psychoanalytic therapy. That is to say, the primary treatment approach inevitably involved that reliable technique, free association, as a method of burrowing beneath the client's intellectual defenses. Free association encourages the expression of irrational thoughts and feelings, the very thing which frightens the intellectualized client, and thereby undermines his rationality. Dream reporting is yet another of the traditional psychoanalytic methods which seem to have some relevance to the intellectualizer and which allow the therapist to get at some of his primordial fantasies. It might be added, in light of our earlier allusion to one upmanship, that both techniques, free association and dream reporting, permit the therapist to remain one-up on the client. In the first case he remains silent, while the client burrows deeper and deeper into his own dynamics, and, in the second instance, he can usually out-interpret the client, although this does not always follow.

But another, and more frequently used technique, is that of concentrating on the dynamics of the client-therapist relationship. This accomplishes two things which are advantageous to the intellectualized client: first, it focuses attention on interpersonal relating (which the client probably has most difficulty with in his day-to-day existence); second, it forces the client to deal with immediate experience. An additional advantage for the therapist is the fact that he is more of an "expert" than the client when it comes to the dynamics of interpersonal relationships. Yet another advantage, related to all the others, is at the level of immediate experience—feelings and thoughts are less separate than when talking about past experience or future expectations. The therapist who deals with the client-therapist relationship places the client in the position of talking about not what is "out-there" where the therapist must take the client's word for it, but about behavior which is observable to the therapist and where the therapist must no longer rely exclusively on the client's interpretation of events.

e. The client who won't let go. Like the intellectualized person, the dependent client also separates thought from feeling, tends to feel guilty for many of his actions and thoughts, and in some sense is still looking at himself as his parents once did. He may be the person who believes that he cannot be loved if he should become strong and independent, and who fears his own separateness from others. He lacks confidence in himself, feels that others can do a better job than he, and feeds his own feelings of inadequacy by continually seeking nurturance from others. One of the hallmarks of the dependent client is the resentment he feels toward those to whom he attaches himself.

At the same time, it should be pointed out that all of us are dependent at times, more or less, and perhaps, in some sense, are always dependent. The dependent client is distinctive in that he tries to fill all of his needs through one or only a few people rather than spreading his dependency around.

Another distinguishing feature of the dependent client is his fear of rejection, attended by his inability to express honestly his feelings toward another person. The dependent client is strangely self-disclosing in the sense that openness for him becomes a tactic in interpersonal relationships and is used to endear himself to others. His openness, in other words, is manipulative rather than fully honest. Uncensored self-disclosure or openness would mean risking the possibility of rejection, and that the dependent client is not willing to risk. He has particular difficulty expressing hostility and any other emotion which he believes might drive others away from him. Consequently, in many instances, he has as much, if not more, difficulty expressing feelings of love and affection. As a result, the dependent client can only be spontaneous and impulsive when absolutely certain that those around him will not move away from him. The dependent client must of necessity worry, since he is continually under pressure to do the right thing. His fear of failure creates undue tension at times and prevents his finding out his real capabilities, which, in turn, inhibits psychological growth.

It seems reasonable to assume that one is not fully independent until he can choose to be either independent or dependent. It is precisely at the point where a person has no choice that his dependency "shows." If he cannot choose independence, that is, if he forces himself against his wishes, and without feeling any real choice in the matter, to "look" independent, or if he is unable to choose independent behavior due to extreme needs for dependency, then we can surmise that regardless of outward appearances he is basically dependent.

Another characteristic which distinguishes the dependent client is his irresponsibility. He is by definition unwilling to assume responsibility for anyone or anything other than himself, and even with himself he seems to lack the skills, i.e., has not acquired the capacity to assume full responsibility for his own behavior. And herein is the beginning point for the psychoanalytically oriented therapist in his work with dependent clients. The counselor helps the client become more responsible for his own actions, but as he does this he must, at the same time, help the counselee deal with the feelings of loneliness and separation which accompany responsibility.

At some point, preferably early in therapy, the therapist may want to allow the client to relate as much as possible to him as an equal. The therapist tries to avoid playing into the dependent client's neurotic system by allowing excessive dependence upon him. With the intellectualized client the therapist may encourage dependency, but with the dependent client most psychoanalytically oriented therapists will discourage it. So the definition of the therapeutic relationship at the beginning of therapy becomes extremely important in the therapeutic management of the dependent client.

Another distinction between the intellectualized client and the dependent client is the level at which they operate. The intellectualized client as discussed in the previous section functions at a highly cognitive level, while the dependent client operates at a highly affective or emotional level of functioning. This difference dictates a difference in understanding as well as in therapeutic approach. It can be said within either a traditional psychoanalytic or an ego psychological framework, that the intellectualized client's behavior is much more under the control of the ego, because of the ego's control of cognitive processes, while the dependent client's behavior is guided more by the id and superego, as indicated by behavioral irrationality and concomitant harsh conscience of the excessively dependent client.

How does the psychoanalytically oriented therapist approach this particular kind of client? We have already mentioned defining the relationship in such a way that the client can no longer get rewards from his dependency on the therapist. Some therapists, incidentally, in their attempt to remain one up on the client, would perhaps encourage *extreme* dependency on the part of the client; that is, they would insist that the counselee be as dependent on them as possible, in order to help him gain control over his own behavior. They would insist on dependency beyond the limits of the client's own toleration, which would sooner or later bring the client to the point where he could no longer contain his hostility and resentment toward the therapist. The client's dependency will ordinarily keep him from withdrawing from the relationship.

The ego of the dependent client has little regard for itself. One of the techniques employed by psychoanalytically oriented therapists is that of analyzing the ego's method of self-derogation, while another very useful approach involves the therapist's devaluating himself before the client (see Variations in Counseling Style).

It seems particularly important with this kind of client to allow them to give something to the therapist. The sense of giving to the therapist can realistically create and nourish feelings of self esteem. Many counselors, by definition of their profession, believe that it is their function to give to the client, although this may not have been thought out in detail by the counselor, and that it is the client's proper role to receive whatever the therapist dispenses as he carries out his professional role.

The dependent client cannot escape the egoistic impulses of pleasure, need-satisfaction, pride, etc. He cannot, in other words, get outside himself; he cannot invest in external tasks which require problem-solving skill, partly because such investments are not drive-reducing (require the postponement of pleasure), and also because of the dependent client's limited skill (which is limited by his dependency, by his inability to accept the consequences of his independent actions, and by his lack of flexibility). The dependent client is, we believe, more flexible at intellectual levels and less flexible at experiential levels. This leads to a kind of inconsistency in his behavior which makes it difficult for him to understand his own dynamics. Consequently, one thing which a therapist might strive for in the therapeutic situation is increased understanding; although, as pointed out many times, awareness by itself is not therapeutically effective. Beyond this, the counselor may wish to reverse the flexibility-inflexibility relationship noted above. He may help the counselee become more flexible experientially while at the same time helping him become cognitively differentiated and unified, in short, less intellectually or cognitively flexible.

Winding Things up with the Client

This is often the most difficult period of therapy for both the client and the therapist. The client usually feels some uncertainty about leaving the safety of the counseling room and venturing out into the outside world to start out on his own. As termination time approaches, the client may suffer an exacerbation of his separation anxiety about leaving a person who has been a good listener, and who has been perceived as being "on the client's side." The prospects of being without this security can be severely upsetting, and many clients will try strenuously to prolong the relationship. Symptoms may be revitalized, helplessness and dependency may once more become dominant themes in the relationship, or the client may try to argue with the therapist that he has made no progress and that more time is needed to unravel the difficulty. In general, the therapist will attempt to be aware of the efforts of the client to continue his life in therapy and to postpone his living in the real world.

The anxieties do not all belong to the client. Therapists too may become anxious as the terminal phase of the relationship approaches. The therapist may have invested himself heavily in the relationship because it has been deeply gratifying to him, and he is now confronted with the fact that it must end. Long-term relationships that end are painful. In addition, there is a sense of urgency that often develops in the therapist. This urgency grows from the therapist's realization that the last few interviews may be extremely crucial. One might conceptualize the therapist's fear as: "I hope I don't do anything wrong."

During this stage, the client realizes that termination is approaching, and this knowledge may uncover aspects of the relationship between therapist and client that had hitherto remained hidden. It is as if the anticipation of separation from the therapist pressures the client to introduce into therapy his feelings about the therapist, both positive and negative, that the client previously felt would ruin the relationship. These feelings may possibly have been expressed before, but in attenuated ways. Now, with nothing to lose, so to speak, the full expression of what the client feels often becomes possible. It is during these last few hours that "real therapy" is apt to occur. Hopefully the client is able to discover completely that the therapist has been able to accept him even when his most destructive feelings or the darkest recesses of his personality have been scrutinized. The therapist has been finally validated, as it were.

Many clients, most in fact, after the anxiety about separation has been worked through, will develop a peer relationship with the therapist. The client may begin to call the therapist by his first name, if he has not been doing so already. The client seems to say by his attitude, that "I don't need you as much any more, and I don't have to preserve you as a potential parent or protector." This is often verbalized. The end of therapy is just around the corner.

A Time for Decision

Most analytically oriented therapists have had the experience of the client who has explored all the nooks and crannies of his personality, who knows his own neurotic life style to a fare-thee-well, who understands his symptomatology, but who still lingers in therapy, and who is unable to invest himself in life in a reasonably happy way. This situation is often perplexing to the therapist and demoralizing to the client.

The client and therapist may both have the feeling that there is little of significance in the client's personality left to be understood. Why then is the client unable to leave therapy and get on with the business of living? In the previous unit, Winding Things up with the Client, the client's fears and apprehensions are focused on the separation from the therapist and the protectiveness of the therapeutic setting. In that sense, the client's anxiety is attributable to specific things in his life, and to that extent is amenable to further insight and exploration. That is, the client really might not be aware of the aspects of the current situation which are making him feel dreadful.

In the case of the client who refuses to "live," the situation described above does not precisely apply. The client will not be motivated to look further for ghosts of the past. There is often an air of waiting within the therapy hour, as if only a decision needs to be made and no additional information is required. At these times the client is often consciously faced with the choice of whether to retain a neurotic life style or to attempt to live life without the neurosis' protective asylum. This gets to be a matter of the client's choosing a responsible way of life for himself.

These may be sad and wistful times for the client, and for the therapist too, if he has allowed himself to empathize deeply with the client. The client is faced with many things during these times. Many clients will experience the feeling that they are taking up life again where they left off, that is, before the onset of the neurotic condition. They may feel that they are becoming reacquainted with a person they themselves used to know years back, and this may be a deeply emotional experience. On the other hand, they may feel a new self is being born for the first time and that no previous real self existed. The individual may express that he feels childlike or young again, and that things feel both sad and delicious. Side by side with the feelings of youthfulness is often a feeling of the here and the now, experienced more keenly than has been felt for several years, perhaps. There is a definite feeling of being a part of humanity with an exciting commitment to the urgency of the present. Here, more clearly than at any other time, is the therapist privileged to see the integration of the past and the present mesh before his eyes. It is a humbling experience. The client, who for defensive reasons had kept the past and the present isolated, now feels the necessity of claiming his experience over the total time dimension of his existence as his own. The client is deeply aware of the emotional continuity of his life. He may express that he feels whole again.

The authors have wondered about the wistful quality experienced by the client when he chooses to shuck his neurosis and reenter the world of the risk-takers. There is a definite feeling of "goodbye" or finality that permeates the situation, which does not seem to be very much related to leaving the therapist. There is an aura in therapy at this time that suggests something is ending and something is beginning. It is the "something is ending" aspect that gives the wistful quality to such occasions. Clients may remark that they feel unsupported, or that they feel they are "standing alone" for the first time, and other similar expressions. A sense of uniqueness, and separateness is communicated very plainly, and diffused with all of this is the feeling of wistfulness mentioned earlier.

When one considers the origination of most neurotic conditions, one fact stands out clearly. The neurosis is a compromise arrangement which is designed to maintain the love and approval of early parent figures in the client's past, or to deny the feeling of being loved by the parents, as well as the love the client has for the parents in return. For such clients, their neurosis comes to stand for their relationship with their parents, and in fact, many clients will relate to their neuroticism in the same manner in which they behaved with their parents. Their neurosis is something they will cower from or feel must be appeased. They may feel that by making themselves a perfect person that it (the neurosis) will leave them alone, or that by feeling guilty and by making efforts to atone is the best way to elicit love and security.

When clients decide—and it is a decision—to give up their neurotic way of life, it is tantamount to saying goodbye to their parents they knew as children, and whom they were trying so desparately to maintain unchanged in their imagery. The wistful quality seems to stem from this "letting go" of the parents, as well as the security they derived from preserving their original childlike relationship with them via their neurotic symbolism. It is by maintaining their stranglehold on the past that clients are unable to relate to their contemporaries as real persons in a real world. In giving up their neuroticism, they fear they will have no relationship and will consequently feel acutely alone. The client is beginning an important process—a process that has far-reaching consequences in his attainment of personal happiness. He now is able to sort people along the time dimension, consigning some people to memories as they existed in his past. This frees him to relate to people as they exist for him presently, which eventuates in a more genuine interaction with others and a more alive way of behaving in the world. It is not unusual for clients at this time to start talking about the future (and quite often the past simultaneously), something they might have neglected for a long time.

Illustrative Case Material

The following counseling interview took place in the counseling center of a large Middle Western university. The client is a nineteen-year-old sophomore, who announced to the counselor during the first interview that he had personal problems and wished the opportunity to discuss them.

The client had been suffering from pronounced feelings of inadequacy and tension for several years, although he felt he had never been happy at any time in his life. The feeling of being pent-up and not getting any enjoyment from life were the crucial feelings that urged him to seek help.

The client's mother and father are both living. The father is a professional man, and the mother is a housewife, with occasional part-time jobs that she seeks to relieve the boredom, rather than because the family needs the money. There is one sister, three years younger than the client, who still lives at home, which is about two hundred miles from the client's university. The client visits home only during holidays.

This is the eleventh interview. Prior to this one, most of the time had been used by the client to communicate his feelings of discomfort and unhappiness in an unproductive and repetitious way. The last three interviews were marked by a noticeable passivity, while he hinted to the counselor that he would be more satisfied if he would diagnose him and plot a course of action for him to pursue.

During the previous interviews, the client presented a sketchy account of his past with no elaboration and little feeling. The client had always been close to his mother, and although he and his father "got along well and without bickering," he always sensed a distance between them. He considered himself rather artistic and sensitive and easily upset. He and his sister were friendly but had drifted further apart in the last several years. He sensed that his family wished him to start out on his own, but felt, at the same time, that they would discourage any effort he made in that direction.

The therapist felt that the client had not committed himself to therapy and was using his passive ego defenses to block the release of emotional material and to prevent any real change in his neurotic attitude. He decided to use the technique of free imagery to circumvent some of the client's defenses by minimizing the controlling influences of the ego, as well as to try to give the client a feeling of therapeutic movement, which might result in a greater investment by him in the therapy process.

Free imagery had been described to him in the last interview and was presented as a method that might move therapy a little faster. He seemed nervous at the prospects of doing it but still wished to try.

The following is a verbatim account of parts of two free-imagery interviews. The comments in parentheses are the thoughts and feelings of the therapist during the hour. CO stands for counselor and CL stands for client. As this was the first time free imagery had been used with the client, the therapist had no previous pattern of images with which to compare the present ones. The picture of the personality ordinarily emerges through repetition of similar themes expressed by the visual fantasies of the client. In this manner, both the client and the therapist gradually build up an understanding of the basic emotional problem as it is operating in the present world and as it originated in childhood. Interpretations and hypotheses by the therapist may be confirmed, modified, or denied by the long-range patterns of recurrent themes played over in these highly symbolic fantasies.

CO: You'll remember last time I said we might try something different today. How do you feel about it now?

CL: Good. I'm ready.

CO: Okay. Why don't you lean your head back against the chair, close your eyes and report all the pictures and visual fantasies that occur to you. It's important that you tell me everything, regardless of how trivial or silly. Try not to censor anything. Also report all the feelings you have or any physical sensations you are aware of. Concentrate upon your body. Attend to the pressure of your hips and legs against the chair. Feel your feet pressing against the floor. Breathe deeply. Please don't open your eyes until I tell you. While you are talking, I will not be speaking, and I will be very quiet, but I am here. Do you understand: This is an effective technique, and it will work for us.

CL: Okay. Are you ready? I'm looking down a valley or some sort of path, or something. It is lined with evergreen trees. It goes down pretty far. It's not cloudy or anything; the sun's shining real bright. A little village. I see a man with glasses on, an old man. He has a big head and a real small chin—kinda ugly. I see some sort of label or plate. I can't see what it says.

CO: (He mentions an old man. I wonder why the age is important. Then he is unable to read the printing on the label—resistance? Resisting something about the old man?)

CL: I see a football, a football player. There's a big shaft or a well. I'm looking down on it from above. There's dark water below; the walls are white. The walls are concrete. The dark waters below sort of fascinate me, yet they seem sort of ... sort of ... nasty. I'm within the shaft now, looking up from the inside, pretty close to the top of the hole. It's night time outside, and there's some sort of light shining over the hole or across it. I see a bunch of arrows, all together—just the points of 'em, and they're sticking into the hole. You said pay attention to what I feel, and I'm beginning to feel frightened, and sort of like I want to cry.

CO: (The therapist reaches over and touches the client lightly on the arm.) Too frightened to go on; if you are, we'll stop now.

CL: No, let's go on. There's a big sewer, like a drain sewer. I'm tempted to walk inside. The sun is just beginning to set. It's dark inside that sewer, and I'm looking into it. I'm not going in there. I feel as if I'd like to run away from it, but I don't, or can't. I see a face, the nose, the eyes, forehead. There are some more eyes over on the right. They're kinda sad like they've been crying, like they're ashamed. There's a woman standing with her back to me. It's dark all around her. She's got her head down. There are the eyes again; they're closed this time, like they're asleep or dead.

CO: (The well shaft, then the inserted arrows—this suggests thinly disguised sexual symbolism. He felt quite anxious here. Some emotional conflict must have been "touched." This is followed by the sewer—this suggests filth to me. I wonder if this conveys his attitude about sex—that it's frightening and dirty? His fear continues, he doesn't wish to go into the sewer, and the sun is setting. This has sort of a morbid feel. He must feel guilty—the eyes are ashamed and sad. Has he seen some episode as a child? The woman has her back turned; he must not wish to identify her.)

CL: I see a tractor or a bulldozer pulling something real big. There are a lot of chains going back to this thing the tractor is pulling. It looks like a big block. Now the scene shifts. I'm looking up the side of a tall building. Now there's a bowl, a black bowl. It has a purple thing coming up from the middle, and it's turning around real fast. It looks like a hand or a gun pointing straight up. There's an alley, a blind alley. It's like it wouldn't do any good to go in there; it doesn't lead anywhere. I feel sort of hopeless right now. Here's a fence; it's all around me. I can't see over on the other side. Now I'm looking down into a basement garage. Cars are coming down a ramp real fast and piling up at the bottom. There's a sun, a big orange sun, like a painting. It's real colorful, red, orange, and purple. Now I'm sitting behind someone in a basket and some slave girls hanging around. There's another basket of peas and carrots, I think. There is something coming out of it, little green stuff, and it's bubbling up like there's something underneath there. It's growing, like. It just keeps bubbling up. I'm looking through a window, seeing the back of someone's head, but they've got their coat collar pulled up. I see a big eye. It's staring real hard. It's real big. Now it seems like someone has turned a room on its side, and the room became real long. And now everything is sort of falling down toward the bottom—table, chairs, spoons, and everything. There's a big mountain standing right below this room. I'm looking up. It's light on top, and there are clouds way up above, but it's light all around them too. It's light all the way up the mountain; nothing's hiding anything. I have the strangest feeling. Like I want to cry again. A few minutes ago if I had cried, it would have been because I was afraid. Now if I cried it would be because ... I don't ... I don't know ... something about that mountain. It would be because I would be, maybe, happy. Like I might dare to climb that mountain. I do want to cry.

CO: (The counselor breaks his silence.) I do understand. (Again the woman is unidentifiable. Wolves' heads—that seems a significant distortion, and the gun barrel, more phallic symbolism? I wonder if wolves have to do with his being lustful. Or maybe they signify danger. The basket of peas and carrots, and the slave girls seem to be in an early Greek or Roman setting. I get the feeling of emotional pressure—the bubbling up. Again the back of someone's head—he rarely sees faces. He must be threatened by whom he will recognize. Then a hint of spatial disorientation—the room on its side—I wonder if that implies emotional chaos? He was quite touched about the mountain. I feel strangely enthusiastic about that too! It seems like he is almost daring to hope that he might be different—to change. I feel he is moved; I share his excitement.)

CL: I'm looking up a ladder or a steel thing. It's light all around; the ladder goes straight up. I feel like I'm going to climb it or something. Climbing must be awfully important to me. (Laughs forlornly.) I see a tiger. He's got something in his mouth—a briefcase or books or something. He's kind of restless. Only it looks like a big cat, not a tiger. There's a telephone. A woman's hand came down to pick it up, and I don't know who she is. Her face is all white. She's yelling over the phone like she's scared. Her eyes are getting real little; her hair is all white—streaked like. She is afraid of something. Now there is a real big bunch of real high chairs alongside of a wall. They're inside a corridor or something, like in the Palace at Versailles in France. The chairs are propped against the wall, and there's a window right above them. As you walk by them, I don't know, the corridor gets foggy. I can't see anymore. I was walking down one side of the corridor, and I looked over on the other side, and there was something like a statue—it's all white. It's a marble statue. It seemed to come around a little corner so quick. It's real hard. It's like a monster or something, and it came around the corner. There are some people in a room; they have beards and mustaches, and they are working on something. They're working on somebody there, lying down. They've all got beards and mustaches. Somebody has lifted up a cover over a casket. Just lifted it up. I can't see anything. It's all just stopped. Everything is frozen. Nobody's moving. I'm looking down from a balcony. There's a light on the floor. There's a door opening just a little bit, and it's opening a little more. There's somebody there with white hair and a white beard. I don't know, he closed the door again.

CO: (All of this sounds significant to me. He appears lost in his production— no acting now. He seems very much a part of his fantasies: "I feel like I'm going to climb the ladder." He must feel freer. Again I sense fear— the tiger must have been too threatening—he reduced it to a small cat. I wonder if the freedom brings on the fear? Does the tiger symbolize a devouring mother who permits no freedom? Or is this castration fear of the father that follows self vigor? The woman is old, like the man. His people are always old or unrecognizable. That surely reduces some threat for him. He seemed almost afraid while talking about the statue—that was followed by the death scene with the casket. Does he wish someone to die? Has he destroyed someone in fantasy? Who? Is this a disguised death wish for himself? The resistance was intense here. Everything froze. The opening door—does that mean readiness for insight? He didn't wish to see what lay beyond. He hasn't gone this far before.)

The interview continues in the usual manner after the client has discontinued free imagery.

CO: How do you feel?

CL: Oh, everyway I guess. Puzzled about what it all means, sort of scared, yet there's also a feeling of happiness. I know it sounds goofy to talk about being scared and happy at the same time, but I do. You know, like I could go either way.

CO: Of course I do.

CL: I really felt . . . felt deeply a couple of times.

CO: Yes, I sensed that. Good. It's sort of good to have feelings, regardless of what kind they are, isn't it? Or does that sound strange?

CL: No, that's true, that's really true. I think I was most frightened about the arrows at the first, remember? And then, near the end, about the casket and the old man opening the door. I really felt scared.

CO: Those two things seemed the most important then—more feeling about those.

CL: Yeah, that and looking up the mountain. You know, it sort of seemed like me in that casket, and then I wasn't there any more.

CO: You sort of had a quick flash of feeling about your own death then—saw yourself there for an instant. That does sound frightening.

CL: It was. You might be wondering if I wish to die, and there have been times when I didn't care, but this didn't feel like that. This felt like I *am* dead. That it's already happened. You know, I think I do feel that—that I am dead in a sense. Life sure hasn't had much meaning for me for a long time. I don't ever feel much anymore. Do you understand?

CO: Sure I do. Something inside died a long time ago. I understand.

After a few more remarks, the interview terminates. Several weeks later the following interview took place. Free imagery had been used during the intervening interviews. The client now is more at ease with the technique and has reported some loosening of his affect within and outside of therapy.

CL: I'm walking now alongside of a woods, and I'm holding my mother's hand. I feel content just to leave my hand resting in hers. I'm playing all around beside her, but I leave my hand in hers. Sort of like I have, well, just so much space to play in—just as far as her arm can reach. And I don't seem to pull away. We are walking beside the woods. It looks scary in there, big trees, dark, and I can see only a little way in. I wish to go in there, but I'm scared. I sort of want to explore, but I know she won't go with me. I'm turning loose of her hand and wandering into the woods alone. I'm just walking down this path—it's a very narrow path. I'm pretty far into the woods now, but I'm just standing there not doing anything. I want to get off the path, but I can't. I'm afraid. There's green grass on both sides of the path and I don't have on any shoes. I want to step over in that grass, but I feel like the ground beneath would be muddy and "oozy." I can't move. I just feel trapped. I feel like I'll stay here forever.

CO: Let something happen. If you need help, let help come. (The counselor breaks silence here in order to break the conflict and allow the imagery to proceed.)

CL: There's a man coming down the path toward me. It's very quiet; nobody's talking. He's very tall and has on a ... sort of woodman's jacket. He's a lumberjack or something. He reaches down and picks me up. I'm sitting on his shoulder, way up in the air. He has on boots, so he can step off the path and not worry about the mud underneath. I'm just sitting there, feeling very secure. I'm sort of ... like up among the branches. I let go of his shoulder and climb around on the branches. He waits below. For some reason I'm peeling some bark off one of the branches. There's white wood underneath where I've peeled it away. He's still there below. Then I climb down on his shoulders again. We're going back to the path now, and he's putting me down. It's very quiet—not a sound. It's like we can't talk. It's real strange. We just can't speak.

CO: (The counselor again feels the need to pierce this resistance and understand the feeling behind this inability to communicate.) Keep your eyes closed, and relax as much as possible. I'm going to hand you a piece of paper and a pencil. Can you see the paper and pencil?

CL: Yes. I take it, but I hand it to the man. He's bending down, writing on it, writing on his knee, kind of. He hands it back to me, but the paper's folded. I can't see what it says. I want to open my eyes. It feels like I want to run out of here. It really seems like I want to run.

CO: I understand. (Soothingly) Keep your eyes closed. Can you still see the paper?

CL: Yes, it's still folded. But I have it in my hand. The paper is real white and clean. It looks like telephone pad paper.

CO: Let's open it and see what it says.

CL: It says "I need you!" (Long silence.) I feel like I want to scream. I feel sort of hot and tingly in my skin, all over. It seems like I could scream and cry at the same time.

CO: I understand how angry and hurt you must feel.

After more remarks in the same vein, the free imagery is interrupted, and the interview proceeds in the normal manner.

CO: Well?

CL: Jesus! We hit something didn't we?

CO: Yes, it seems like it.

CL: Do you know what it means?

CO: Not really. I guess I feel you have the answer to that. I am sure of one thing, you felt very intensely about something. If I'm getting it right, sort of real angry and real hurt—side by side.

CL: I think that's right. Where do those feelings come from? All of a sudden they're there.

CO: Something you've needed to feel for a long time, I suppose.

CL: M-hm.

CO: Was there anything that seemed important that you haven't told me about? So much happened it might be hard to say.

CL: Yes, there was (definitely). You know when the guy was waiting for me under the tree.

CO: Yes.

CL: He was tapping his foot. Just tapping it on the ground.

CO: Like he was irritated or impatient?

CL: No, he wasn't mad or anything; it was just a mannerism. Just something he was doing.

CO: I got it. Go on.

CL: Well, it's something my dad used to do a lot—just tap his foot. He wouldn't be mad or anything like that, but he just had the habit of doing it. Tapping his foot. I don't know whether you realize it or not but you do that a lot too. Do you know you do?

CO: I hadn't been aware of it, but now that you point it out, it seems that I do. Yes, I do. Isn't that odd? We are sort of a threesome then—the man in the dream, your dad, and me. It's something that sort of links us together, this foot tapping business.

CL: That's right. You know I always feel so uneasy when I bring you into things.

CO: Yes, I know. You want to keep me in place as just a psychologist and not have any human feelings about me.

CL: But that's goofy, isn't it. You are human. It's obvious you are.

CO: Yes. Indeed I am.

CL: You know, right at the start there was something about you that reminded me of dad. Even before the foot tapping. Something, I don't know what. But one time, when I was leaving, and you hit me on the back as I went out the door. Remember that?

CO: Yes.

CL: Well, I felt like I wanted you to put your arm around my shoulders, or give me a hug, or something like that. Does that sound too crazy?

CO: Not at all. Somehow it would have been very satisfying or reassuring if I could have responded to you like this. Is this sort of what dad used to do?

CL: Well, some, but not as much as I wanted him to—I wanted him to a lot more than he did. I always felt there was so much unsaid between us.

CO: You mean like in the dream.

CL: Yeah, just like that. I always wanted to feel—I thought how nice it would be if dad wanted to be with me like I wanted to be with him, but he never did. Or he didn't seem to. (Sighs deeply.)

CO: You never could get the deep commitment from him that would have been so satisfying. That sort of explains the note, I guess. You wanted to be needed and loved as much as you loved him, but it didn't ever happen that way.

CL: Oh, Lord. I tried harder than you know.

CO: I know you did.

After a few remarks, the interview terminates. Much of the symbolism of the waking dream is explained in the interview after the free imagery has ended. The client's need for his father as a model for identification and his wish to be loved by him seem apparent.

The therapist by this time has made a tentative formulation of the client's problem, but always subject to modification as the client produces newer and deeper material. At first, the formulation of the problem is sketchy and incomplete. In many instances the therapist is uncertain of the meaning of the symbolism and the articulation of the various aspects of the maladjustment.

During the early stages, the therapist selects certain sequences in the imagery that appear to him to be important in the dynamics of the client. He attends to the male and female sexual symbolism scattered throughout the interviews. He is aware that this symbolism is often followed by scenes of catastrophe, danger, or morbidity. He is also aware that the client chooses to see in the imagery decidedly old persons who appear with their backs turned or situations in which their faces are unrecognizable. The therapist senses the frequent references to contrasting shades of light and dark throughout the production but does not understand the meaning of this symbolism. Fear seems to be a significant feeling for the client, and the therapist, at this juncture, wonders if it is connected with a wish for someone to die or a masochistic internalization of this wish—that is, a wish for himself to die.

By the time of the second recorded interview (there were six or seven unrecorded intervening sessions), an emerging picture of the client's personality has become clear. The therapist tentatively—and it should be repeated for emphasis, *tentatively*—formulates the problem as one in which repressed sexual elements play an important part, perhaps with incomplete sexual identification with the father and consequently with the male role. The client's attitude toward sex seems to be one of morbidity, guilt, and fear. Death seems in some way connected with this complex, either as an urge to self-destruction or, perhaps, at a deeper level, a death wish for someone else. The therapist conjectures the narcissistic personality makeup of the client's mother plus the unapproachability of the father, which combined to keep the client (1) dependent on his mother, (2) fearful of exploring and pursuing masculine interests and, thereby, unable to crystallize a masculine identification, (3) constantly searching for safety and support, and (4) narcissistically regressed. The client is seen as fixated at the phallic stage of psychosexual development, suffering from anxiety centering around the Oedipal complex and his assumption of an independent and masculine life role. His diagnosis, at this time, would be that of psychoneurosis, anxiety reaction, mild, with no appreciable impairment, and with dependent behavior.

Passivity and dependency on the therapist would seem to be the line the client's resistances will follow. The client wishes to solve his problems, and there are signs that he will achieve some significant insights soon in therapy in addition to those he already has. The therapist anticipates being used as a transference target for the feelings the client has for *both* his mother and his father. The therapist would expect the client, during the latter stages of therapy, to recapture the original feelings of fury and hurt when he as a child came to the dawning realization (later repressed) that the strangulation of his potential self and his adulthood was the price he had paid for his safety and continued union with his parents. The therapist would also anticipate an emancipation from his infantile dependency on adults (parent surrogates), the resurrection of his own values, and a reincorporation of the parents with an acceptance of their neurotic limitations—a human understanding, in other words.

To make significant gains on his emotional problem, the therapy process will probably require not less than weekly interviews for an academic year.

Some Research Possibilities

Few theoretical disciplines have captured the imagination of men more profoundly than psychoanalysis; yet the psychological researcher, for all of its dramatic appeal, sees it as a system in which it is abysmally hard to do research. Freud's theories, some of them at any rate, almost seem beyond investigation. Little research can be done on the death wish, as it is practically impossible to derive any empirical propositions from it. Almost as exasperating is his concept of reaction formation, which permits the analyst to explain behavior in terms of a direct expression of forces within the id or the polar opposite of these forces. Research is difficult when opposite behaviors can be explained in terms of the same unconscious impulse. Scientifically trained psychologists attempting to do research in the field of psychoanalysis have been exasperated and impeded by such knotty problems.

Attempts to validate psychoanalysis have developed along two lines. The most obvious one is the clinical validation of the postulates of psychoanalysis, which are observed by the analyst during the therapy hour. This usually takes the form of interpretations offered by the analyst and confirmed by the patient, which reduces his anxiety and allows him to put to use parts of his personality that were lying dormant and ungratified. This is usually enough validation for the practitioner.

The other method is by subjecting psychoanalytic hypotheses to experimental investigation, and here, researchers run into the problems mentioned earlier. Researchers also face opposition from the analysts themselves, who are decidedly nonexperimentally oriented, and who are accused of being frightened by any attempts at quantification.

In general, there have been four kinds of attention given to researching psychoanalytic principles. One sort of attention has been the actual doing of research, mostly carried on by clinical and experimental psychologists who have been familiar with Freudian theory. The majority of these studies have unfortunately emphasized repression and its derivatives, with other postulates of the system suffering neglect.

A second kind of attention has been that of defending the reasons research has not been done, and this comes from the analysts themselves. They point out the idiosyncratic development of the individual, the ethical problems that arise in research, and the superior means of understanding behavior afforded by the introspective method.

A third sort of attention comes again from the analysts. Some of them recognize the need for research and even mention ways in which research on psychoanalytic theories might be methodologically improved, but they wish that psychologists indoctrinated in analytic methods would do it.

The fourth sort of attention also comes from the analysts, who examine their own motivations for wanting to do, but not doing, research. They find that the doing of research is an expression of more basic aims within the researcher, and they are apparently freed from the need to do research after this insight.

Rather than reviewing for the reader the research on psychoanalytic theory and attempting to arrive at conclusions about the validity of its postulates in a few pages, we have decided to discuss several areas within psychoanalysis, or derivatives of it, that present researchable possibilities.

The whole area of ego psychology seems fraught with research opportunities. The work of Kroeber seems to need perpetuation. His work on delineating the differences between ego coping and ego defensive mechanisms appears important, and the information such research may yield should be useful to the therapeutic aims of counseling and clinical psychologists. Some experimental questions that seem worthy of investigation are:

What behavioral correlates of the therapist or client precede the changing of defensive into coping behavior for the client? What are the physiological correlates of defensive and coping behavior; for example, are there differences in GSR readings under both conditions? Are outside judges able to discriminate the differences between coping and defensive behavior within the interview? What is the ratio of coping behavior to defensive behavior at different stages of therapy? What are the ratios of coping to defensive behavior during the child's developmental years, for example, from three to five, or from five to eight. What coping behaviors are common to optimally adjusted adults; that is, are some types used more frequently than others?

New ego therapies are being mentioned in the literature. Ego therapists speak of Shapiro's subself type of therapy, or of "devaluating the object," etc. Are certain types of ego therapy more efficacious with certain types of clients? Can certain subselves be made operable through posthypnotic suggestion? If so, do different subselves have different psychometric manifestations, for example, on the MMPI? Are behavioral modification approaches able to reinforce or extinguish the existence of subselves, providing most of the behavioral cues that pertain to a subself could be specified? How does subself therapy relate to the modeling approach currently being employed by many behavioral therapists? With television equipment now available to many therapists, is the process of therapy speeded up by watching the client's subself being acted out in the therapy room? What behavioral rating techniques are applicable to measuring subself change? What therapist or client behavioral correlates precede subself integration?

Much work has been done on conditioning anxiety or fear to external cues in the environment. A fruitful area of investigation is the conditioning of anxiety states to other internal cues, such as thoughts or feelings. Is neurotic tension experimentally produceable by conditioning anxiety to anxiety free states of the organism? Is the termination of different intensities of cognitive organismic arousal able to act as reinforcers of behavior? Does anxiety or arousal always accompany the stoppage of a behavioral plan?

One of the important dimensions of the counseling or therapy situation is the structure, or lack of it, within the interview situation. Very little experimental work has been done in the area of ambiguity in therapeutic interaction. Bordin (1955) has theorized on the subject, but we have little empirical data.

How is the ambiguity of the interview related to the development of transference as rated by judges? What sorts of clients are likely to use therapeutic ambiguity to advantage? In what stage of the therapy process is ambiguity most effectively employed?

Dr. Joe Reyher, Michigan State University, has been conducting research for several years in the area of free imagery, or emergent psychotherapy, as he has recently entitled the process. Free imagery offers some intriguing possibilities of speeding up the process of therapy and providing a method of personality restructuring at the deepest levels. The process has not received a lot of experimental attention, and the use of the method, at this point, has probably exceeded the technique's empirical verification.

Does the use of free imagery speed up the process of therapy when compared to insight-oriented methods of psychotherapy in which free imagery is not used? Does the use of free imagery provide for a deeper level of personality reorganization than when it is not used? What types of clients are able to use free imagery most effectively? For example, are persons with paranoid trends in their make-up able to use this method as well as clients who are characterized by anxiety reactions? How is visual imagery related to cognitive style? How is visual imagery related to arousal states of the organism, as measured by EEG apparatus? How is the employment of emergent psychotherapeutic techniques related to client's and judges' perception of various dimensions of the therapist's behavior?

Answers to most of these questions are needed. The purpose of this brief section was to stimulate investigation into these areas that, heretofore, have been insufficiently researched.

Psychoanalytic theory, with all of its complex assumptions, has obviously not stimulated the research that one would expect from such a system. The men and women who work as practitioners in this discipline apparently have not been research oriented, and many of them simply do not possess the necessary skills to carry out research programs. A few experimental and clinical psychologists have attempted to verify specific Freudian hypotheses with some success, but the difficulty of developing research methodologies that capture the full flavor of psychoanalysis has been apparent. Regardless of the research validation of the theory itself, during our introspective moments, most of us are able to sense in ourselves the dark and mysterious elements of which Freud wrote, to be aware of the vigilance of parts of ourselves to ward off threat, and to feel the defensive maneuvering we maintain to ensure our self-regard. We are alternately despairing and elated, confident and cringing, self-loving yet feeling tender for others. For many people, Freud's clear identification of such things that were heretofore only half sensed provides a basic validity for the system.

Bibliography

Alexander, F. M. *Fundamentals of psychoanalysis.* New York: Norton, 1963.

Allport, G. W. *Pattern and growth in personality.* New York: Holt, 1961.

Arlow, J. A. Silence and the theory of technique. *J. Amer. Psychoanal. Ass.,* 1961, **9,** 44-56.

Baura, M. Freud and Horney on anxiety and neurosis. *Samiksa,* 1955, **9,** 93-103.

Bellak, L. Research in psychoanalysis. *Psychoanal. Quart.,* 1961, **30,** 519-548.

Bobbitt, R. The repression hypothesis studies in a situation of hypnotically induced conflict. *J. abnorm. soc. Psychol.,* 1958, **56,** 205-213.

Bordin, E. S. Ambiguity as a therapeutic variable. *J. consul. Psychol.,* 1955, **19,** 9-15.

Bordin, E. S., Nachmann, B., & Segal, S. J. An articulated framework for vocational development. *J. counsel. Psychol.,* 1963, **10,** 107-117.

Brenner, C. Panel on the validation of psychoanalytic techniques. *J. Amer. Psychoanal. Ass.,* 1955, **3,** 496-505.

Brill, A. A. (Ed.) *The basic writings of Sigmund Freud.* New York: Random House, 1938.

Colm, H. A field theory approach to transference and its particular application to children. *Psychiatry,* 1955, **18,** 324-326, 339-352.

Evan, S. The compensatory work of transference. *Psychoanal. Rev.,* 1961, **48**(2), 19-29.

Federn, P. The ego as subject and object in narcissism. *Ego psychology and the psychoses.* New York: Basic Books, 1952.

Fenichel, O. *The psychoanalytic theory of neurosis.* New York: Norton, 1945.

Fleming, J. What analytic work requires of an analyst: A job analysis. *J. Amer. Psychoanal. Ass.,* 1961, **9,** 719-730.

Ford, D. H., & Urban, H. B. *Systems of psychotherapy.* New York: Wiley, 1965.

Fountain, G. Adolescent into adult: An inquiry. *J. Amer. Psychoanal. Ass.,* 1961, **9,** 417-434.

Geleerd, E. R. Some aspects of ego vicissitudes in adolescence. *J. Amer. Psychoanal. Ass.,* 1961, **9,** 394-406.

Grossman, D. Ego activating approaches to psychotherapy. *Psychoanal. Rev.,* 1964, **51,** 65-88.

Haley, J. *Strategies of psychotherapy.* New York: Grune & Stratton, 1963.

Hall, C. S. *A primer of Freudian psychology.* Cleveland: World Publishing, 1954.

Hartmann, H. *Essays on ego psychology.* New York: International Universities Press, 1964.

Hefferline, R. F. Learning theory and clinical psychology—An eventual symbiosis. In A. J. Bachrach (Ed.), *Experimental foundations of clinical psychology.* New York: Basic Books, 1962.

Jacobson, E. The affects and their pleasure-unpleasure qualities in relation to the psychic discharge processes. In R. M. Loewenstein (Ed.), *Drives, affects, and behavior.* New York: International Universities Press, 1953. Pp. 38-66.

Jones, E. *The life and work of Sigmund Freud.* Garden City, N.Y.: Anchor Books, 1963.

Jourard, S. M. *The transparent self.* Princeton, N.J.: Van Nostrand, 1964.

Kaywin, L. An epigenetic approach to the psychoanalytic theory of instincts and affects. *J. Amer. Psychoanal. Ass.,* 1960, **8**, 613 659.

Kelly, G. *The psychology of personal constructs.* New York: Norton, 1955.

King, P. T., & Neal, R. *Ego psychology in counseling.* Boston: Houghton Mifflin, 1968.

Kris, E. Ego psychology and interpretation in psychoanalytic therapy. *Psychoanal. Quart.,* 1951, **20**, 15 30.

Kubie, L. S. *Practical and theoretical aspects of psychoanalysis.* New York: Praeger, 1950.

Kuhnel, G. Transference in group analysis. *Acta Psychotherapeutica Psychosomatica Orthopaedogogica Suppl.,* 1955, **3**, 196 200.

LaForge, R., Leary, T. F., Naboisek, H., Coffey, H. S., & Freedman, M. B. The interpersonal dimension of personality. Part II. An objective study of repression. *J. Pers.,* 1954, **23**, 129-153.

Lilly, J. C. The psychophysiological basis for two kinds of instincts. *J. Amer. Psychoanal. Ass.,* 1960, **8**, 659-671.

Loomie, L. S. Some ego considerations in the silent patient. *J. Amer. Psychoanal. Ass.,* 1961, **9**, 56-79.

Lowenstein, R. M. Conflict and autonomous ego development during the phallic phase. *The Psychoanalytic Study of the Child,* 1950, **5**, 47 52.

Lundin, R. W. Behavioristic psychology. In R. W. Heine & J. Wepman (Eds.), *Concepts of personality.* Chicago: Aldine, 1963.

McGinnies, E. Emotionality and perceptual defense. *Psychol. Rev.,* 1949, **56**, 244-251.

Marmor, J. Panel on the validation of psychoanalytic techniques. *J. Amer. Psychoanal. Ass.,* 1955, **3**, 496-505.

Meerloo, J. A. M. The dual meaning of human regression. *Psychoanal. Rev.,* 1962, **49**(3), 77-86.

Mullan, H. The existential matrix of psychotherapy. *Psychoanal. Rev.,* 1960, **47**, 87-99.

Munroe, R. L. *Schools of psychoanalytic thought.* New York: Holt, 1955.

Nacht, S., & Levovice, S. Indications and contra-indications for psychoanalysis. *Rev. Franc. Psychoanal.,* 1955, **19**, 135-204, 279, 304-309.

Nagelberg, L., and Spotnitz, H. Strengthening the ego through release of frustration and aggression. *Am. J. Orthopsychiat.,* 1958, **28**, 794-801.

Poetzl, O. Experimentelle erregte traumbilder in ihren beziehungen zum indirekten sehen. *Zfl. ges. Neural. Psychiat.,* 1917, **37**, 278 349.

Rangell, L. On the psychoanalytic theory of anxiety: A statement of a unitary theory. *J. Amer. Psychoanal. Ass.,* 1955, **3**, 389-414.

Riviere, J. *Freud's introductory lectures.* New York: Liveright, 1958.

Rogers, C. *On becoming a person.* Boston: Houghton Mifflin, 1961.

Rosenstock, I. M. Perceptual aspects of repression. *J. abnorm. soc. Psychol.,* 1951, **46**, 304-315.

Ruesch, J. Transference reformulated. In J. Fiasch & N. Ross, *Annual survey of psychoanalysis.* Vol. 6. New York: International Universities Press, 1955.

Sanford, N. *Self and society.* New York: Atherton, 1966.

Schmidl, F. The problem of scientific validation in psychoanalytic interpretation. *J. Psychoanal.,* 1955, **36,** 105-113.

Shapiro, S. B. A theory of ego pathology and ego therapy. *J. Psychol.,* 1962, **J3,** 81-90.

Siegman, A. J. A reaction to positive transference. *Psychoanal. Rev.,* 1955, **42,** 172-179.

Silverberg, W. V. Acting out versus insight: A problem in psychoanalytic technique. *Psychoanal. Quart.,* 1955, **24,** 527-559.

Skinner, B. F. Critique of psychoanalytic concepts and theories. *Scient. Mon.,* 1954, **79,** 300-305.

Stern, M. The ego aspect of transference. *Int. J. Psychoanal.,* 1957, **38,** 146-157.

Strean, H. Difficulties met in the treatment of adolescents. *Psychoanal. Rev.,* 1961, **48**(3), 69-80.

Truax, C. B., & Carkhuff, R. R. *Toward effective counseling and psychotherapy.* Chicago: Aldine, 1967.

Wepman, J. M., & Heine, R. W. *Concepts of Personality.* Chicago: Aldine, 1963.

White, R. W. *Lives in progress.* New York: Dryden Press, 1952.

White, R. W. Ego and reality in psychoanalytic theory. *Psychol. Clues,* 1963, **3** (3).

Zeligs, M. The psychology of silence: Its role in transference, counter-transference and the psychoanalytic process. *J. Amer. Psychoanal. Ass.,* 1961, **9,** 7-44.

Zeller, A. F. An experimental analogue of repression: Part I. Historical summary. *Psychol. Bull.,* 1950, **47,** 39-51.

Zeller, A. F. An experimental analogue of repression: Part III. The effect of induced failure and success on memory measured by recall. *J. exp. Psychol.,* 1951, **42,** 32-38.

Zetzel, E. R. The concept of anxiety in relation to the development of psychoanalysis. *J. Amer. Psychoanal. Ass.,* 1955, **3,** 369-388.

6

Behavioral Views of Counseling[1]

LEONARD D. GOODSTEIN

The scientific study of learning, or the changes in behavior as a function of experience, has been and continues to be a major concern of experimental psychology. Psychologists' interest in the phenomena of learning can be traced back to the pioneering work of Ebbinghaus (1885), Bryan and Harter (1897, 1899), and Thorndike (1898). Thorndike's later work (1911, 1932) in demonstrating the crucial importance of rewards and punishments in the learning process, particularly his statement of the "law of effect," has become one of the most significant factors influencing the development of contemporary experimental psychology. Thorndike proposed that learning occurred because responses that were accompanied by or resulted in a satisfying state were "stamped in" and consequently were more likely to be repeated in the future. This statement of the empirical law of effect or principle of *reinforcement* marked the introduction of concern and interest in motivational variables into theoretical conceptualization of the learning process, a concern and interest that characterizes many current behavior theories of learning. More recently, B. F. Skinner (1938, 1953) has been concerned with the theoretical and practical implications of how patterns or *schedules of reinforcements* affect behavior.

A great deal of contemporary psychological research also stems from the work of the Nobel prize winner Ivan Pavlov (1927), who demonstrated that the simultaneous presentation of an unconditioned stimulus (meat paste) and a conditioned stimulus (sound of a tuning fork) would eventually

[1] The author is indebted to a number of his professional colleagues for their careful reading and critical comments of earlier versions of this chapter. The author would like to especially thank Drs. I. E. Farber, Samuel N. Harrell, and Janet T. Spence for their considerable expenditure of time and effort.

result in the conditioned stimulus eliciting the response (salivation) which previously could only have been elicited by the unconditioned stimulus. This phenomenon, termed *conditioning*, together with Thorndike's research on the law of effect became the basis of an objective psychology which dealt only with observables and avoided the subjectivity and intuition which characterized much of the then current psychological approaches.

John B. Watson (1913, 1919) was the foremost proponent of this vigorous objectivity based on conditioning, a position which has been labeled *behaviorism*. While the original meaning of behaviorism was at one time rather clear to virtually all students of psychology, the many changes, modifications, and alterations in contemporary *behavior theory*, or neobehaviorism, have obliterated this clarity. As Bergmann (1956) has pointed out, almost all contemporary psychology reflects Watson's influence by demanding objective scientific evidence for elucidating psychological theories, but no contemporary psychologists are true Watsonians. While much of Watson's methodological behaviorism underlies current American psychological theories, few if any of such theories have adopted his original extreme position in rejecting the significance of inferred motivational states and the importance of constitutional factors. Indeed, it was noted above that an emphasis on inferred motivational state, following Thorndike's seminal work, is characteristic of much current behavior theory, particularly that of Clark Hull.

The work of Clark Hull (1943, 1951, 1952) may be seen as the most highly developed and comprehensive theory which follows in the tradition of an objective, empirically based science of psychology. His work, primarily based on the *stimulus* (S) and *response* (R) concepts of Pavlovian conditioning and the motivational concepts of Thorndike's reinforcement principle, is better anchored in objective laboratory investigations than any other current theoretical position. This position has been extended by some of Hull's colleagues, especially Dollard and Miller (1950), to the field of personality and to counseling and therapeutic relationships. The work of Dollard and Miller thus represents a comprehensive attempt to apply the behavior-theoretical approaches developed in the experimental study of learning to the understanding of the complexities of human personality development and personality change.

Most current behavior theories stem more or less directly from the laboratory tradition in psychology and have their empirical roots in Pavlovian studies of conditioning and Thorndikian studies of reinforcement and have their methodological roots in the objectivity advocated by Watson. Since, however, they tend to deviate from Watson's original position, the terms behavioral or neobehavioristic are probably more appropriate. The former term, behavioral, will be used throughout the remainder of this chapter in the interests of simplicity of presentation. It can be noted that the singular importance of the terms *stimulus* (S) and *response* (R) in such approaches has also led to their being labeled S-R *theories,* while the emphasis on learning has led to labeling these *learning-theory* formulations. Finally it should be noted that there is no single behavioral approach or S-R formulation of behavior (or of counseling), but rather there are several theories. All resemble each other to a greater or lesser degree especially in their emphasis on the importance of learning and in their attempt to explicate the learning process in objective and quantifiable ways. The interested reader will find Hilgard and Bower's *Theories of Learning* (1966) a useful summary of the most prominent of these theoretical positions as well as of those that have quite different orientations.

The Nature of Current Behavior Theory

The basic assumption of most current behavioral conceptualizations is that behavior is a function of its antecedents and, consequently, that behavior is lawful. Although constitutional or innate factors are not ignored, the emphasis is almost always on the effects of prior experiences or happenings on the events under scrutiny. It is taken for granted that these antecedent events are identifiable by some observational procedures and that the relation between antecedents and behavior is regarded as open to study by the procedures and methods of the other natural sciences. The study of the relationships between antecedents and behavior is seen as the major task of psychology in these behavioral approaches, and it is assumed that such relationships, that is, the laws of behavior, are potentially discoverable by such an approach. Such an assumption does not presume that these laws or relationships are currently available but merely that they should be and will be available as the body of empirical information relating antecedents and behavior is built up. Once these laws of behavior are available, human behavior can then be predicted and, to the extent to which the antecedents can be manipulated and controlled, human behavior is potentially controllable.

Determinism and Behavior Theory

It is important to note that such an assumption does not involve a fatalistic view of human behavior, a view that human destiny is irreversible. While it is assumed that certain determinants or antecedents do lead to a certain behavior or a particular consequent, it is always further assumed that changes in the antecedents, that is additional antecedents, may lead to changes in the consequences. The influence of later events may always change the consequences of some earlier event. Indeed, behaviorally oriented counseling and psychotherapy stem directly from this assumption.

This modification by later events of the effect of a particular antecedent on behavior does not deny the validity of an observed law but would
simply suggest that the operation of a particular determinant of behavior is
complex and interacts with other determinants. As a hypothetical example,
let us suppose that it has been found that early weaning (antecedent) leads
to thumb sucking (consequent) but that the psychological climate of the
home, the affection and respect of the parents for each other and the child,
may also affect the amount of thumb sucking. Early-weaned children from
happy homes, those with a warm psychological climate, were thus found to
suck their thumbs less than those early-weaned children from psychologically cold homes. The latter finding would not destroy the validity of the
former law, that early weaning leads to thumb sucking, but only suggests
that the law is rather complex in its operation, as it is dependent also on the
psychological climate of the home. Most of the laws of human behavior will
almost certainly include such complex relationships involving several determinants of behavior which interact with each other rather than just simple
one-to-one relationships.

It is often argued that such lawfulness in human behavior is somehow
forced or coercive because the antecedent is seen as requiring or forcing
some particular behavior. This notion usually results from a confusion between
the nature of scientific and legislative laws. While enacted or legislative laws may have the effect of forcing or requiring certain behavior,
scientific laws are seen as merely statements of observable relationships
among events in the natural world. In our hypothetical example the observation of the relationship between weaning and thumb sucking did not
make the child suck his thumb; this would have occurred with or without
the relationship having been observed or known. The statement of the law
in such cases simply makes explicit certain relationships which help the
scientist understand the natural relationship between antecedents and behavior. It can be noted in this example that manipulation of the age of
weaning would provide some measure of control over thumb sucking, suggesting the practical utility of having such behavioral laws available.

Is Behavior Theory Mechanistic?

There are some who insist that this behavioral or S-R view of human
behavior is too mechanistic, too deterministic for them to accept. They
argue that such a view of behavior reduces man to the level of an automa-
ton with no active role in the choosing of his own destiny, a robot merely
responding to changes in the environment over which one has no control.
These critics insist that such a view is inconsistent with man's experience of
his own behavior in which he sees himself as actively deciding what responses to make and what courses of action to follow. While these protago-
nists may accept the validity and usefulness of such a naturalistic approach

for understanding the physical world, they argue that the complexities of human behavior, particularly the intricacies of human personality functioning, defy such a simple-minded and direct analysis. While granting the strength of the emotional appeal of the opponents' arguments, the behavior theorist insists on the usefulness of his approach in the understanding of human behavior and, as noted above, insists that this approach includes ways of comprehending the complexities of human behavior and personality.

One aspect of these objections to a behavioral view deserves special consideration, namely, the contention that human behavior is a function of active decision making, of higher mental activity, on the part of the behaving person. Farber (1964) has noted that there is disagreement among behavior theorists as to whether or not such decision making or thinking responses are important determinants of much human behavior, but at least some behavior theorists, including Dollard and Miller (1950) and Farber (1963) insist that these *mediational* responses, thinking or higher mental activity, do importantly influence human behavior. Much of Dollard and Miller's theory of both personality development and personality change is concerned with the nature and operation of these mediational or thinking responses. It should be noted that the acceptance of the importance of such mediational responses in these behavior theories does not change the thoroughgoing deterministic nature of the theories. These mediational responses are regarded by Dollard and Miller as having antcedents, some of which they attempt to identify; they do insist that such higher mental activity or decision making partially serve as a determinant of other, subsequent behaviors.

The Role of Language and Thinking

Dollard and Miller, following Hull, distinguish two types of responses, those which are direct and instrumental and have some immediate effect on the environment, and those which have no direct effect on the environment but rather mediate or lead the way to another response. These mediational, cognitive, or thinking responses frequently involve language behavior, although the language may not be spoken or overt.

Labeling

Labeling or naming aspects of the environment, labeling particular events or certain experiences, is an important aspect of these mediational or cognitive processes. Giving two aspects of the environment the same label or name, for example, labeling or identifying two situations such as crossing the street and playing with a ferocious dog both as "dangerous," increases the probability of the person's responding the same way, with caution, timidity, avoidance, and so on, in these two rather dissimilar situations. Conversely identifying two rather similar aspects of the environment with different labels, for example, naming two similar appearing men as "father" and "uncle," increases the probability of a dissimilar response. These examples illustrate the role of mediational language or labeling responses in enhancing *generalization* and *discrimination* in behavior, respectively.

Language Rewards

Another important property of language, not directly related to its mediational function is the capacity of language responses, both by the responding person and by others, to reward or reinforce responses. Verbal rewards, praise, commendations, and approbations serve to enhance the frequency of occurrence of responses in the manner suggested by Thorndike's statement of the law of effect. Such statements as "That's a good thing to do" or "You've done the right thing" after a particular response, whether made by others or by the person himself, have important consequences for the repetition of that response by the individual. How such verbal statements acquire reward or reinforcement value is itself an important theoretical problem with which behavior theorists have concerned themselves (cf. Brown, 1961). In general, it may be noted that behavior theories typically attempt to explain acquired motivation as a consequence of the socialization of organic drives, but a presentation of such conceptualizations is beyond the scope of this chapter.

The Incentive Value of Language

Still another function of language is to facilitate the incentive or potential reward value of events which will occur in the future. Generally, the effectiveness of a reward on a response is dependent on the time intervening between the termination of the response and the delivery of the reward, with lengthy delays diminishing the reinforcing value of the presumed reward. Anticipatory language responses maintain the effectiveness of delayed rewards which would otherwise be dissipated over time. Thus language can mediate the reward value of such events as a candy bar to be received later in the day and the diploma to be received at the termination of school. It is these primarily human language responses which make human behavior so sharply distinct from that of the lower animals and simultaneously make human behavior so complex and difficult to explain.

Vicarious Problem Solving

Thinking or reasoning is the substitution of internal mediational responses for more overt behavior. The adult human can utilize his reasoning for more efficient solutions to his problems. He can rehearse his responses symbolically rather than overtly, anticipating at least some of the consequences of alternative responses. He can both plan his future behavior, anticipating some of the difficulties that various responses will pose and the rewards such responses can perhaps yield, and he can also analyze his past behavior, recognizing the limitations in effectiveness posed by his prior responses as well as his successes. The application of efficient higher mental processes can do much to eliminate responses which raise more problems than they solve and responses which may be temporarily satisfying but ultimately lead to undesirable consequences for the individual. The inability of the individual to think straight and to use his higher mental processes in this way is one of the primary identifying characteristics of the maladjusted person in our culture, according to at least some behavioral points of view (Dollard and Miller, 1950; Shaffer, 1947). Such failure of thinking to yield adjustive solutions to one's problems can frequently be explained in terms of the inhibiting effects of fear or anxiety on the higher mental processes, a problem to which we shall return later.

Language and Counseling

The above emphasis on the far-reaching effects of the mediational aspects of language behavior or thinking on other behavior provides one behavioral view of the counseling process. Shaffer (1947) has presented a relatively explicit statement of such a view of the counseling process. His formulation suggests: (1) that an outstanding characteristic of the maladjusted or disturbed person is his inability to control his own behavior, (2) that normal persons control their behavior by the use of a variety of language signals, or mediational responses, including subvocal and gestural ones, and (3) that counseling or therapy can be seen as a learning process through which the individual acquires an ability to speak to himself in appropriate ways so as to control his own behavior. Human behavior is seen as partially dependent on the individual's mediational or self-signaling language responses which can be changed in therapy or counseling with a resultant change in other behaviors.

The Self Concept

One set of mediational or self-signaling language responses that is very important in both current personality theory and current counseling theory is the *self-concept*. Within a behavioral framework one can conceptualize the self-concept as those organized mediational or language responses that a person uses in describing the continuity of his motivational patterns, the underlying or genotypical pattern of his motives, and his prevailing interpersonal relationships (Hilgard, 1949). In such a conceptualization, such specific self-concept or mediational responses as "I am a failure" or "I am a success" are regarded as important determinants of the subsequent behavioral response. To the extent that such expectations of success or failure are generalized and constitute an organized set of expectancies about the consequences of one's behavior, they operate as a part of a person's self-concept.

In one study (Aronson and Carlsmith, 1962) those subjects who expected to do poorly on the experimental task (had an initially low self-concept) but who were told that they had performed well on the task were found to be surreptitiously lowering their performance records, while those subjects who had expected to do well on the task (had an initially high self-concept) and who were told that they had performed poorly surreptitiously raised the record of their performance. On the other hand, those subjects whose performance was in line with their expectations or self-concept made few changes in their records. Although there are obvious additional reality considerations such as aptitude or skill also involved in determining the adequacy of the consequent response, these would not preclude the importance of the self-signaling language responses also affecting such responses. Such an interpretation of the role of the self-concept in behavior theory highlights the importance of counseling-induced changes in the self-concept without the necessity of accepting a phenomenological view of the self-concept advocated by the Rogerians (Rogers, 1951; Combs and Snygg, 1959).

One behavioral view of the counseling process focuses on the verbal language or symbolic behavior of the client, not because of some intrinsic interest in verbal behavior per se, but because of the profound and far-reaching consequences of modifications in the mediational language system or thinking processes of the client. It is assumed that these changes in cognitions initiated or acquired in the therapeutic situation will be generalized or applied in other situations, just as the effect of all educational experiences are expected to transcend the narrow confines of the situation in which they were acquired. Thus the client, as a function of counseling, learns to reason better, to analyze more carefully, to see new relationships between antecedents and behavior, to modify his self-concept, etc., and to use these new understandings not only in discussing his problems with his counselor but in changing other aspects of his life.

The Role of Fear and Anxiety

While the concept of fear or anxiety has long been of interest to psychologists, most of psychology's contemporary interest in anxiety as an important determinant of behavior stems from the work of Cannon (1929) and Freud

(1936).[2] Mowrer (1939) appears to have been the first to translate their notions of anxiety into the language of S-R reinforcement theory. According to Mowrer, fear or anxiety[3] is a learned or acquired emotional reaction to originally neutral stimuli which were presented a number of times together with a noxious or painful stimulus. This anxiety is the acquired capacity by new stimuli or cues to evoke strong affective reactions, reactions acquired according to the classical conditioning conceptions of Pavlov. This conceptualization of anxiety as learned emotionality or affectivity plays a central role in several behavioral views of human motivation and behavior (Brown, 1961; Dollard & Miller, 1950) partially because of the clearly observable and profound effects of fear or anxiety on behavior and also because acquired fear is better understood than any other learned motivational state.

The Generalization of Fear

Both the controlled experimental research with animals and clinical reports with humans clearly indicate that the cues or stimuli that have been previously paired with painful or noxious stimuli now themselves can elicit the emotional reactions previously aroused only by the original or unconditioned stimulus. It may be further noted that this anxiety may be generalized or transferred to other than the original stimulus or cue and that this generalization can be enhanced or inhibited by labeling in the fashion discussed above. For example, a child may have been badly frightened by a particular dog, and the acquired fear of this dog can then generalize or spread to all similar appearing dogs (large, black, or growling ones), to all dogs, to all animals, etc., depending on the labeling or mediational behavior that follows the original experience.

Fear or anxiety can be attached in this way to virtually any stimulus or cue, and the socialization process presents innumerable opportunities for humans to acquire anxiety or fear reactions to a variety of cues. Dollard and Miller (1950), Whiting and Child (1953), and Bandura and Walters, (1963) present analyses of the socialization process and of how anxiety is acquired through early childhood learning experiences to a variety of social stimuli. Fear or anxiety, acquired in this way, is characteristic of the maladjusted individual, and an understanding of how these anxiety reactions were acquired is crucial to an understanding of maladjusted and neurotic behavior. The "inexplicable" or "silly" fears of the neurotic, his fears of success, of studying, of making decisions, and so on are explained in terms of

---

[2] Much of Freud's work on anxiety precedes 1936 but this 1936 book is his most widely cited English-language reference on this topic.
[3] While some writers attempt to differentiate fear and anxiety, this distinction is not necessary for the purposes of our discussion.

learned anxiety reactions to the cues involved in these situations. It is our inability to observe the circumstances of learning involved in the acquisition of these fear and anxiety reactions that makes much neurotic and maladjusted behavior difficult to comprehend. The maladjusted person himself cannot recall the occasion of acquisition because of the inhibiting effects of anxiety on thinking, a problem which is discussed more fully below, or because the learning may have occurred early in life, before the language or mediational responses were sufficiently developed to permit such verbal recall.

The Drive Properties of Fear

A very important theoretical consideration is that anxiety or fear operates as a secondary or acquired drive. Increases in activity level are characteristic of individuals in the presence of drive cues, and there is considerable evidence (cf. Brown, 1961, pp. 144–168) that anxiety cues do function precisely in this way. The presence of acquired anxiety cues operates both as generalized energizers of behavior and as cues for particular responses. It is beyond the scope of this presentation to differentiate between these two functions.

The Reinforcing Effects of Fear Reduction

Not only does anxiety appear to function as an instigator or energizer of behavior, but its prompt reduction after a response leads to facilitation of that response (a case of the operation of the previously noted empirical law of effect). The elimination or cessation of an anxiety-arousing cue thus has reinforcement value and leads to the repetition of any response which has led to anxiety reduction. Anxiety cues lead to increases in activity, and provided that the initial response made does not lead to anxiety reduction, a variety of responses are made; such variable or trial-and-error behavior will continue until a response is made which reduces the anxiety. The nature of the response which results in anxiety reduction will depend on a variety of factors, including the particular situation.

How Fear is Reduced

It should be clear that there are many potential anxiety-reducing responses in any situation and that there will be considerable variability among individuals as to which response is acquired. Some individuals will leave the situation and avoid it in the future, some will deny the existence of the anxiety cues, and so on, covering the entire gamut of the so-called "defense mechanisms" or responses to anxiety. These responses which serve the individual best as anxiety reducers become acquired as an important part of his behavioral repertoire or personality. It can be noted that many anxiety-reducing responses have later undesirable consequences, although they do serve as immediate anxiety reducers. Such responses as compulsions, hysteria, and alcoholism can be seen as strong immediate tension or anxiety reducers, although they later raise difficulties for the individual. Symptoms are those responses whose immediate anxiety-reduced effects are outweighed by their later nonadaptive consequences.

It might be asked why individuals do not simply avoid these anxiety-producing cues and thus avoid the possibility of developing such self-defeating responses. In some situations, as in the case of phobias, this is exactly what does occur. If the anxiety-producing cue can be easily avoided, as in not swimming or not flying in airplanes, the individual has little difficulty in arranging to avoid these cues. However, many of these cues are not so easily avoided because they are highly generalized fears such as fear of people, fear of competitive situations, and so on, and because adequate functioning in such situations is regarded by society as essential for normal daily life. Persons who are successful in interpersonal relationships or in competitive situations are highly reinforced for such success, and persons with acquired fears of these situations are in strong conflict between their incompatible desire to function effectively and their strong fear of the situation. Thus, fears lead to conflicts that are also very characteristic of the neurotic in our society.

In summary it can be noted that certain cues or stimuli can acquire the capacity to serve as the signal for complex emotional responses, called anxiety, and these responses then themselves serve as cues or stimuli for still other responses. Anxiety is therefore both a response and a signal for other behavioral responses. Anxiety operates as a drive, instigating or impelling the individual to respond, and its reduction will reinforce those responses associated with the reduction. Those responses which have led to the prompt reduction of anxiety will be repeated even though they may lead to later maladaptive consequences.

Unconscious Processes

We have previously presented a conceptualization of the important role of cognitive or mediational responses, language and thinking, in behavior. Such mediational responses, especially those involving foresight and planning, are regarded as important in determining the adaptive quality of the individual's behavior. Those responses which are not under language control or where the language control is faulty are important in maladjustment of behavior pathology. These behaviors which are not under mediational or language control are regarded as *unconscious*, a formulation which is quite consistent with psychoanalytic notions.

It is possible to differentiate two different types of unconscious responses in behavior theory. The first of these includes the responses acquired early in life, prior to the development of language behavior, and for which there are no adequate cultural labels provided such as kinesthetic or visceral responses. Our inability to label accurately such complex motor behavior as that involved in driving an automobile or playing tennis partially accounts for the difficulties we encounter in teaching these skills to others.

Repression

The second type of unconscious process, which is far more important for understanding maladjustive behavior, involves those responses for which anxiety or fear prevented the acquisition of labeling responses or for which the mediational responses were available but could not be used because of the inhibiting effects of fear or anxiety. Fear and anxiety can become attached to thought or language responses in exactly the same way that any previously neutral cue can acquire value; this process has been labeled as *repression* by Dollard and Miller (1950, pp. 198ff.). Repression is thus seen as the avoidance of certain thoughts which have acquired anxiety effects and the response of not thinking or repression is reinforced by anxiety reduction. Repression therefore is explained by the same principles of learning through drive reduction as the other symptoms discussed above. Memories of painful events are avoided because of their capacity to reevoke the pain or anxiety experienced in the original situation.

The Effects of Repression

This repression of the antecedents of behavior, the inability to recall the circumstances of how certain behaviors were learned, is one of the elements that make maladjusted behavior appear silly or unreasonable. The individual evidences responses which are clearly maladaptive, frequently even to himself, and cannot explain why he is responding in this fashion. For example, this occurs in phobias where the individual cannot remember, i.e., has repressed, the original learning experience leading to the phobic reaction although the resultant reaction of terror and dread is clearly present. Recall of the original learning situation is not necessary for the effects of learning to be present, although in ordinary social intercourse we almost always expect persons to be able to offer some acceptable reasons for their behavior. It is suggested here that the person's inability to justify behavior involving repression may actually raise his anxiety level, for he is now viewed by others as peculiar or stupid because of his inability to explain why he is behaving in this fashion. This state of affairs often gives rise to the development of socially acceptable but often either incomplete or inaccurate explanations of one's own behavior, the so-called "rationalizations." Such faulty labeling or inadequate thinking may be self-satisfying and socially acceptable but inhibits adequate self-understanding.

It should be noted that in our culture we tend to punish others not only for overt acts but also for having the thoughts or impulses that led to the overt act. This type of punishment is particularly evident in our child-rearing practices where we sometimes punish children more severely for the "dirty" thoughts that led to the aggressive or sexual behavior than for the behavior itself. Because we frequently punish children more for having such "evil" thoughts than for the deed or act itself, we may actually inhibit thinking without inhibiting the actual behavior. Thus an individual responds sexually or aggressively without being able to adequately label his own behavior as such. In such cases the anxiety has been attached only to the verbal or mediational responses and not to the overt ones.

The tendency to avoid certain anxiety-producing thoughts varies along a continuum depending on the strength of the fear involved. Strong fears may result in a complete inability to think about particular topics and is evidenced by blocking and generalized avoidance of the subject, while milder fear will result in a weaker tendency to avoid the anxiety-producing topic. We frequently see instances of this type of avoidance of anxiety in group discussions of illness or death when one member of a group suggests, on a more conscious level, that the topic be changed to a more pleasant one.

Some Examples

The avoidance by an individual of thoughts about certain responses will also lead to a failure to see connections between responses or patterns of behavior. For example, an underachieving high school student may not be able to see that his scholastic failure serves as a way of expressing his hostility toward his father. All previous direct expressions of hostility as well as the thoughts underlying such expressions previously may have been severely punished. The youngster, while recognizing that the father is upset and angry, can deny any direct responsibility for his father's upset, blaming his academic difficulties on a variety of other circumstances. Since the son is unable to correctly label his own failure as a subtle form of hostility because such an admission would be anxiety arousing, he continues to fail, much to his own dismay as well as that of his teachers who find such behavior inexplicable. The father, although himself upset and angry, is typically not able to punish the adolescent for his hostility but only for his underachievement. These unconsciously determined responses are typically seen by the psychologist as maladaptive because of the long-term consequences of such responses, although they may have short-term reinforcing properties.

In still another example of the interfering effects of repression on thinking, a vocationally undecided college junior is unable to choose among several major fields for which his aptitudes and interests would qualify him, although he has available considerable information about the fields and the opportunities these fields present. The counselor to whom he turns for assistance with this problem recognized that the client is unable to take responsibility for making any important decisions which affects his life and, further, that there is a pattern of such responsibility avoidance running through the client's self-reported history. The client, however, is unaware of this pattern and is consequently unable to conceptualize remedial courses of action. Under such circumstances the counselor would be concerned about the client's dependency problems and how the client's anxiety about dependency was presumably interfering with his seeing the pattern of his own behavior.

In both examples we can observe that repression, that the avoidance of certain thoughts that are anxiety producing, leads to the failure by the individual to label adequately his own maladaptive behavior and see certain connections among his responses or between environment events and his responses. This failure to develop adequate mediational or language responses, the inability to "think straight," can lead to the failure of any response to appear, to the making of inappropriate responses, to faulty generalizations or discrimination, to an inadequate or unrealistic self-concept, and to the entire gamut of maladaptive and neurotic behaviors.

Counseling and Psychotherapy

Thus far this chapter has been concerned with an explanation of maladjustive behavior, using the concepts and terms of traditional general or experimental psychology. It is this methodological behaviorism that characterizes the behavioral approach to all problems and, naturally enough, extends to the behavioral views of counseling and psychotherapy. Behavior theory regards human behavior as primarily rooted in the experiential history of the organism, as having been learned, and as susceptible to modification by psychological means. The emphasis of behavior theory is thus on the nature of the learning processes that underlie this behavioral change, and these processes are regarded as essentially identical to those involved in any other kind of complex human learning. Such an approach not only does much to remove the mystique surrounding counseling and psychotherapy but also permits the application of understanding gained through traditional laboratory and educational psychology to the therapeutic interaction.

It should be noted in this context that there is no single behavioral view of counseling or psychotherapy but rather that there are a number of such views. Just as there is no single behavioral view of learning, even in the case of rather simple learning phenomena, there is no single behavioral view of the process of therapy or counseling, which is more complex and far less understood than the general process of learning. What characterizes such divergent views as behavioral or S-R, is their conceptualization of counseling as a situation involving the application of the general laws of learning. Behavioral analyses of the therapeutic interaction use the same constructs and language derived from laboratory psychology that were used in the earlier section of this chapter to describe the development and maintenance of nonadaptive responses and behavior. Thus a behavioral view of counseling is one characterized by methodological behaviorism, rigorously defined concepts, and operational language rather than by any particular counseling or therapeutic technique.

Two Behavioral Approaches to Counseling

Contemporary behavior theorists interested in counseling and psychotherapy advocate two quite different approaches to the problems of behavior change through counseling. One such group (Shoben, 1948; Dollard and Miller, 1950; Murray, 1964) has advocated using the rather traditional procedures and techniques typically involved in psychodynamically oriented counseling, but has attempted to translate this traditional approach into the language of behavior theory. Rather than attempting to develop new techniques, these writers have attempted a rapprochement between typical counseling practice and behavior theory, a goal they regard as both feasible and desirable. Another group of writers (Eysenck, 1960; Bandura, 1969; Wolpe, 1969), operating from a highly similar behavioral orientation, has advocated a quite different course. This latter group has insisted that an acceptance of the full implications of behavior theory must lead to a counseling approach that is very different in its procedures from the usual psychodynamically oriented interview. They argue for more direct intervention in and manipulation of the client's behavior, much like the procedures advocated by traditional directive counselors. While some of their presentations suggest that the techniques they are proposing are both new and stem directly from behavior theory, it would appear that many of these procedures predate contemporary behavior theory (cf. Bagby, 1923).

Both groups, although they advocate apparently dissimilar approaches to the process of therapeutic change, are quite consistent with behavior theory. Rather amusingly both sets of writers tend to insist that their position is *more* consistent with behavior theory than the other and thus more "scientific." Breger and McGaugh (1965) have reviewed many of these arguments and have concluded that such discussions overlook the many complexities involved in behavior theory and are essentially futile.

The more important issue, of course, is which approach is more effective for therapeutic change, an empirical problem that can only be answered by research studies. But this is a more complex problem than it might appear. As Kiesler (1966) has noted, clients who seek counseling help, and the problems which they present, are quite heterogeneous. It would be quite naïve to suppose that, in view of this diversity of clients and problems, any single approach would be found to be universally more effective. The student who presents a school phobia may be successfully treated by quite a different approach than one who has difficulty in choosing a major field or one who is overwhelmed by feelings of futility about life.

Krumboltz (1966) has suggested that the goals of counseling be stated in behavioral terms, that is, as specific and directly observable behaviors much as an increase in grade point average or frequency of dating or a decrease in family arguments rather than in general and difficult to define terms, such as self-understanding or self-acceptance. A rather substantial body of research utilizing such behavioral goals has compared the relative efficiency of the direct and indirect approaches to counseling (Krasner and Ullman, 1965; Paul, 1966; Martinson and Zerface, 1970). The results of these studies clearly support the efficacy of the direct approach in realizing behavior goals. As a matter of fact, the literature review done in preparation for this chapter did not uncover a single empirical study that demonstrated the superiority of the indirect approach, or even its clear equality, to the direct approach. The typical rebuttal to this evidence is that behavioral change is not sufficient; that insight, self-understanding, self-acceptance, even peace of mind are the "real" goals of counseling. Certainly no one would argue against such goals, but with terms as vague and general as these, it is difficult to ever obtain agreement about when such goals are achieved.

Throughout the remainder of this chapter an effort will be made, wherever possible, to contrast the implication for counseling practice of these two approaches. The former, with its emphasis upon verbal reports of behavior and on changing mediational responses, will be termed the *indirect* or traditional approach, while the latter, with its emphasis upon actual, overt responses and the direct control of behavior, will be termed the *direct* approach. We will direct more of our attention throughout the remainder of this chapter on the direct approach because almost all the innovative developments have occurred here and most of the behaviorally oriented practitioners and writers have stressed this approach. The theoretical roots of both these approaches in current behavior theory, however, should be recalled.

The Behavioral View of Client-centered Counseling

There have not been any systematic attempts to translate client-centered or Rogerian concepts into the language of behavior theory. The successful attempts by Murray (1956) and Truax (1966) to analyze in behavioral terms the counseling behavior of a number of client-centered counselors, including Rogers himself, suggests that this could be done. Using previously published cases of client-centered counseling, they demonstrated how counselor responses could be regarded as reinforcements for particular classes of client statements, suggesting the process was anything but client centered. It should appear equally feasible to translate virtually any psychologically based theory of therapeutic change into behavioral terms but, it would be noted, such translations are typically far more satisfactory and rewarding to the translator than to the original proponents of the system who almost invariably claim that the translation has damaged the original theory beyond any hope of recognition. The client-centered approach with its emphasis on the verbal interaction between client and therapist and on the resultant changes in self-concept is far closer to that advocated in the indirect approach than that of the direct approach. One common element involved in both the direct and indirect approaches is a concern with anxiety as an important factor in maladjustive behavior and its modification.

Anxiety as a Counseling Problem

One general characteristic of the client who requests therapeutic help, be it called counseling or psychotherapy, is the presence of anxiety. In general, diffuse anxiety or the so-called "free-floating" anxiety typifies the anxiety neurotic, or, on the other hand, it may be more delimited anxiety which is anchored in some rather circumscribed area, such as vocational or educational choice, marital, educational, or occupational adjustment. Even when the anxiety cues can be crudely identified by the client, he usually has difficulty in precisely delineating or differentiating the circumstances of anxiety arousal. The client may also have developed a variety of techniques or "mechanisms" for attempting to cope with his anxiety, obsessions, compulsions, rationalizations, denials, and so on (see Dollard & Miller, 1950, p. 157ff., for a behavioral analysis of how such mechanisms are learned), but these mechanisms are always operating ineffectively, or the client would not voluntarily seek help. The mechanisms may not be operating efficiently, and the individual is thus still experiencing anxiety; or the anxiety level has suddenly been increased by some new threat, and the mechanisms cannot handle the additional load; or the mechanisms are themselves maladaptive and anxiety producing. Compulsive or obsessive defenses that actually interfere with a person's attempts to study, work, or play are examples of this last type of failure of the mechanisms to work.

There are two general reasons for the nonadaptive behavior seen in counseling, both of which involve anxiety. In one instance, the individual has never had sufficient opportunity to acquire or learn adaptive or adequate responses, and his inadequate behavior stems from a limitation of experience. Thus a client may be seen as having poor social skills, no vocational plans, or inadequate study habits, simply because of the failure of his prior experience to provide adequate opportunities for the learning of such responses. In such cases the anxiety observed in counseling is regarded as stemming from the failures which have resulted or can result from this lack of skills, skills which the client recognized that others possess but that he does not. This anxiety coupled with shame and guilt stops the client from seeking assistance from nonprofessional sources, friends or relatives, and turns him instead to the counselor or therapist. The person may not have developed such friends or acquaintances. This observation has led Scofield (1964) to label psychotherapy (and counseling) as "the purchase of friendship." The person who is not anxious about such inadequacies rarely seeks professional help, while the anxious client turns to professional help because of the paucity of social resources available to remedy such personal inadequacies. The popularity of such skills-oriented self-improvement courses as public speaking and social dancing partially attest to the social need for such resources. In such cases, once the anxiety due to not having the skills available is alleviated, the skills can typically be promptly acquired.

Vocational Indecision As a Function of Lack of Information

Rather typical vocational *guidance* may be seen as an example of this type of treatment. The client's initial anxiety about not having made a vocational choice is quickly alleviated, and the counselor then sets about to provide information about the client's abilities and interests and also about the world of work so that the client can now integrate these data into a vocational decision. In such a circumstance, the client's failure to have previously acquired such information is regarded as stemming from a prior lack of exposure to such educational experiences. The very interesting problem of how persons can avoid such experiences in the normal course of events is ignored and the focus is on the client's acquiring the necessary skills. In this first instance the anxiety evidenced by the client is seen as a consequence of the client's failure to have developed the appropriate skills. The anxiety is seen as playing a rather minor role in the etiology of the problem, being primarily responsible for the client's not availing himself of the other noncounseling resources available for problem solving.

Vocational Indecision as a Function of Anxiety

In the second instance, anxiety is regarded as playing a central role in the development of the problem. In this instance, the client's failure to develop or learn the appropriate response is not regarded as resulting from the failure of opportunity but rather from the failure to use the opportunities which were provided because of the interfering effects of anxiety. Thus the client who is vocationally uncommitted is undecided not simply because of lack of information either about himself or the world of work but because making a decision or commitment is strongly anxiety arousing. He may have such information but be unable to utilize it, or he may not have such information, his anxiety preventing him from taking advantage of opportunities to acquire it. For example, making a vocational decision may involve breaking away from parents or defying them; it may represent an act of independence for which the client is not yet ready; it may mean a commitment to an academic career for which the client may feel inadequate, and so on. In each of these hypothetical examples the client avoids the anxiety by avoiding making a decision. But there are strong social pressures on adolescents and young adults to make a vocational choice, at least on the verbal level, and the client cannot completely avoid this anxiety-producing situation as can the phobic individual who is made fearful by airplanes or bodies of water. In the case of the vocationally indecisive client, there are strong pressures to symbolically approach the source of his conflict. Simply consider as one example of this social pressure the number of times adolescents and young adults are asked, "What are you going to be?" It is often this *conflict* of opposite tendencies, one to avoid the anxiety involved in a decision and the other to yield to the social pressure and decide, that serves as the drive that brings the client to counseling or therapy. If the situation that arouses the anxiety could easily have been avoided, the client would have avoided such situations and the anxiety arousal and never come for help.

In this latter instance it is the anxiety which has been previously attached to otherwise neutral cues (see above for a more detailed discussion of how anxiety acquisition is typically explained by current behavior theorists) that prevented the client from using the previously available opportunities to acquire the skills which he now lacks. One of the goals of diagnosis in counseling and therapy with such cases is the identification of the cues that arouse this anxiety so that the anxiety can be eliminated or reduced, permitting the client to now learn appropriate skills. The counselor's mere provision of current opportunities for learning the skills may be not sufficient in this latter instance since the anxiety will still be aroused by the cues in the learning situation. In this latter instance the anxiety is regarded as a cause of the client's problem. But, as noted in the first instance, the lack of such adequate responses is itself anxiety arousing, and the client is often only able to discuss this consequent anxiety without noting the interfering effects of the antecedent anxiety. Indeed, since discussing the type of experience, even in counseling, involves anxiety-producing thoughts, repression or the avoidance of such anxiety-producing thoughts may operate, producing a distorted or incomplete picture of the development of the client's problem. It is, therefore, sometimes rather difficult for the counselor to decide exactly how anxiety did enter into the etiology of the client's problem.

An Example

A twenty-one-year-old male college junior applied for counseling help with a presenting problem of very poor social skills, especially in heterosexual relationships, a history of rather limited heterosexual experience, and considerable anxiety and concern about the implications of this problem for his general adjustment in the future. A diagnostic problem which confronted the counselor was the assessment of the role of anxiety in this case. If he decided that the client's lack of heterosexual skills was the result of a lack of opportunity to develop such skills, an example of the first instance, he might have encouraged the client to avail himself of the several opportunities for acquiring social skills now available to him. The counselor might have arranged for the client to take social dancing lessons at the campus union or join a social group that would permit the client to develop some social skills. The counselor's role would have been to reduce the client's initial anxiety, provide the opportunity for the skills to be acquired, and wait for the development of more adequate social behavior to be reinforced by society. If, however, this was a case of the second sort, where anxiety initially interfered with the acquisition of the response, the client would still become extremely anxious when confronted with the opportunity to learn how to dance or interact with girls, and unless the cues arousing the anxiety were identified by the counselor and this anxiety eliminated or reduced, the client could not profitably use these counselor-provided opportunities for social learning. This was indeed the case with this particular client who, upon contact with girls, became sexually aroused which, because of his particular learning history, served as the cue for strong anxiety. Thus, for this client the opportunity to develop heterosexual social skills only served as an opportunity to become extremely anxious. Only when the anxiety was reduced through counseling was the client able to acquire the skill he previously lacked in this area.

A diagnostic problem confronting the counselor is the assessment of the role of anxiety in the etiology of the problem. In the above example the decision that anxiety was an important antecedent to the problem was based on the counselor's ascertaining that the client had many opportunities for heterosexual relationships throughout high school and college but never used them because he felt tense and anxious when confronted with such opportunities. Further he evidenced strong anxiety and powerful repression when asked about his sexual interests in females, explaining that his puritanical religious background would never permit him to think about girls "in that way" prior to marriage, if even then. The counselor therefore reached the diagnostic decision that anxiety had led to the development of this client's problem and must be weakened or eliminated prior to the acquisition of any new skills. Let us now turn to the critical problem of the elimination or reduction of anxiety in counseling.

The Elimination of Anxiety

Anxiety has been previously defined as a learned or acquired emotional reaction to an originally neutral stimulus. Earlier sections of this chapter have highlighted the central role of anxiety in the etiology of maladjustment and have discussed the importance for reducing or eliminating anxiety in order to effect behavior change in counseling. The issues, both theoretical and practical, involved in a behavioral analysis of such anxiety elimination or modification are highly complex and beyond the scope of this chapter. The following is a necessarily abbreviated attempt to explain the process of anxiety elimination, especially as it applies to the counseling interaction.

Anxiety, like other learned responses, may be weakened or extinguished when the response is made to occur without any primary reinforcement. The fear or anxiety was originally acquired by pairing a previously neutral stimulus or cue with a painful or noxious stimulus. Such learned fear or anxiety can be weakened by now presenting the learned anxiety cue without the primary reinforcement of the painful or noxious stimuli. The child who has learned to be frightened of a large black dog because he had been bitten or knocked down by this dog will have his fear reduced if on his next meeting with this animal, he is not bothered by it.

Why Anxiety Is Difficult to Extinguish

In comparison with many other responses, however, fear or anxiety is extremely resistant to extinction. The experimental research on fear reduction in animals as well as clinical reports on anxiety reduction in humans offer unequivocal support for this contention. Explanations of the resistance to extinction of fear or anxiety responses is based on empirical observations that fear is a strong drive and that fear reduction is a powerful reinforcer (see Brown, 1961, p. 144ff.). The strength of responses or habits learned as a function of the reduction of such a powerful drive should themselves be quite powerful and consequently very resistant to extinction.

There is the additional element that many responses can serve as anxiety reducers, and because the anxiety is temporarily reduced, these responses operate to prevent any final extinction of the acquired anxiety response. Thus, the learned anxiety cue elicits the anxiety, and the anxiety, in turn, elicits some maladaptive but anxiety-reducing response. This vicious circle prevents any permanent extinction of the anxiety-arousing properties of the cues.

Further, the resistance of anxiety to extinction is affected by any circumstance that would serve to enhance the anxiety, such as reinforcement by a more painful stimulus or additional reinforced trials, particularly if these reinforced trials occur after extinction has started. This process is an instance of *partial reinforcement,* where the primary-reinforcement is not paired on every trial with the learned or conditioned stimulus but occurs together less frequently and leads to responses that are exceedingly resistant to extinction. Thus, in the example of the boy and the dog, if the dog were to again knock the boy down or bite him after several experiences where the animal had appeared harmless, the boy's resulting fear of the dog would now be very much more difficult to extinguish than it had originally been. If it is assumed that most human fear responses are acquired under exactly such conditions of partial reinforcement, the resistance of such anxiety to extinction becomes more understandable.

Three Theoretical Approaches to Anxiety Reduction

Guthrie (1952) has noted that, in general, there are three ways of presenting a stimulus or cue that are likely to lead to extinction of a learned response, such as anxiety, to that stimulus. There are (1) adaptation or desensitization, (2) inhibitory conditioning or internal inhibition, and (3) counterconditioning. Before we attempt to define each of these and give examples of each, from the laboratory and from the counseling office, it should be noted that these three methods are not clearly distinguishable from each other, especially in practice. Most real-life attempts to eliminate or reduce anxiety would seem to involve some combination of these methods, and it is difficult to find pure procedures. All three methods are aimed at eliminating the acquired capacity of a cue to arouse the anxiety response. This is accomplished by interfering with the capacity of the previously neutral cue to elicit the emotional response originally elicited only by the noxious stimulus.

Desensitization

Adaptation or desensitization involves the presentation of the anxiety-arousing stimulus at very weak strengths so that it will not be strong enough to actually elicit the anxiety response. The strength of the stimulus is then gradually increased, always taking care to keep the strength of the stimulus below that which is required to elicit anxiety. Eventually even the presentation of the stimulus at full strength is no longer an effective cue for eliciting the response. One way of reducing the effectiveness of the stimulus in such a desensitization process is to present the stimulus at some distance from the organism and then gradually decrease the distance. In the previously cited example of the boy and the dog, the dog could be brought into the boy's sight and gradually brought closer each time but never close enough on any occasion actually to elicit an anxiety response.

The widest use of counseling by direct application of desensitization involves the development of *anxiety hierarchies,* following Wolpe (1952). In this procedure the client, with the counselor's help, develops a list of cues or behavioral situations that are anxiety arousing for him and then arranges these cues in rank order from the most to the least anxiety arousing. Counseling involves having the client imagine or think of those situations which are only moderately anxiety producing and then moving up the hierarchy over sessions until the situation highest on the hierarchy can be imagined without the experience of anxiety. The role of the counselor is to assist the client in "producing" his anxiety provoking images without experiencing undue emotional arousal. As soon as the counselor begins to detect such arousal, either by the client's report or from the counselor's observation of the client, especially of such signs as flushing, perspiration, and so on, the counselor must move the client to a situation which is lower in the hierarchy.

In a study of desensitization of secondary school students with test anxiety, Laxler, Quarter, Kooman, and Walker (1969) used items such as "going into a regularly scheduled class," "being called upon to answer a question in class by a teacher who scares you," "cramming at home for an exam the night before," "entering the room where an exam is to be given," "receiving a marked exam paper back from a teacher," "seeing an exam question and not being sure of the answer," and "having to tell your parents you failed" for constructing the anxiety hierarchy. The clients were told to imagine scenes when each of the items from the hierarchy were read to them and to indicate whenever they felt anxious. Further, they were told to close their eyes to heighten the vividness of the scenes. The authors reported that this procedure, applied in group settings, was effective in reducing the test anxiety of the clients, using several different indices of anxiety reduction. The counseling and psychotherapy literature now includes numerous examples of the successful application of this procedure to such diverse anxiety problems as public speaking, dating, and other heterosexual problems, and a variety of specific phobias, such as to snakes, dogs, and school.

It should be noted that desensitization also occurs in indirect or traditional counseling as well, although it clearly is of a more informal sort. In the indirect approach the client approaches anxiety-arousing material in his counseling sessions; and the counselor, either implicitly or explicitly, encourages this approach behavior by his interest, sympathy, and concern. Anxiety extinction begins to occur when the client experiences some mild anxiety while approaching these causes and while the anxiety is *not* reinforced by the counselor. The permissive, accepting counselor does not punish or intensify the client's anxiety under these circumstances, but he reflects or interprets the feeling and attempts to clarify the relationship between the emotional response and the precipitating thoughts.

It must be recognized that extinction would not ordinarily occur with a single experience, even when rather intense feelings are expressed, the relatively permanent extinction of anxiety is thought, by adherents of both the direct and indirect approaches, to require several exposures to the anxiety-arousing material. The similarity of such extinction procedures to the psycho-analytic process of "working through" may be apparent. One practical problem involved in this kind of desensitization of anxiety-arousing cues is the frequency with which such cues can be presented in the counseling session. Counselors are typically concerned lest the client's anxiety level become so high during the counseling session that he withdraw from counseling because counseling has become too painful for him to continue. The client centered counselor (Rogers, 1951) takes the extremely cautious position of giving the client the major responsibility for setting his own dosage of anxiety. Most indirectly oriented counselors take a somewhat more active role than Rogers in the dosing of anxiety, but most take extreme care to promote extinction without losing clients because of the overdosing of anxiety. We will note, however, in the following section on internal inhibition that there is an alternative view of this problem, one that leads to a very different set of procedures.

Inhibitory Conditioning

The second method of extinguishing anxiety is called inhibitory conditioning or *internal inhibition.* The present view of this process of internal or reactive inhibition involves presenting the anxiety-producing cues in sufficient strength to elicit the anxiety response, and these cues are either continuously presented or are presented for periods of time, without any additional primary reinforcement, but with only brief intervals of rest interspersed between their presentation. The continual or very frequent presentation of such stimulation will result in a virtually continuous response; such continual responsiveness will in turn lead to fatigue and other changes in the organism, which will eventually lead to the cessation of the response despite the continued presence of the anxiety-arousing cues. An important factor in extinguishing anxiety through internal inhibition by frequent presentation of the anxiety cues is the length of the interval between the presentation of the anxiety cues. If the interval between these presentations is very brief, more technically termed the *massing of trials,* the internal or reactive inhibition builds up quite rapidly and extinction of the anxiety response is facilitated. This procedure is the *experimental extinction* process of classical Pavlovian conditioning and can be applied to any conditioned response, presumably including anxiety.

If, on the other hand, these rest periods are sufficiently lengthy or distributed in such a way as to permit dissipation of the reactive inhibition, then little extinction will occur. Simply stated, extinction of anxiety will occur as a function of internal inhibition if the stimulus-arousing anxiety is continually presented to an organism with only brief time intervals between these continual presentations.

One reason for the failure of anxiety responses to extinguish through internal inhibition in the natural course of events is that individuals tend to avoid anxiety-provoking cues in real life, particularly if they have recently been exposed to such cues. The massing of extinction trials, with no opportunity for internal inhibition to dissipate, rarely occurs naturally when fear or anxiety is the drive involved. For example, the individual who has a phobic fear of heights rarely will continually ride up and down the elevator in the tallest building in town to rid himself of his anxiety by such a massing of trials. Quite the reverse is more likely to happen: If he can bring himself to ride the elevator once, his relief at arriving safely on the ground will lead to a quick leave taking of the premises. In our earlier example of the boy and the dog, for internal or reactive inhibition to lead to the extinction of anxiety, the boy would have to be presented with the sight of the dog again and again with only brief lapses of time intervening between these presentations, although he would probably evidence signs of strong anxiety and make several attempts to withdraw from the situation. The difficulties in arranging for extinction to take place under such circumstances, especially if a protective parent was present, should be readily apparent to the reader, although there is little question that such a procedure will often be efficacious in eliminating the anxiety.

There seem to be at least two applications of internal inhibition to counseling methodology. The first of these, termed *implosive therapy,* by its inventor and chief advocate, Thomas Stampfl (Stampfl and Levis, 1967), involves the reduction of anxiety by the repeated presentation of the anxiety-arousing stimulus and the expected arousal of anxiety, but *without* the antici-pated physically hurtful consequences. According to Stampfl, anxiety is best extinguished by symbolically reproducing the cues to which anxiety has learned, but in the absence of the primary reinforcement, the actual hurt. The implosive therapist thus vividly describes and asks the client to imagine the most revolting and terrifying experiences conceivable. An obsessive client, with real concerns about cleanliness, is asked to imagine himself reaching into a wastepaper basket and then taking his hand from the basket to find it covered with the most revolting mixture of feces, mucus, saliva, blood, dirt, and urine. Even further in the session, the client is asked to imagine himself endlessly swimming in such a horrifying mixture, perhaps even living there. According to Stampfl, the stronger the anxiety elicited by such materials, the greater the need for continuing the presentation of these materials. It is only when these materials no longer arouse any affective response from the client does the counselor terminate the procedure. Over sessions, the distressing and anxiety provoking scenes are repeated, again and again, until they have lost their capacity for emotional arousal and there is a clear reduction in the presenting symptoms.

This procedure has been applied to other sources of anxiety as well, such as aggression, bodily injury, loss of control, and so on. While these techniques are rather new and the research evidence on their effectiveness not at all clear (Bandura, 1969, pp. 403–405), it is interesting to note that there are *no* reports in the literature of this implosive process producing an overall or generalized increase in anxiety, although this is what many of Stampfl's critics would predict. Nevertheless, it is clear that this is not a counseling procedure that will appeal to every counselor, especially the more fastidious ones, but it does suggest the very much increased range of counseling behaviors that are involved in behaviorally based techniques.

The second application of internal inhibition is directed at the elimina-tion of responses which are anxiety-reducing for the client but which are maladaptive. Many neurotic symptoms, such as handwashing, other com-pulsions, tics, and other obtrusive behaviors, fit into this category. Yates (1958), following the early research of Dunlap (1932) on negative practice, has offered the following method, which he regarded as an example of the application of the principle of internal inhibition. If the symptoms (compul-sions, tics, etc.) are voluntarily evoked by the counselor's instructions under conditions of massed practice followed by periods of prolonged rest, these symptoms will be extinguished, and this extinction will be generalized beyond the immediate confines of the counseling situation.

Both of these two approaches obviously stem from the direct behavior-al approach. The indirect approach, with its more traditional orientation, tends to be far more cautious in the dosing of anxiety. There is, however, some similarity between implosive therapy and the psychoanalytic reports of "abreaction" in which the client will begin to act out in imagination the situation underlying the emotional conflict. The major difference would appear to be that abreaction occurs spontaneously. Nevertheless, the previous discussion of internal inhibition would suggest that a massing of interviews, with only brief periods of time intervening, might maximize the process of anxiety reduction.

Counterconditioning

The third procedure discussed by Guthrie, *counterconditioning,* involves the presentation of the anxiety cue in sufficient strength to elicit the anxiety response; however, this occurs when the organism is making some other response that is incompatible with the anxiety response. For example, eating and the satiation of hunger are partially incompatible with fear, providing the fear is not too strong. In a new classical experiment using this method of competing responses, Jones (1924) eliminated a young boy's fear of a rabbit by showing the boy a rabbit while the boy was eating. Under these circumstances, the child did not evidence any fear, although it was evidenced under other circumstances. The rabbit was kept at a distance during the early phases of the extinction process so that the responses involved in eating inhibited the anxiety responses rather than the reverse occurring. One of the dangers inherent in such procedures is that the opposite result may occur, and the child may learn through a process of higher-order conditioning to become anxious at the sight of food.

In the foregoing example it should be clear that desensitization is also involved but the effects of desensitization or adaptation are augmented by the effects of counterconditioning. Thus, in one sense, counterconditioning is a more powerful technique because it may involve two separate processes. Certainly counterconditioning is the most popular of the procedures advocated in the direct behavior approach.

In one clear example of counterconditioning, again one that also involves desensitization, Lazarus (1960) has reported treating a child's strong fear of moving vehicles by reinforcing each of the child's "positive" comments about trains, cars, buses, and so on, by giving him a piece of candy. After the child was able to talk about moving vehicles without experiencing anxiety, the child and the therapist began to play with toy cars and, during the play, the child was again reinforced with chocolates. He then was fed chocolates in a stationary auto until he no longer experienced anxiety and finally was driven in a car to a candy shop where he was fed chocolate. At the conclusion of this series of treatments, the child was sufficiently free of anxiety to be able to go driving with his parents, although, for a time, he insisted on being fed chocolates during such drives.

Nonadjustive anxiety-reducing responses may also be treated by a process of counterconditioning, using pain or other noxious stimulation, so-called *aversion therapy.* In such counterconditioning the maladjustive responses, which previously served as anxiety reducers, now become the cues for anxiety increments. Blakemore, Thorpe, Barker, Conway, and Lavin (1963) report successfully treating a male transvestite by systematically providing a very unpleasant electric shock at irregular periods to the patient while he was dressed in woman's clothing; the series of shocks were terminated only when he had removed all of these clothes. Thus, being dressed in women's clothing became the cue for anxiety, which was reduced when he divested himself of these clothes. Under such circumstances the transvestism became anxiety producing, and the patient gave up this maladaptive response. Feldman (1966) has reviewed the literature on the application of aversive procedures to sexual deviates and concluded that such procedures are most effective when coupled with positive rewards for socially appropriate behavior.

Not all the procedures recommended by advocates of the behavioral approach are quite as impersonal as those discussed above. Indeed, one of the most widely used and strongly recommended techniques is that of desensitization coupled with counterconditioning by relaxation. Wolpe (1958, 1969) recognized that the responses involved in relaxation were incompatible with those of anxiety. If, therefore, the anxiety cues could be presented while the patient was in a state of more or less complete relaxation, the capacity of these cues to elicit anxiety would be consequently reduced. Wolpe also used sexual and assertive responses in his *reciprocal inhibition* therapy since such responses are also physiologically antagonistic to and therefore inhibitory of anxiety, but the use of relaxation appears to be the most widely adopted of his procedures (see Eysenck, 1960). The relationship of these procedures to the concept of counterconditioning should be obvious to the reader.

On the basis of his examination of the patient, particularly his assessment of the current sources of the patient's anxiety, Wolpe develops a list of the cues that elicit anxiety in rank order of strength, the anxiety hierarchy. The patient is then taught relaxation procedures, frequently involving the use of hypnotic suggestion, and is then told to think of or imagine situations involving a very weak anxiety-producing cue. If anxiety is evidenced, a still weaker cue is chosen until the client can imagine the anxiety-producing situation without experiencing anxiety, while still in a state of relaxation. In later sessions stronger and stronger anxiety-producing cues are presented until the entire anxiety hierarchy can be imagined without disturbing the patient's relaxation. Thus, through reciprocal inhibition therapy or counterconditioning, relaxation rather than anxiety is attached to the cues in the anxiety hierarchy.

Counterconditioning is regarded as a potent factor by those who advocate the indirect approach as well. Shoben (1948, 1949), in an analysis of the counseling process based upon the principle of counterconditioning, has pointed out that the nonanxiety responses of acceptance, warmth, and security experienced by the client in working with a counselor can now become attached to the verbal symbols which previously elicited anxiety. The basic similarity of this position to that of Wolpe should be readily apparent.

In the indirect approach, it is argued that the client's anxiety has its roots in his socialization experience and is, therefore, interpersonal in nature. Maladjusted individuals in our culture learn to be anxious about their interpersonal relationships, in particular about expressing such thoughts as hostility, dependency, and sexuality. Such interpersonal anxiety can best be extinguished in an interpersonal relationship with a warm, permissive counselor who provides an opportunity for the client to desensitize these anxiety-producing thoughts by not punishing the client when such thoughts are expressed. The extinction of the client's anxieties in his relationship with the counselor may thus well be seen to some extent as a direct reconditioning experience. For example, a client with anxiety about dependency may have such anxiety reduced as dependency responses occur in his relationship with the counselor in such a way that they elicit anxiety which is identified or labeled but not reinforced by the counselor. Thus, reduction of dependency anxiety is occurring in a kind of direct reconditioning, even though the counselor is an advocate of the indirect approach.

In the indirect approach the client typically is conceptualized as symbolically approaching anxiety-producing material in the counseling session through the discussion of his symptoms and their etiology. This may involve the discussion of hitherto unverbalized thoughts, the recall of unpleasant experiences, the vicarious rehearsal of anxiety-arousing behavior, and so on. The choice of language in permitting the client either to approach or avoid the emotionality or anxiety is noteworthy is this context. The client may discuss the same material on a very abstract, impersonalized level or on a highly specific, detailed, personal level which is far more likely to arouse anxiety. Consider the differential consequences of having the client say "My father and I don't get on" versus "I hate my old man." Anxiety elimination can only occur when the client is able to discuss anxiety-producing material with emotionality actually occurring in the counseling situation. The similarity of this conceptualization to the psychoanalytic notion of *catharsis* can be noted. It has been frequently noted, most recently by Hobbs (1962), that the therapeutic development of "insight" or a change in cognitive behavior that does not also involve changes in emotionality or anxiety is not likely to be very useful to the client in modifying his adjustment pattern.

A Comparison of the Direct and Indirect Approach to Anxiety Reduction

The process of anxiety reduction in both the direct and indirect approaches concentrates upon the presentation of the anxiety-arousing cues without any primary reinforcement, but there are several differences in the manner which these cues are presented in the two systems. In the indirect approach the cues are always presented by the client verbally and symbolically, imbedded in his own conversation; in the direct approach, the cues are often presented by the counselor, often independent of the client's ongoing conversation, and, consequently, may appear in much sharper relief than in the indirect method. Further, in the direct approach the counselor may actually present the anxiety-producing stimulus or a picture or photograph of the object, a process which almost never would occur in the indirect approach. For instance, the counselor might actually produce a snake, or pictures of snakes, if the problem were one of a snake phobia.

The question of the efficacy of these two approaches, the direct or the indirect, in the elimination of anxiety, especially the problem of the necessity of reexposing the client to the actual anxiety-arousing cues, as part of counseling is quite complex. Some anxieties are highly generalized, such as anxiety about authority relationships or heterosexual interactions, and because of repression, the client cannot identify the original source of the anxiety. Further, it often would be impossible to provide the original anxiety-producing cues in counseling because of practical considerations, for example, the cues involved in anxiety learned on a battlefield in wartime or those acquired in an interaction with a deceased parent. Such considerations would appear to limit the application of such direct reconditioning procedures to fairly circumscribed anxiety reactions to relatively common objects, the so-called phobic reactions.

Under such circumstances the question of the relative effectiveness of these two approaches is an empirical one still to be answered by research. In one experimental study dealing with this problem, Peck (1951) compared the effectiveness of counseling on anxiety reduction, both with and without the actual anxiety-producing cues being present. She found that the relative efficacy of these two procedures depended on the general anxiety level of the client, with those persons originally classified as nonanxious showing anxiety reduction only when reexposed to the original anxiety-arousing cues as part of counseling. On the other hand, anxiety reduction in those persons originally classified as anxious occurred when only the verbal cues were presented. For these anxious subjects, reexposure to the actual anxiety cues in counseling tended to intensify rather than reduce the anxiety. This single study is, of course, not definitive but does suggest that the question of the adequacy of these procedures is more complex than is typically suggested by advocates of either approach.

In summary, we have reviewed the three theoretical approaches to the process of anxiety reduction: desensitization or adaptation, internal inhibition or inhibitory conditioning, and counterconditioning. For each of these three approaches we have attempted to contrast the direct and indirect procedures which stem from that position. It now must be clear to the reader that these three approaches are not clearly distinguishable from each other, especially in practice. Most counselors' attempts to eliminate anxiety involve some combination of these methods, and it is difficult to find instances of a pure method. Unfortunately for contemporary counseling practice, there have been few studies of the relative effectiveness of these three procedures. Further, since the mechanisms underlying these procedures are not clearly understood at this time, it is not possible to decide upon their relative efficacy on theoretical grounds either.

Beyond Anxiety Reduction

It should be noted, however, that the mere elimination of anxiety does not directly or invariably lead to the development of these previously unlearned responses, even when anxiety is the antecedent of the failure to learn. The extinction of anxiety now makes the client teachable, but the acquisition of skills, particularly such complex social skills as dancing or dating, still requires specific learning experiences directed at the development of such skills. The failure of counselors and therapists to help the client find such opportunities, especially in a culture with few such opportunities generally available, leads to less effective counseling results than would otherwise be the case. The resolution of the client's problem in the above example involves not only a reduction of his anxiety but also an acquisition of the proper skills. While it is obviously beyond the interests and perhaps even beyond the skills of the average counselor or therapist to provide these learning experiences himself, he should not overlook the client's need for finding and using such opportunities to achieve an adequate resolution of his problem.

In actual counseling practice, the two processes of reducing the interfering anxiety and initiating the acquisition of skills frequently overlap in time. The counselor continuously evaluates the changes in the client's anxiety level. When, in the counselor's judgment, sufficient anxiety reduction has occurred so that the client may now approach the anxiety-producing cues without severe discomfort, some counselors will urge the client to test his freedom from anxiety by entering into a program of acquiring new socially adequate responses. The client can regularly discuss his progress in these real-life situations, with the therapist serving both to reduce the antecedent anxiety further and to reinforce the reported gains.

The previous discussion takes the view that neurotic or maladaptive behaviors are responses to internal and largely hypothetical states of emotionality which are typically called anxiety. Following Dollard and Miller (1950), it was argued that counseling typically requires some elimination of anxiety before desirable patterns of behavior can be learned. Some behavior theorists (e.g., Eysenck, 1960), however, would contend that such anxiety elimination should not be the counselor's primary concern but rather that therapy should be directed at the elimination of nonadjustive behavior pattern and/or providing conditions for learning more adjustive responses. In actual practice, however, it is often difficult to decide to what extent a therapeutic procedure involves anxiety extinction along with retraining. It would also appear that there may be some cases in which anxiety extinction is necessary prior to retraining.

The Role of the Counselor as a Reinforcer

The important point which we have been stressing in the preceding section is that effective counseling would appear to require more than anxiety reduction. What is required, either in addition to or instead of anxiety reduction, is constructive behavior change. The student who poses a study-skills problem must be helped to learn how to study; the vocationally undecided client must be helped to make his decision; the socially awkward client must develop social skills, and so on. The role of the counselor is to facilitate the development of such socially appropriate behavior by systematically reinforcing this kind of client behavior.

In almost all views of the counseling process, as the therapeutic relationship develops, the responses of the counselor to the client become increasingly important. Without recourse to such complex concepts as the psychoanalytic one of *transference,* it should be clear that the counselor's interest, attention, and approval, or contrariwise, his disinterest and disapproval increase in importance to the client over time and are best regarded as reinforcers of client behavior. The positive reinforcers may range from statements of direct approval such as "I'm glad you did (or told me) that," to such indirect and subtle procedures as head nodding or the client-centered "Mm-Humm." The negative reinforcers range from a failure to make any response to direct threats to discontinue the therapeutic relationship. These reinforcers are primarily interpersonal and social in nature and involve the language behavior, verbal and gestural, of the counselor, frequently without his complete awareness. Some counselors, especially those of the direct persuasion, may utilize material rewards such as candies, but this is most typically done only with children or severely disturbed mental patients.

These reinforcers help determine the client's behavior both in the counseling sessions and in real-life situation. In the counseling session, the counselor tends to reinforce the client's approaching anxiety producing material by his interest and sympathy, if not by more direct verbal approval. The counselor especially rewards talking when the client is anxious or afraid because, as noted previously, it is the experience of anxiety while verbalizing about the anxiety-arousing material in a permissive situation that leads to the extinction of anxiety.

The behavioral counselor tends to interpret counselor responses in the actual counseling hour as reinforcing the particular topics being discussed by the client. As both Murray (1956) and Truax (1966) have noted, this view can be extended to the work of the client-centered counselors as well. In these analyses, those topics which were rewarded by the counselor's interest, such as independence, tended to increase through the course of the interview; those that were "punished" through disinterest, such as dependence and sex, tended to decrease in frequency. There is considerable experimental support for this interpretation in the counseling and therapy "analogue" research literature. In the analogue studies (Lanyon, 1967; Hoffnung, 1969), subjects are asked to role-play clients coming for counseling. The experimenter attempted to reinforce. through his attention and interest, either the content of the interview, like the dealing with parental relationships, or the emotional involvement of the subject. There is also the experimental literature on verbal conditioning (see Bandura, 1969, pp. 566–579 for a systematic review of this work) in which subjects are reinforced by an experimenter for making up sentences using certain words, but the several methodological problems involved in this work make its direct applicability to the counseling situation rather doubtful. On the basis of this work, however, it seems quite safe to conclude that the counselor, consciously or unconsciously, deliberately or accidentally, does influence the client's behavior in the counseling session.

The counselor not only tends to control through reinforcement the client's behavior in the counseling situation, but this control tends to extend to the client's extracounseling behavior as well. The counselor rewards certain responses that the client reports performing in real-life situations and punishes others. These rewards are approval, interest, and concern, all of which have been developed in the course of the counseling relationship. Such reinforcement would be especially important during the period when the client is trying out new responses or behavior that is as yet not regularly reinforced by others in the client's life. Indeed, one of the important reasons that counseling fails is that there are insufficient reinforcements for the new or emerging behaviors that the client attempts. The socially awkward client who tries his first date will need a fair degree of reinforcement that might not be gained in that situation.

An awareness of the potency of reinforcements delivered by the counselor has led to what Krumboltz (1966b) has termed a "revolution in counseling." By this he means the development by counselors of a variety of helping programs that are based upon the application of reinforcement to problem behaviors. More recently Krumboltz and Thoresen (1969) have prepared an edited volume that presents a wide variety of applications of reinforcement procedures to counseling problems, including managing over-active and aggressive classroom behavior, improving academic perfor-mance, making educational and vocational choices, learning job-interview skills, and improving study habits. The role of the counselor is seen not only in the direct application of these techniques but also in the training of others, including classroom teachers, to use these procedures.

In the application of reinforcement it is important to recognize that what is being changed is not only the client's verbalizations during the counseling hour but his extracounseling behavior as well. For example, Krumboltz (1963) has clearly demonstrated that the counselor's reinforcing of his client's statements that he intended to seek occupational information in the school library actually led to sharp increases in their information-seeking behavior. This was accomplished by such counselor reinforcements as, "It's good that you are thinking about it now because you should find this out before you make a decision." This study is also important in that it demonstrates that counseling does change the client's mediating or thinking responses, in this case his thinking about post-high school planning, which in turn affected his overt behavior.

Social Modeling and Vicarious Learning

One of the fundamental processes by which we learn new behaviors is through *imitation*. Imitation is sometimes termed social modeling, vicarious or observational learning. Recent research on this process (see Bandura, 1969, pp. 118-216 for a thorough review of this literature) clearly indicates that virtually all of the learnings that can be acquired through direct expe-rience can also be acquired vicariously, that is, through observation of other people's behavior and its consequences for them. Thus, for example, skills can be learned by observing the behavior of appropriate models; emotional reactions, such as anxiety, can be acquired by watching the emotional reactions of others undergoing painful experiences; emotional reactions, acquired either directly or vicariously, can be extinguished by observing others approach feared objects without experiencing painful consequences for this behavior; inhibition of responses or "self-control" can be learned through observation of others being punished; and people generally are strongly influenced by the behavior of models who are high in status or prestige for the observer.

If social modeling is an effective procedure for producing behavior change it should have considerable relevance for the counseling process. There recently have been concerted efforts to develop and evaluate a va-riety of applications of social modeling procedures for counseling and there are a number of such procedures of tested usefulness now available. Both Bandura (1969) and Krumboltz and Thoresen (1969) described such techniques in some detail.

In one such example of the application of social modeling techniques to counseling, Krumboltz and Schroeder (1965) played a 15-minute audio tape recording of a counseling session to clients early in the first session. These clients, all of whom were male high school juniors who were undecided about their post-high-school plans, were told, "... I thought you might be interested in hearing an edited tape of a boy who had a problem similar to yours. He was quite successful in his decision regarding his future and he gave his permission to let other high school students listen to it." The recording was a role-played counseling session in which the male student expressed concerns about his impending decisions and wanted additional information relevant to college and occupational choice. On the tape the counselor expressed approval of the client's information-seeking and led him to consider other relevant sources of information. Those clients who were initially exposed to the model showed significantly more information-seeking behavior than did those clients who were only counseled. This indicates a facilitating effect for the social modeling procedure.

In another and rather different procedure, children who were afraid of dogs were exposed to several different treatment conditions with the aim of extinguishing this particular avoidance behavior (Bandura, Grusec, and Menlove, 1967). Those children who were permitted to observe over several trials live peer models "fearlessly" approach a dog demonstrated significantly more stable and generalized avoidance reduction than did those children who simply observed the dog "in a positive context" or those who were simply exposed to the positive environment without either the dog or the model being present. A subsequent study (Bandura and Menlove, 1968) demonstrated that similar reductions in avoidance reactions could be obtained by showing dog-fearful children a series of motion picture films showing peer models playing with a dog. In this latter study when the model was shown playing with several different dogs, there was sufficient anxiety reduction so that the previously fearful children were themselves later able to play with dogs, without any additional counseling.

These and other empirical studies strongly support the conclusion that social modeling can have important positive effects as part of a counseling program. In general, it would appear that social modeling is most effective when the model is attractive, high in prestige, and rather similar to the subject in some important ways, like age, race, and sex. Obviously the characteristics that will determine the prestige of a model will depend upon the particular subject population. The effects of social modeling can be produced by live models, by films, by video tape presentations, and even by audio tape. One of the important advantages of these latter techniques is that they provide the counselor with greater control over the presentation and insure that the desired consequences will be observed for the behavior to be demonstrated. This is not always possible using live models.

There is still another aspect of social modeling that is very much involved in all counseling, including that of the more traditional, indirect sort, namely, the counselor himself as a role model for the client. The counselor, as previously noted, typically becomes an important person to the client and often becomes a model for imitation. The counselor is typically seen as a well-adjusted, successful person who is very worthy of emulation. It thus should not be surprising to find the client imitating the counselor, especially in such critical behaviors as attitudes, values, and a prevailing philosophy of life. An awareness of social modeling not only suggests that such *identification* is impossible to avoid but that such imitation is an important ingredient of any successful counseling relationship. The counselor should be alert to this phenomenon and should recognize that certain aspects of such imitation are undoubtedly healthy, such as appearing well-adjusted; however, other aspects are more worrisome, such as having the client decide to become a counselor himself although he lacks college aptitude. It is suggested that the counselor should be prepared to help the client discriminate between those aspects of his behavior which are reasonable for the client to model and those which are not.

It can be noted in this context that many counselors have used role-playing as a technique to heighten behavior change. The counselor might ask the client to role-play a job interview with him, or a family quarrel, or some other important event. In the typical use of role playing the client and the counselor will switch roles, so that the counselor can provide the client with some feedback on his behavior and also to provide a model of more adequate behavior. Our previous discussion of social modeling as an important aspect of the counseling process would suggest that such role playing as one kind of social modeling is very useful. Those readers with some knowledge of psychodrama will also note that one aspect of this procedure is to provide the client with more appropriate models for their behavior.

Discrimination Learning and the Counseling Process

In addition to anxiety extinction, another important function of the counselor or therapist is teaching the client to distinguish or differentiate the cues that elicit anxiety. As noted earlier, anxiety learned to a specific cue can be generalized to an entire class of cues so that the person is fearful of all dogs rather than a particular dog, is made anxious by all members of the opposite sex rather than a particular person, is anxious about any dependent relationship rather than a specific one, and so on. The counselor not only helps extinguish such anxiety but also helps the client learn that the anxiety has been generalized and is inappropriate in some of the instances in which it occurs. The counselor may point out that all dogs do not bite, that all heterosexual or dependent relationships do not necessarily lead to rejection. This discrimination learning, coupled with some anxiety reduction, should lead to attempts by the client to try out in real life responses which were previously inhibited by anxiety. The client may attempt to approach a dog, secure a date, or become involved in a dependent relationship outside of the counseling situation.

Too often it is these tentative and fumbling attempts by the client to try out new responses that lead to a failure of counseling. If these tentative attempts result in a reinforcement rather than a reduction of the anxiety—if the dog does bite, or if the date is a monstrous failure, or if the dependency leads to rejection—then, because of this additional reinforcement, the resultant anxiety will be more difficult to extinguish than was the original anxiety. Some discussion of the possibility of failure, some vicarious rehearsal of the consequences of failure, can be attempted by the counselor. Successful counseling, however, usually involves the positive reinforcement of the emergent responses by society rather than the enhancement of the anxiety. Fortunately, these tentative responses are usually ones that are regarded by our society as socially appropriate and useful and are typically more likely to be rewarded than punished.

One type of discrimination learning involved in the indirect counseling process deserves special consideration, namely, discriminating between thoughts and actions. The anxiety which has been previously acquired because of prior punishment inhibits not only the overt behavior but the thoughts and impulses which mediate the overt responses. This repression interferes with the client's higher mental processes, his thinking about his internal state, and how he should respond as a consequence of this internal state. Not only are aggressive behaviors inhibited by anxiety, but even the recognition that one is angry or aggressive under conditions of frustration or conflict may be inhibited. This type of repression leads to inappropriate and maladaptive behavior because the individual is unable to correctly label or identify how he feels. The counselor's task under such circumstances is to help the client recognize and correctly identify such feelings but at the same time discriminate between having such aggressive feelings and acting aggressively. The counselor will attempt to point out that such aggressive feelings are natural and acceptable but that aggressive behavior is not usually regarded as acceptable. Thus, the counselor attempts to teach suppression rather than repression, again emphasizing the role of the client's cognitive behavior in mediating his overt responses.

This discussion of mediational processes highlights another interesting difference in the positions held by the advocates of the direct and indirect approaches to counseling. In the direct approach the client's symptoms are not regarded as resulting from any underlying historically based neurosis but rather as "simple learned habits" (Eysenck, 1960, p. 9). Since there is no conflict or neurosis underlying the symptom but merely the symptom itself, the elimination of the symptom should be the counselor's only concern, at least according to Eysenck. In this concept there is little concern with the learning of the symptoms, only with their unlearning or reconditioning. This lack of concern with the etiology of the client's problem typically extends to the mediational or language responses that mediate the client's anxiety and his efforts to manage his anxiety. The proponents of the direct approach believe that the elimination of the symptoms is the critical element of counseling and that appropriate changes in mediational and language behavior will follow the elimination of the symptoms.

In contrast, the proponents of the indirect approach take the view that changes in the language processes or mediational processes that steer or direct human behavior must first be accomplished. Changes in the more overt responses will typically follow these cognitive changes. These changes in cognition or language may be termed as "developing a more realistic self-concept," "the growth of insight into one's personality," etc., depending upon the particular frame of reference of the counselor. In the indirect approach, the counselor's efforts are concentrated on these self-signaling language systems, with the expectation that changing these mediational processes in the direction of clearer thinking will lead to more effective behavior.

Thus the indirect approach views changes in overt behavior as following changes in the mediational responses, while the direct approach views the changes in the mediational responses as following the changes in the overt responses. The problem of whether changes in the direction of a more positive self-concept must precede or follow actual positive experiences is a case in point. The advocates of the indirect approach argue for initial attention to such mediational responses prior to having the client attempt more overt responses in real-life situations; the reverse is argued by the direct adherents. To some extent, this argument may be resolved on empirical grounds; an underlying, and more irresolvable, problem is the differential importance placed on mediational processes by these two groups.

The Counseling Relationship

It would seem appropriate to conclude this exposition of behavioral counseling with a discussion of the role of the counselor in such relationships. While there may be a tendency on the part of some critics to characterize the role of the counselor in behavioral counseling as impersonal and manipulative, this is not a necessary aspect of this point of view. Several writers in this area, especially Wolpe (1958, 1969), point out the need for establishing a good interpersonal relationship as an integral part of the treatment process. Indeed, it has been noted that an essential role for the counselor to play is that of a reinforcing agent, a role that depends upon the developing counseling relationship.

It was previously noted that many of the client's difficulties involve his interpersonal relationships, including problems of aggression, affection, dependency, and so on. As the therapeutic relationship is an interpersonal relationship between two persons, many of the client's interpersonal difficulties may be activated in this relationship with the counselor. Indeed, the permissive, accepting atmosphere of counseling probably facilitates the direct and overt expression of thoughts and feelings that are partially inhibited in more typical social interactions. The counselor thus has an opportunity to observe directly some of the client's interpersonal behavior and the problems involved in such behavior in addition to having the typical indirect knowledge based on the client's discussions and analyses of his own behavior. The diagnostic usefulness of such direct behavioral observation, for example, seeing the client when he is angry or depressed or dependent, over relying entirely upon the client's report of such behavior should be immediately apparent. Such a firsthand understanding of the client should greatly facilitate the counselor's attempts to modify these behaviors as well as extinguish the underlying anxiety which may motivate these responses.

The counselor must help the client develop a warm, close, and rather dependent relationship wherein the counselor becomes the dispenser of important secondary rewards. The counselor becomes a significant person to the client, and his approval or disapproval become important factors mediating the client's behavior. Snyder (1961) has concluded that the client's positive feelings for the counselor, feelings that the counselor respects the client and is attentive, warm, and empathetic are essential for successful counseling to occur. Snyder has further noted that such positive feelings must be reciprocal, that is, the counselor must indeed like and respect the client, for the counseling to have a successful outcome. While undoubtedly some of the reward value of the therapist's behavior stems from his cultural role as a professional expert, his reinforcement value would appear to be substantially enhanced by a close interpersonal relationship with the client.

The therapist or counselor must also play a diagnostic role, assessing the role of anxiety in the client's symptoms, evaluating the client's capacity to handle anxiety, and then dosing the anxiety in the counseling situation by symbolically exposing the client to anxiety-arousing cues. The counselor must have considerable understanding about the various sources of anxiety in the culture and how it may be best extinguished. He must be able to facilitate the client's psychologically approaching anxiety-arousing materials without becoming anxious himself. Bandura, Lipsher, and Miller (1960), using anxiety about aggression as the case in point, were able to demonstrate that counselors who were themselves anxious about aggression avoided discussing the client's feelings about aggression, while the counselors without anxiety in this area encouraged such discussion. The avoidance of discussion by the anxious counselors of both the client's aggressive impulses and his anxiety about these impulses precluded any extinguishing of the client's anxiety, reducing the usefulness of the counseling interaction in this area.

The counselor not only exposes the client to anxiety cues, but he also reinforces, directly or indirectly, consciously or unconsciously, the client's behavior both in the counseling sessions and in extracounseling situations. It should be clear that an awareness and understanding by the counselor both of the client's need for these counselor-dispensed secondary rewards following certain responses and of the importance or reward value of such counselor behavior would greatly improve the efficacy of such reinforcing behavior. For example, there may be a need for the counselor to reinforce the client for discussing some particularly anxiety-provoking topic or for attempting some especially fear-arousing response in a real-life situation. The experienced counselor would, however, refrain from such attempts to reward the client until he was reasonably certain that, on the basis of the therapeutic relationship, his approval would have some reward value to the client.

In addition to extinguishing anxiety and differentially reinforcing client behavior, the counselor also attempts to teach the client to think more effectively, to approach situations with a problem-solving attitude, and to substitute vicarious problem solving for overt trial-and-error behavior whenever possible. As the counselor helps the client to discriminate more accurately between realistic and unrealistic fears, between thoughts and actions, he enhances the client's capacity for developing intelligent, rational solutions to his problems and reduces the client's need to discuss new problems with the counselor as such problems arise in the future. Such an approach emphasizes the client's problem-solving ability rather than simply providing the client with the solution to a particular problem.

A Summing Up

Contemporary behavioral counseling represents the attempts of psychologists to extend the knowledge and theoretical insights obtained in the psychological laboratory to the counseling situation. The empirical roots of behavior counseling are in the Pavlovian studies of conditioning and the Thorndikian studies of reinforcement, while the methodological roots of behavioral counseling are in Watsonian objectivity. Based upon the assumption that behavior is a function of its antecedents and, consequently, is lawful, behavioral counseling attempts to explain behavior problems in learning terms and also to develop strategies of behavior change based upon the principles of learning.

In general there are two different positions involved in behavior counseling. The first of these, the *indirect* approach, involves the attempts to reanalyze and explain traditional, psychodynamically oriented counseling and therapy procedures, using the concepts and language systems of laboratory psychology. Advocates of this indirect approach primarily have attempted a rapproachment between typical counseling practices and behavior theory, a goal they regard as both feasible and desirable. The second of these approaches, the direct approach, involves direct intervention in and manipulation of the client's behavior, utilizing techniques much like those previously used by directive counselors. Included among such procedures would be the use of relaxation training and the direct reinforcement by the counselor of behavior change.

Behavioral counseling of both the direct and indirect varieties tends to place much importance upon anxiety as a counseling problem. Anxiety or conditioned emotionality to previously neutral cues becomes the central explanatory concept in most behaviorally oriented theories of counseling, and the reduction or elimination of anxiety is typically seen as the major problem for the counselor. There would appear to be three general ways of anxiety reduction based upon a theoretical analysis of the process. The first of these is *desensitization,* or adaptation, where the anxiety-arousing stimulus is presented at very weak levels so that it will not be strong enough to actually elicit anxiety. The strength of the stimulus is gradually increased over time so that eventually the client will not respond anxiously even when the stimulus is presented at full strength. The second method of anxiety extinction is *inhibitory conditioning,* or internal inhibition, where the anxiety-arousing stimulus is continuously presented at full strength over a rather lengthy period of time. Such a continual or frequent presentation presumably will lead to fatigue and the eventual permanent cessation of the anxiety response. The third method of anxiety extinction is *counterconditioning,* which involves the presentation of the anxiety-arousing cues in sufficient strength to elicit the anxiety response but when the client is making some other response that is incompatible with anxiety. For each of these three theoretical approaches a number of specific techniques were presented, including some from both the direct and indirect positions. It was noted that, in practice, these three theoretical approaches are not clearly distinguishable from each other, and most counseling procedures involved some elements of each approach.

In addition to anxiety extinction, the other important function of counseling was seen to be the promotion of effective behavior change. Included here was the client's ability to effectively cope with his real-life situation and his ability to think more effectively about his life. The role of the counselor as a reinforcer of effective behavior change was stressed and a number of different strategies for both initiating behavior change and sustaining such changes were presented. Perhaps the characteristic of behavior counseling which most distinguishes it from other counseling approaches is the willingness of behavioral counselors to attempt new and different procedures in order to effectively assist the client in obtaining his behavioral goals.

Bibliography

Aronson, E., & Carlsmith, J. M. Performance expectancy as a determinant of actual performance. *J. abnorm. soc. Psychol.,* 1962, **65**, 178-182.

Bagby, E. *The psychology of personality.* New York: Holt, 1928.

Bandura, A. Psychotherapist's anxiety level, self-insight, and psychotherapeutic competence. *J. abnorm. soc. Psychol.,* 1956, **52**, 333-337.

Bandura, A. *Principles of behavior modification.* New York: Holt, 1969.

Bandura, A., Grusec, J. E., & Menlove, F. Vicarious extinction of avoidance behavior. *J. pers. soc. Psychol.,* 1967, **5**, 16-23.

Bandura, A., Lipsher, D. H., & Miller, P. E. Psychotherapists' approach-avoidance reactions to patients' expressions of hostility. *J. consul. Psychol.,* 1960, **24**, 1-8.

Bandura, A., & Menlove, F. Factors determining vicarious extinction of avoidance behavior through symbolic modeling. *J. pers. soc. Psychol.,* 1968, **8**, 99-108.

Bandura, A., & Walters, R. H. *Social learning and personality development.* New York: Holt, 1963.

Bergmann, G. The contributions of John B. Watson. *Psychol. Rev.,* 1956, **63**, 265-276.

Blakemore, C. B., Thorpe, J. G., Barker, J. C., Conway, C. G., & Lavin, N. I. The application of faradic aversion conditioning in a case of transvestism. *Behavior research and therapy,* 1963, **1**, 29-34.

Breger, L., & McGaugh, J. L. Critique and reformulation of "learning theory" approaches to psychotherapy and neurosis. *Psychol. Bull.,* 1965, **63**, 338-358.

Brown, J. S. *The motivation of behavior.* New York: McGraw-Hill, 1961.

Bryan, W. L., & Harter, N. Studies in the psyiology and psychology of the telegraphic language. *Psychol. Rev.,* 1897, **4**, 27-53.

Bryan, W. L., & Harter, N. Studies on the telegraphic language. The acquisition of a hierarchy of habits. *Psychol. Rev.,* 1899, **6**, 345-375.

Cannon, W. B. *Bodily changes in pain, hunger, fear, and rage.* New York: Appleton Century Crofts, 1929.

Combs, A. W., & Snygg, D. *Individual behavior.* (Rev. ed.) New York: Harper, 1959.

Dollard, J., & Miller, N. E. *Personality and psychotherapy: An analysis in terms of learning, thinking, and culture.* New York: McGraw-Hill, 1950.

Dunlap, K. *Habits, their making and unmaking.* New York: Liveright, 1932.

Ebbinghaus, H. *Memory* (1885) H. A. Ruger & C. E. Bessenius (Trans.), New York: Teachers College, 1913.

Eysenck, J. H. (Ed.) *Behavior therapy and the neuroses.* New York: Macmillan, 1960.

Farber, I. E. The things people say to themselves. *Amer. Psychologist,* 1963, **18,** 185-197.

Farber, I. E. A framework for the study of personality as a behavioral science. In P. Worchel & Byrne (Eds.) *Personality change.* New York: Wiley, 1964.

Feldman, M. P. Aversion therapy for sexual deviations. *Psychol. Bull.,* 1966, **65,** 65-79.

Freud, S. *The problem of anxiety.* New York: Norton, 1936.

Guthrie, E. R. *Psychology of learning.* (Rev. ed.) New York: Harper, 1952.

Hilgard, E. R. Human motives and the concept of the self. *Amer. Psychologist,* 1949, **2,** 374-382.

Hilgard, E. R. & Bower, G. H. *Theories of learning.* (3rd ed.) New York: Appleton Century Crofts, 1966.

Hobbs, N. Sources of gain in psychotherapy. *Amer. Psychologist,* 1962, **17,** 741-747.

Hoffnung, R. J. Conditioning and transfer of affective self-references in a role-played counseling interview. *J. consult. clin. Psychology,* 1969, **33,** 527-531.

Hull, C. L. *Principles of behavior.* New York: Appleton Century Crofts, 1943.

Hull, C. L. *Essentials of behavior.* New Haven: Yale, 1951.

Hull, C. L. *A behavior system.* New Haven: Yale, 1952.

Jones, M. C. The elimination of children's fears. *J. exp. Psychol.,* 1924, **7,** 383-390. Reprinted in H. J. Eysenck (Ed.) *Behavior therapy and the neuroses.* New York: Macmillan, 1960.

Kiesler, D. J. Some myths of psychotherapy research and the search for a paradigm. *Psychol. Bull.,* 1966, **65,** 110-136.

Krasner, L., & Ullman, L. P. *Research in behavior modification.* New York: Holt, 1965.

Krumboltz, J. D. Counseling for behavior change. Paper read at the Annual Convention of the American Personnel and Guidance Association, Boston, April, 1963.

Krumboltz, J. D. Behavior goals for counseling. *J. counsel. Psychol.,* 1966, **13,** 153-159. (a)

Krumboltz, J. D. (Ed.) *Revolution in counseling: Implications of behavioral science.* Boston: Houghton Mifflin, 1966. (b)

Krumboltz, J. D., & Schroeder, W. W. Promoting career planning through reinforcement. *Personnel guid. J.,* 1965, **43,** 19-26.

Krumboltz, J. D., & Thoreson, C. E. (Eds.) *Behavioral counseling: Cases and techniques.* New York: Holt, 1969.

Lanyon, R. I. Verbal conditioning: Transfer of training in a therapy-like situation. *J. abnorm. Psychol.,* 1967, **72,** 30-34.

Lazarus, A. A. The elimination of children's phobias by deconditioning. In H. Eysenck (Ed.) *Behavior therapy and the neuroses.* New York: Macmillan, 1960.

Laxer, R. M., Quarter, J., Kooman, A., & Walker, K. Systematic desensitization and relaxation of high test-anxious secondary school students. *J. counsel. Psychol.,* 1969, **16,** 446-451.

Martinson, W. D., & Zerface, J. P. Comparison of individual counseling and a social program with nondaters. *J. counsel. Psychol.,* 1970, **17,** 36–40.

Mowrer, O. H. A stimulus-response analyses of anxiety and its role as a reinforcing agent. *Psychol. Rev.,* 1939, **46,** 553–565.

Murray, E. J. A content-analysis method for studying psychotherapy. *Psychol. Monogr.,* 1956 (13, Whole No. 420).

Murray, E. J. Sociotropic-learning approach to psychotherapy. In P. Worchel & D. Byrnne (Eds.) *Personality change.* New York: Wiley, 1964.

Paul, G. L. *Insight versus desensitization in psychotherapy.* Stanford, Calif.: Stanford, 1966.

Pavlov, I. P. *Conditioned reflexes.* G. V. Anrep (Trans.), London: Oxford, 1927.

Peck, R. The influence of anxiety factors upon the effectiveness of an experimental "counseling" session. Unpublished doctoral dissertation, University of Iowa, 1951.

Rogers, C. R. *Client-centered therapy.* Boston: Houghton Mifflin, 1951.

Scofield, W. *Psychotherapy: The purchase of friendship.* Englewood Cliffs, N.J.: Prentice-Hall, 1964.

Shaffer, L. F. The problem of psychotherapy. *Amer. Psychologist,* 1947, **2,** 459–467.

Shoben, E. J. A learning theory interpretation of psychotherapy. *Harv. educ. Rev.,* 1948, **18,** 129–145.

Shoben, E. J. Psychotherapy as a problem in learning theory. *Psychol. Bull.,* 1949, **46,** 366–392.

Skinner, B. F. *Behavior of organisms.* New York: Appleton, 1938.

Skinner, B. F. *Science and human behavior.* New York: Macmillan, 1953.

Snyder, W. V. *The psychotherapy relationship.* New York: Macmillan, 1961.

Thorndike, E. L. Animal intelligence: An experimental study of the associative processes in animals. *Psychol. Rev., Monograph Supplement,* 1898, **2,** (8).

Thorndike, E. L. *Animal intelligence.* New York: Macmillan, 1911.

Thorndike, E. L. *The fundamentals of learning.* New York: Teachers College, 1932.

Truax, C. B. Reinforcement and non-reinforcement in Rogerian psychotherapy. *J. abnorm. soc. Psychol.,* 1966, **71,** 1–9.

Watson, J. B. Psychology as a behaviorist views it. *Psychol. Rev.,* 1913, **20,** 158–177.

Watson, J. B. *Psychology from the standpoint of a behaviorist.* Philadelphia: Lippincott, 1919.

Whiting, J. W. M., & Child, I. L. *Child training and personality.* New Haven, Conn.: Yale, 1953.

Wolpe, J. *Psychotherapy by reciprocal inhibition.* Stanford, Calif.: Stanford, 1958.

Wolpe, J. *The practice of behavior therapy.* New York: Pergamon, 1969.

Yates, A. J. The application of learning theory to the treatment of tics. *J. abnorm. soc. Psychol.,* 1958, 175–182. Reprinted in H. J. Eysenck (Ed.), *Behavior therapy and the neuroses.* New York: Macmillan, 1960.

7

A Summing Up

BUFORD STEFFLRE

Having examined four current counseling theories and the place of such formulations in counseling settings, we may now be ready to make some observations regarding their similarities and differences. An unexpected similarity may lie in the extent to which they fail to qualify as "theories" by any rigorous definition of that term. They attempt to account for relatively few of the phenomena observed in the counseling relationship, and their explanations are characterized by little precision and certainty. Perhaps, a more accurate designation of these statements would be "counseling systems" or "counseling positions" or "points of view on counseling." However, the value of boggling at strained terminology is not great, so, theories or not, let us proceed to a consideration of their usefulness, likenesses, and uniqueness. And, as we do so, it is but honest to acknowledge a frankly relativistic bias which militates against ever actually finding the Holy Grail, while it continues to point out promising hiding places. A bias against the question "Which theory is best?" and for such questions as "Who will feel most comfortable using which theory?" and, "Which clients and problems are most apt to be helped by which procedures?" The true believer will not be comforted by such a view, but true believers find their comfort in other ways.

The substantive elements expected in a theory of counseling, as specified in Chapter 1, will establish the framework for a summary comparison of the theories.

The Nature of Man

Although no clear philosophical or theological beliefs about the nature of man are found in the theories, some plain implications emerge. Although unstated assumptions may be difficult to clarify, several differences are apparent.

287

One way of categorizing these differences is found in Ford and Urban's *Systems of Psychotherapy,* in which they refer to conceptions of man as a "pilot" and conceptions of man as a "robot" (1963, pp. 595-598).

The pilot conception sees man as capable of determining his course and assuming responsibility for his voyage. The externals of wind, reefs, and currents are secondary to his subjective decision to select and make for a port of his own choosing. The client-centered position seems most completely to embody this view, although a case could also be made that the trait-and-factor theory is built on the implicit assumption that given the necessary data (facts about the self and occupations), the individual is capable of wisely charting his course.

Those who are said to view man as analogous to a robot believe that he only appears to be self-directing while, in fact, his behavior is determined by the nature of his mechanism and perhaps by the signals emanating from a power outside himself. Focus is on the field of forces—events, situations, other people—that call into motion those responses that occur from among all those that are theoretically available but do not occur. Theorists subscribing to the robot view of man attend to ways in which behavior becomes acquired, selected, and generalized. Proponents of this position include those espousing the psychoanalytic and behavioral views.

Unfortunately, this neat dichotomy is mussed by further examination. The pilot described by those of the client-centered persuasion appears to choose a port but in reality sails to the only available harbor compatible with his phenomenal chart of the world and his conception of himself as a captain. He selects the choice that seems most self-enhancing as surely as a computer calculates the sum of squares on command. It is only from our external frame of reference that he looks as if he were choosing, and indeed it may *look* the same to him, for he adopts our framework in describing himself to us as an actor. Beck (1963, pp. 66-70) has done an excellent job of considering choice as a pseudoconcept in phenomenology.

Conversely, the psychoanalytic and behavioral students, although agreed that past and present actions are determined, seem to be working toward a situation in which greater choice is possible. By relieving the hiccupping effect attendant upon anxiety with its ineffective and damaging repetitions and by providing the client with lessons in psychological map reading, they imply that the individual will become less a robot and more a pilot.

Not surprisingly, none of the theories have been able to unravel one of mankind's oldest, most snarled Gordian knots—free will versus determinism. They explain behavior in robot terms, while they hope for future adventures in piloting.

Another dimension to be examined in determining the nature of man is his basic trustworthiness. Left to his own devices, will man woo Lilith or

Eve? The client-centered theorists posit a fundamentally "reliable," "constructive," and "good" man. They say that when nature takes its course,
good results are obtained, for human beings are to be trusted. A gyroscopic
self-enhancing mechanism enables man to do the right thing for himself and
his fellows. An ethical phototropism is innate in all of us, and counseling is
designed to remove the deterrents to the proper functioning of this
characteristic.

The psychoanalytic schools, particularly the Freudian, are less san-
guine about man's basic nature and have less difficulty in seeing the skull
beneath the flesh. Evil is seen as not only something done *by* man but as
something natural *to* him. Counseling, then, has the function of the proper
housebreaking of the part of man's nature which loves to romp. One goal
becomes awareness, acceptance, and control of primitive drives so that they
serve both society and the self.

Later psychoanalytic thinkers, as well as advocates of the trait-and-
factor and behavioral positions, seem to see man as having a wider repertoire of responses and as possessing much talent for both good and evil.
This more neutral view of man suggests that he has in common with the
little girl with the little curl right in the middle of her forehead a tendency
when he is good to be very, very good, and when he is bad to be horrid.
Counseling may then release potentialities of all kinds, though; since it is
given within a societally defined structure, it should tend to shape behavior
in a way that permits and acknowledges the presence and rights of others.

How Behavior Is Changed

Counseling is a form of purposeful intervention into the lives of clients. The
purpose of the intervention includes the changing of behavior—in the broad-
est sense. Such change may replace a vague uneasiness regarding a choice
of classes with greater certainty regarding the decision. It may replace panic
and anxiety about the purpose of life with greater focus and acceptance.
The client as well as the counselor expects differences to result from the
counseling, although the client's overt desire for change may be unex-
pressed and minimal. Being concerned with changing the ways in which the
client behaves, the counselor will presumably act from some theoretical
base which includes a point of view on how change is best accomplished.

The trait-and-factor theorists suggest that behavior changes when new
information is made available to the client. The emphasis, then, becomes
one of providing facts about the individual (largely through test information
and a consideration of past events) and facts about the world of work
(largely through information and occupations and the style of life accompanying them). The notion that people behave rationally leads to concern for

providing facts which they will take into account in guiding their behavior. Behavior is changed by information and thinking.

The client-centered theorists suggest that behavior is changed by the restructuring of the phenomenal field that takes place when an individual is placed in a setting of maximum security and minimal threat. Under such conditions the client can reexamine his views of himself and his world and let the self-enhancing tendencies inherent in him be operative. Behavior is changed by creating a situation where it can change itself. The counselor does not act directly on the behavior in order to change it but establishes a climate conducive to the self-actualizing and at the same time societally valued behavior which is the natural expression of man.

Behavioral theorists have the most clear and explicit plan for changing the behavior of clients. They diagnose the situation to determine the responses to be extinguished and those to be encouraged. By a form of conditioning, they set about systematically to induce more appropriate responses. Most self-conscious and aware, this position knows what it is trying to change and how it hopes to accomplish its goals. Behavior is changed somewhat in accordance with classic Pavlovian conditioning that rewards responses which are desired, places in contiguity unconditioned and conditioned stimuli to link the latter with a response occasioned naturally by the former, and punishes to extinction, or permits to occur until extinction, undesired responses. Their concern with changing behavior is focused on problems of anxiety which are seen as primary blocks to sensible, successful instrumental acts. The nature of the behavior change for this school will be in the form of less anxiety and therefore freer and more effective responses.

Similarly, the psychoanalytic theorists are clearly committed to a reduction of anxiety in the belief that more flexible and discriminating behavior will result. Counseling is needed when much energy is being used in intrapsychic conflict caused by forces blocking the immediate—and often socially unwise—discharge of primitive forces. Verbalization in counseling leads to the substitutive discharge of controllable quantities of energy. Pent-up feelings are thus recognized, accepted, and canalized. Behavior is changed in that it becomes less feared, blind and restructed. A clear commitment to change behavior is a hallmark of this theoretical position.

In various degrees these four counseling systems recognize that the counselor is a change agent. Some hope to induce change by accretion of information, some by providing a client with maximum opportunity for change, some by explicitly specifying areas and direction of change, and some by sensitizing the client to the depths of his nature and thus inducing change. All would seem to be committed to furthering change, although the client-centered advocate finds it more difficult to openly accept the responsibility that accompanies this function.

Goals of Counseling

The general goals of counseling are sometimes phrased at a rather high level of abstraction. Client-centered: The client is more congruent, more open to experience, less defensive. Psychoanalytic: Ideally the number of cues to which the patient may respond is multiplied. His restrictions on both perception and response are minimized and are subjected eventually to an altered and increased conscious control (Snyder, 1963).

The trait-and-factor counselor seeks, "To aid the individual in successive approximation of self-understanding and self-management ... " while the behavioral practitioner removes anxiety so that the client may function more effectively and less blindly. Little disagreement is evident in these statements of general goals—all seek liberation from the forces of darkness and ignorance so that rational, flexible, and satisfying behavior can result. That the model of psychological health varies somewhat for different theorists, however, is suggested by Glad who contrasts values related to the psychoanalytic and client-centered view by suggesting that the former strives for an individual who is an "internally organized, emotionally controlled, parent-like person" and the latter for an "internally articulated, comfortable selfhood, prizing his own individuality, and democratically understanding the individuality of others" (1959, p. 62).

When these high-level abstractions are traced to specific referents, some contradictions and confusions may eventuate. That is, when we ask the question "How can we tell if the client is better off than he was?" we get less unanimity regarding the answer. (This question, incidentally, is not the same as "How can we tell if counseling helped?" an even more difficult query which will be discussed later.)

Behavioral manifestations of having been helped might include such diverse outcomes as educational and vocational achievement (measured by such criteria as grade-point average, attendance, staying in school, money earned, promotions received, etc.); different and more pleasing behavior as viewed by friends, teachers, and employers; establishment of vocational goals seen as more "suitable" by judges; absence of apparent symptoms previously present. The difficulty with such criteria is that for any one individual any single criterion might be completely inappropriate and misleading. For example, educational achievement in the aggregate is desirable, but perhaps Mary is investing too much time in school and not enough on other activities. Pleasing others is often desirable, but Riesman's concept of the consequences of extreme other-directed behavior and Fromm's concern with the "marketplace" aspects of some nonproductive orientations would suggest that *not* pleasing others may sometimes be more healthy. A panel of judges might well have viewed Gauguin's decision to leave a fine job in banking for the vicissitudes of art as clearly "unsuitable." Perhaps for such reasons "goals" tend to be stated in mystical, sonorous ambiguities, and research tends to turn to investigations of process rather than outcomes. The consideration of the extent to which counseling goals are achieved is perhaps at a stage parallel to that of considerations being given to the extent to which teaching goals are achieved. Judgments need to be suspended until we know more about the practitioners' characteristics and the practitioners' behavior (process). Estimation of effectiveness must be preceded by (1) descriptions of behavior, (2) judgments and consensus regarding which behaviors manifest effectiveness, and (3) studies of the relationship among characteristics, behavior, and accepted evaluative criteria (Ryans, 1963).

Role of the Counselor

The counselor, regardless of the theoretical framework he favors, may be met by expectations from the client similar to those faced by counselors of other and differing persuasions. The client's expectations will vary with his sophistication and current needs but will rarely if ever be completely fulfilled as originally presented to the counselor. The expectations themselves may change as the client enlarges his view of himself and the presenting problems; the counselor's uniqueness will preclude his fulfilling precisely the preconceived role expectations; finally, the counselor's greater professional knowledge will usually result in behavior unforeseen and unexpected by the client. In spite of the literally unique nature of the interaction between any one counselor and any one client, there are counselor role expectations common to the theoretical positions considered, although the patterns of role fulfillment will vary with the counselor, the client, and the hour on the face of the sociopsychological clock that measures their changing relationship. More clearly, what the counselor does is a function of (1) his own personality, including knowledge, skills, and needs, (2) the client as perceived by the counselor, (3) the instant in the history of their relationship in which the counselor is acting, and (4) the counselor's notion of what he *should do* which is a value related to his total theoretical position on counseling.

Tests

Although the client may approach counseling expecting that tests will be prominent in the experience, the type of tests given and the centrality of their use to the total experience will vary with the orientation of the counselor. The trait-and-factor theorist is most apt to make use of cognitive measures because of his greater emphasis on this aspect of problem solving. The use of "objective and verified data" to permit greater self-understanding and exploration is a hallmark of this position in which measures of interests and aptitude are particularly prominent. The adaptation of the client-centered method for school and college settings, in which educational-vocational concerns are frequent, makes room for the use of tests, and excluding the most orthodox doctrinaire, counselors taking this stand will give tests at least occasionally. Here, however, tests are apt to come late in counseling and are rarely used routinely. The other two theories seem to view testing as largely a phase of diagnosis rather than of solution. Consequently, the tests used may more generally be of a projective nature than of the kind associated with the work of the trait-factor adherent. Again, however, the use of tests late in counseling to help with educational-vocational matters does not appear to be specifically excluded but rather is peripheral to the counselor's main purposes.

Case Histories

Although perhaps varying in completeness and focus, case histories appear central to the conception of the trait-factor, psychoanalytic, and behavioral views. Especially in the latter two they would serve to provide information to enable the counselor to decide whether his skills, orientation, and institutional responsibilities are such that he should undertake to counsel the individual who has presented himself. The focus of the case history would likely be personal adjustment and perhaps cover such areas as family relationships, peers, attitudes toward authority, and emotional expressiveness and appropriateness. The trait-factor orientation would seem to call for more attention to educational-vocational successes, failures, and perceptions although other aspects of life might well be included. The client-centered formulation leaves no place for case-history taking but does raise the problem of which clients should be dealt with, and a solution to this problem would seem to rest in part on information gleaned from the case history. This formulation might be said to (1) do no diagnosis because it might interfere with a desired structure of the relationship or (2) diagnose everyone who appears for counseling as someone who could benefit from the client-centered approach as practiced by the counselor he happens to see.

Values

The once widely held belief that the counselor's position on values should be eunuchoid was generally and effectively shattered for many by Murphy's 1954 address to the convention of the American Personnel and

Guidance Association in which he said, " . . . while no one knows enough to construct a philosophy of life, nevertheless, if he who offers guidance is a whole person, with real roots in human cultures, he cannot help conveying directly or indirectly to every client what he himself sees and feels, and the perspective in which his own life is lived" and went on to call for an emphasis in counselors on " . . . sound, rich, generous, and wise personality" rather than "tricks of the trade" (Murphy, 1955).

Now the usually held view is that the counselor's values are not only present and consciously held but constitute an important part of his armamentarium. The debate has shifted from the question "Should the counselor's values be apparent to the client?" to the question "Should the counselor have in mind values which he will attempt to implant in the client?" The affirmative position is clearly stated by Williamson in his chapter on trait-factor theory and elsewhere (1958).

A persuasive case against counselor neutrality toward values is made by Samler who writes,

> One can list a set of troubles, the therapies of choice and their underlying orientation:
>   For the demanding and infantile—assumption of responsibility;
>   For the vocationally disorientated—assumption of a working role congruent with the picture the client will develop of himself;
>   For the guilt ridden—tolerance for himself and life's reality;
>   For the unloved and unloving—self acceptance and kindliness;
>   For the achievement and power-ridden—appreciation of the rich resources in human beings;
>   For the highly controlling—reduction of anxiety and a more trusting and optimistic outlook (1960).

The negative position on the implanting of values has come to be associated with the client-centered counselor and is characterized by a belief that the client must freely accept or reject the moral and ethical values of the counselor who would leave to such social institutions as the church, the family, and the school the teaching of values (Patterson, 1958).

Because there is agreement that the counselor's intervention is a stimulus that affects the client and because the nature of the intervention must be a consequence of the counselor's values system, some rapprochement would seem possible. The apparent difference may lie in the client-centered counselor's lesser reliance on societally constructed signposts in finding viable values. That is, the value communicated may be a consequence and a meriting of personal standards to a greater extent than is true with other theories placing greater (although, of course, not exclusive) reliance on social consensus. If so, it follows that recognition must be given to the fact that personal responsibility, self-determination, and freedom to reject the counselor's values are themselves a value commitment, and the counselor's behavior may be designed to inculcate this position in the client.

Group Procedures

All the theoretical positions have some history of group counseling activity. The trait-and-factor position has been used in high school classes—variously labeled "occupations," "vocational problems," or "orientation"—designed to learn about aptitudes and occupations. Analytically orientated group therapy, behavioral counseling, and client-centered therapy provide models for group counseling sometimes supplemented by individual sessions. Conditioning plays a large part in the rationale for group counseling; because of his responses, the client is enabled to act out new ways of behaving and achieve reinforcement from the other group members. He learns that it is possible to say things which previously he has suppressed, to think thoughts which previously he has rejected, and to perform in new ways with support from group members and success in maintaining their regard. While obvious modifications are called for in moving from an individual to a group procedure for theoretical framework would seem to hold and to provide clues for the counselor's behavior.

Research Support

The discouraging state of research support for the notion that people are helped by talking is most forcefully presented by Eysenck, who, after a review of the literature, concludes that, with the possible exception of treatment of the behavioral type, there is no evidence that people get better as a result of therapy (1961). (In discussing the difficulties of obtaining objective consideration for such research, he includes a delightful quotation, "To some of the counselors, the whole control group idea ... seemed slightly blasphemous, as if we were attempting a statistical test of the efficacy of prayer ... ")

In reviewing three years of counseling research Callis writes that, "Trends in the data indicate that experienced counselors may produce better results than neophytes and that most experienced counselors choose their methods to fit the task rather than a stereotyped school of conviction" (1963).

Such a conclusion gives little optimism to those who have been attempting to find research support for their favorite counseling theory especially since in this same article Callis adds, "In many instances, the outcome against which counseling was evaluated was not the intended goal of the counselor but an incidental by-product."

Patterson seems to agree that there is little present and unassailable evidence of the value of counseling but believes that the situation stems not from the basic worth of counseling but from inadequacies of research design.

From the analysis of the deficiences of current research, a number of suggestions or recommendations for future research are apparent:

1. Consideration must be given to the goals and objectives of counseling and guidance services and to the criteria relevant to the attainment of these goals and objectives developed and used in future studies.

2. Attention must be given to specifying and to defining the nature of the treatment variable in order that studies may be replicated and in order that one may know to what variable what results may be attributed. Study of specific, defined methods or services in terms of specific criteria will lead to knowledge of what leads to what and will enable investigators to select methods or approaches that will lead to desired criteria or outcomes.

3. An adequate test of the effects of counseling, especially when criteria of personality changes are used, must provide counseling services that are sufficiently extensive and intensive to provide realistic expectations for such changes. It is unreasonable to expect superficial one-interview counseling to have such effects.

4. Any adequate test of the influences or effect of counseling must be based upon the use of counselors who are trained and experienced and who have competence in the methods or approaches they use.

5. Although it is of interest to study the effects of counseling on unmotivated clients or on clients who do not apply or volunteer for counseling, the primary concern is with individuals who are interested in or desirous of receiving counseling. Studies using involuntary clients are not a test of the effects of counseling in a normal counseling situation.

6. Long-term follow-up is necessary to ascertain the nature and persistence of effects. In some instances, there are delayed effects; in others, there may be superficial effects immediately following counseling which will not persist.

Controlled experiments which meet these requirements are difficult and expensive to conduct, not only in terms of experimental design and controls, but also in terms of time, including the duration of the experiment and the follow-up. It would appear that, as in other areas of research, an adequate study requires more than the resources of a single investigator. The time is ripe for an extensive, long-term investigation with adequate financial support, in which existing knowledge may be applied to the conduct of meaningful research on the effects of counseling and guidance services (1963).

An evaluation of the state of counseling research, particularly as it applies to educational settings, indicates that we are far from definitive answers (Stefflre, 1963).[1]

---

[1] Much of the remainder of this section is adapted from this article by the author.

The present relationship between research and practice in counseling is much like the relationship between research and practice in other areas of education. If we did in the name of counseling only those things which research has proved to be worth doing, we should have a good deal of free time on our hands.

Present knowledge in counseling can be divided into three categories. There is a very small category of knowledge which we know to be true as a result of sound research evidence. There is an extremely large category of "knowledge" which we "know" from common sense or scholastic revelation; such knowledge may be said to be a part of the "conventional wisdom." Finally, there is a category of knowledge, which is growing rapidly, that indicates what we do not know! Well-designed research in counseling typically results in transferring "knowledge" from the second category to the third one. The most common conclusion reached as a consequence of carefully designed research in counseling is the verdict "Not proved."

To be more specific with regard to our present situation, let us take a look at the research which deals with the value of counseling.

In reviewing the research which deals with the value of counseling, Stefflre and Matheny in the *Encyclopedia of Educational Research* (1969, p. 263) state that the following observations appear justified: (1) evidence that counseling is clearly superior to the unspecified happenstances of life in the treatment of complex personality problems remains to be demonstrated; (2) counseling appears to bring about changes in the self concept, as measured by Q-sorts, but accompanying behavioral changes have frequently not been shown; (3) counseling has sometimes proved valuable in promoting satisfactory occupational selection and adjustment, but it remains to be shown that it is valuable in improving academic achievement; (4) many studies have failed to obtain positive results either because their goals were too ambitious or because their treatments were too brief; and (5) variation among rates of improvement claimed by different theoretical orientations is probably related to the kind of client problems characteristically dealt with by a given orientation and the degree of specificity employed by the orientation in the establishment of goals.

Crucial Determinants

The practical consequences of commitment to a given theoretical position continue to be unclear. Relevant studies are concerned with frankly psychotherapeutic activity and may not be generalizable to counseling. In an important early study Fiedler (1950) found that experienced psychoanalytic, client-centered, and Adlerian therapists tended to resemble each other in their behavior more than experienced therapists of any one of these orientations resembled inexperienced therapists of the same orientation.

Fiedler also speculated that knowledge of theory helped a practitioner feel more secure and hence released him to attend to the patient's needs in ways that experienced practitioners would tend to regard as effective. Strupp (1955a), however, found sharp differences in the types of responses given by the client-centered as opposed to psychoanalytically oriented therapists, although with greater experience and with personal analysis, the client-centered workers' responses become more similar to those of the psychoanalyst.

In another study, Strupp (1955b) found support for Fiedler's finding that greater experience leads to a diversification of technique.

The present state of research would, therefore, suggest that intensive training, personal therapy, and experience are greater determinants of counseling behavior than are stated theoretical positions. It is possible, however, that familiarity and comfort with a counseling theory is a necessary but not sufficient condition for the emergence of a relationship between the counselor's background and his counseling behavior.

Common Elements

At the risk of some violation of niceties within the four schools of thought let us search for common elements as a corrective against the possible magnification of differences. This consideration does not constitute a synthesis but rather a recognition that "counseling," of whatever style, is apt to use bricks which are basic and solid regardless of the esthetic principles advanced by the architect. Ten facets of counseling which seem both crucial and common will determine the structure of our examination of commonalities.

1. Flexibility

Although counseling procedures are most clearly seen in extremes approaching caricature, they are apt to be used by any one counselor along several continua—from active to passive, directive to compliant, cognitive to affective, etc. The hallmark of the experienced counselor seems to be the ability to fit his style to the unique character of the client and the relationship at any one time. All schools imply that some variation in style is advisable, although they differ in their emphasis on this matter. No theory advocates fitting a client to a mold, all presuppose reasonable flexibility in the application of theoretical principles.

2. Motivation

While not always made explicit, it would seem that the several theories are agreed that the clients who want counseling are more apt to profit from it than those who don't. The unmotivated client may be dealt with, but the likelihood of success is felt to be minimal. The school or college which drags the reluctant client to the counselor's door will find little optimism in the counselor's assessment of his chances of being helpful. Motivation for counseling would appear to be a necessary condition for behavior change and counseling "success." Research which has not taken this crucial variable into account is open to much criticism.

3. Relationship

From time to time one theory or another tries to claim the concept of "relationship" as its personal discovery, and all are agreed that it is a most important element. Some might say it *is* counseling; all would agree that it plays a crucial role in counseling. The concept includes, but goes beyond, the notion of rapport to take in (1) improved interpersonal relationships as a goal of counseling, (2) practice in relating to another person during the interview, and (3) relationship as the base on which the entire structure of counseling must be built. To attempt to create a relationship is to give an earnest of caring; to establish a relationship is to make counseling possible; to continue a relationship is to permit growth and change.

4. Respect

Again, respect for the individuality, humanness, and wonderful complexity of the client is shared by all counselors. This respect for the other grows with self-respect and an appreciation of the command to love others as you love yourself. For the counselor to appreciate the client, he must first appreciate himself so that out of his self-acceptance, out of his deep understanding of his virtues and weaknesses, and out of the recognition and control of his own needs comes the skill, the wit, and the love to respect another in a way that makes counseling result in growth.

5. Communication

Whether through words or nonverbal cues, through symbolizations or plain speaking, through physical arrangements or limited time, the counselor and client must communicate, and all four theories are concerned with this problem. The sensitivity and objectivity of the counselor will greatly determine the extent and accuracy of communication. If the counselor with his "third ear" can hear and understand the story of the client's personal world, if he can help find a Rosetta stone to aid in the translation of the client's private language and symbols, and if he can detect the presence and meaning of nuances of tone, word choice, and bodily gestures, then communication and counseling become possible. The greatest sensitivity needed by the counselor, however, may be that reserved for his self-understanding. Why does he press testing onto the client or alternately blind himself to the service it may sometimes perform? Does his silence mean support, approval, or anxiety? Is his restraint in the face of client provocation the result of maturity shown by the control of impulses in the interests of work to be done or is it the result of that narcissism, that higher smugness, expressed as an angelic air of patience and forbearance which has been called the vocational disease of counseling (Wyatt, 1948)?

Sensitivity to self and sensitivity to the client is a necessary condition for the kind of communication required in counseling.

6. Learning

Although the psychoanalytic adherents may tend to be skittish about the use of the term and the trait-and-factor adherents to embrace it too fervently, the concept of learning is present in all four theoretical formulations. Basically the client learns more about himself and his world and, therefore, performs better. The explanation of why he learns may vary from the client-centered emphasis on the climate for emotional learning to the trait-and-factor belief in the value of the structured lesson and plan. The fact that this learning has so often defied measurement would seem to be related to differences in subjects being taught (information or release), in teachers (counselors), in readiness (motivation and maturity), and in the tests used to measure the results of counseling. However, all counselors face and answer, openly or covertly, the basic pedagogic question "What do I want this person to learn?" (Sometimes, of course, it is expressed—"How do I want him to be different after counseling?" or "What is the justification and purpose of my intervention into his life?")

7. Direction

Although once serving as a psychological litmus paper thought capable of clearly differentiating types of counseling, the concept of direction of the client by the counselor is now more frequently seen as an omnipresent aspect of all counseling. All but the client-centered group have recognized and consciously used their capacity for direction. The client-centered have, on the contrary, resisted the view that their presence or behavior in any way directs the client. (The term "nondirective," as noted in a previous chapter, was originally used to label the point of view in which the client-centered roots are found.) The consideration of the counselor's responses as a stimulus in a conditioning sequence has resulted in an extensive literature. After a review of such literature, the conclusion is reached that the majority of studies demonstrate that such responses as "mmm-hmm," or "I see" do positively reinforce the making of affective statements (Krasner, 1958).

Concern now shifts from the presence or absence of direction to the extent, method, and purpose of direction. Some direction may be explicit and clear (trait-and-factor and behavioral), some subtle and tentative (psycho-analytic), and some intuitive and unrecognized (client-centered), but most would agree that it is always present. Perhaps the struggle should shift to the arena of social direction. Perhaps we should ask—Does the counselor direct the client's attention to societally established (external) or personally derived (internal) sign posts? Answers to such a question result in much overlapping among the theories (for like most dichotomies this one is un-stable) but directs the dialogue to a more meaningful level of disagreement.

8. Support

The presence, interests, and activity of the counselor are seen by theorists of all schools as supporting the client. The counselor gives the client support by acting out for him such messages as "You are deserving of my time and concern," "We can talk and by doing so can 'touch' and teach each other," and "You will be able to cope with the decisions, crises, and problems facing you." The openness and form of the support would likely vary with the personality of the counselor and the perceived needs of the client as well as the moment of interaction more than with the theoretical orientation of the counselor. By cultural definition the counselor is one who provides support, but he may do so unconsciously and incidentally or deliberately and directly.

9. Rewards

The counselor rewards the client for his presence and for some of his behavior. (For the argument that the counselor rewards all the client's behavior equally, or perhaps not at all, as suggested by the client-centered practitioners—see Direction, number 7 above.) Such consequences may go beyond support as discussed in the previous section to the kind of conditioning mentioned previously. An aspect of reward sometimes overlooked, however, is the reward received by the counselor from the client. If he does not understand the basis in his own need system for the rewards he feels, the counselor may be in danger of exploiting the client out of insatiable psychic greed. The counselor who refuses to recognize the limitations of his training and role and therefore undertakes to counsel those whose needs are beyond his training to deal with is probably best explained by his failure to be significantly cognizant of the nature of the rewards that have "hooked" him.

All four theories have room in them for an explanation of the mutually rewarding nature of the interaction between the counselor and client, although the psychoanalytic system is most explicit about the genesis, dangers, and function of this reward. The superior status of the counselor and the counseling relationship is so unmistakable that the client would have to be completely outside our culture not to be affected by it. This status is active in direction, support, and reward. It cannot be cast off: It can only be consciously used, partially neutralized, or blindly denied.

10. Purposes

The discussions of counseling goals show us many elements of commonality among the system with regard to this dimension of counseling. All seek a free, informed, responsible person conscious of himself—his strength and weaknesses, his sickness and health—and capable of viewing the world unblinking and unafraid; capable, too, of making decisions for himself in harmony with his unique nature and at least minimal societal requirements. It is not true, as their enemies may contend, that the client-centered counselor seeks anarchy, that the psychoanalytic counselor seeks an orgy of impulse gratification, or that the trait-and-factor and behavioral counselors seek a brave new world of controlled robots.

Conclusion

The beginning counselor may need to remind himself that, although theories are best separated by concentrating on their differences, successful counseling is best accomplished by attending to their similarities. What they have in common needs to be learned and put into practice before fine doctrinal disputes distract us from the core activity, which is helping the client to find his identity in a culture that like the human condition itself is both baffling and beautiful.

Theory is needed to help us conceptualize the interrelationship of data, to help us temper intuition and rigidity, and to help us examine the efficacy of our actions. Reasonable freedom from theory is also needed if we are to overcome the smugness of the "in" counselor, if we are to free the individual to add himself to the counseling equation, and if we are to be capable of making that higher synthesis which results in better and more inclusive theories. The learning of theory may be likened to the learning of the descriptive rules of grammar. Only after they are known, understood, examined, and evaluated may they be safely breached.

Bibliography

Barry, R., & Wolf, B. *Modern issues in guidance—Personnel work.* New York: Teacher's College, 1957.

Beck, C. *Philosophical foundations of guidance.* Englewood Cliffs, N.J.: Prentice-Hall, 1963.

Callis, R. Counseling. *Rev. educ. Res.,* 1963, **33** (2), 184–185.

Coleman, J. S. *The adolescent society: The social life of the teen-ager and its impact on education.* New York: Free Press, 1961.

Encyclopedia of educational research. (4th ed.) New York: Macmillan, 1969.

Eysenck, H. J. The effects of psychotherapy. In *Handbook of abnormal psychology.* New York: Basic Books, 1961. Pp. 697 725.

Fiedler, F. E. A comparison of therapeutic relationships in psychoanalytic non-directive and Adlerian therapy. *J. consult. Psychol.,* 1950, **14,** 436-445.

Ford, D. H., & Urban, H. B. *Systems of psychotherapy.* New York: Wiley, 1963.

Glad, D. D. *Operational values in psychotherapy.* Fair Lawn, N.J.: Oxford University Press, 1959.

Jahoda, M. *Current concepts of positive mental health.* New York: Basic Books, 1958.

Krasner, L. Studies of the conditioning of verbal behavior. *Psychol. Bull.* 1958, **55** (3), 148-170.

Murphy, G. The cultural context of guidance. *Personnel guid. J.,* 1955, **34** (1), 8.

Patterson, C. H. Program evaluation. *Rev. educ. Res.,* 1963, **33** (2), 222.

Patterson, C. H. The place of values in counseling and psychotherapy. *J. counsel. Psychol.,* 1958, **5** (3), 216-223.

Rothney, J. W. *Guidance practices and results.* New York: Harper & Row, 1958.

Rothney, J. W., & Roens, B. A. *Guidance of American youth: An experimental study.* Cambridge, Mass.: Harvard, 1950.

Ryans, D. G. Assessment of teacher behavior and instruction. *Rev. educ. Res.,* 1963, **33** (4) 415-441.

Samler, J. Change in values: A role of counseling. *J. counsel. Psychol.,* 1960, **7** (1), 36.

Snyder, B. K. Student's stress. In Terry F. Lunsford (Ed.), *The study of campus cultures.* Boulder, Colo.: Western Interstate Commission for Higher Education, 1963.

Stefflre, B. Research in guidance: Horizons for the future. *Theory into practice,* 1963, **2** (1), 44 50.

Strupp. H. H. An objective comparison of Rogerian and psychoanalytic techniques. *J. consult. Psychol.,* 1955, **19,** 1 7. (a)

Strupp, H. H. Psychotherapeutic technique, professional affiliation, and experience level. *J. consult. Psychol.,* 1955, **19,** 97 102. (b)

Williamson, E. G. Value orientation in counseling. *Personnel guid. J.,* 1958, **36** (8), 520 528.

Wyatt, F. The self-experience of the psychotherapist. *J. consult. Psychol.,* 1948, **12,** 83-87.

Name Index

Subject Index